EXCAVATIONS WITHIN EDINBURGH CASTLE

ST DRISCOLL & PA YEOMAN

EXCAVATIONS WITHIN

EDINBURGH CASTLE

in 1988–91

STEPHEN T DRISCOLL & PETER A YEOMAN

with contributions by

Jane Clark

and

Denise Allen, A Akhtar, Sheila Boardman, Stephen P Carter, David Caldwell, Ann Clarke, Jennie Coy, Anne Crone, John Dore, William Finlayson, Sally M Foster, Thea Gabra-Sanders, Dennis Gallagher, Doreen Grove, Richard Grove, Sheila Hamilton-Dyer, Brian Hartley, Nicholas Holmes, Finbar McCormick, Donald Mackreth, Ann MacSween, Coralie Mills, D Pollock, Alix H Powers, Susan Ramsay, Nigel Ruckley, Nancy Russell, R Michael Spearman, R Tipping, Robert S Will.

Illustration

Marion O'Neil & Keith Speller

SOCIETY OF ANTIQUARIES OF SCOTLAND

MONOGRAPH SERIES NUMBER 12

Edinburgh 1997

SOCIETY OF ANTIQUARIES OF SCOTLAND
MONOGRAPH SERIES

EDITOR • ALEXANDRA SHEPHERD

This volume is published with the aid of a generous grant from

British Library Cataloguing-in-Publication Data.

A catalogue record for this book is available
from the British Library.

ISBN 0 903903 12 1

Produced by Sutton Publishing Limited, Stroud, Glos.

Printed in Great Britain by Henry Ling Ltd., at the Dorset Press, Dorchester, Dorset.

CONTENTS

FOREWORD

Castles, it is popularly believed, were built to keep people out; nowadays, they are expected to admit as many as possible. Nowhere is this more true than at Edinburgh Castle.

For centuries this mighty royal fortress dominated its surroundings with an awesome majesty. Today, it is seen as a powerful symbol of Scotland's past, and hundreds of thousands of people from all over the world are attracted each year to its rocky perch.

The castle's new role as Scotland's premier paying tourist attraction has inevitably put a great deal of pressure on the venerable citadel. In 1984, Historic Scotland, who maintain Edinburgh Castle on behalf of the Secretary of State for Scotland, began to investigate how the castle's facilities might be improved. Five years later, following wide-ranging discussions and public consultation, a four-phase, multi-million-pound development programme was initiated.

The chief element in the first phase was the construction of a vehicle tunnel for business traffic into the castle, leaving visitors free to amble up to Crown Square and the heart of the castle by the traditional route. Much of the tunnel was driven through the hard basalt, but at either end was a length of 'cut-and-fill' which required to be investigated archaeologically. This volume is a record of the archaeological discoveries made by Peter Yeoman and Stephen Driscoll and their team between 1989 and 1991 during the course of that work.

Before excavation began, none of us had much idea what might be encountered beneath the grey granite setts, excepting perhaps for certain 17th-century structures known from the surviving plans. What the team discovered exceeded all our expectations. Not only did they put flesh on the bones of the 17th-century castle, but they also cast considerable light on the nature of the medieval fortress, and quite incredibly unearthed significant remains from the Iron Age stronghold. By the time they had finished, they had succeeded in pushing the story of the inhabitants of the Castle Rock back to the Late Bronze Age.

As the project manager for the archaeological works, I can testify to the energy, dedication and forbearance of Peter Yeoman, Stephen Driscoll and their team throughout the works, and often in very trying circumstances. At one stage, between Christmas and New Year 1989, they were working two 12-hour shifts around the clock in appalling weather conditions so that the programme might be kept on schedule. The fruits of their labours are among the most important archaeological discoveries ever to have been made in Scotland, and they are evident for all to see in this fascinating report.

Chris Tabraham
Principal Inspector of Ancient Monuments

ACKNOWLEDGEMENTS

Edinburgh Castle supports a large community, embracing Historic Scotland, the Scottish United Services Museum, the National Museums of Scotland, the Scottish National War Memorial, the Scottish Office Reception Facility and the Army – truly a town within the city. For a short time the archaeological team became part of that special community and we enjoyed the comradeship and support of these more permanent residents.

Naturally to carry out complex excavations required the assistance, support and co-operation of a large number of individuals. Special thanks are due to the Historic Scotland staff in the Castle: the General Office Staff, Alan Armstrong, the then Area Superintendent, Willie Smith, the Castle Superintendent of Works, Davie Stanley, the Castle Squad Foreman, and all his staff, and particularly to the Castle Warders who put up with the mess and who showed great interest in the work. The administration of much of the archaeological work was expertly co-ordinated by Bert Tasker of Historic Scotland.

Tremendous cooperation was received from the many consultants and contractors, especially the staff of James Williamsons, Engineers. The Lilley construction company, the main contractor, provided assistance beyond that which could have reasonably been expected, and special thanks are expressed to the site agent, Graham Mack, and to Willie Thane, the foreman.

None of this could have been achieved without the archaeological team, whose expertise, commitment and hard work ensured that high quality results were extracted from every area, no matter how difficult the circumstances. The team comprised many but some should be singled out: Susan Bain, Alan Braby, Alan Bradwell, Jane Clark, David Easton, Pauline George, Gordon Turnbull and Bob Will.

Numerous specialists have produced valuable reports for this publication, and thanks are expressed to them all, not the least because several of them had to re-write reports as a consequence of continuing discoveries. Special mention is due to Jane Clark who processed and analysed the greatest bulk of the finds, the unglamorous iron, bronze and worked bone, as well as co-ordinating the coming and going of the finds between the authors, the specialists and the lab. She performed this complicated job wonderfully. We would also like to acknowledge the help of Dr Richard Fawcett in compiling the architectural stone report and Katherine Forsyth for advice on the early medieval literary material.

The two main illustrators, Marion O'Neil (finds) and Keith Speller (plans and sections) are due particular thanks for having to endure the continually changing programme of work. Both contributed substantially to the interpretive effort through their observations during the post-excavation work.

During the course of the excavation we benefited from the close support and co-operation of Historic Scotland's then in-house environmental and conservation unit (AOC) which provided advice on sampling strategy, gave consultations in the field and undertook the programme of artefact conservation. Most of these individuals have contributed specialist reports, but we would single out Dr Coralie Mills for her effective co-ordination of the environmental studies. Ian Mate generously provided additional advice on soil science.

While preparing this report we received many invitations to present the results of the excavation to learned bodies, local archaeological societies, conferences and seminars. We have benefited immensely from the critical responses received from the audiences. In particular we would cite the Edinburgh Castle Conference, the Society of Antiquaries London, the University of Glasgow Post-graduate Seminar, and the First Millennium Study Group.

Finally the authors would like to express the special debt of gratitude owed to Chris Tabraham, Principal Inspector of Ancient Monuments, who more than anyone ensured the success of the excavation and post-excavation programmes by providing expert and good humoured management. His critical comments on the first draft, together with those of David Breeze, have improved this text considerably.

SPECIALIST ACKNOWLEDGEMENTS

Ann Clarke would like to thank Dr Alec Livingstone of the Dept of Geology, National Museums of Scotland for identifying all the rock specimens and Mr Trevor Cowie, Dept of Archaeology, National Museums of Scotland for his comments and advice on the quern stones.

Robert Will would like to thank George Haggarty and Graeme Cruickshank for their help and encouragement.

Dennis Gallagher is grateful to the following for their help with the identification of finds: David Caldwell of the National Museums of Scotland; Adrian Oswald, for his comments on the armorial pipe and especially Alan Carsewell, of the United Services Museum, Edinburgh Castle, for his invaluable assistance with items of military dress.

Sheila Boardman and Coralie Mills would like to thank all those who have assisted in the environmental sampling, processing, sorting, assessment and analysis of the Edinburgh Castle material; besides the authors of the environmental reports, these include Galo Ceron-Carrasco, Ruby Ceron-Carrasco, Alan Duffy, Juliet Hall, Ann Kerrigan, Phil Miller, Jane Peet, Phil Simpson, Rab Smith, Jennifer Thoms. The advice and assistance of John Barber, Harry Kenward, Ann MacSween, Ian Mate, V J McLellan, and Richard Welander is also warmly acknowledged.

Finbar McCormick would like to thank Dr Coralie Mills, Catherine Smith and Dr Brian Moffat for help with the report on the faunal remains.

Dick Grove would like to thank Dr Santini of the Dept of Conservative Dentistry, Edinburgh University who kindly provided advice on the dental pathology of this group.

LIST OF CONTRIBUTORS

Denise Allen – Andover, Hants
A Akhtar – AOC Scotland Ltd
Sheila Boardman – AOC Scotland Ltd
Stephen P Carter – AOC Scotland Ltd
David Caldwell – National Museums of Scotland
Jane Clark – National Museums of Scotland
Ann Clarke – North Berwick
Jennie Coy – Department of Archaeology, University of Southampton
Anne Crone – AOC Scotland Ltd
John Dore – Newcastle upon Tyne
Stephen T Driscoll – Dept of Archaeology, University of Glasgow
William Finlayson – Centre for Field Archaeology, Edinburgh University
Sally M Foster – Historic Scotland
Dennis Gallagher – Edinburgh
Doreen Grove – Historic Scotland
Richard Grove – Melrose

Brian Hartley – Dept of Classics, University of Leeds
Sheila Hamilton-Dyer – Dept of Archaeology, University of Southampton
Nicholas Holmes – National Museums of Scotland
Finbar McCormick – Queen's College, Belfast
Donald F Mackreth – Peterborough Museum
Coralie Mills – AOC Scotland Ltd
Marion O'Neil – Kirkcaldy, Fife
Alix H Powers – Dept of Archaeology, University of Sheffield
Nigel Ruckley – British Geological Survey
Nancy Russell – AOC Scotland Ltd
Michael Spearman – National Museums of Scotland
Keith Speller – Glasgow University Archaeological Research Division
Richard Tipping – University of Stirling
Peter A Yeoman – Planning Service, Fife Council
Robert S Will – Glasgow University Archaeological Research Division

LIST OF ILLUSTRATIONS

LIST OF TABLES

CONTENTS OF THE MICROFICHE SECTION

PROLOGUE

The excavations presented in this report were the first archaeological investigations at the Castle since 1912. They were far more productive than anyone might have guessed at the outset and have made significant contributions to our understanding of the Castle's history. Five main themes emerged from analysis of the excavation results: these are introduced in this prologue in a visual format to allow readers to familiarise themselves with the major aspects of the site, enabling them to appreciate more readily the detailed results in the body of the report.

1
A view of Edinburgh Castle from the east (c 1696) illustrating the extent of the basalt plug, with annotation about the softness of the rock (Crown Copyright PRO MPF 245).

THEME 1

THE PREHISTORIC SETTING AND ORIGINAL SIGNIFICANCE OF THE SITE

Among the most dramatic revelations of the excavation was the discovery that the formidable defences were built upon deposits which extended back to the late Bronze Age. During the excavations this great depth of chronology was apparent in a number of areas; illustration 2 shows excavation in progress beneath part of the deep accumulation in the Mill's Mount area. Arguably this discovery makes the Castle the longest continuously occupied site in Scotland. Castle Rock (illus 3a) is only one of a number of ancient hilltop settlements in the Edinburgh area (illus 3b). The longevity and significance of the settlement encourages us to look at the location of the Castle Rock for clues to its ultimate success.

2

Excavation of later prehistoric levels and a medieval causeway at Mills Mount with the Inner Traverse on the summit in the background.

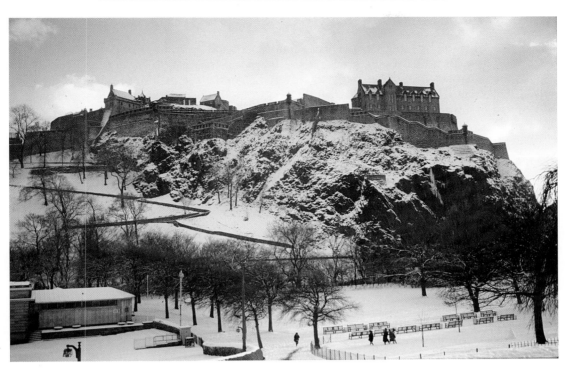

3a
View of Edinburgh Castle and the Rock, in the snow, from the north.

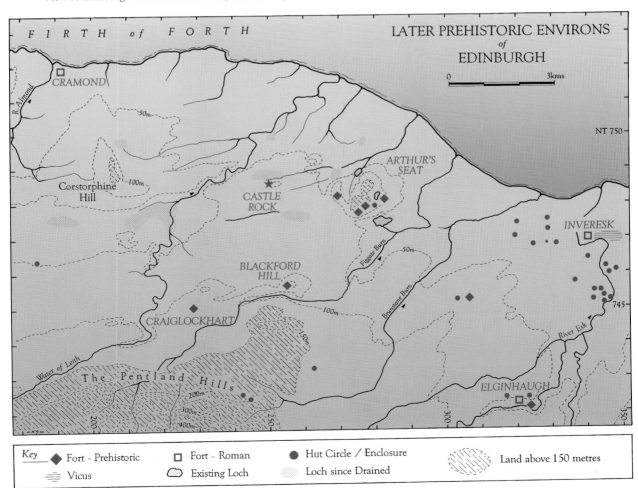

3b
Map to show the later prehistoric environs of Edinburgh.

THEME 2

THE POLITICAL GEOGRAPHY OF THE CASTLE IN ROMAN TIMES

It is first possible to start assessing the political significance of the Castle during the Roman period. Its significance can be evaluated by setting it against the other later prehistoric settlements and early medieval settlements in the area (illus 4a). The artefacts recovered from the site provide another way of assessing its significance. The quality and quantity of small finds from the Roman period such as the bronze brooches (illus 4b) help create the impression of the Castle as a high-status site.

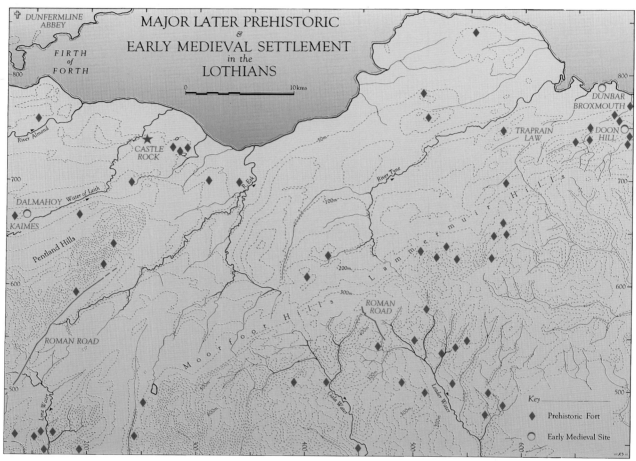

4a
Map to show the later prehistoric and early medieval settlement in the Lothians.

4b
Three Roman period brooches.

THEME 3

THE DARK AGES AND THE QUESTION OF CONTINUITY

The dominance of the landscape which the Castle exhibits (illus 5) is underlined by the earliest documentary references to the site in *The Gododdin* which suggest that the Castle Rock was the residence of an important British king. Unfortunately, the archaeological evidence for this settlement is scant; only a few small finds such as this comb (illus 6a), which is scarcely regal, were recovered. Nevertheless, the site is likely to have been home to warriors such as that represented on the early medieval Govan sarcophagus (illus 6b).

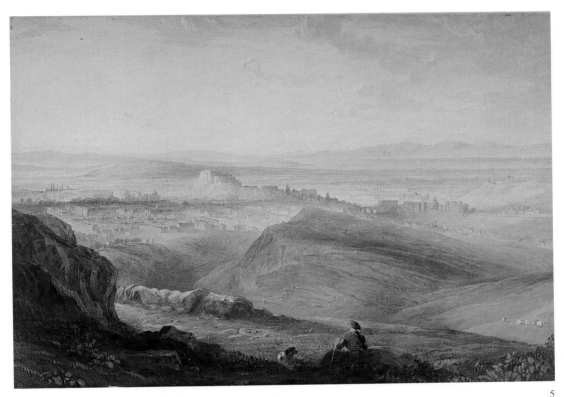

5
View of the Castle from Arthur's Seat by Hugh William Williams.
(Reproduced by kind permission of the City Art Centre, Edinburgh.)

6a
A double-sided comb of the early medieval period.

6b
The horseman: a detail from the Govan sarcophagus.
(Photograph courtesy of Tom Gray.)

THEME 4

THE CASTLE ECONOMY AND DOMESTIC LIFE

Revealing the domestic life of the varied phases of the site was one of the major achievements of the excavation. Evidence for the agrarian economy of the Roman and early medieval periods was particularly rich because of the presence of primary midden deposits such as the one which preserved the segment of cattle spine in illustration 7. There was ample evidence for the dietary practices of the later Middle Ages, some of which was in a primary context such as the dump of oyster shells (illus 9), although much of the evidence may not necessarily relate to the royal household itself.

7
Cattle spine from Mills Mount Roman period midden.

8
A selection of Roman fine and coarse wares from Mills Mount.

Consumption patterns of material goods were extremely well represented, not the least by the large quantities of pottery which date from the Roman period (illus 8) onwards. The range of post-medieval pottery was just one of the categories of evidence which provide direct insight into the daily lives of the garrisons which served in the Castle (illus 10).

9
Oyster shells in the Mills Mount medieval midden.

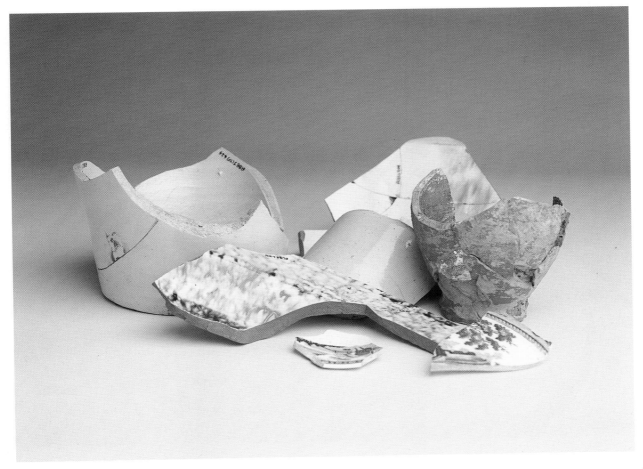

10
A selection of the post-medieval pottery sherds.

THEME 5

EVOLUTION OF THE DEFENCES FROM THE ROYAL CASTLE TO A GARRISON FORTRESS

The battered stumps of rebuilt walls revealed in the excavations provide key evidence for early schemes of the Castle's defences. Historic views are invaluable for interpreting these remnants. The earliest view of the Castle, made by an English spy for the Earl of Hertford's army in 1544 (illus 11), shows the defences of the Castle at the height of their medieval development. The later view of the Castle (illus 12) was made between 1689 and 1707 and is attributed to Capt John Slezer who was intimately familiar with the interior of the Castle, having redesigned some of its defences.

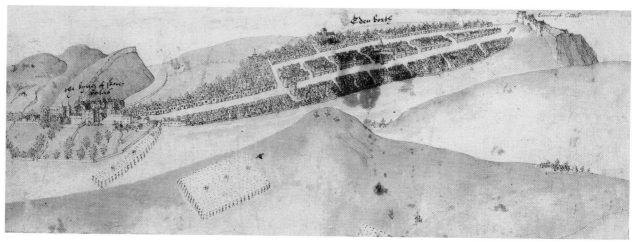

11
View of Edinburgh showing damage by Hertford's army 1544 (by permission of The British Library; Mss Cotton Augustus I, vol ii ant 56).

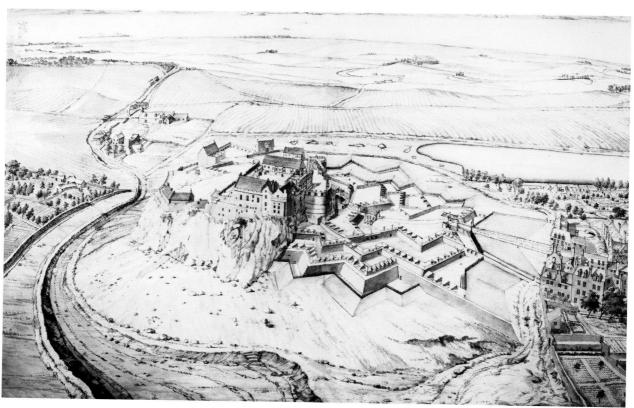

12
Bird's-eye view, probably by Capt John Slezer *c* 1700 (By permission of The British Library; Map Library K Top XLIX.74). Slezer's knowledge of the interior suggests this perspective on that area is extremely reliable but, since it includes an external set of defences which were never built, his treatment of the exterior circuit is less dependable.

INTRODUCTION

Edinburgh Castle, unlike most historic monuments, has maintained a functional relevance to each successive age, being transformed, as the excavations have shown, in turn from hillfort, to castle, to royal palace, to garrison, to ancient monument. The Castle has become a national symbol – an icon of Scottishness, and the archaeological agenda was aimed at cutting through this to reveal the reality of the development of the Castle and the lives of the occupants.

The rescue excavations described in this volume were prompted by a major programme of refurbishment (illus 13) designed to provide much improved visitor facilities within existing accommodation. The siting of the excavations was determined by the location of the works involving the construction of a vehicle tunnel, new toilets, a new shop, and a restaurant. These areas were all on the northern perimeter, at some remove from the core of the Castle, the Royal Palace, on the summit, which is where the most important buildings have always been sited, and where any archaeologist creating a research design to address the interpretation of the site would have chosen to excavate. It is not surprising, therefore, that scepticism was expressed, before commencement, about the possibility of the survival of significant deposits.

Over thirty separate trenches were excavated during the period from 1988 to 1991. Most of these were small trial trenches dug to evaluate survival of archaeological strata, some of which were followed up with larger excavations. This volume is concerned only with those trenches dug as part of the improvement scheme which included the fitting out of the Inner Barrier Guard House as a shop, the refitting of the Cartshed at Mills Mount as a restaurant and the construction of a vehicle tunnel from the NE of the Esplanade to the Western Defences behind Mills Mount (illus 14).

2.1 THE STRUCTURE OF THE REPORT

The volume consists of six sections of text:

1) the introduction,
2) the archaeological structures and their historical background,
3) the artefact assemblages,
4) the environmental studies,
5) the human skeletal remains,
6) the discussion.

In addition there are microfiche sections containing specialist reports and catalogues. The intention has been to provide a manageable and readable report which is not overly burdened with technical description. Those wishing more detail than this report contains should consult the site archive housed in the National Monuments Record of Scotland and the artefact assemblage under the care of the Secretary of State for Scotland.

The two main areas of excavation were located at either end of the tunnel. By and large it has been convenient to retain the trench labels even for adjacent areas such as L and M, because these areas were usually defined by the presence of standing buildings and consequently both the standing buildings and buried deposits had a coherence of their own. The numeric phasing employed in each area is therefore not equivalent. We have not produced a single cross-site phasing, because only in the later, historically attested, structures could chronological links between areas be established with confidence. For these features of the 17th century or later it seemed more helpful to emphasise the absolute dating information rather than to

Illus 13
Constructing the roof of the new shop within the former entrance Flanker (Areas G, J and K); from the W, looking towards Arthur's Seat.

impose an abstract phasing scheme. The historic structures are, after all, elements of more or less well-documented construction programmes.

The historical commentary interspersed throughout the structural account is a distillation of years of detailed work by Historic Scotland on the documentation for the Castle's fabric. They do not constitute a 'history' of the Castle, but conveniently bring the relevant textual evidence together for comparison with the appropriate archaeological evidence. Iain MacIvor's *Edinburgh Castle* (1993) is the authoritative account of the history and development of the Castle and provides a far more comprehensive perspective than has been possible in this study. Not only does MacIvor discuss the architectural aspects of the many buildings, he also explains the circumstances of their construction. In this report we will presume a familiarity with this book, the RCAHMS *Inventory* of Edinburgh (1951) and the Buildings of Scotland volume on Edinburgh (Gifford *et al* 1984) which will allow us to focus on the finer details.

Naturally much of the important historical material consisting of accounts, architectural plans, maps and state records relates to the post-medieval fortifications. Where appropriate these have been reproduced, others can be readily obtained in the RCAHMS *Inventory* and in MacIvor's volume.

In the text, where it has been necessary for clarity to refer to context or feature numbers these are enclosed in parentheses. Close attention should be paid to the illustrations where all significant features are illustrated, because for the most part dimensions have not been provided in the text. The area plans and sections have been drawn for reproduction at convenient scales (1:40, 1:50, 1:100, etc) and where appropriate are supplemented with detailed drawings of specific features. The reconstruction drawings all have been produced after the final consideration of the excavation data. A key to the conventions used is attached to the foldout sections at the back of the volume.

The length of the excavation programme allowed the analysis of the structures, artefacts and environmental samples to begin before the excavations were complete. While this led to some frustration on the part of the specialists, who probably thought they would never complete their work, it had the benefit of allowing the excavators to direct subsequent phases of excavation towards resolving specific questions raised by the initial discoveries. This was particularly true for the environmental studies, which were conducted by Historic Scotland's Archaeological Operations and Conservation Unit.

Naturally a work such as this is the result of the collaboration of many authors. Wherever possible we have attempted to blend the separate articles into a coherent text by standardising structure, terminology and systems of referencing. However, some variations are likely to remain. This is particularly true for the main portions of the structural account. Different approaches were adopted when dealing with the areas dominated by buildings (the Entrance Flanker, the Inner Barrier, the 1801 Main Guard and the Mills Mount Powder Magazine) as opposed to areas of 'soft' archaeology. The historical record of the different building episodes frequently provided a tight chronological control, which allowed a firm phasing. In the areas where the archaeology was predominantly of layers and dug features (Mills Mount and the Coal Yard) a more fluid approach was adopted.

2.2 THE CIRCUMSTANCES OF EXCAVATION

The archaeological programme can be summarised as follows: the team had the whole of 1988 to carry out excavations in advance, while 1989 was devoted to mounting watching briefs, to excavating those areas which required engineering support during the construction work and those where unexpected discoveries dictated further work. Peter Yeoman was excavation director and archaeological consultant to the development from November 1987 until October 1989, when he was succeeded by Stephen Driscoll who oversaw the completion of the main fieldwork to January 1990 and the watching briefs conducted through 1991. The programme was managed by Chris Tabraham of Historic Scotland who responded marvellously as the excavations produced unexpectedly high quality discoveries and deep deposits, requiring considerable extra funding and resources.

The excavations were conducted in unusually difficult situations, which often involved the use of shoring and powered hoists. Spoil disposal varied between the inconvenient and the demanding. Work at the Inner Barrier (Area L) had to proceed in confined spaces beneath a temporary bridge which carried all the traffic into the Castle. This bridge had to be lifted by a 100 tonne crane to allow the final photos of the discoveries to be taken. The final stages of the excavations at Mills Mount (Area X) involved digging underneath the shop while it was still in use, which necessitated modifications to the engineering plans to allow excavation during the construction programme. For a short period shift work was instituted to enable excavation to take place for twenty hours a day and avoid delays to the building timetable. It is quite clear that without the support provided by a large scale engineering programme (illus 14) the majority of the deposits would have remained inaccessible.

In several cases, excavation in certain areas had to be interrupted, generally because special engineering support was required. As a result, work in a particular area might span a period of months. The work was carried out by a small team and it was rare that more than one area was being actively investigated at the

Illus 14
Drilling and blasting the tunnel below St Margaret's Chapel; from the N. Left: the early stages of work; right: the west portal begins to take shape.

same time. The various areas that were excavated are introduced below and are listed in the broad sequence in which they were examined.

1801 MAIN GUARD (Area F)

The foundations of the Guard House were known to exist under the grassed area opposite the Argyll Battery. These were excavated so that they could be displayed and interpreted for the benefit of visitors to the Castle.

GUARDROOM (Area G), CO's STABLES (Area J), DETENTION CELLS (Area K) AND PRINCES STREET GARDENS (Area R)

The various components of this block were excavated prior to their conversion into the new shop (illus 13). All of the areas were found to be within what had been a medieval flanker (entrance fortification) which originally projected further to the N. It contained an early access road into the Castle. This flanking area was reduced in size and infilled with massive dumps of soil when the new entrance and higher roadway were constructed in the 17th century. The great depth of infilled soil, revealed by the archaeological work, enabled the shop to have two sales floors, rather than the one originally planned.

Two opportunities for excavation were available: a 2.5m wide trench was cut N–S to a depth of 7m through the interior of the Guardroom (Area G) in March 1988. This was followed by work to the W of this in the Detention Cells (Area K) in May 1988. The excavation was done in advance of demolition and construction work on the new gift shop.

Further watching briefs, minor excavations and structural surveys took place throughout this area up to Summer 1989. Construction work involved mechanically removing some 7m of soil and some bedrock from

Illus 15
The works at Mills Mount showing the W rock-cut portal in the foreground and archaeological excavation in progress in front of the Cartshed; from the S.

Areas G and K to accommodate the shop interior. This revealed the inner walls of the Flanker. The level in the Stables Yard (Area J) was not significantly altered, although man-hole construction offered a chance for limited archaeological excavation.

MILLS MOUNT AND CARTSHED (Areas H and X) illus 15

These trenches examined the West tunnel portal, where it was built using the cut-and-cover method, and the section. Every episode in the life of the site over three millennia was uncovered here, from the late Bronze Age to the present day. Paved yards and stone-walled houses of the Iron Age were sealed by middens, dumped by British, Anglian and Scottish occupants from the 2nd to 11th centuries. A road and smithy of the medieval fortress replaced the middens, before being swept away by buildings and artillery fortifications of the 17th and 18th centuries. The Bronze Age deposits were buried 4m beneath the present day surface.

The irregular trench layout for this area reflects a much modified programme of archaeological investigation in this area. Much of this modification can be attributed to minor alterations to the line of the tunnel made during the course of the project. The need to mount the awkward excavations under the Cartshed was dictated by the fine preservation of earlier deposits. As a consequence of conducting several forays into Mills Mount a certain amount of the evidence has been lost, particularly where the edges of different cuttings come together. In some instances the ambiguity about the correspondence between contexts from different cuts is a direct consequence of conducting excavations months apart.

Illus 16
View, from the E of the Coal Yard, of the construction of the E tunnel portal with the entrance Flanker to the right.

INNER BARRIER FORECOURT (Area L) illus 16

This portion of the tunnel was also a cut-and-cover section, which runs obliquely under the existing road. The well-preserved remains of the later 17th century inner defences together with a guardhouse of the same period were examined, before they were partially removed by the tunnel works.

COALYARD (Area M)

The East tunnel entrance apron is just inside the Castle over the North dry ditch bridge. Two infilled massive medieval ditches were found, together with a fragment of an angled bastion related to the medieval entrance. These were overlain by a late 17th-century cemetery. Here trial trenches failed to identify the presence of either the cemetery or the defensive ditches (all of the trial trenches struck the post-medieval rubble which made up the latest ditch fill). As a result, the excavations were conducted under the most urgent conditions, in the midst of the construction programme. Because the Coalyard provided the main site access for the contractors, the excavations were dug as space became available. As in the case of Mills Mount, gaps in the record have resulted.

APPROACH TO WEST TUNNEL PORTAL (Area T)

The West tunnel exit apron is to the N of Mills Mount and the Cartshed. Excavation of this area took place in July 1989 in advance of the construction of the vehicle tunnel exit. The archaeological strategy was to recover information concerning the two known major construction phases: the 17th-century defences, and the Powder Magazine of the 19th century. Information was also sought to relate the development of this area to that of Area H (Mills Mount) and Area X (Storekeeper's House), immediately to the S. In doing so it was hoped to identify the remains of pre-17th-century defences.

Following the completion of the main contract, a number of other small excavations and watching briefs have taken place since the completion of the main programme. Where relevant, the results have been incorporated into the main report.

Key aspects of the excavations can only be fully understood by reference to the geological formations upon which they are built. For that reason a short discussion of the geology was commissioned as part of the post-excavation programme. It has been included in the introduction rather than with the other environmental studies since it provides information necessary for a full appreciation of the archaeological structures.

2.3 THE GEOLOGICAL SETTING
Nigel A Ruckley

Edinburgh Castle is situated on an easily defendable prominence which has cliffs on three sides that rise up to over 50m above the surrounding area. The location and subsequent development of the Castle were directly controlled by the local geology, and the strategic value of the site, close to and commanding the capital city, has always been considered sufficiently important to outweigh any resulting logistical problems, such as the provision of a satisfactory water supply.

2.3.1 GEOLOGY

The Castle Rock is the eroded remnant of a basaltic plug of an ancient volcano intruded almost vertically through a sequence of Cementstone Group sedimentary rocks of Lower Carboniferous (Dinantian) age (345 Ma). Subsequent glacial erosion of the area during the Pleistocene (2.0 Ma to about 10,000 years BP) has created a classic example of a landform known as a 'crag and tail' (illus 17). The over-deepened valleys surrounding the crag on three sides are partially filled with glacial and post-glacial drift deposits, leaving the Castle Rock and most of the 'tail', extending towards the E from the plug, comparatively free of drift (Sissons 1971) (illus 18).

The Castle Rock is oval in shape and elongated in a NW – SE direction. The axis of the plug is tilted slightly from the vertical towards the SE (Cheeney 1977). The plug may represent a series of intrusions, as the chilled margins of the basalt plug are not confined to the intrusion's outer limit (Tait nd). This is illustrated by the chilled surface on the inner side of the partly opened vertical fissure that separates the main portion of the Castle Rock from the crag on which lie the ruins known as Crane Bastion.

The plug consists of a Dalmeny type microporphyritic basalt of Lower Carboniferous age, and has a fine-grained groundmass, consisting of plagioclase feldspar, augite and magnetite, with phenocrysts of slightly altered olivine and augite. The rock exhibits weathering at two outcrops on the E side of the plug near the Fore Well, elsewhere it is in a fresh and unaltered condition. To the W of the Governor's House, the rock exhibits a more doleritic, coarser grained texture (Price & Knill 1967, 411–432).

The extent of the basalt to the N and S of the Castle is difficult to define, as the junction with the sediments is masked by post-glacial drift deposits. The W edge of the plug can be traced in the gardens on the E side of King's Stables Road below the cliff, where marls, marly shales and sandstones of the Cementstone Group are exposed.

On the E side, the sedimentary rocks form an irregular terrace, utilised by the Eastern defences, that rises from near the SE part of the plug in a NW direction to within 7.3m of the summit. These rocks consist

Illus 17
The solid geology of central Edinburgh (based upon the 6" edition of map sheets NT 27 SW and SE, British Geological Survey, 1965).

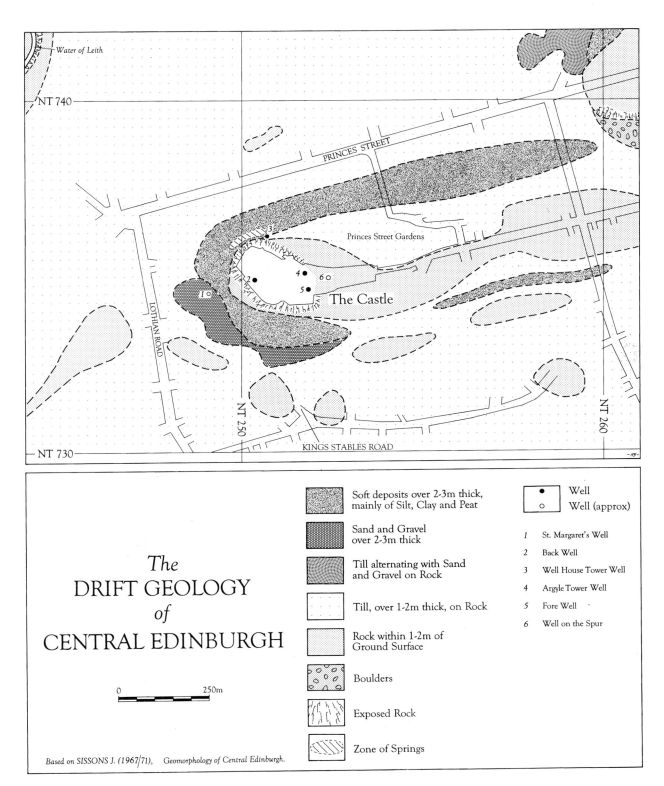

The
DRIFT GEOLOGY
of
CENTRAL EDINBURGH

0   250m

Based on SISSONS J. (1967/71), Geomorphology of Central Edinburgh.

	Soft deposits over 2-3m thick, mainly of Silt, Clay and Peat
	Sand and Gravel over 2-3m thick
	Till alternating with Sand and Gravel on Rock
	Till, over 1-2m thick, on Rock
	Rock within 1-2m of Ground Surface
	Boulders
	Exposed Rock
	Zone of Springs

● Well
○ Well (approx)

1   St. Margaret's Well
2   Back Well
3   Well House Tower Well
4   Argyle Tower Well
5   Fore Well
6   Well on the Spur

Illus 18
The drift geology of central Edinburgh (after Sissons, 1967) showing the locations of wells.

Illus 19
Geological section of the S side of the Esplanade, showing the rock exposed during the construction of Johnston Terrace in 1829 (from Greenock 1833).

mainly of beds of sandstone between 0.3 to 0.6m thick, which are interbedded with cornstones and friable greenish grey marly shales. In places, these rocks are hardened by metamorphic contact at the near vertical junction with the E side of the plug (Tait 1942, 28–33).

Further E, near the W end of the Esplanade, the sequence of sedimentary rocks is cut by the NE tending Castle Hill Fault of Late or Post Carboniferous age. The only visible exposure of the fault lies on the grassy slope below the S side of the Half Moon Battery. Here the downfaulted sandstones, cornstones and baked sandy marls between the Castle Hill Fault and the E margin of the plug, dip steeply to the NW at angles of between 30 and 40 degrees. At the E of the fault, the sediments dip gently to the E and can be seen in the S-facing bank below the Esplanade (Greenock 1833, 39–45; BGS 6" Geological Sheets NT27 SW & SE) (illus 19).

Glacial and post-glacial deposits in the vicinity of the Castle consist of till, sand and gravel, lacustrine sediments and made ground, which are in places up to 30m in thickness (Sissons 1971).

Although no glacial or post-glacial deposits have been positively identified on the summit of the Castle Rock, the tail of rock on which the medieval burgh stood was covered by an uneven and usually thin cover of till which has been masked in parts by human deposits, often of considerable depth.

Lacustrine deposits in the area now occupied by Princes Street Gardens may have represented part of an earlier post-glacial lake. The artificial Nor' Loch that provided a defensive barrier on the N side of the Castle and city, occupied part of this area from its formation early in the 15th century until it was drained early in the 19th century (Tait 1942, 28–29).

2.3.2 GEOLOGICAL AND GEOMORPHOLOGICAL FACTORS AFFECTING THE LAYOUT OF THE CASTLE

The majority of the Castle's inner defences lie within the confines of the basalt plug. The Eastern defences, on the weaker side, utilised all the available high ground. The 16th-century Half Moon Battery and David's Tower lie partially on the plug and partially on the uneven terrace of incompletely metamorphosed and often weathered sedimentary rocks.

The former medieval ditches (see 3.9 Area M) of the outer defences occupied what is now the W portion of the Esplanade, where the faulted sedimentary rocks would have made their construction easier. When the defences were remodelled in the 16th century to form an earthen spur work, material would have been available for its construction.

Because of the hardness of the basalt plug – first recorded in a siege engineer's report of 1572–3 as 'a massy substance' (RCAHMS 1951, 6) – any mining and counter-mining has been restricted to the tunnelling of the sedimentary rocks underlying the Esplanade (Douglas 1898, 199–210). The relative softness of these eastern rocks is one of the factors which has allowed this approach to be altered in post-medieval times.

Only the E face of the castle was ever considered for infantry assault following the successful destruction of the Eastern defences by mine or bombardment. The late 17th-century survey of the castle suggests that the sedimentary rocks in the vicinity of the Half Moon Battery were of a less formidable appearance than their present artificially steepened counterpart (illus 1 and 22, PRO MPF 245 (4021 [1696]).

2.3.3 BUILDING STONE

The basalt of the Castle Rock was never a primary source of building material for the majority of the buildings still extant on the Rock today. Only the Well House Tower, constructed in 1362, uses local basalt rubble for its walls, with freestone dressings (RCAHMS 1951, 17).

Although basalt is durable, it is not easily worked into ashlar or freestone and, as a result, Carboniferous sandstone from local quarries was the preferred building material from an early date in the Castle, as well as in the city of Edinburgh (McMillan 1987, 89–117). The 12th-century St Margaret's chapel and the 14th-century David's Tower are both constructed of sandstone ashlar, whilst the 16th-century Half Moon Battery is constructed mainly from rough-dressed sandstone blocks.

Published building accounts between 1529 and 1649 indicate that at least four named sandstone quarries were utilised for either new work or repair of existing structures (Paton 1957; Imrie & Dunbar 1982). Between 1615 and 1617 the substantial rebuilding of the Palace used sandstone from Craigleith (NT 226 745) and St Cuthbert's quarries. The latter quarry was opened specifically for the work and proved very subject to flooding. Two other named quarries, Maidencraig (near Blackhall) (NT 223 745) and Craigmillar (NT 285 709) are specifically mentioned in the accounts of 1628 and 1639 respectively (Imrie & Dunbar 1982, lxxix–lxxxv).

2.3.4 WATER SUPPLY

The locations of the wells in Edinburgh Castle were dictated by the geology (illus 18). The difficulty in obtaining sufficient water is related to the type of rocks on which the Castle stands and caused considerable embarrassment and expense from the construction of the castle until the introduction of mains water in the 19th century (Ruckley 1990, 14–26).

The basalt, on which the major part of the fortress now stands, is naturally a very poor aquifer. In 1967 during rock stabilisation work, a level of permanent water saturation was recorded about 15m above the footpath W of the Well House Tower. As none of the wells on the plug is sunk to this depth, the internal flow of water into the well shafts is therefore controlled by the number, size and orientation of the joints and fractures within the rock that communicate with the well shafts from the rain catchment area. Any prolonged dry spell, coupled with increased water consumption, would severely deplete the amount of water present in the wells.

Numerous springs have been reported at the foot of the Castle Rock or close to its base which would indicate that the natural ground water table in the sedimentary rocks and superficial deposits surrounding the plug is on, or very close to, the natural ground level (SRO Map RHP 35690; NLS MSS 8027, f.14v; NLS Map Z2/8a).

Under siege conditions, topography determined which wells the garrison could use to their advantage. Wells, although of limited capacity, within the defences on the summit would be more easily defended and

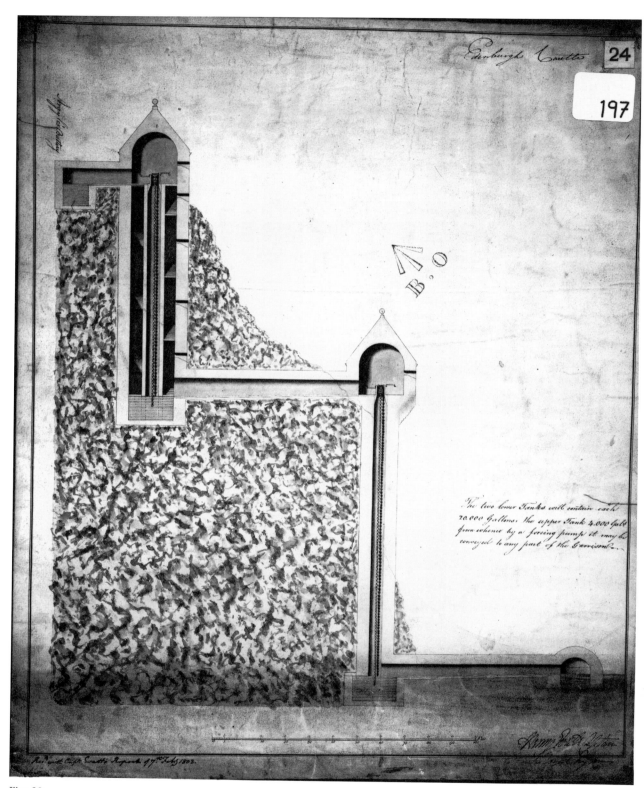

Illus 20
Designs for bomb-proof towers to lift water into the Castle from the Well-House Tower (Reproduced courtesy of the Keeper of the Records of Scotland; Scottish Record Office RHP35774).

presented fewer logistical problems of transporting water than an abundant supply of water situated at the base of the Castle Rock. For example, in 1381 when war with England seemed imminent, the Fore Well was restored to working order as there had been no water available from the only well on the summit of the rock since its deliberate slighting in 1314. (Exch Rolls III, 81–2).

The medieval Castle's water supply falls into two distinct groups. The lower wells surrounding the base of the Castle Rock consist of St Margaret's Well (often confused with the well at the Well House Tower, but probably in the vicinity of the Castle Terrace Car Park), and the well and springs at the Well House Tower. The higher wells consist of one on the Esplanade associated with the Spur (Bannatyne Misc II, 72–80), the Argyll Tower well (J Elphinstone Plan of Edinburgh Castle, British Library Map Library K Top XLIX.73), the Fore Well, and the Back Well (Ruckley 1990, 25).

Acute water shortages were experienced, not only during the 1572–3 and 1689 sieges, but with increasing frequency during the mid 18th century when large garrison numbers severely stretched resources (Rae 1966). Several schemes to alleviate the water shortage were proposed in the late 18th and early 19th centuries including estimates and plans for the construction of cisterns (National Library of Scotland, Board of Ordnance Plans MS.1649. Z.3/53 and Z.3/54a&b). Two rainwater cisterns were constructed under the Half Moon Battery, probably between 1779 and 1785.

An elaborate scheme proposed in 1803, which illustrates the extent of the concern, although not implemented, called for the construction of two bomb-proof towers sited on the N face of the Castle Rock (illus 20, Scottish Record Office Plan RHP. 35774). Each tower contained a reservoir in its base together with a windlass and an endless chain of buckets. The cistern was to be filled from springs situated to the W of the Well House Tower. Once within the castle the water was to have been stored in a cistern within the Argyll Battery and a force pump was to have distributed the water throughout the Castle.

Uncertainty remains regarding the longevity of the two late 18th-century rainwater cisterns within the Half Moon Battery. It is not clear whether these tanks continued to collect rain water after the installation of a pumped water storage scheme using water from the Fore Well. A third water tank was added after 1858. A re-examination of all available data since the publication of Ruckley 1990 has led to a revised date of early to mid 19th century for the introduction of the Fore Well pumped water storage scheme utilising a triple cylinder pump of late 18th-century design (Ruckley 1990, 19; James Wood pers comm).

Mains water began to be piped in to the Castle in the early 19th century and around 1850 mains water was brought into the upper castle and stored in a circular metal tank near Foogs Gate (Ordnance Survey Map 1854).

THE EXCAVATIONS: THE STRUCTURES AND THEIR HISTORICAL CONTEXT

3.1 DEFINITION AND CONCORDANCE OF PHASING

In this report the numerous individual trenches have been grouped into six larger areas for ease of discussion. Three of these were located in the W interior: Mills Mount (Areas H and X), the 19th-century Powder Magazine (Area T) and the 1801 Main Guard (Area F) and three near the E entrance: the Entrance Flanker (Areas G, J, K and R), the Inner Barrier (Area L), and the Coal Yard (Area M) (illus 21). The discussion of the historical background focuses on the two general excavation locations and they precede the detailed accounts of the W interior areas and the E entrance structures. At the beginning of each section an abstract account is provided of the major structures found in each area and the chronological scheme which has been employed to interpret these structures. Where dates have been provided for phases, it should be understood that they are approximate. The dating evidence is discussed in detail for each phase individually.

The internal complexity found in each area and the uncertainty of the dating of particular phases was a discouragement from applying a single set of numbers to all the excavated phases. However, wherever possible corresponding phase numbers are used for developments in associated areas. Unfortunately it has not proved possible to link the chronology of all of the separate phases for each area; table 1 provides a concordance of the various areas and their phasing. A more detailed concordance is provided for the complex deposits in the Mills Mount area (Table 4, 1:A2–B4).

Table 1 Concordance of phasing between the excavated areas

The string of equal signs indicate that there are stratigraphic links between the phases in the separate areas. Question marks indicate that the phase is only loosely dated. No stratigraphic link existed between the W interior and E entrance.

		WESTERN INTERIOR				EASTERN ENTRANCE				
Area	H/X		T	F		G, J, K & R		L		M
Phase	1									
	2									
	3		1?							
	4									
	5									
	6					1				1
	7		2?			2	===	2	===	2
	8			1?		3	===	3	===	3
						4	===	4	===	4
	9	===	3			5	===	5	===	5
	10	===	4			6	===	6	===	6
			5	===	2					
			6							
			7	===	3	7	===	7	===	7

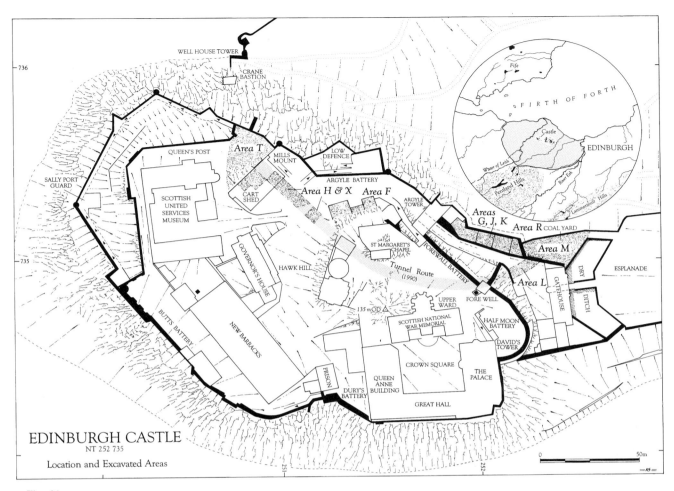

Illus 21
Edinburgh Castle: location plan and excavated areas.

3.2 HISTORICAL BACKGROUND TO THE WESTERN INTERIOR
Doreen Grove

3.2.1 MILLS MOUNT (Areas H and X) AND THE POWDER MAGAZINE (Area T)

Evidence for the medieval use of the W part of the Castle is scarce. In 1093 Queen Margaret's body was carried out of the Western postern of Edinburgh Castle by her son, in an attempt to escape capture by his uncle who was besieging the Castle's front entrance (Anderson, 1922, II, 86). They escaped along a road to the W of the Castle, but that postern may have been in the Upper Ward wall and is not evidence for the enclosure of the W part of the Rock. There is a possibility that the area below the summit was used for the repair of siege engines, but there is no firm evidence to support the theory. However the area was certainly used with the coming of the royal arsenal. Guns were both manufactured and repaired in the Castle (Caldwell 1983), somewhere to the S of the W plateau near the vaults which support the S and W sides of Crown Square. The use of guns required the storage of gunpowder, because of the dangers attendant on the storage this was done as far as possible away from the centre of the Castle. The building visible low in the W on the Gordon of Rothiemay drawing of 1647 was probably a powder magazine (see illus 73).

The connection between the Castle and the Well House Tower of David II, built in the late 14th century, may also have necessitated some form of defended approach from the W of the citadel, at a point near Mills

Mount. But it is not clear from the surviving structures how this approach was made, or indeed whether the water was lifted by some mechanical means or was carried.

For most of the history of the Castle there is no specific mention of this part of the rock. Captain John Slezer was the first to produce a plan to systematically consolidate and utilise the Western Defences (MacIvor 1993, 82–3). He began his work in the early 1670s and continued for more than thirty years. His earliest plans show an intention to use the space for accommodation as well as storage and manufacturing, with the whole being defended by an improved encircling wall, to enable 'the sentries to pass round it at night', and the approach road strengthened by the building of an Inner Traverse, an anti-personnel device which channelled the traffic through a narrow gate overlooked by musket loops, much like those in the walls adjacent to Foog's Gate (MacIvor 1993, 83 illus 52). He, and successive Board of Ordnance Engineers, built and rebuilt batteries on all sides to protect the back of the Castle, on Hawk Hill, at Mills Mount, along the Butts and at Dury's battery on the S.

Among the first buildings documented in the W part of the Castle was the two-storeyed structure which seems to have been used as gunners accommodation from the late 17th century (illus 22, British Library Map Library, K Top XLIX.69, PRO WORK 31/18). The gunners were trained artillerymen, formed into companies, who provided the main garrison for the castle. By 1725 the building was being used as a Storekeeper's House with a small extension to the W (illus 62). The external stairway visible on the S side of the building on the late 17th-century drawing seems to be enclosed on the later plan (illus 60). The storekeeper will have lived here alongside and above the stores. The slope of the site allowed a basement storey to be set into the hill.

A plan drawn by William Adam in 1746, shows the site empty; both the Storekeeper's House and the Inner Traverse were removed at this time. Adam's workmen had removed the structures as part of the upgrading of the defences which he was currently under contract to complete. The site was not long allowed to remain vacant. In 1746 a plan was drawn up by the engineer Dougall Campbell of a building to replace the Storekeeper's House. The new building was to be for bread carts, to supply the army on the move. Presumably this was prompted by the inadequate supply machinery available to respond to the troubles of the previous year. It was to have five gabled double doorways, with the multi-pitched roof being held up internally on a series of pillars. This created a large, open, single-storeyed Cartshed, clearly ignoring the existence of the basement which had existed in the earlier building.

The Cartshed was extended to the NW at the beginning of the 19th century. Because of the topography the extension incorporated two storeys, the upper one level with the existing structure, but only four bays wide, unlike the original building which had five. There was no access between the two areas. The original sheds became an armoury and ordnance store and the new area to the rear was a fire-proof magazine, containing cartridges for small arms (SRO, RHP35687). By 1852 the cartsheds had also been adopted for use as an expense magazine, storing cartridges and ammunition. Before the re-survey by the OS in 1877 the magazine had been altered into a barrack block. A central corridor was built just inside the old sheds, to provide access into barrack rooms in the old and the new parts of the building. Within the two sides of the building, partition walls were built separating the bays along the lines of the pillars, creating eight long narrow barrack rooms. Each room was fitted with a fireplace in the centre of one of the long walls.

The extension to the rear of the cartsheds was demolished to make way for the alterations to the N Ordnance Stores block by E Ingress Bell in 1897, which was transformed into a hospital (MacIvor 1993, 117–8). The Dougall Campbell building survived to go through further lives as a junior ranks club and most recently as a shop and is now serving as a restaurant for visitors to the Castle.

3.2.2 1801 MAIN GUARD (Area F)

The building at the foot of the Lang Stair was purpose-built as a Guard-House in 1801 (PRO WO5/818), to a design by Major Stratton. It consisted of a large room in the W, the main guardroom with four double beds; two small central rooms; a larger Orderly Room and, to the extreme E, a small guardroom squeezed into an awkward corner to overlook the Lang Stairs. One of the central rooms will have been a lock-up cell. This building replaced the Main Guard which had stood at the top of the

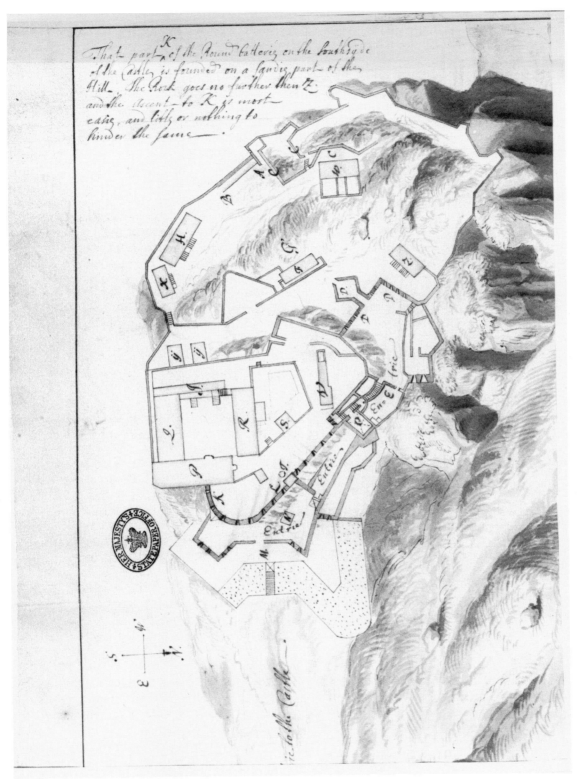

Illus 22
Plan of Edinburgh Castle *c* 1696 with annotation commenting upon the accessibility of the Rock in the event of assault (Crown Copyright PRO MPF 245).

Lang Stairs since before Slezer's arrival in Edinburgh. It is possible that it dates from as early as 1575 as part of Regent Morton's work undertaken after the 1573 siege when the Constable's Tower was replaced by the Portcullis Gate. It is shown on Slezer's drawing of 1674 and despite an attempt to move its function to a new building on the site of the present Governors House in the late 17th century so that it would overlook the new Inner Traverse designed by Slezer, the site at the top of the stairs continued in use.

Both the Main Guards were probably abandoned in 1853 when the Flanker was converted to a Guardhouse and by 1877 both had been demolished (Ordnance Survey, second edition). The port guard served the Flanker Guardhouse until the existing gatehouse was built in 1886–8. The upper guardhouse, which spent the last 70 years of its life as a barrack store, was demolished to make way for a skittle alley.

The Main Guard performed several functions: the position of the building enabled the soldiers of the Main Guard to monitor traffic into and out of the Castle; it was the duty station for the officer of the guard, who issued instructions to the subordinate guard posts at the port guard, the sally-port Guard (while such existed) and the guard for Palace Yard (Crown Square); it was also where soldiers were taken when they were put on a charge and their immediate fate was decided. Depending on how serious the charge was they received either a summary punishment or time in a lock-up until a court martial was due to sit. The soldiers serving on guard performed regular tasks, either as sentries at the gate, on a patrol around sections of the wall or as guards at the lock-up cells. Once that duty was completed each returned to rest on the beds provided, covered only with the blanket brought from his barrack room, but at all times men on guard slept fully clothed to be able to respond quickly to emergencies.

3.3 MILLS MOUNT (Areas H and X)

3.3.1 ABSTRACT SEQUENCE (illus 23)

Individual plans are provided in the main text for each phase and the main sections from each side of the trench are contained in the fold-out sheet at the back of the volume (illus 24). As a ready guide within the text, the description of each phase contains a key logo of the section with the appropriate portion highlighted.

PHASE 1 Late Bronze Age – early Iron Age (900 BC–200 BC

Occupation represented by a group of pits, scant cobbled surfaces, soil hearths, a stone-built drain and few artefacts. These earliest traces only survived in the deepest part of the trench and even here had been damaged by the Phase 2 Iron Age building works. The most striking features were two pits containing substantial portions of smashed pots.

PHASE 2 Late Iron Age (200 BC–AD 100)

Occupation in this phase is represented by fragments of three round houses and extensive paved surfaces. No complete buildings lay entirely within the trench. All appear to have been substantially demolished and to have had timber superstructures. The period of occupation is likely to have spanned the last couple of centuries BC to the 1st or 2nd century AD, although arguably the buildings were in an advanced state of decay by the Roman times. A small number of abraded sherds of local Iron Age pottery and a few Roman sherds come from contexts attributed to this phase.

PHASE 3 Roman (AD 100–300)

The deposits attributed to this phase can be described as primary midden. The layers are composed predominantly of ash and hearth sweepings, containing copious amounts of animal bone. Extensive areas were covered with matted vegetable matter (perhaps thatching) which had been buried before it

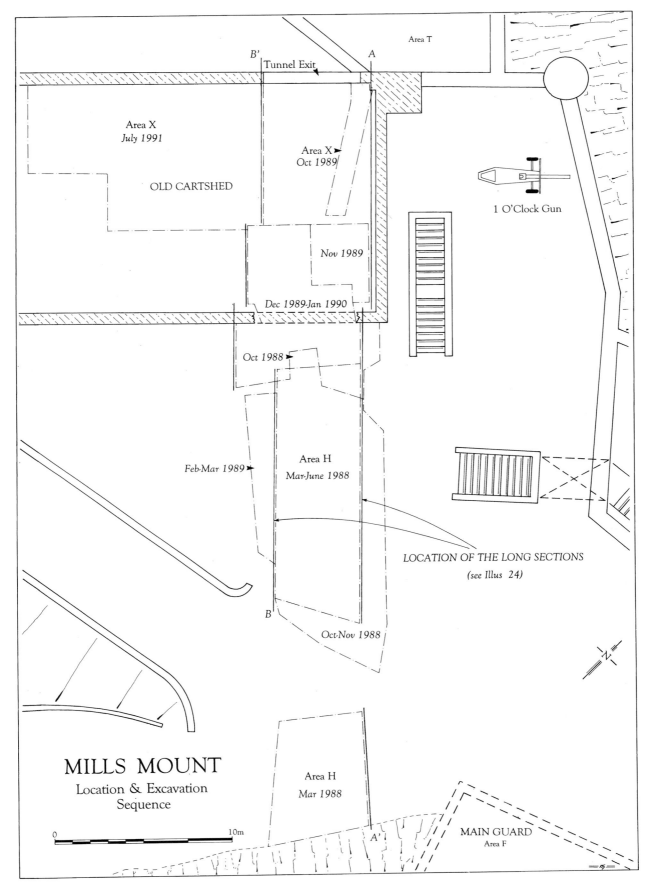

Area T

B' Tunnel Exit A

Area X
July 1991

Area X ►
Oct 1989

OLD CARTSHED

Nov 1989

Dec 1989-Jan 1990

1 O'Clock Gun

Oct 1988 ►

Feb-Mar 1989 ►

Area H
Mar-June 1988

LOCATION OF THE LONG SECTIONS
(see Illus 24)

B

Oct-Nov 1988

MILLS MOUNT
Location & Excavation
Sequence

0   10m

Area H
Mar 1988

A'

MAIN GUARD
Area F

N

Illus 23
Mills Mount location plan and excavation sequence. For sections see illus 24.

had fully decayed. The major part of the Iron Age pottery and the Roman material comes from these midden layers. The Castle Rock was clearly still occupied, but the dwellings were not located at Mills Mount.

PHASE 4 Late Roman – early medieval (AD 300–?1000)

There was no discernable break in the continuity of the Mills Mount midden. Material continues to be deposited, but some slight evidence for activity in the area was provided by stakeholes and rough walls. The main occupation of the Castle Rock was probably still confined to the summit.

PHASE 5 Medieval (?AD 1000–1325)

At some point which is impossible to define with precision, the dumping of rubbish ceased. The paucity of closely dated finds makes it impossible to provide a tight chronology for beginnings of this reuse of Mills Mount. A cobbled pathway was built over the midden towards the west end of Castle Rock. This seems to be associated with iron-working, which was conducted in the open air and appears casual and informally organised.

PHASE 6 Medieval (AD 1325–1400)

A substantial blacksmith's workshop was constructed at Mills Mount. All of the main features of the smithy were located and most were well-preserved; in addition, some traces of the rather insubstantial workshop building were identified. Large quantities of industrial debris were recovered including much scrap iron.

PHASE 7 Late medieval (AD 1400–1550)

This phase saw the end of the smithy and the refurbishment of the workshop building and its reuse for some unknown purpose. It also saw the demolition of the building and the importation of substantial quantities of soil evidently to level off the site. This levelling material probably came from outwith the Castle and contains a jumble of 15th- and 16th-century artefacts.

PHASE 8 Early Modern (AD 1550–1675)

Two episodes of earthwork defences were revealed, neither of which is documented. The first was represented by a rubble and clay rampart of which only the base survived. This probably dates to the mid-16th century and was replaced by a ditch and rampart on a different orientation during the early 17th century.

PHASE 9 Late 17th century (1675–1745)

The defensive ditch was filled in and a set of formalised artillery defences known as the Inner Traverse were constructed. These defences, which included a semi-subterranean casemate (a bomb-proof shelter) and the Storekeeper's House, are all part of a programme of works attributed to Capt John Slezer.

PHASE 10 18th century (1745–1800)

The final building event on Mills Mount was the demolition of the Storekeeper's House and the Inner Traverse to allow the existing Cartshed to be built as part of the military reorganisation following the Jacobite Rebellion of 1745.

MODERN

All evidence of small-scale landscaping and services subsequent to the construction of the Cartshed have been described as modern.

3.3.2 THE RADIOCARBON DATES (illus 25)

Three batches comprising a total of eight samples were submitted to the Glasgow University Radiocarbon Dating facility based at the Scottish Universities Research and Reactor Centre in East Kilbride. The rationale for selecting the samples emerged from the preliminary analysis of the structural remains and was intended to help to provide an absolute dating framework for the earlier phases of Mills Mount (Areas H and X). All of the samples were of burnt wood except for GU-2913 which comes from a sample of the matted vegetable material from Phase 4. In addition to these samples several other samples made up of animal bones were submitted. These would have helped to date the midden deposits. However, although there was ample bone from secure contexts, the bones themselves had insufficient collagen to be dated. This is particularly unfortunate in view of some of the results. The specific contexts of these samples are discussed in the details of the archaeological structures below, while the charcoal identifications are the subject of a specific report (5.3 below). The calibrations quoted here are derived from the application of the OxCal Radiocarbon Calibration and Statistical Analysis Program from the Oxford Research Lab for Archaeology version 2.01.The complete references for datasets and intervals used may be found in Stuiver *et al* (1993). The details of the calibrated calibrated dates are quoted below with an errors which do not include a laboratory error multiplier.

Table 2 Radiocarbon dates and calibrations

Lab No.	Phase/ Context	Radiocarbon Age in Years	Cal Age One Sigma 68.2% confidence	Cal Age Two Sigma 95.4% confidence
GU-2579	Ph1/592	2740+50BP	912BC (1.00) 825BC	990BC (0.09) 955BC 944BC (0.91) 806BC
GU-2580	Ph2/535	1770+50BP	AD224 (0.93) AD345 AD361 (0.07) AD375	AD141 (1.00) AD396
GU-2661	Ph2/534	2040+70BP	112BC (1.00) AD60	333BC (0.00) 328BC 199BC (1.00) AD126
GU-2663	Ph2/1225	1550+50BP	AD444 (0.93) AD558 AD582 (0.07) AD591	AD420 (1.00) AD617
GU-2581	Ph3/522a	1540+50BP	AD449 (0.27) AD485 AD498 (0.15) AD518 AD530 (0.58) AD598	AD425 (1.00) AD625
GU-2664	Ph3/522b	1770+70BP	AD151 (0.03) AD158 AD214 (0.97) AD384	AD89 (0.01) AD96 AD118 (0.99) AD422
GU-2913	Ph3/511	1870+80BP	AD68 (1.00) AD247	31BC (0.01) 19BC 7BC (0.98) AD345 AD360 (0.01) AD375
GU-2662	Ph4/461	1680+160BP	AD151 (0.02) AD159 AD214 (0.98) AD553	AD20 (1.00) AD661

What is immediately clear from the inspection of these data is that at the two sigma (95.4%) level of confidence only the Phase 1 date can be distinguished. However it is possible to select the best dates for each Phase based upon stratigraphic considerations. These do not eliminate the overlap, but probably give a more accurate guide to the actual formation date of the various deposits. The reasons for favouring the specific contexts are discussed in the appropriate section of the sequence discussed below.

Table 3 Preferred radiocarbon dates for Mills Mount phasing

GU-2579	Phase 1 (592) 912–825BC	GU-2913	Phase 3 (511) AD68–AD247
GU-2661	Phase 2 (534) 112BC–AD60	GU-2662	Phase 4 (461) AD214–AD553

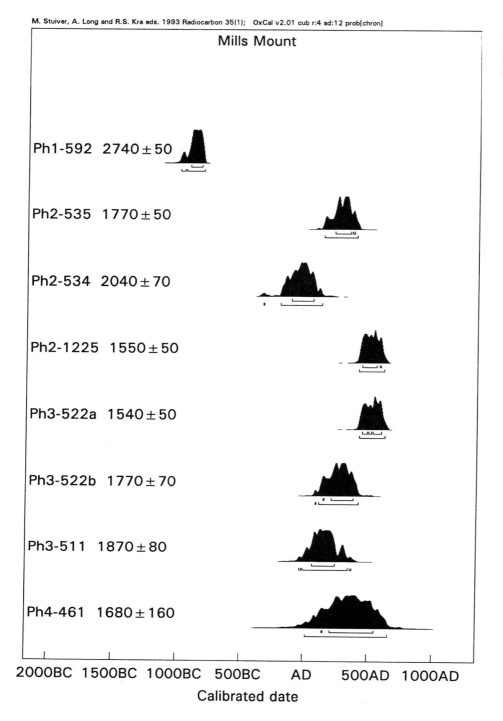

M. Stuiver, A. Long and R.S. Kra eds. 1993 Radiocarbon 35(1);   OxCal v2.01 cub r:4 sd:12 prob[chron]

Mills Mount

Ph1-592 2740±50

Ph2-535 1770±50

Ph2-534 2040±70

Ph2-1225 1550±50

Ph3-522a 1540±50

Ph3-522b 1770±70

Ph3-511 1870±80

Ph4-461 1680±160

2000BC 1500BC 1000BC 500BC   AD   500AD 1000AD

Calibrated date

Illus 25
Display of calibrated radiocarbon dates for Mills Mount.

If the calibrated dates are examined at the one sigma level of confidence (68.2%) and we focus our attention on those samples with the securest provenances, we are left with four distinct dates, one for each of the first four phases. These preferred samples provide a sequence of time spans, which on the available evidence, should be regarded as indicative of the ages of the phases. This sequence is broadly in agreement with the artefactual evidence, but in some cases the artefactual record indicates that the phases lasted for a longer time, for example the 3rd-/4th-century material from Phase 3 and the 7th-/8th-century comb from Phase 4.

It would be unwise to read too much into four radiocarbon dates from a single trench from a large site which was occupied for close to three thousand years. In addition to their scarcity there is another reason why these dates cannot be used to examine either the question of whether there is continuity of occupation from the late

Bronze Age to the late Iron Age or from the Roman period to the medieval. One of the main truths to emerge from the excavations at Mills Mount is that the usage of the area changed dramatically from age to age. While this helps us to recognise the passage of time in the archaeological record, the different uses created different opportunities for dating evidence to be deposited and identified.

3.3.3 MILLS MOUNT: DETAIL OF THE ARCHAEOLOGICAL STRUCTURES

PHASE 1

The Late Bronze Age/Early Iron Age Settlement (900 BC–200 BC)

PHASE 1 FEATURES (illus 26)

Phase 1 describes the earliest prehistoric settlement on the Rock which is dated to the late Bronze Age or early Iron Age. A hearth (F592) produced a radiocarbon age estimate calibrated to 912–825 BC (see 3.3.2). Artefacts from these deposits include pottery (see 4.1.2) and worked stone objects such as a saddle quern (see 4.1.3). The archaeological features document a range of domestic activities and other features less easily explained.

The natural configuration of the rock surface and the later accumulation of protective strata determined where the oldest deposits survived. The best preserved and the thickest prehistoric layers were found towards the NW end of the trench where the bedrock surface was lowest and the medieval soil accumulation greatest. Further SE within the trench, where the rock level was closer to the modern surface, the earliest deposits tended to survive only as pockets of soil in depressions and crevices in the irregular bedrock surface. The relative lack of protective soil also made these shallower deposits more prone to contamination and disturbance.

The basic soil matrix which characterised the earliest occupation levels was difficult to distinguish from the natural clay (536, 1081, 1395) which was observed to directly overlie the rock. This yellow brown silty clay (592, 1470) contained minute flecks of charcoal and its heavily trampled appearance identified it as an occupation surface. Set upon and cut into this surface were features which included a small area of pebble pavement, a stone-built drain, soil hearths, postholes and pits.

The major accumulation layer (597/1470) was a slightly modified natural clay-silt. It overlay the natural clay and was distinguished from the natural by its darker brown colour which in places imperceptibly graded into undisturbed natural soil. This layer contained features,

like the paving, and had features cut into it, such as the postholes. The Phase 1 deposits were stratigraphically distinct from the Phase 2 deposits which sealed the early horizon. There was little evidence of contamination among the finds and a period of abandonment or minimal activity may be inferred between Phases 1 and 2. This layer (597/1470) would appear to represent accumulation during and immediately following the earliest recognised features.

The small area investigated and the restrictions naturally imposed by the limited survival of early deposits prevents any overall interpretation of the pattern of features, but the types of feature serve to characterise the range and intensity of the earliest prehistoric activity on the rock. Broadly speaking, the drain, paving, postholes and hearth can be described as domestic, but not all features can be comprehensively interpreted.

Of the two types of features, the pit group appeared to be earlier, although the pits' stratigraphic situation with respect to the domestic features were ambiguous. The pit group (illus 26 and 27) was confined to an area some 3m by 1.5m and contained four irregular, intercutting pits (1430, 1432, 1438, 1426) and a shallow scoop (1435), which overlay and truncated several of the pits. The globular and undercut profile of the pits argued against interpreting them as large postholes, as did the contents of two of them.

Pit 1430 was the only one of the group not to have been cut by another pit or the scoop (illus 28). It was also notable because it contained the greater portion of a thick-walled bucket-shaped vessel (SF417, illus 111) and the base stone of a saddle quern (SF418, illus 113), which had been set on edge and projected above the rim of the pit (illus 29). This projecting quern ultimately came to be incorporated into the Phase 2 paving (1388). Pit 1432 also contained a large portion of a pot, an everted rimmed vessel (SF419, illus 111). It is clear that each pit was dug separately and backfilled before the next was dug. There is no way of knowing over how long a period this pit digging took place. Whereas the contents of at least one of these pits may be regarded as unusual, the fill of F1426 seems rather mundane. It contained crushed shell, patches of burnt vegetable matter, flint and potsherds, all of which could be regarded as domestic rubbish. Other pits also contained some of these objects as well as a tight packing of stones.

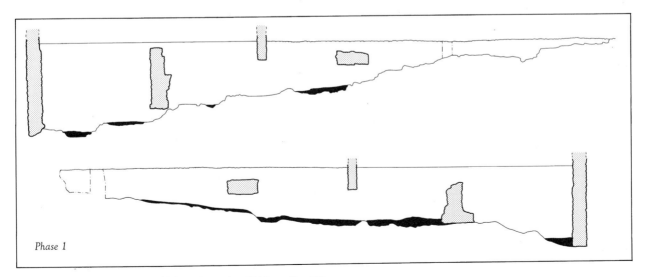

Phase 1

Phase 1: key to relevant layers within main section (fold-out illus 24).

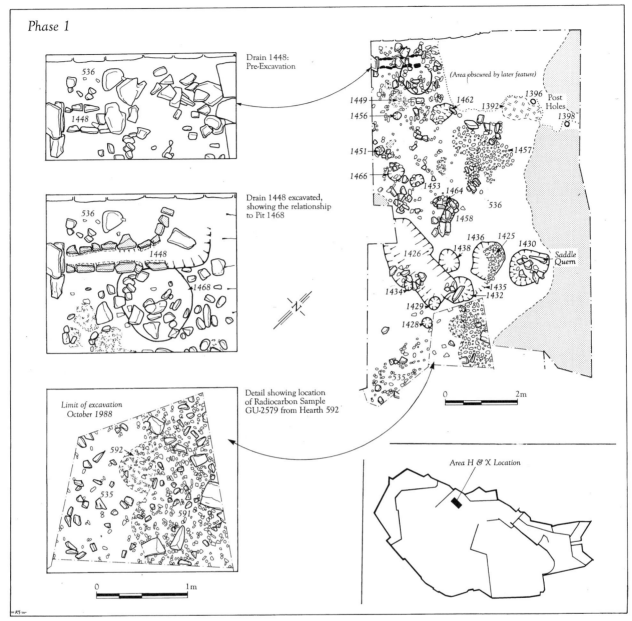

Phase 1

Drain 1448: Pre-Excavation

Drain 1448 excavated, showing the relationship to Pit 1468

Limit of excavation October 1988

Detail showing location of Radiocarbon Sample GU-2579 from Hearth 592

(Area obscured by later feature)

Post Holes

Saddle Quern

0   2m

Area H & X Location

0   1m

Illus 26
Mills Mount (Areas H & X): plan of Phase 1

Although these pits have been separated from the domestic features there is no compelling reason to regard them as having a ritual function. The possibility exists that the pots were placed into the pits, for instance while cooling, to provide them with additional support. Their smashed presence in the pits may simply be the result of breakage *in situ*.

Most of the remaining features can be categorised as elements of structures which were, at least partially, timber-built. These include postholes, small patches of pebble paving, a stone-built drain and three ground hearths, that is patches of intensely burnt soil with scant evidence of any hearth structure. There was insufficient evidence to determine how many buildings are represented or where the wall(s) may have run. Late Bronze Age/early Iron Age houses in SE Scotland are typically about 10m in diameter (Harding 1982; Rideout *et al* 1992), if the fragments revealed at Edinburgh are also from a typical house then only a fragment has been revealed in this trench. The domestic features seem to post-date the pit group, but the evidence is circumstantial.

Three relationships were observed which suggest the sequence of pits was followed by domestic activity. One of the pits in the group (1436) was covered by a skin of cobbles. Another pit (1468), which was separate from the rest, was cut by the drain (1448). The elongated pit or ditch (1426) was cut by a posthole (1429).

Of the domestic features, the hearths suggest the presence of more than one structure, not necessarily at the same time. The hearths themselves may not have been strictly 'domestic', since traces of fine droplets of iron-working clinker were recovered from one of the hearths (592). This is the only hearth from this phase to have been analysed for metalworking. It is exceptional also because the dating for this phase depends upon charcoal recovered from it. Unfortunately this hearth (592, illus 26) was encountered when only a small area of the trench was available for investigation. When a larger area was available it proved impossible to make a stratigraphic link between this hearth and the other Phase 1 features.

The building features were concentrated just to the N of the pit group,

Illus 27
Mills Mount Phase 1: pit group fully excavated; from the S.

Illus 28
Mills Mount: view of pit 1430 partially excavated.

Illus 29
Mills Mount: lifting the pot from pit 1430.

Illus 30
Mills Mount: view of drain 1448 excavated; from the E.

and ultimately being destroyed by a later scoop (Phase 2, 1455). The drain was constructed of flattish irregular stones set on edge and roughly capped. It had no basal stones and was completely silted-up, but produced no finds.

PHASE 1 DATING

The majority of features attributed to this phase cannot be closely dated. The most securely stratified artefacts from the early pit group include two types of pottery and a saddle quern and rubber, all of which are broadly datable to the late Bronze Age and early Iron Age. The single radiocarbon date comes from a hearth at the same absolute level as the pit group, but was not stratigraphically linked. The date of 912–825 cal BC provides the securest basis for believing that the Rock was occupied in the late Bronze Age, but the length of that occupation is impossible to gauge. In the absence of any evidence for the end of this phase it has been extended until the start of Phase 2 as indicated by radiocarbon evidence.

PHASE 1 INTERPRETATION

The Phase 1 artefactual finds are consistent with a later prehistoric settlement. The assemblage includes pottery, flints, shale bangles, worked bone and antler, a saddle quern and other worked stone objects (see 4.1.2–4.1.5). Like the structural features they are fundamentally domestic in character.

Given the location of the site on Castle Rock and character of the finds and structures, it seems likely that these early remains are those of a hilltop settlement, presumably enclosed, of the sort known to be a characteristic feature of the Lothians during most of the first millennium BC.

which they appear to post-date. They include six postholes (1451, 1452, 1456, 1428, 1462, 1464) and three possible postholes (1427, 1458), all of which varied between 0.25–0.45m in diameter. As a group they are too few to interpret as a building plan or to serve as the basis for an estimate of size. Irregular patches of tightly laid fine cobbles (591, 1421, 1425 and 1457) stand out from the background trampled surface (536) with its randomly scattered larger stones bedded in the packed, natural clay. These paved surfaces could be either interior or exterior features.

The most distinctive architectural feature was a stretch of stone-lined drain (1448 illus 30) which ran for 1.3m before splaying out

PHASE 2

The Late Iron Age Settlement (200 BC–AD 100)

PHASE 2 FEATURES (illus 31)

The structures of the second major phase are similar to those which characterise Phase 1, but they were better preserved, more extensive and more substantial. The better structural preservation made it possible to identify parts of three domestic buildings amongst the excavated features. The most substantial surface

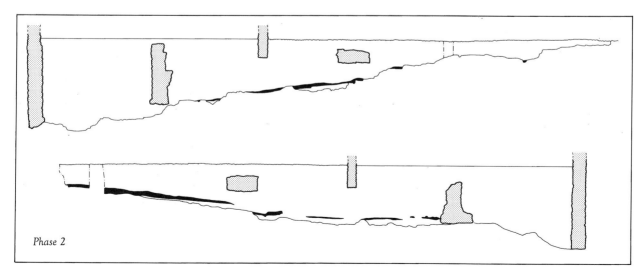

Phase 2

Illus 31 (opp)
Mills Mount (Areas H & X): plan for Phase 2 with (above) key to relevant layers within main section (fold-out illus 24).

Phase 2

HOUSE FRAGMENT 1
Sunken Cobbled surface 1391 surrounding Box Hearth 1389

1391

1389

1388N

HOUSE FRAGMENT 2
Southern spread of Flags 1388S surrounding Threshold 1420

1420

1388S

HOUSE FRAGMENT 3
Box Hearth 1222 and Pit 1226

535/1228

1226

1227

1223

1222

531

Pit 1455

Post Hole 1423

1419

Post Hole 526

(Area obscured by later feature)

Post Hole 1224

531

498

489

Pit 517

(Area obscured by later feature)

0   1m

0   2m

Area H & X Location

Illus 32
Mills Mount Phase 2: paving slabs 1388S and rough cobbling 1419; from the S. The large white rectangle on the left side is the concrete underpinning to support the E Cartshed Wall.

Illus 33
Mills Mount Phase 2: large paving slabs 1388N; from the E.

Illus 34
Mills Mount Phase 2: paving 1388S showing entrance kerb 1420.

Illus 35
Mills Mount Phase 2: paving showing hearth 1222, unexcavated pit 1223 and excavated posthole 1225; from the W.

encountered was a paving of large slabs (1388). This was in fact constructed of large unworked blocks of whinstone and 'mudstone' (sandstone bearing rippled surface), which were usually far from flat overall but had been set with the irregular side down so as to provide a level upper surface. In some instances this involved cutting through earlier (Phase 1) deposits into the natural clay to accommodate the more irregular shapes (illus 31). In excavation the paving (1388) was treated as a single feature, but subsequent analysis suggests that it represents two episodes of paving belonging to separate buildings (illus 31; 32).

The N area of slabs (1388N, illus 33) runs up against the kerb of large stones set around a sunken cobbled surface (1391) approximately 0.3m lower than the slabs with a polygonal stone setting (1389). This stone box probably served as a hearth, but only scant traces of charcoal and ash (1390) were recovered from the soil within the box. No other features in this phase can be definitely associated with the hearth and pavings, but it is most likely that the sunken area formed the central area of a house constructed with a stone and timber superstructure. The sunken area and the associated features were all buried by a soil composed of both humic material and a large proportion of the natural

yellow clay. This infilling was presumably deliberate and provided a soil surface which became trampled hard.

Moving away from the scooped area the edge of 1388N was poorly defined. The large slabs of 1388N graded into an area of rough cobbles and packed earth (1419, illus 34). A second area of paving (1388S) consisted of noticeably smaller slabs and focused on a setting of three slabs set on edge in a line (1420). These three stones formed a slightly curving kerb 1.1 × 0.2 × 0.1m (illus 34). A similar structural element in House IV at Broxmouth has been interpreted (with the benefit of a complete house plan) as a threshold (Hill 1982b, 172). The different sizes of the slabs (in 1388N and 1388S) and orientation of the kerb (1420) to the sunken cobbled area (1391) indicated that they belong to different structures. There was no definite stratigraphic relationship but it would seem that the threshold feature (1420) post-dated the infilling of the sunken floored structure. Also post-dating the infilling was a posthole (1455) set against the former edge of the sunken area.

Elements of a third house were detected around a second box-hearth (1222), which again produced scant evidence of fire (illus 35). Here the surrounding area was of beaten earth (535/1228) rather than cobbles or slabs. Adjacent to the hearth was a large pit (1226) capped by irregular stones and slabs (1223). It appeared to belong to this phase, although circumstances did not allow for its excavation. On the opposite side of the hearth was a large, 0.6 × 0.6 × 0.3m, posthole (1224) containing masses of charcoal (1225) which provided material for the radiocarbon date, GU-2663. Although the posthole was originally thought to be contemporary with the hearth, its calibrated date range of AD 420–617 appears to be too late, given the quantity of Roman period artefacts in the subsequent Phase 3 deposits. It must be regarded as a probability that the feature belongs to a later phase and that its top was missed during excavation. The best radiocarbon date for this phase derives from charcoal recovered from the matrix of the packed earthen surface (534). It provides a calibrated date range of 112 BC to AD 60 which is more in line with the recovered artefacts (see below).

Further up the slope various sizes of cobbling were found, the most extensive being layer (531) which graded into the finer cobbles (489) at the top of the trench. The distinctions between the areas of beaten earth (eg 535) and the rough cobbling (531) were not definite or clearly marked and the boundaries between them are arbitrary. At the top of the slope, where the soil depth was at its shallowest, some of the cobbles (489) may have been exposed during the Middle Ages when the area was used as a smithy (see below Phase 6).

On the E side of the trench much of the bedrock was apparently exposed during Phase 2. In places the surface showed clear signs of wear and contemporary surfaces survived only as isolated pockets of cobbles in crevices. Not only was the rock worn but in places it appears to have been worked. In the SE corner an irregular pit (517) had been cut into the rock for an unknown purpose. It produced no artefacts and had been infilled with loose chippings, probably soon after it was dug.

PHASE 2 DATING

There are three radiocarbon dates for this phase, but only one of these (GU-2661 from 534) seems to provide an accurate indication of the age of the structures. It was difficult to find deposits with appropriate dating material. Sample GU-2663 came from a large posthole (1225) adjacent to one of the box-hearths, with which it was believed to be contemporary. Unfortunately the calibrated date range AD 444–591 is in conflict with the age estimates for the artefacts recovered from this phase. This posthole was located in the narrow strip on the W side of the trench which was excavated separately from the main trench. To maximise the time spent working on the early deposits, the top layers were machined off. This may account for a failure to notice that the post had been cut from an earlier level.

The second radiocarbon date which seems somewhat out of phase with the artefactual evidence (GU-2580) came from a bulk soil sample of the deposits (535) used as bedding for the rough cobble paving (531). This cobbling appeared to be contemporary with the buildings, but was very rough and easily disturbed. As a consequence the calibrated date range of AD 224–375 may relate to final use and dismantling of the buildings.

The most secure radiocarbon date (GU-2661) also came from a bulk sample, but from a layer (534) which was sealed by later areas of burning which did not exhibit much disturbance. Based upon the scant architectural evidence the calibrated date span of 112 BC to AD 60 seems about right, but the stratigraphic relationship with the built features is remote.

Although there were very few artefacts recovered from Phase 2 contexts, none of which were closely datable ones, they suggest a period of activity in the later Iron Age. In particular the rotary quern, points towards the later Iron Age, while the scarcity of Roman finds suggests that these buildings went out of use by the 2nd century AD, when relatively large quantities of pottery appear on the site. The three Roman sherds recovered from Phase 2 contexts could all be intrusive: there is evidence for burrowing

animals. On balance it seems most reasonable to consider that these structures date to the last centuries BC and 1st century AD and that by the time the Roman military arrived the population of the settlement had significantly diminished.

PHASE 2 INTERPRETATION

Given the unsatisfactory, not to say contradictory, dating evidence and the fragmentary survival of distinctive structural features, detailed interpretations about the nature of the settlement are not justified. What is clear is that during the later Iron Age, a community with a tradition of building stone-floored round houses occupied the NW shoulder of the Castle Rock. This occupation was long-lived enough to allow a sequence of three houses to be built in succession. Given their topographical situation, this settlement must be considered as a hillfort.

It is most likely that the features of this phase represent elements of a hillfort interior, given the ubiquity of enclosed later prehistoric settlements in SE Scotland (well-documented in RCAHMS 1956, Harding 1982 and Rideout et al 1992). The range of features encountered in this phase are typical of other later prehistoric settlements in SE Scotland, which consist of buildings constructed with substantial stone elements. These features include areas of stone flagging, cobbled surfaces, and stone-built 'box-hearths', while surprisingly few settings for timber elements were noted. Although preservation in this phase is superior to that of the preceding phase, and the survival of remains more extensive, an additional post-depositional factor to consider is the apparent dismantling of the buildings. Given the use of stone in the structures, one would expect more stone to be present in the layers of post-occupation debris. The relatively stone-free deposits in Phase 3 (see below) suggests that the buildings were deliberately dismantled, perhaps so the stone could be used elsewhere.

Unfortunately there were few deposits which could be regarded as representing debris associated with the occupation of these houses, hence the small number of artefacts (for example there were only four prehistoric sherds to go with the three Roman ones). On balance it seems as though the houses were abandoned at the start of, or during, the 2nd century AD. The predominance of Roman material in the subsequent deposits of Phase 3 indicates that this area was unoccupied by the time of the midden formation.

PHASE 3

Roman Period Midden (AD 100–300)

PHASE 3 FEATURES (illus 36)

Some of the richest and most intriguing deposits on Mills Mount are those which signal the abandonment of the buildings occupied in Phase 2. All of those features clearly relating to the settlement were sealed by extensive layers of artefact-rich midden. These deposits accumulated over a period of decades if not centuries and provide the clearest evidence for continuity of settlement on the Castle Rock from the late Iron Age to the early medieval period.

The midden was represented by broad horizons of soil composed mainly of the ashy remains of burnt vegetable material with a relatively small mineral component (illus 36 inset and 37). These deposits varied in colour from dusky reddy browns to bright pinks and in texture from a soft, sticky loam to a stiff, fine silt approaching a clay-like fineness (for detailed discussion of the soil micromorphology see 5.5 below). Animal bones and artefacts were present in large quantities (illus 38 and 39).

Originally an attempt was made to make fine distinctions between the discrete dumps of burnt material (eg 516, 520, 522, 523), but the 'stop and start' nature of the excavations (see illus 23) made

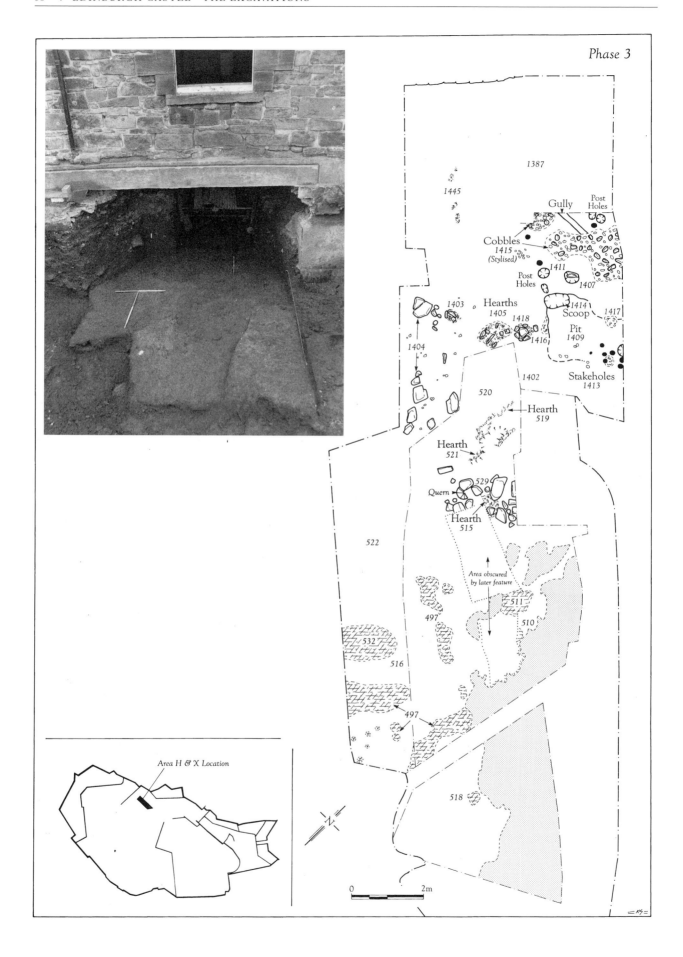

Phase 3

Area H & X Location

0   2m

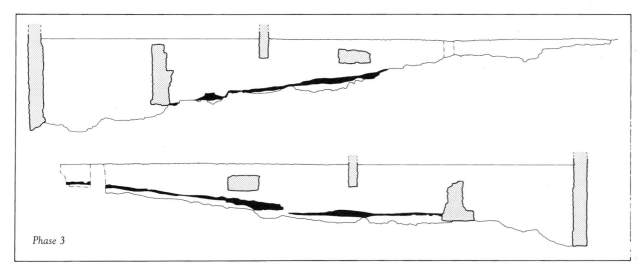

Phase 3

Illus 36 (opp)
Mills Mount (Areas H & X): plan for Phase 3 with inset showing primary midden 1387 running under the Cartshed; from the S; above, key to relevant layers within main section (fold-out illus 24).

Illus 37
Mills Mount Phase 3: section showing build up of primary midden 1387 over paving 1388; from the W.

distinctions difficult to trace from one adjacent area to the next. In any event because of the complexity of the deposition such distinctions were imperfect and of indeterminate significance chronologically. As the excavations were expanded to tunnel beneath the former Cartshed, the greater depth of deposit and the better preservation here allowed a broad distinction to be drawn between a lower, less disturbed horizon (1387) and an upper horizon (1392) which had been more disturbed by both animal and human activity. To some extent the distinctions between these two levels was arbitrary, but texture and the disposition of the animal bones provided a coarse subjective indicator. The lower levels were much less disturbed, with several instances of bones surviving in their articulated position. These upper levels are considered in the next section on Phase 4.

The midden deposits survived wherever the depth of bedrock protected them from disturbance in the late medieval period. In

places the midden was 0.8m deep and the micromorphology analysis (see 5.5) suggests that an additional unknown depth has been lost from the top during the Middle Ages. The analysis of the soil micromorphology indicates that the lower layers (516, 1387) were formed by rapidly deposited multiple dumps which in places consist of almost pure hearth sweepings (vegetable ash with a high component of quartz, which probably derived from sandstone used as hearth stones). In addition there was a relative lack of disturbance as demonstrated on the macro level by articulated animal bones (illus 7 and 38) and potsherds (illus 40), and on the micro level by sharp boundaries between the layers. These sharp boundaries indicate that the midden was formed rapidly enough to prevent these characteristics from being disturbed by invertebrates or plant roots forming perhaps over a matter of months. (The post-depositional history has further complicated the picture: the graphic interpretation of the formation of the midden (illus 41) is intended to clarify these processes).

Within the midden there were several points of interest. Perhaps most interesting were the dark brown-black matted fibrous deposits which were originally interpreted as decayed timber or a buried turf horizon (373, 382, 384, 400, 497, 511, 518, 532). The thin section analysis of the soil showed these deposits to be the residues of decayed grass culms or leaves. This is likely to represent matted straw derived from thatching, bedding or floor covering. This matted layer was both thin (about 0.02m) and extensive, being spread over an area at least 8 × 4m.

As indicated above, the soil micromorphology detected much more complexity within the midden deposits than the few context numbers used in the field would suggest. For example context 522, one of the more extensive layers, was seen at the micro level to consist of two distinct horizons. The lowest, which had accumulated on the former Phase 2 living surfaces (eg 531), essentially consisted of the natural soil as found directly on the bedrock with many small fragments of charcoal, ash, bone and other signs of human activity trampled in. The upper horizon within 522 was composed predominantly of ash, which was characteristic of the midden elsewhere. In the field such distinctions were not observed and 522 appeared as relatively homogenous in colour, texture and inclusions.

Despite the dumping of domestic rubbish and hearth sweepings on Mills Mount, this did not lead to absolute avoidance of the

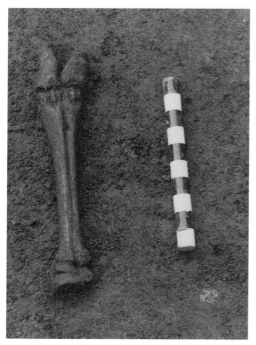

Illus 38
Mills Mount Phase 3: articulated shin bones of a sheep
as excavated from midden deposit 1382; 10cm scale.

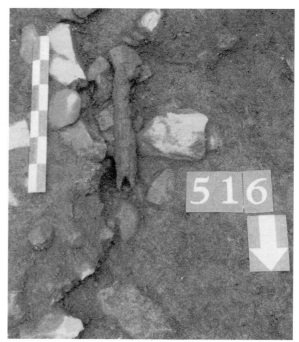

Illus 39
Mills Mount Phase 3: possible spear-butt (SF183) as discovered
during the excavation of midden deposit 516; 30cm scale.

area for other purposes. There is evidence of sporadic short term
use of the area, which consisted of several hearths built directly
on the midden surface with little or no evidence of associated
structures. These 'ground-hearths' may be distinguished from
the relatively common pockets of burnt soil within the ashy
deposits (eg 519, 588, 1403, 1422, 1445) by their coherence
which is indicated by gradual variation in colour from a bright
orange centre to a dusky, sooty halo. The most substantial of
these (515) measured: 0.5 × 0.3 × 0.05m (illus 42). Contexts
1400 and 1405 were both soil hearths, the latter was
distinguished by having a rough stone setting on three sides.
Context 521 was also probably an *in situ* hearth, but had suffered
from animal disturbances. Elsewhere the powdery grey ash of
context 532 indicates where a fire had been set on the matted
straw after it had been laid down. These should perhaps be
regarded as serving industrial purposes; 521 contained traces of
iron slag and 519 included coal amongst its fuel.

Further down the slope was a shallow scooped feature with a
packed earthen 'floor' (1409), although small (1.4 × 0.7m)
this may represent an interior space. Nearby a cluster of
stakeholes (1413) and several postholes (1417) hint at the
presence of a timber structure without providing any clear
indication of a plan. Also nearby was a small (0.5m across)
setting of stones (1418), which may have provided a solid
work surface of some sort. Further S patches of rough
cobbling (1415) provide further indication of use of part of
this area.

In addition there are faint suggestions of structures constructed in
the midden during its deposition. Two possible postholes (524
and 526) were noted but neither was definite; they may have been
animal burrows. Context 1423 has more integrity and is likely to
be a small post-setting (max 0.07m diam).

Stone in any concentration was unusual in these deposits
and with the possible exception of the dubious stone setting
around soil hearth 1405, the stone that was present must be
regarded as rubbish. In two locations, structureless dumps
of stone were excavated. Context 1404 contained flat stones

which could have served as flags but were a jumbled mass.
Context 529 was also a dump of stones, within 522, which
contained the discarded half of the upper quern (SF204,
illus 43).

PHASE 3 DATING

The rich organic elements of these deposits provided the best
samples for radiocarbon dating of any of the prehistoric phases. A
sample (GU-2913) from the matted grass or straw (511) has
provided a calibrated date range of AD 68–247 at one sigma.
Three other dates have been obtained from the charcoal recovered
from bulk samples taken from the burnt soil layers. Context 522,
as was explained, is a complex deposit which is not as uniform as
was thought at the time of sampling (and of submitting radiocarbon samples). It has provided two with scarcely any overlap.
The earlier of the two (GU-2664 522b) provided a calibrated age
range of AD 151–384 at one sigma and derives from immediately
above the Phase 2 slab-built hearth (1222), but is unlikely to
represent material from that specific hearth. The other sample
from 522 (GU-2581 522a) calibrates to AD 449–598 at one
sigma and derives from midden which accumulated over Phase 2
cobbling (531).

On balance the date derived from the matted grass or straw (AD
68–247) is to be preferred since it is likely to represent a single
year's growth and almost certainly represents material from a
primary deposit, whereas the bulk samples contain an inherent
uncertainty since the origin of the material being dated is
unknown.

The calibrated dates are in broad agreement with those suggested
by the artefactual analysis. Large quantities of Roman pottery
from the 1st to 3rd centuries was present (see 4.2.3 and 4.2.4).
This was also the phase with the greatest quantity of Romano-
British metalwork, including some relatively well-dated brooches
which have been dated to that era (see 4.2.5). Although the bulk
of the Roman material dates to the time of the Antonine
occupation, there are small quantities of material from both before

Illus 40
Mills Mount Phase 3:
midden deposit 522
under excavation
adjacent to the W section
with a nearly complete
pot (SF360) in a heap
above the N arrow.

and afterwards. The most closely datable artefact was the denarius of Hadrian (AD 117–38) (see 4.3.8), from the burnt layer (1406), which was probably introduced to the Castle during the Antonine period, but as with all of these imported goods there may have been a big gap between the date of manufacture and the date of deposition.

PHASE 3 INTERPRETATION

It is possible then to characterise the use of Mills Mount in the 2nd and 3rd centuries as a rubbish tip which apart from the dumping of refuse saw only casual use. By the time that the

midden began to accumulate the houses of Phase 2 had been partially dismantled leaving only the floors and hearths. The formation of the midden indicates that the Castle Rock remained inhabited and it is reasonable to suppose that this occupation was nearby and focused on the summit. The content of the midden indicates that the settlement was of exceptional status with access to a wide range of imported goods. The organic contents of the midden may also reflect the status of the site – the disposal of the debris of conspicuous consumption alongside the main approach to the summit may have been a deliberate announcement of the wealth of the residents. Whatever the nature of the settlement which attracted the fine collection of imported materials, it did not include habitation on Mills Mount.

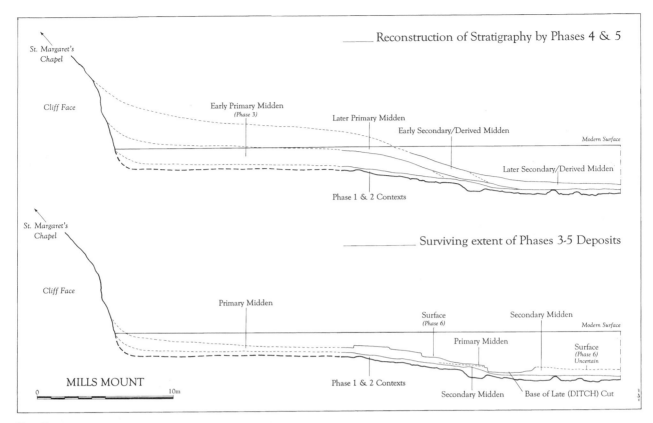

Reconstruction of Stratigraphy by Phases 4 & 5

St. Margaret's
Chapel

Cliff Face

Early Primary Midden
(Phase 3)

Later Primary Midden

Early Secondary/Derived Midden

Modern Surface

Later Secondary/Derived Midden

Phase 1 & 2 Contexts

St. Margaret's
Chapel

Surviving extent of Phases 3-5 Deposits

Cliff Face

Primary Midden

Surface
(Phase 6)

Secondary Midden

Modern Surface

Primary Midden

Surface
(Phase 6)
Uncertain

MILLS MOUNT

Phase 1 & 2 Contexts

Secondary Midden

Base of Late (DITCH) Cut

0   10m

Illus 41
Mills Mount: interpretive reconstruction of the deposition and erosion processes affecting the survival of the midden deposits Phases 3–5.

Illus 42
Mills Mount Phase 3: section through ground-hearth 515; 30cm scale.

Illus 43
Mills Mount Phase 3: dump of stones 529, within deposit 522, containing broken rotary quern upon which the Phase 5 Causeway was built; 1m scale.

PHASE 4

Late Roman – Early Medieval Midden
(AD 300–?1000)

PHASE 4 FEATURES (illus 44)

This phase represents a continuation in the history of the use of Mills Mount as a midden. The contexts of this phase have been distinguished from those in Phase 3 for two reasons. First, while digging, definite but subtle distinctions were recognised between the later layers (431, 461, 493 and 1382) and the earlier layers (516, 522, 1387); these distinctions were first noted in the deeper end of Area H (outside the Cartshed) and later confirmed in Area X (under the Cartshed), where an effort was made to test the initial distinction during excavation. Secondly, upon analysis of the finds from the two sets of layers, a few artefacts of early medieval type were noted in the upper layers. Thus, although the distinctions between the particular layers were at times unclear and contexts were sometimes defined instinctively, if not arbitrarily, the basic distinctions seem to have been valid. It should be stressed that there was no suggestion of a hiatus in the deposition of material upon the midden between Phases 3 and 4. Rather, it looks as though similar rubbish continues to be deposited throughout the early to middle centuries of the first millennium AD, with changes only being recognised though the types of artefacts and faunal remains.

As with the Phase 3 layers, the main soil deposits consist of dark brown clayey soils with grey to pink patches and highlights (431, 461, 493, 1382), which were slightly darker in colour than the layers which lay below. All of these layers consisted largely of plant ash, with the characteristic quartz grains, in other words, hearth sweepings and domestic rubbish including conspicuous quantities of animal bones and charcoal. The presence of animal burrows and other minor disturbances was much more pronounced in the Phase 4 layers. This observation was particularly clear the second time that these layers were excavated (ie contexts 1382 & 1397), where the later layer was seen to be less compacted and more burrowed than the earlier. However, it was probably true that the midden was infested with rats during both phases.

Fewer features are attributed to this phase than to the previous one, but at least three are of interest. Only two hearths were built on the midden surface. One (1385) was typical of the slight hearths from Phase 3, but the other (1211) was more substantial. This hearth contained the usual orange-fired soil, with a substantial build-up of ash (1214), which had formed on a stone base made of flat slabs set in a shallow concave basin (0.3m in

diameter) (1221 & 1229). The stonework and ash build-up indicate that the hearth had been used repeatedly.

Other suggestions of more permanent use of the area include a fragment of wall (494). This is of interest because it was the first of a series of stone built features which, like the hearth (1221), hint at a more regular use of the area. The wall fragment (494) was composed of fractured, undressed stone blocks up to 0.3 × 0.3 × 0.3m in size and pockets of yellow clay which may have served as bonding. The wall was 0.7m wide and stood only 0.1–0.2m high, but extended for 1.6m before running out of the excavation area. The low flimsy structure may indicate that the wall was the footing or raft for a timber structure. Without wishing to attribute too much significance to this small scrap of wall, it does seems to belong to a different architectural tradition than that observed in Phases 1 and 2.

Several features apparently marked the position of timber uprights. None can be associated with the wall or are particularly remarkable. The posthole (508) was 0.4 × 0.3 × 0.2m, while the stakeholes (512, 513) were 0.06m in diameter. The only other feature not thought to have been caused by animals was a formless dump of stone (530), which appeared to be discarded rubble. In view of the late radiocarbon date from the sample from posthole (1224), this large posthole should perhaps be assigned to Phase 4 rather than Phase 2.

PHASE 4 DATING

Dating for this phase is provided by charcoal extracted from a bulk sample of soil from context 461, and by the artefacts. The radiocarbon date (GU-2662) calibrates to AD 151–553 at one sigma, which has an overlap with the preferred Phase 3 sample (GU-2913 511: AD 68–247) and is indistinguishable from the two less secure dates from Phase 3. The artefacts however point to a later date. In addition to the occasional sherds of native Iron Age pottery (4.1.2) and less frequent Roman pottery (which was more common in Phase 3) and glass, there were three artefacts of possible early medieval date. SF191 (context 493) is a simply decorated, bone/antler comb, of Pictish or Anglian form, which has been ascribed to the period 7th to 10th century (4.3.3 below) and SF355 (context 493) a D-shaped bronze buckle of a type common from the 7th to 13th centuries (4.3.4 below). The third artefact is possibly a fragment of a fire-steel (SF193) the form of which, although incomplete, would not be out of place in a 7th–9th century context (4.3.5 below). It should also be noted that, aside from the Roman and a few minute fragments of later Medieval pottery (probably introduced by burrowing animals),

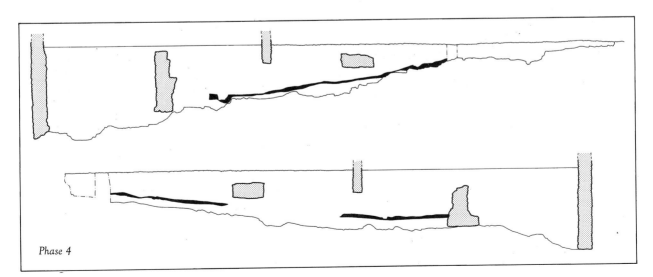

Phase 4

Phase 4: key to relevant layers within main section (fold-out illus 24).

Illus 44
Mills Mount (Areas H & X): plan for Phase 4

Phase 4

Disturbed

Hearth
1385

1382

493

*Area obscured
by later feature*

461

431

462
Post
Holes
508

Post Hole
1224
?(Phase 4)

Wall Base
530

513

512 Stakeholes

Wall Base
494

*Area obscured
by later feature*

1211 Hearth
1229

Area H & X Location

0   2m

there was very little pottery. Nevertheless there is a slight suggestion that a type of coarse hand-made pottery dates to this era (see discussion 4.1.2).

PHASE 4 INTERPRETATION

While in many respects our understanding of these Phase 3 and 4 deposits remains inadequate, they at least indicate that activity persisted on Castle Rock through the end of the Roman period into the early Middle Ages. What form the early medieval settlement took can hardly be addressed on the basis of the evidence from Mills Mount. The use of Mills Mount as a rubbish tip implies a smaller settlement than in the Iron Age, in which the focus of occupation was perhaps confined to the summit. As the animal bone report makes clear (5.4 below), the occupants at that time favoured the consumption of wild species in contrast to the higher proportions of domesticated livestock in both preceding and subsequent assemblages. Given that hunting in the Middle Ages was a noble prerogative and that the settlement was more compact, we may infer that Phase 4 saw the development of the site as a royal British stronghold, which was subsequently held by Anglian and even perhaps Pictish rulers.

PHASE 5

Medieval Causeway and Industrial Activity (?AD 1000–1325)

PHASE 5 FEATURES (illus 45)

This phase marks a dramatic change in use of the Mills Mount area. Although the deposits of this phase included large quantities of the burnt soils which were also seen in the previous phases, these soils were not the undisturbed midden of the previous phase, but had been churned up and redeposited as a result of intensive industrial activity in the area (illus 41). The most outstanding feature of this phase was the cobbled pathway (402, 430, 450, referred to as the Causeway) which runs diagonally across the length of the trench. This track may be regarded as the precursor to that now located on Hospital Brae which leads to the W end of the Castle Rock. Also notable at this level were a number of intensely burnt hearths (496, 417, 1361, 1372), which were apparently used for iron smithing, in

part fuelled by coal. In addition to the hearths there were other signs of more permanent activity in the area including a stone-built drain (1371) and numerous post-settings.

In Area H the main layer designations used in this phase were 433 and 418, which superficially were very similar to the layers which they sealed (ie 431, 461). In Area X the equivalent redeposited layers of burnt material were not seen and the contemporary features were found on the surface of 1382. Evidently the erosion of the midden which was responsible for the formation of 433/418 did not extend so far down slope (5.5 below). The downhill boundary of the erosion unfortunately fell in the gap between Areas H and X which was only partially excavated.

Layer 433 was a fine, almost silty, soil with similar colour and textural qualities to the ash-rich burnt soil layers of Phases 3 & 4. When first encountered, the stone-free softness and homogeneity suggested that it had been cultivated. However the micromorphology discounted the cultivation theory and also identified the structural differences between the Phase 5 soils and the earlier burnt soils. The fine layer distinctions (visible only at the microscopic level), which are characteristic of undisturbed individual dumping events, were absent. Thus, although the 433 deposits derive from similar midden materials, they have clearly been greatly transformed by subsequent human activities before final deposition.

The Causeway was built across the Phase 4 midden deposits (431 & 461) and was engulfed by the similar material redeposited as layer 433. This can only have happened if the redeposition of midden material continued. We can suggest that further up the hill, *in situ* late Iron Age/Dark Age midden deposits were allowed to erode and cause silting down-slope. Such an interpretation would be consistent with the presence of artefacts in the Phase 5 soils which were initially deposited in the late Iron Age and were later exposed to heavy traffic and redeposited, perhaps during the early Middle Ages. This general process has been represented schematically (illus 41).

THE CAUSEWAY

The cobbled track we have named the Causeway was composed of contexts 402, 430, 450. It was a complex structure which had evidently been built in two stages, with subsequent repairs (illus 45 inset; 46 a & b). The most substantial elements consist of irregular flat slabs (430) and a kerb of similar slabs set on edge (402). These slabs were of mudstone identical to stones found in some of the

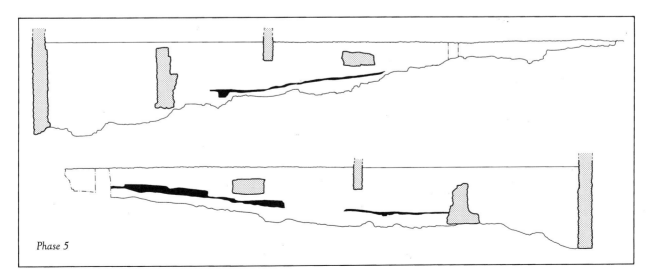

Phase 5

Phase 5: key to relevant layers within main section (fold-out illus 24).

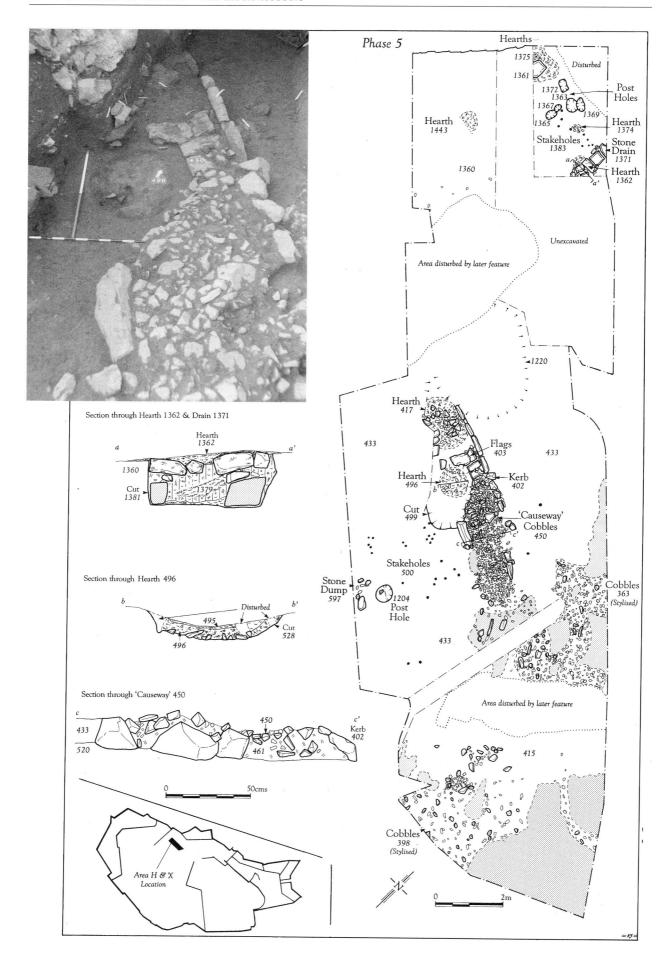

Phase 5

Hearths

Hearth 1375 1361 Disturbed
1443
1372 1363 Post Holes
1367 1369
1365 Hearth 1374
Stakeholes 1383 Stone Drain 1371
Hearth 1362
a
a'
1360

Unexcavated

Area disturbed by later feature

1220

Section through Hearth 1362 & Drain 1371

Hearth 1362
d a'
1360
Cut 1381 1379

Hearth 417

433 Flags 403 433

Hearth 496 Kerb 402
b
Cut 499 'Causeway' Cobbles 450
c c'

Section through Hearth 496

b b'
Disturbed
495
Cut 528
496

Stakeholes 500

Stone Dump 597 1204 Post Hole

433

Cobbles 363 (Stylised)

Section through 'Causeway' 450

c c'
450 Kerb 402
433
520 461

0 50cms

Area H & X Location

Area disturbed by later feature

415

Cobbles 398 (Stylised)

0 2m

Illus 45 (opp)
Mills Mount (Areas H & X): plan for Phase 5 with inset of a view from the S of the lower part of the Causeway showing where hearth 496 has burned through it.

Illus 46
Mills Mount Phase 5: upper part of Causeway 450 and stakeholes 500; from the N.

Phase 2 structures (eg 1388N). They may have been robbed from Iron Age structures. The area of slab paving was restricted to the downhill, N, end of the Causeway where it was bedded directly on to the ashy midden. The remaining, uphill, part of the path was paved with tightly packed cobbles (fist-sized and larger, context 450) which was retained on both sides by irregularly unworked stone blocks. The slab kerb (402) was present only on the N side of the path (the S kerb was probably removed by later disturbance). The kerb for the cobbles was preserved on both sides for much of its length. At the lower end the cobbles were bedded within the soil of layers 431 and 461. In section it appeared that a slight trench had been excavated for the kerb stones which, during its digging, had exposed the matted straw of 511. Moving further S and up slope, the cobbles rested largely on the bedrock and as the slope flattened near the top of the trench the Causeway lost definition and merged with the cobbled surfaces (363, 398, 415) which practically spread across the full width of the trench.

It was clear from excavation that the cobbling of the Causeway had been repaired on several different occasions as indicated by alternate layers of stones and soil. What is less clear is the relationship between the cobbles and the flagging. At their juncture some of the cobbles spilled onto the flagging. It may be that the slab-built part of the Causeway was constructed first to provide access across an area which undoubtedly would have been a quagmire in wet weather. Only later, as eroded Iron Age midden accumulated on the slope, was the cobbled path added. The alternative explanation may be that the difference in build simply reflects the subsoil conditions; where the ground was soft and the soil deep enough, slabs were laid, and, where the bedrock poked through the surface, cobbles and rough blocks (which could be wedged into crevices in the bedrock) were more suitable. Whatever the case, the Causeway provided a sturdy track over a

stretch of ground that was periodically treacherous. There can be little doubt that the main intention was to provide a firm footing for crossing the area of accumulated midden. That the Causeway was built to provide access to an area increasingly being used for industrial activities seems altogether likely.

On all sides of the Causeway there were clear signs of intensive occupation represented by cobbled surfaces, packed earth floors, post-settings and particularly hearths. The silting and erosion of the burnt ash midden continued once the Causeway had been built. Evidence of activity was found within this silt accumulation and on its surface. The surface of 433 was typically very hard-packed as would be expected if it had been a well-trodden earthen floor. Although this trampled level was ascribed a number of labels (389, 407, 409, 1360, 1360, 1402) as it was encountered, it was a consistently distinctive horizon which was seen across the whole of the site, excepting the S end where bedrock was highest and there were cobbles. Presumably this formation represents the end of the erosion, because either the midden was exhausted, removed or covered over. The erosion however did not end until after the slab end of the Causeway had been buried by up to 0.1–0.2m of silt which obscured all but the kerb (402).

INDUSTRIAL ACTIVITY

There are several sets of features which seems to indicate industrial activity on this packed surface. These features can be most conveniently described as they occurred, moving from the top of the slope downhill to the W. About midway along the length of the cobbled Causeway there was an array of post- and stakeholes, which as a group were roughly aligned perpendicular to the Causeway on its S side (illus 46). These timber settings included two substantial postholes (462 and 1204), both of which would have held posts on the order of 0.2–0.3m diameter. Upwards of 20 stakeholes were recorded (cf contexts 476 & 500) in the immediate vicinity of the postholes. Although some of these smaller holes may well be animal burrows, a majority were truly vertical and must mark the positions of real stakes which on average were 0.05m in diameter. Clearly there is no way to determine which of these features were contemporary, but as a group they suggest the presence of a linear barrier such as a hurdle fence which was rebuilt on more than one occasion. Indeed two parallel lines may be discerned, perhaps indicating two episodes of fencing. Only a few stakeholes were seen N of the Causeway; this is perhaps best explained by the presence of bedrock very near to the contemporary ground level. Because of the trampling of the surface 389/409, these timber settings were not all visible until the final traces of the trampled soil had been removed. Nevertheless it suggests the presence of a boundary that was approximately respected when the later smithy was laid out (see below Phase 6).

As was mentioned, the lower end of the Causeway was engulfed by layer 433. Once the flagging (430) had been obscured, the area directly above the (buried) Causeway was used for iron-working. A substantial hearth (496, 495, 499) was built directly on the ground on the SW side of the flagging and contained perhaps the most intense evidence of burning seen during the entire excavation (illus 45 inset; 47). This has been interpreted as the base of a furnace which appears to have had a superstructure of wattle and daub and to have been fuelled by charcoal. The furnace was set in a sub-rectangular depression (499) which evidently removed some of the Causeway itself.

Although not directly linked, a second ground-hearth (417), adjacent to 496, was found at a slightly higher absolute level and apparently post-dated the first. This second hearth was built directly above the former centre of the Causeway up against some of the protruding kerbstones (402). This second hearth (417) was not as intense as the first (496) but did have some form of a superstructure. This was represented by a jumble of stones (403), some fire-reddened, which were found covering the centre of the hearth. This hearth seems to have been fuelled by coal rather than charcoal. Although primitive, these features were technically adequate for the smithing of iron (see Iron-working and industrial residues report 4.3.7).

Immediately NE of these two hearths is one of the more enigmatic features on the site: a slight depression which may represent a building. The area occupied by the depression (1220) was excavated in two stages, separated by many months, and was partially truncated by a later ditch (see below Phase 8), so only a partial plan was recovered. The depression defines a sub-rectangular area, which originally was probably about 3.2 × 2.5m in size. The depression itself was only 0.10–0.15m deep at most, but had a particularly hard-packed surface which may represent a beaten earth floor. There was no evidence for any superstructure or of any internal fittings. It is possible that this may be the location of a small workshop or shed.

Evidence of more permanent structures was found further down slope at the S end of the trench. Part of a rough stone drain (1371), built of slabbed sides and rectangular capstones, was traced for only a short length (illus 48). Circumstances prevented excavation of its full length, but it seems likely that it was built to carry waste from the general area around the hearths (496 and 417) and the beaten floor (1220). There are two remarkable features of this drain. First, one of the capstones was a door or window hood-moulding (1378, SF468). This type of detail cannot be closely dated but is unlikely to be pre-13th century (below 4.3.6). Vague though this is, it is one of the few pieces of dating evidence for this phase. The second point of note is that

Illus 47
Mills Mount Phase 5: detail of section through hearth 496.

Illus 48
Mills Mount Phase 5: detail of section through drain 1371.

some of the capstones of the drain were subsequently utilised as a base for a hearth (1362). The hearth seems to indicate that here, as elsewhere, iron-working was being practised. The capstone which served as the hearth stone was Old Red Sandstone (ORS) and had crumbled due to the exposure to the heat.

Immediately adjacent to this hearth was a number of features including: a dump of coal, nine stakeholes (1383) and five postholes or timber settings (1363, 1365, 1367, 1369, 1372). Some of these could represent a frame for bellows set next to the hearth. Two of them were particularly interesting. The fill of one posthole (1369) was approximately 40% coal, while the other posthole (1372) had a regular-shaped, rectangular plan, 0.35 × 0.27 m, and only 0.1m deep. This may have been the setting for some piece of smithing equipment rather than a structural timber.

Further down-slope from these features was a sequence of two other hearths. The later hearth (1361) was built upon an ORS slab which lay on the ashes of the previous hearth (1375). Both fires had been very intense to judge by the scorching of the soil and the stone. They are presumed to have been used for smithing. Lying between these two hearths and the hearth built on the drain was an isolated dump of ash and burnt soil which may have come from one or other of these fires.

PHASE 5 DATING

The activities represented by these features apparently spanned a considerable period to judge by the silting and repositioning of hearths. It is extremely difficult to provide a tight chronology for this phase. The hood-moulding reused as the drain cap points to a period during or after the Wars of Independence. There are no coins from this phase, but there are two Edwardian pennies (4.3.8 Coin catalogue nos. 2 and 3), which were minted between 1310–22 and give a loose terminus ante quem of the mid-14th century. The artefactual range is not particularly helpful. The spearhead (SF172, 4.3.5) is not particularly distinctive and is most closely compared with Anglo-Saxon ones of the mid-6th century or with the example from Lagore, Ireland dating to the 7th–10th centuries. The socketed arrowhead (SF558, 4.3.5) is too fragmentary to be dated closer than 13th–15th centuries. A significant group of pottery from the deposits was found at the base of 433 sealing the Causeway, which included a number of locally produced cooking pot rims. These date to the 14th century. Probably the most economical reading of the evidence would be to regard it as activity dating to either the English occupation of the early 14th century or the restoration of the Castle in the middle of that century. However the Causeway could be much earlier and romantics may make a special case for regarding it as the path taken on Queen Margaret's last journey. In terms of the absolute dating sequence the Causeway could well have been constructed as early as the 11th century.

PHASE 5 INTERPRETATION

As a group, all of these features are consistent with use of the Mills Mount area for industrial purposes. These industrial activities seem to have centred around iron-smithing, although other materials such as bronze may have been worked in small quantities. However the recovered remains appear to represent elements of several different working set-ups and it is not possible to define a coherent plan of any single smithy as was possible for Phase 6. This out of doors smithing would be consistent with working on large objects such as siege engines or castle gates.

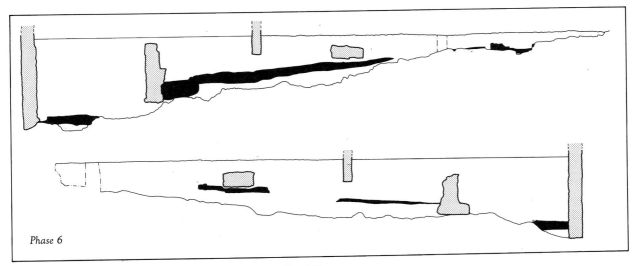

Phase 6: key to relevant layers within main section (fold-out illus 24).

PHASE 6

Medieval Blacksmith's Workshop
(AD 1325–1400)

PHASE 6 FEATURES (illus 49)

The presence of industrial activity on Mills Mount was already a notable aspect of the previous phase, but during Phase 6 iron-working appears to be the principal activity on Mills Mount. Along with evidence of greater industry there is an appearance of increasing formality in the organisation of the craft. This is most clearly seen in the construction of a substantial blacksmith's workshop. It would be wrong to over-stress the formality because there still were hearths built directly on the ground with little or no superstructure which contained residues of iron-working. Nevertheless, it is significant that the ground-hearths were being built in the shadow of the first solid buildings to be constructed on Mills Mount since the Iron Age. This building appears to have been a purpose-built smithy and occupied the entire S half of the trench.

SURFACES AND SOIL ACCUMULATION: EARLY AND LATE ACTIVITY

At the S end of the trench, in the area immediately around the forge (296), the bedrock was close to the surface and exposed in

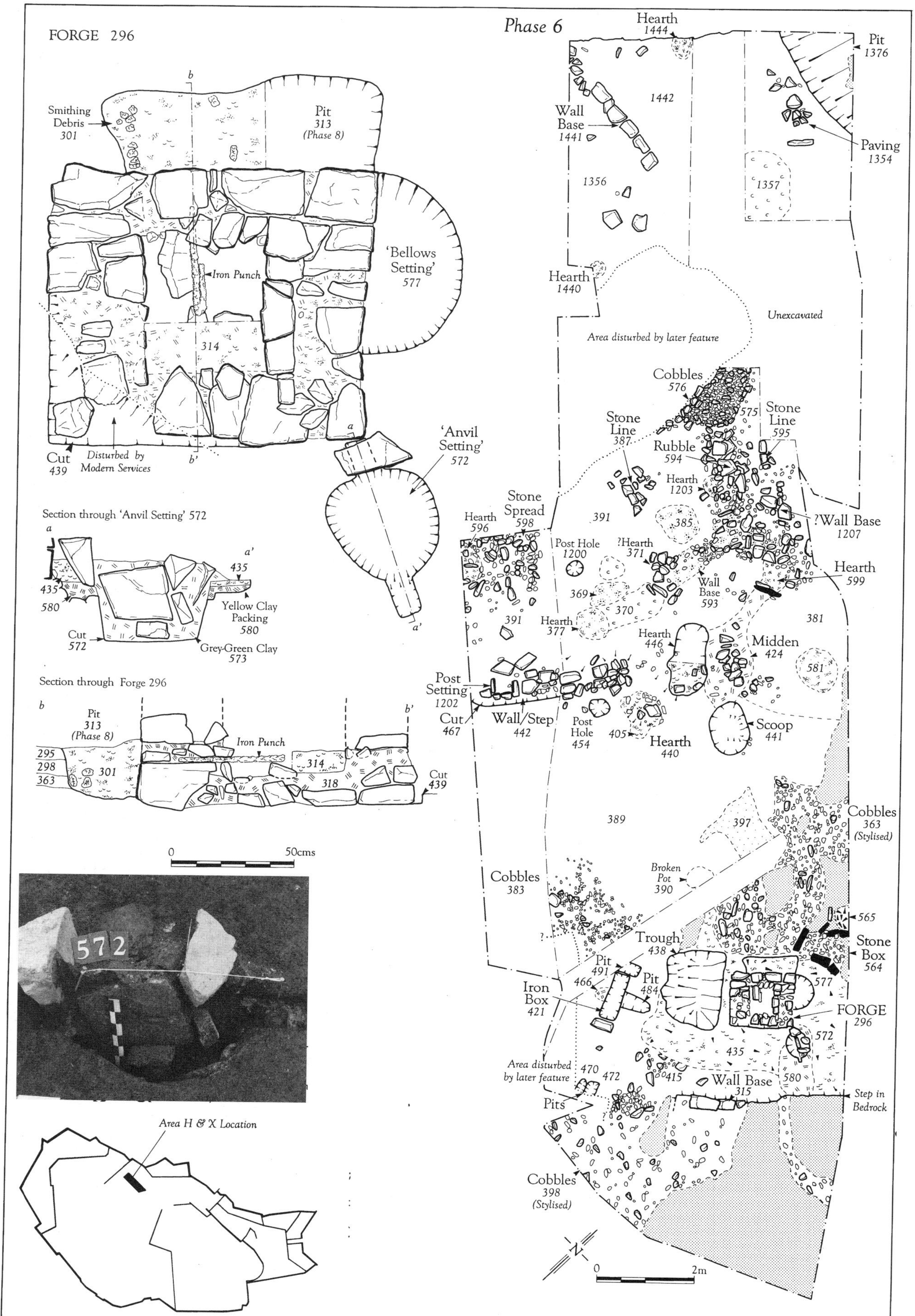

FORGE 296

Phase 6

Hearth
1444

Pit
1376

Wall
Base
1441

1442

Paving
1354

Smithing
Debris
301

Pit
313
(Phase 8)

1356

1357

Iron Punch

'Bellows
Setting'
577

314

Hearth
1440

Unexcavated

Area disturbed by later feature

Cobbles
576

Cut
439

*Disturbed by
Modern Services*

Stone
Line
387

575

Stone
Line
595

'Anvil
Setting'
572

Rubble
594

Hearth
1203

Stone
Spread
598

?Wall Base
1207

Section through 'Anvil Setting' 572

Hearth
596

391

385

Hearth
599

a

a'

435

435
580

Post Hole
1200

?Hearth
371

Wall
Base
593

381

Yellow Clay
Packing
580

369

370

Cut
572

Grey-Green Clay
573

391

Hearth
377

Hearth
446

Midden
424

581

Section through Forge 296

b

Post
Setting
1202

Post
Hole
454

Scoop
441

b'

Pit
313
(Phase 8)

Iron Punch

Cut
467

Wall/Step
442

405

Hearth
440

295
298
363

301

314

318

Cut
439

389

397

Cobbles
363
(Stylised)

0   50cms

Cobbles
383

Broken
Pot
390

572

565

Trough
438

Stone
Box
564

Iron
Box
421

Pit
491

466

Pit
484

577

FORGE
296

435

572

Area disturbed
by later feature

470   472

415

Wall Base
315

580

Step in
Bedrock

Pits

Area H & X Location

Cobbles
398
(Stylised)

N

0   2m

—KJ—

places. Elsewhere cobbles (363, 415), probably from earlier phases, were utilised and some new ones laid down (383). But moving down the slope the surface upon which much of the activity in this phase took place was the trampled earth surface of 433/461 (which during the excavation was labelled variously 389, 407, 409 and 1360 and is discussed above under Phase 5). Indeed some of the industrial activity which characterised the end of the previous phase probably helped to produce this well-trampled surface and the distinction between the end of Phase 5 and start of Phase 6 is somewhat arbitrary. Only within the immediate vicinity of the forge did a distinctive deposit (435), indicative of smithing, build up. Elsewhere deposits of soil with quantities of smithing debris accumulated on the slope, in places directly over 389/409/1360. These deposits were less hard-packed and were identified variously as 381, 391, 575, 1356; they were less well-trampled than 389 and equivalent surfaces.

However, it is clear that smithing was continuing even as more material was being deposited in the N end of the trench and that new structures were being built at this later stage. In effect then we can distinguish between structures which were primary to the 'main' smithy centred on the forge (296) and later activity. To attempt to refine the chronology with more precision than early

and late would be demanding too much of the available evidence.

Beyond the extent of the ash, coal dust and hammer scale (435) from the forge was an area of relatively hard-packed earth (389) and cobbles (363, 383) which may represent the extent of the interior since it was fairly level and free of other features (illus 50). This relatively open area extended up to the N wall (442) (see below). The shallow pit (441) filled with a dump of stones (425) was an exception. On the surface were, however, a scattering of artefacts associated with smithing, like the small dump of iron scrap (404), the only recognisable components of which were a few nails. Another deposit with a possible industrial function was the thin spread of yellow-brown sand (397) on the N side of the forge.

The layers which built up during the active period of the main smithy (381, 391, 575 and 1356) were broadly similar. They consisted of dark-brown clayey soils with ample traces of burning. Some of this may ultimately have derived from the same parent materials as produced the post-Iron Age midden which characterised Phases 3 to 5. These Phase 6 layers certainly contained Roman and Iron Age artefacts. It is nonetheless clear that much of the evidence of burning was medieval and in some cases of an industrial nature.

Illus 49 (opp)
Mills Mount (Areas H & X): plan for Phase 6 with inset half section through anvil setting.

Illus 50
Mills Mount Phase 6: view from the S of the smithy showing the extent of floor deposits 435; forge 296 (to the right of the scale with 10cm divisions) has been half-sectioned and trough 438 has been emptied.

Layers 381 and 391 were the first of this build-up encountered and the most meticulously observed. The total depth that the two layers occupied varied between 0.2–0.3m, but was composed of many discrete lenses and dumps of soil. Except where these were particularly distinctive, either because of having been burnt or having high proportions of shell, stone, mortar or clay, no attempt was made to record these lenses. As time became scarcer during the excavation even these two distinctions were dropped and grouped into a single context 1356. Clear distinctions could be drawn between 381/391 and both earlier and later build-ups of soil. The main difference between this and the later levels was the absence of post-medieval pottery and the relative scarceness of animal bone. The most striking qualities which distinguished these layers from earlier, lower levels were the presence of mortar spreads (385, 388) and coal. In places the coal was the dominant component within the soil and served as a valuable marker horizon (eg layer 575).

The plan which accompanies this phase has compressed into one drawing (illus 49) many features which were not precisely contemporary. Only a few of the small hearths (eg 377, 392, 396, 581, 596) found within 381/391 were visible at any given moment. Similarly not all of the stone features shown within 391 towards the middle of the trench are likely to have been in use at any given moment.

THE BLACKSMITH'S WORKSHOP – PRIMARY FEATURES

The forge

The forge (296) was the central element of the smithy; this furnace was used to heat the iron for working (illus 51a). Only the base of the forge survived and only to a maximum height of 0.5 m. This represents perhaps the bottom third of a structure that would originally have been waist high. At its base the forge was rectangular in plan (1.2 × 1.5m) and rested directly on the bedrock. It was built of whinstone bonded with a bright yellow clay. The walls were two stones thick leaving a central hollow which at the time of discovery was filled with burnt clay and smithing debris (314). Originally the interior would have been hollow to improve the draw of air and collect ash and clinker. It also contained a large punch for working iron (SF081). At the base of the interior was a tightly packed layer of irregular stone (318) which had been keyed into the bedrock to provide a secure foundation.

There was no sign of scorching or intense heat on the surviving masonry of the forge, nor was there any evidence of a rake-out opening for the fire box. Both of these points confirm that the forge originally stood much higher, with a fire box at waist level.

The evidence for the position either of the bellows or of any chimney hood is ambiguous, but the overall working arrangement can be inferred from the position of two key features associated with the forge. Immediately off the SE corner of the forge was an approximately circular (0.56m diameter), flat-bottomed pit (572) some 0.25m deep (illus 51b). This pit was lined with the same yellow clay that was used to bind the forge and it seems likely that it represents the location of an anvil mounted on a section of tree trunk. Just such an arrangement, where the timber survived intact, has been observed at the post-medieval iron works at Fasagh, near Loch Maree (Lewis 1984, 444).

The other curious feature was a pit (577) found centrally on the E side of the forge. This steep-sided semi-circular pit (0.7 × 0.45m) was cut down into the bedrock and undercut the forge itself (illus 51b). It was filled with more smithing debris (578) but may have been open while the forge was in use. No passage to the interior of the forge was located, so it certainly is unlikely to have been a flue. The function of the pit is unclear, however it is possible that a support for a bellows stood in it, supplying blasts of air to the waist-level fire box. An assistant could have worked the bellows on the E side, while the other evidence points to the 'working side' of the forge being to the S.

The rock-cut trough

The most impressive feature within the smithy was a rock-cut trough (438) on the W side of the forge (illus 50). At ground level this was rectangular in plan (1.35 × 1.15m). It retains its full length to its base some 0.75m below ground level while its width tapered down to no more than 0.1m at the bottom. Its irregular V-shaped profile was to a large extent determined by the natural faults within the rock. Once empty of smithing debris (451) and other rubbish (432), this substantial pit quickly filled with rainwater, providing a visual confirmation of its interpretation as a quenching trough. At its nearest, the trough was only 0.25m from the forge base. A spread of the yellow clay (580), used to bond the forge and to bed the post in 572, extended from the forge beyond the putative anvil setting to the artificial step in the bedrock (315).

Identifying the trough and putative anvil setting provides an indication of the layout of the smithy and helps to interpret two more enigmatic features related directly to the forge. Running along the entire W side of the forge was a pit (313) filled with clinker, ash, fired clay and other smithing debris (illus 51a). The fill of this pit (301) was clearly deposited some time after the forge had gone out of use and the ground level had risen some 0.2–0.3m. The pit was very straight-sided and seems likely to represent a void created when something built adjacent to the forge was removed. In view of the fill's composition which is very similar to that of the forge (314) it seems most likely that the void

Illus 51a
Mills Mount Phase 6: W portion of the stump of the forge 296 with pit 313 half excavated on the right.

Illus 51b
Mills Mount Phase 6: E portion of forge 296 and associated features after removal of W. portion.

(pit) was filled during the final demolition of the forge (during Phase 7). It may therefore be that this marks the position of a support for a hood.

To the NE of the forge was a setting of stones on edge (564) which formed a shallow, c 0.1m, box (1.0 × 0.75m). This box rested on bedrock and on the ashy build up (435) which spread out from the forge. It was also relatively free of smithing waste, so it is not clear what function this may have served. Its relationship to a spread of smithing debris (566) suggests that this rough stone box was constructed during the working life of the smithy.

The iron-lined box

A more remarkable feature associated with the smithy was a box (421) built of wood, lined with a sheet of iron and set into the ground (illus 52 a & b). The box was rectangular (0.97 × 0.30m) with slightly (10°) splayed sides, which tapered down to 0.80 × 0.22m at the base. Its top was not well preserved but its full depth was about 0.25m and does not appear to have

protruded above floor level. Set into the ground at the S end of the box was a stone (about 0.1 × 0.3m) which protruded some 0.1m from the floor. None of the timber frame of the box survived, but the sheet metal lining preserved clear impressions of a wood grain identified as oak. The void left by the decayed timber was filled with highly organic soil deposits (422 & 445) which suggest that the box was about 0.02m thick. The wood grain impressions, which varied between 0.18 and 0.25m apart, confirm this thickness. One puzzling aspect of the box was its shape. When discovered the sheet metal lining exhibited a pronounced bulge mid-way down each side, which protruded some 0.02–0.03m inwards. It seems that the bulge was simply distortion caused by movement during the process of decay. Detailed inspection of the lining during conservation revealed no evidence that it was part of the original form.

The most striking thing about the box is its lining with a sheet of iron, which appears to have been about 2–3mm thick. An effort was made during conservation to identify seams or joins, but none was found. The rounded corners would indicate that the iron lining had been knocked into the box. This particularly difficult

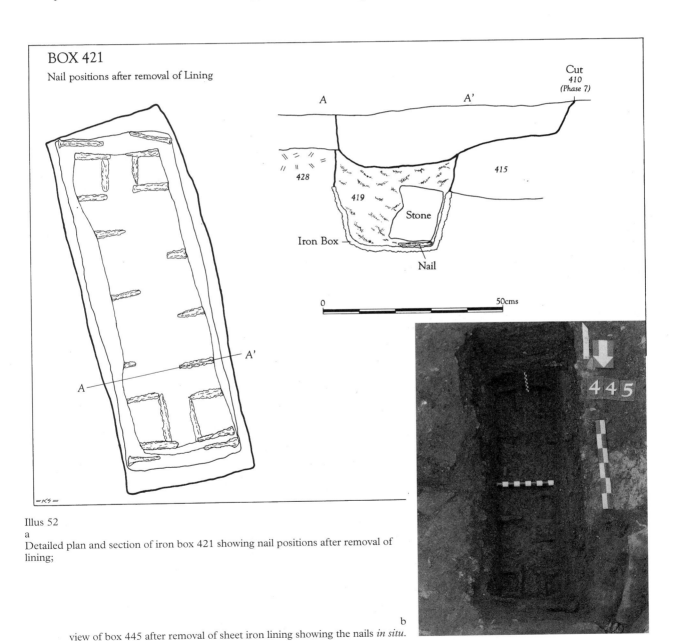

BOX 421

Nail positions after removal of Lining

Illus 52
a
Detailed plan and section of iron box 421 showing nail positions after removal of lining;

b
view of box 445 after removal of sheet iron lining showing the nails *in situ*.

method may have been adopted so that the box would be water-tight. The presence of clay within the lining of the hole dug for the box, might be taken to support this notion.

The box would have to have been sturdily built to withstand the punishment of installing the lining. It was held together by 26 or 27 nails (445a–445z). The nailing pattern was fairly regular and allows us to suggest how the box was actually put together. All of the sides overlapped the base and were nailed into it. From the direction of the nails it looks as though the end pieces were first attached using two nails, then the sides were attached to the base with five nails on each side. The sides evidently overlapped the ends, for each corner was fastened with three nails driven through the sides into the grain of the end pieces.

There is no complete explanation for the box. It apparently was water-tight so is perhaps best explained as a second trough used in the smithing and annealing process. Since both it and the stone-cut trough appear to have been primary features of the smithy, it may be that they served slightly different purposes. It is even possible that this was a secure box, capable of being locked, in which valuable materials or tools might be stored.

SMITHY INTERIOR

The original floor of the smithy is hard to identify. It seems likely that some of the cobbling which formed the floor was already present at the time of its construction. For instance, the cobbles on the N side of the forge (363) were probably laid down at the same time as the Causeway (450). Similarly, the cobbles to the N of 363, near the edge of the proposed smithy building (383), may predate the smithy itself. Some of the cobbles are likely to be significantly earlier than the smithy itself. Those from the area around the trough and box (398) may in fact be Iron Age. It is impossible to know which of these cobble spreads were earlier surfaces revealed by erosion and which might have been laid down for the smithy. What is clear is that they were soon obscured by a black layer of smithing debris.

An accumulation of smithing debris testified to the main purpose of the smithy – the working of iron. This surface (435) was extremely black and composed of fine particles of coal, charcoal and iron fragments which had been trampled into a hard-packed layer which was only 0.01–0.02m thick. The surface of the layer was particularly hard-packed and in section it could be seen to be made up of a great number of very fine layers laminated together by constant traffic.

Towards the bottom of the layer the presence of small iron fragments was more pronounced. On and within this layer were many larger pieces of iron, which had apparently been lost or discarded. In addition to the iron scrap, there was a small quantity of scrap trimmings from working sheet copper or bronze. In one spot, iron filings and scraps (447) spread in an irregular heap approximately 1.0m in diameter and 0.2m high. Judging from the fineness of the material within the heap, this may mark the location where certain finishing jobs were carried out. Elsewhere a large number of iron fragments (many unidentifiable) were recovered from this surface.

Three shallow pits were discovered within the smithy itself, which appear to date to the primary use of the structure. Although the samples from these pits have been analysed no specific explanation for these pits can be offered. They were not particularly large or deep. Two very similar ones (470 and 472) were adjacent (intercutting) and look to be roughly contemporary, although 470 had been backfilled before 472 was dug. Both look to have been filled in quickly and deliberately with significant quantities of slag and clinker. Neither pit was particularly large (between 0.25–0.35m) and only 0.08–0.12m deep. It seems likely that they represent settings for minor internal features. Both were sealed by layer 435.

The third pit (484) was adjacent to the iron box (421) and had been truncated by the cut (429) for the box. This pit was also truncated by a later feature, so only a small portion (0.5 × 0.3 × 0.22m) of this steep-sided pit remained. In addition to being more deliberately dug, this pit also had a more structured fill than the other two mentioned above. It contained three different elements. The lower fill (486) was chiefly redeposited Iron Age hearth sweepings (Phase 3); above this was a high concentration of iron corrosion which resembled a thin pipe which had been squashed. This in turn was sealed by a loose dark brown soil (485) containing both coal and charcoal as well as iron stains. This lapped over the edge of the pit. Its position between the rock-cut trough and the box suggests that it might have provided some link for transferring water, but its purpose remains unclear.

SMITHY BUILDING (illus 53)

Although it seems clear that the structures of the smithy were sheltered, we have scant evidence for the building in which they may have been housed. As in the previous phases, this is to a large

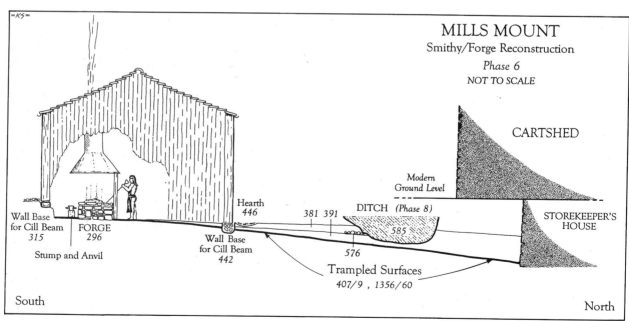

Illus 53
Mills Mount: smithy reconstruction.

extent a consequence of the limited dimensions of the excavation: it was not possible to expose the entire building plan and thus make all the features intelligible. For example, the E side of the trench was probably too close to the forge to have included the E wall, but in other directions structural evidence was revealed. Unfortunately this evidence is ambiguous and in some cases dates to the succeeding phase.

The wall (442) served to define the extent of layer 389 on the downhill (N) side (and thus the interior) and slot 315 on the uphill (S) was a good candidate for the S wall of the smithy. A length of approximately 3.5m of the wall footing (442) survived (illus 2). The wall was bedded on a step (467) cut into the slope and consisted of unbonded roughly shaped blocks facing up rubble. When built, the facing stones would have been visible. It seems most likely that this stonework footed a timber wall (perhaps based on a sleeper). A square, stone-faced setting for a post (1202) was an integral part of the construction. The internal dimensions of the setting (0.35 × 0.35m) would have accommodated a substantial timber. One end of the wall ran out of the trench to the W. No continuation of the wall to the E was identified, but if the smithy had a barn-door sized entrance perhaps none should be expected. Just to the putative inside of the wall (442) was a posthole (454) (0.4m diameter × 0.15m deep) which may have been contemporary with 442.

Evidence for the S wall was equally slim. It consisted of a step cut into the bedrock to the S of the forge, built up with a single course of unbonded stone (315). The alignment of the step deviated from the natural orientation of the bedrock and approximated to that of the wall (442) and the forge. The alignment was continued in a later trench (356) which may have held a timber wall during Phase 7. This later trench unfortunately removed the evidence for any continuation to step and wall (315) in this phase.

The smithy seems therefore to have been an insubstantial timber building measuring about 8.0m N–S with an unknown width. Rather than a well-enclosed workshop it should probably be thought of as a shed with partially open walls and free-standing timbers providing support for the roof.

LATER HEARTHS

Some of the industrial features look as though they were not inside and recall the less well-organised arrangements of the previous phase. These include a number of very intense hearths built directly on the ground. These seem to post-date the main smithy since they are built after layer 391 had started to form and while layer 381 was being deposited. Moreover, the close proximity to one another argues against more than one being in use at a given time. The most substantial of these ground-hearths was a roughly rectangular scoop (446) located in the possible doorway of wall (442). This substantial scoop (1.4 × 0.75m) contained layers of charcoal and ash (420), and burnt soil (406) with smithing debris. The build-up of ash and waste suggests that it was used for some time.

A second, equally intense ground-hearth (599) was located 3m to the NE, outside the smithy. This had been truncated but its surviving dimensions (0.75m × 0.7m) could be those of a similarly shaped hearth, An added feature was a vertically set stone slab (0.6 × 0.1m) on the short side. The depth of the ash build-up of 0.3m was again indicative of lengthy use. The third hearth (1203) in the vicinity was much less intense and probably used only occasionally.

LATER STRUCTURES

Immediately to the downhill side of wall 442, there was a second concentration of building evidence. This activity post-dates that in the area of the forge and those hearths just described. Because of their poorly preserved quality, it is

impossible to know how they may have been used. As with the smithy building itself, the main the problems of interpreting these structural remains are the consequence of the effective demolition during later periods. The thoroughness of this is well demonstrated by the extremely degraded nature of the stone features which were encountered to the N of the N wall (442) of the smithy.

In the case of feature 598, all that survived was a structureless layer of rubble, while elsewhere slightly more coherence was seen (illus 54). The complex of stony deposits (593, 594, 595, 576, 1206, 1207) in the middle of the trench are indicative of a building which was at least in part built of mortared masonry. However only a corner of the building fell within the trench. The overall impression is of a timber building on mortared rubble foundations. Some of the unmortared stone is probably no more than demolition rubble, while some is certainly paving or cobbling. Ultimately too little remains to justify any further discussion, although this does represent the earliest mortared structure encountered on Mills Mount.

A similar problem hampers interpretation of those features at the extreme N end of the trench. These included more of the ubiquitous, but relatively insubstantial ground-hearths (1355, 1416, 1444). The best preserved hearth (1355) was 0.4m in diameter and was apparently charcoal-fired; but there was also plenty of coal in the surrounding deposits. An indication of the ephemeral nature of some of these hearths is that they were relatively small. Probably contemporary with the hearths and the earliest built structures in this phase was a spread of rough cobbles (1415) which lay directly on the trampled surface 1360, making it approximately contemporary with the main smithy.

The rest of the features occur late in the phase, after or during the deposition of layer 1356 (equivalent to 381/391). The

Illus 54
Mills Mount Phase 6: view from the N of possible wall footings 593 and 594.

Illus 55
Mills Mount Phase 6: view of wall footing 1441 and terminal of ditch 585 (Phase 8) on extreme left with the scale marked in 10cm divisions.

most substantial feature was a massive pit or ditch (1376) most of which fell outwith the trench. Its minimum dimension was likely to have been in the order of 4–5m and it had been cut down to bedrock, a depth of just over a metre. The orientation of the fills was more consistent with a pit than a ditch, but these fills (1359, 1377) give little indication as to its purpose. The most striking thing about the fill, apart from the presence of much coal and charcoal, was the presence of fragments of yellow sandstone which was not seen elsewhere on the site.

Near to the pit and probably contemporary was a dump of coal (1357) within coal-rich layer (1356). This spread of pure coal (1.0 × 1.25m) was the largest concentration discovered anywhere on the site. Probably slightly later than these features (perhaps contemporary with 576 and the other later stone features) was a linear setting (1441) which was one stone wide which ran from the edge of the section some 3.0m before terminating abruptly (illus 55). These unbonded, rough blocks had been simply set into the ground and may have served as the footing of a timber structure. It certainly overlay hearth 1443 and produced a differential deposition of soils. The soil (1442) deposited to the NE of the line had a higher content of shell and domestic rubbish than noticed in the surrounding deposits of 1356. The impression was that this had accumulated in the interior up against the stone line (1441).

PHASE 6 DATING

All of the evidence points to the mid-14th century as the period of the construction and use of the smithy. As mentioned above the pottery in the layers which are contemporary with the structure contained 14th-century forms. From the soil accumulation (381) N of the smithy, there came a penny of Edward II (SF151) minted between 1320–35. Any datable small finds associated with the smithy appear to be 14th century. None is so precisely datable as to resolve the question of whether the smithy was built during the English occupation of the Castle or after its recapture.

PHASE 6 INTERPRETATION

The finds from the smithy indicate that much of the work undertaken on Mills Mount was to satisfy domestic and building requirements (4.3.5 below). This is hardly surprising in view of the scale of the rebuilding work being undertaken during the middle of the 14th century. What is perhaps surprising is the scarcity of weaponry. There is little evidence that the smithy was part of the armoury.

The Castle smithy is unusually well-preserved which helps us to appreciate the technical qualities of 14th-century iron-working; what is not clear is how significant the slight evidence for armour or weapons is. The smithy building is more substantial than those which have been excavated elsewhere. For example, Hen Domen castle (Barker & Higham 1982, 33) and Bramber Castle, Sussex (Barton & Holden 1977) both produced smithing residues but no forge. Neither of these castles was royal or as important as Edinburgh, so the relatively meagre evidence from their smithies is not surprising, but it may point to the real measure of the importance of a smithy. The Mills Mount smithy was a far more substantial structure and this in itself may be evidence of the intention to produce more demanding and specialised objects such as weapons. The erratic patterning of hearths outwith the building may have been to produce items too large to be accommodated within the smithy or to cope with extraordinary demands.

PHASE 7

Late Medieval Reuse of the Smithy Building (AD 1400–1550)

PHASE 7 FEATURES (illus 56)

This phase saw the end of smithing in the building constructed to house the forge, but witnessed a considerable refurbishment, and saw its continued use for an unknown purpose. It also marks the beginnings of a comprehensive remodelling of the topography of Mills Mount into a level area by importing quantities of soil, either from elsewhere in the Castle or from the burgh.

The end of the active life of the smithy is very clearly marked by a spread of dense, red-brown clay (366) which was laid in a thick layer around the forge (296), presumably to seal in the deposits of coal, ash and clinker (435) which had built up on the floor of the smithy. At the same time, the trough (438) was filled in with red sandstone blocks (432) which included two architectural fragments, quantities of smithing debris (451) and other stones and soil and clay (434) (illus 56 inset). The red clay capped part of this infilling. The iron box (421) was also filled in at this time with a large stone (423) and soil (419) (illus 52a). This fill was capped by a mixed layer of clay and midden material (399), which derived from a combination of the capping clay (366) and the midden material which had been used to level up the slope of Mills Mount (344, etc). We will return to this levelling process later.

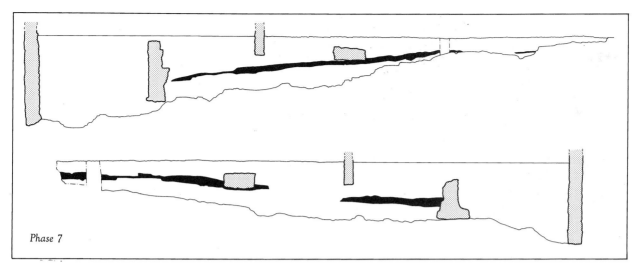

Phase 7

Phase 7: key to relevant layers within main section (fold-out illus 24).

There is no real clue as to the new use for the smithy building. In most places the floor was a well-trampled mixture of clay and redeposited midden which incorporated small fragments of coal, shell and domestic rubbish. In the SE corner, near to the S wall (315), this surface was labelled 368; on the opposite side of the trench it was 399. Ultimately (during Phase 8) a depth of soil built up (to over 0.10m deep in places). This build-up (339) was very similar in colour, texture and inclusions to the redeposited midden (344) which had been placed on the slope to the N of the smithy. As a result, it is difficult to determine the relationship between this build-up (339) and the levelling (344).

The relative sequence is not in doubt, because over the SE corner of the infilled trough (438) a small quantity of the midden material (identical to 344) overlay the red clay capping (366) to the infilled trough. This small pocket (0.4 × 0.4 × 0.15m) of redeposited midden (449) provides the clearest key to the sequence of deposits within the former smithy.

At this point it is worth clarifying the distinction between this redeposited midden and the *in situ* midden (433) of the earlier phases. The main difference between the two is that the earlier midden was representative of the activity within the Castle, while (as will be argued below) the later midden is probably derived from elsewhere and its contents do not necessarily derive from activities conducted within the Castle.

A distinction can also be drawn between those contexts which accumulated inside the former smithy and those which built up outside. The interior deposits (eg 339) were more mixed and the inclusions were more broken up than was the case in the exterior deposits (eg 344). This distinction reflects the greater degree of trampling to which the interior surfaces were subject.

The accumulation of dark clayey soil on the new floor (366, 399) of the smithy was the result of large-scale deposition of material on the slope N of the smithy. The intention was apparently to level up the natural slope of Mills Mount by importing soil. Large quantities of soil were involved: in places the layer (344) was up to 0.3m deep. This mass of material was apparently deposited in cart loads. Although several context numbers were used during the excavation (344, 346, 1353), after a short period of digging no attempt was made to keep track of individual dumps except where they were composed of distinctive material such as stone or shell.

This redeposited midden was essentially composed of dark brown clayey soil in which domestic rubbish was homogeneously mixed. This rubbish contains unremarkable domestic material, but within the rubbish component there were smaller features which probably relate directly to activity within the Castle. For the most part these represent small dumps which were found within the major dumps of 344/346, between cartloads as it were. In this category were several stone features including two structureless dumps of angular stones (379, 393), as well as the rough platform of stone slabs (394) of indeterminate purpose. Other deliberate but obscure constructions include a linear stone setting (395) and a dump of clay (386) covering two blocks of dressed sandstone (401). Only a single post-setting was noted within the body of the midden (1212).

Familiar from the previous phases were the two hearths built directly on the ground. One is a small patch of burnt soil (408) with no apparent stone furniture, while the other (440) was built on a flat stone (0.3 × 0.25m) and surrounded by a jumble of stones, some of which were fire-reddened. Also familiar are the small spreads of mortar (436), of mixed clay and coal (434). Most distinctive of these small dumps were those composed of oyster shells (354, 437). All of these deposits reflect brief periods of activity during the levelling with the redeposited midden. Some features, like the oyster shells, may signify no more than the lunch of one of the labourers handling the midden material.

A final feature within the redeposited midden, which is significant for our understanding of life in the Castle was the animal burrow (452) clearly seen as a brown trail running through the fired orange soil under a hearth (440). This was one of many such features, which attest to the freshness of the midden and the state of cleanliness of the Castle. These burrows were present in all the softer deposits and account for the minor degree of mixture of pottery assemblages.

This attempt at levelling raises two particular questions. Where did the material come from and why was the area being levelled? As the pottery analysis makes clear, the large quantities of domestic rubbish, bone, shell, pottery within this midden are unlikely to be within a primary context. The pottery was very well broken up and there were surprisingly few joins to be found between the sherds. Indeed the material was sufficiently broken up to suggest that it represented tertiary deposition. The origins of this midden material is indicated by the remarkably mundane quality of the pottery, very little in the way of fine or imported material was present. Taken together these points suggest that the most likely source for the bulk of this material lay outwith the Castle, either from the digging of defensive works or else from within the burgh. These large quantities of soil were carted into the Castle for a specific reason, presumably landscaping. We certainly know that a similar process took place following the re-construction of the entrance Flanker (below 3.7.2).

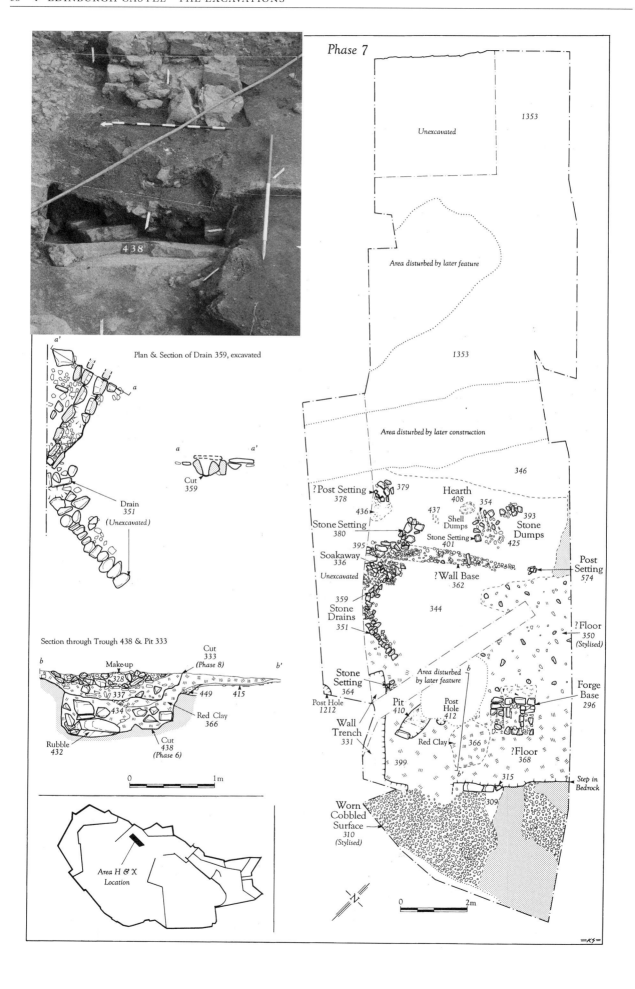

Phase 7

1353

Unexcavated

Area disturbed by later feature

1353

a'

Plan & Section of Drain 359, excavated

a

Area disturbed by later construction

a   a'

Cut
359

346

?Post Setting
378   379

Hearth
408   354

436   437   393

Drain
351   Stone Setting   Shell
380   Dumps   Stone
Dumps
425

(Unexcavated)   Stone Setting
395   401   Post
Setting
574
Soakaway
336   ?Wall Base
362
Unexcavated

359   344   ?Floor
350
Stone   (Stylised)
Drains
351

Section through Trough 438 & Pit 333

Cut
333   Stone   b   Forge
(Phase 8)   Setting   Base
b   Make-up   b'   364   296
328   Post Hole   Post
337   1212   Pit   Hole   ?Floor
449   415   410   412   368
434   Wall   Red Clay   315
Trench   366   b'
Red Clay   331
Rubble   366   399   Step in
432   Cut   Bedrock
438   309
(Phase 6)   Worn
Cobbled
0   1m   Surface
310
(Stylised)

Area H & X
Location

N   0   2m

=KS=

Illus 56 (opp)
Mills Mount (Areas H & X): plan for Phase 7 with, inset, a view from the W of the section through the infilling of the trough 438 and partially removed layer of red clay 366 (under the right-hand scale).

After the redeposited midden had been brought onto the site and allowed to settle, the smithy building was remodelled before its final demolition. It is not clear whether this involved a complete rebuilding or an extensive repair to the structure. The key elements in this are slots dug through the floor (399) presumably to hold timbers. One of these (342/356) continues the alignment of the putative footing for the S wall (315). The other slot (331/360) appears to be a partition which runs at right angles to the S wall for some 3m before terminating. At the junction of the two slots was a setting of stone slabs (364) which may have performed some structural function.

This building technique is a departure from the cill-beam system suggested for the original structure built during Phase 6. The relationship between cuts 342 and 356 implied independent posts, but was not definitive. However the evidence for individual posts was noted in the other slot (331/360). The fill of the posthole (540), seen in 331, contained substantial quantities of coal (541). It was 0.4m in diameter and 0.25m deep. The other posthole (538) was seen in slot (360) and was 0.3m in diameter and 0.25m deep. The fill (539) of this second post was distinguished from the surrounding slot by the concentration of charcoal it contained. Neither posthole fill preserved any sign of the post itself, but the differences in fill may indicate that these were replacement posts which were installed at different times.

Only two features were recorded in the vicinity of the working area of the former forge. Posthole (412) (0.28 × 0.30m) was an early feature which was removed before the midden (339) started to form on the floor (366). Another internal feature only partially recovered was a shallow oval pit (0.7 × 0.6 × 0.3m) dug next to the iron box (421).

Slightly to the N of the terminal to the partition slot (360) were two channels of a stone-built drain. The main line of the drain (359) was built of vertically set slabs capped with flat slabs, but, apart from a few packed pebbles, it was without a base. Its overall width was 0.35 but was only 0.15m deep. This ran out of the section and terminated in a mass of stones (336) (0.1–0.2m diameter), which served as a soakaway. Feeding into this at a right angle was a simply-built branch drain (351). This was represented by a line of stones (some cobbles, some angular) set in a shallow ditch. The single row of stones became double as it approached the main drain (359). The junction lay outside the excavation area and was not observed. The main drain was completely silted (372) and a spread of material (367) which may have come from drains was also noted. The main drain is likely to relate to another workshop, immediately W of the smithy (and outwith the excavated area).

The N extent of the remodelled smithy may have been marked by a linear spread of small stones adjacent to relatively stone-free areas. The line (362) lay just N of the soakaway (336) at the end of the drain (359) and small (less than fist-sized) stones. It ran across the full width of the trench in a spread about 0.5m wide and was about 0.15m deep. Within this line of pebbles was contained a stone setting (574) which could have held a timber post 0.16m square, which would seems to support the suggestion that these stones mark the position of the N wall of the rebuild smithy. There is no conclusive explanation for the stones, but at the time of excavating it was thought they might have accumulated against an insubstantial wall.

PHASE 7 DATING

Neither the decommissioning nor the refurbishment of the smithy can be satisfactorily dated from the evidence provided by the features from this phase. The contents of the pottery and other small finds within the midden material used to raise the ground level cannot be used to date the time of the levelling. For instance, the pottery from the redeposited midden material is very well mixed and sherds from the 15th and 16th centuries were found side by side. The only coin from this phase was a penny of Edward II issued between 1310–14, which was one of the few items of 14th-century date and must have been some age when it was deposited at Mills Mount.

PHASE 7 INTERPRETATION

The refloored smithy apparently continued in use for some period of time. The duration of the continued use cannot be accurately gauged by the artefacts recovered, but the depth of deposit which accumulated on the floor, and the degree of repair and alteration, give the impression that it continued in use for as much as a half a century until perhaps as late as 1550. It may be that the construction of the defences described in Phase 8 precipitated its final demolition.

The reason for the large-scale deposition of soil at Mills Mount is not revealed in any documentary account, nor is it apparent from the archaeological evidence. The damage to these levelling layers caused by later features built in the N end of the Mills Mount trench complicates the interpretive process (see Phases 8 & 9 below). There is no archaeological evidence relating to the line taken by the Medieval curtain wall, but by the late 15th century it would seem that the Castle was provided with a complete circuit. It may be that the importation of soil was related to the construction or repair of the curtain wall or for the need to provide a more gently graded road for guns.

PHASE 8

Early Modern Demolition of the Smithy and Earthwork Defences (AD 1550–1675)

PHASE 8 FEATURES (illus 57)

This phase sees the final demolition of the smithy building, the continued deposition of midden material and the construction of earthwork defences. The first of these was a rampart which was replaced by a massive ditch set at right angles to the rampart. This ditch was approximately on the line of the later 17th-century Inner Traverse attributed to Capt John Slezer. During this phase the entire area examined in the Mills Mount trench appears to have been free of buildings.

FINAL DEMOLITION OF THE SMITHY

The final demolition of the smithy is clearly recorded in the stratigraphy of Mills Mount. Around the stump of the forge spread a mottled green-yellow clay layer (305) deriving largely from the clay used to bind the forge itself together. This layer was thickest (0.10m) nearer to the forge base. It ran over the edge of the filled-in stone-cut trough and pit. At only one point was it clearly seen to overlie the trampled midden (339); elsewhere the relationship was ambiguous. This blurring of the relationship probably reflected the chaos of the general process of the demolition. In addition to the clay spread, there was a dump of

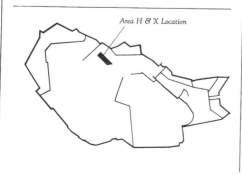

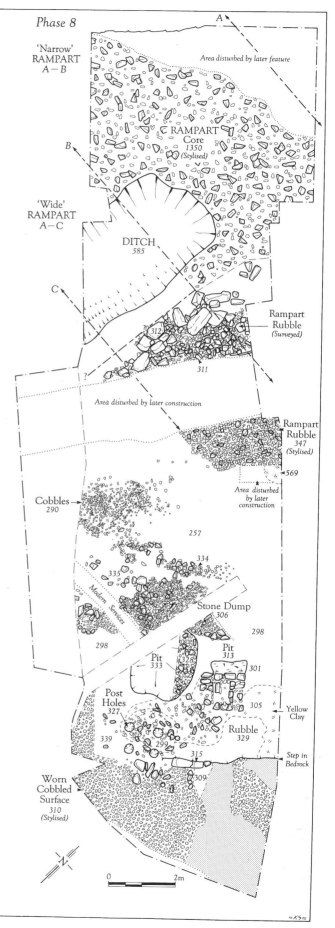

Area H & X Location

Phase 8

'Narrow' RAMPART A – B

Area disturbed by later feature

RAMPART Core 1350 (Stylised)

'Wide' RAMPART A – C

DITCH 585

Rampart Rubble (Surveyed)

312

311

Area disturbed by later construction

Rampart Rubble 347 (Stylised)

569

Area disturbed by later construction

Cobbles 290

257

334

335

Modern Services

Stone Dump 306

298

298

Pit 333

Pit 328

Pit 313

301

Post Holes 327

339

299

305

Rubble 329

Yellow Clay

315

Step in Bedrock

309

Worn Cobbled Surface 310 (Stylised)

N

0   2m

Phase 8

Illus 57 (opp)
Mills Mount (Areas H & X): plan for Phase 8 with insets: top, view from E of four-posted structure in reused smithy building; middle, detail of base of the ditch 585 showing primary infilling; bottom, detail of rubble in upper fill of ditch 585; the foundations of the Inner Traverse are visible on the far left; (above) key to relevant layers within main section (fold-out illus 24).

rubble and yellow clay (329) that represented part of the demolished forge. A spread of similar yellow clay (338), located a few metres NW of the forge, was judged to have come from the forge. The spread of stones (334), which seemed to respect the edge of the clay, may represent the stones from the forge which were dumped before being salvaged. They spread in a band which parallels the putative line of the N wall (362). The nearby spread (335) of pale brown clay and flat stones at this level may also be demolition debris.

It was after the forge (296) had been demolished that the apparent pit (313) on the N side of the forge was created. As was argued in Phase 6, this pit was in fact a void created by the withdrawal of one or more timbers which may have supported a hood for the forge. Into the void fell the ash and clinker (301) which had remained within the body of the forge. It is presumed that this marked the end of the smithy building.

The demolition debris of the forge and the associated levels were soon covered in more midden. For the sake of clarity this has been termed the Upper Midden to distinguish it from the Phase 7 Redeposited Midden, but there was little significant difference in these layers and they probably represent the same general levelling operation. Several context numbers were used to designate slight local variations within the Upper Midden (298, 330, 300, 317). The Upper Midden levels were more variable and if anything more mixed than the Redeposited Midden.

Two types of activity were observed in association with the demolition or shortly thereafter. Over the stone-cut trough an irregular oval pit or scoop (333) (1.8 × 1.5 × 0.6m) was formed, which in the first instance was filled with more of the Redeposited midden, capped with a thick layer of irregular stones mixed with the midden (328). The edges of this stony fill were not very well-defined and probably include the stones (308) above the pit/hollow. The purpose of this pit is unknown, but on balance it seems most likely that it was deliberately dug and did not result from subsidence over the rock-cut trough.

About 0.5m S of this pit was a set (327) of four shallow postholes set in an approximate square of side c 0.5–0.7m. The four holes (319, 321, 323, 325) were very similar in size, between 0.2–0.3m in diameter and only about 0.1m deep. This had been a small, temporary four-post structure (illus 57 top inset).

While these posts were being dug, cobbles were also being laid within and on the Upper Midden in various locations. Some, like those at the S end of the trench (310), are readily explained as metalling for an earlier version of the existing road up to the citadel. Others, such as (306 & 350) which are both within the area of the former smithy, may be part of the final stages of the levelling which elsewhere on the site saw successive layers of cobbles laid down.

CONTINUED MIDDEN DEPOSITION

In addition to the cobbling, the site of the smithy was covered by more of the Upper Midden material. By and large this tended to be stonier and contain less bone than the earlier midden levels. It is probably to be seen as levelling material. Some of the components were distinctive, being spreads of charcoal (299) or mortar (569), but by and large the distinctions between (295, 298, 297, 357) seem of little importance. Apart from that, these final layers of midden material seem to lap over stoney spreads (290, 347) which are associated with the top level of the rampart (1350) discussed below.

DEFENSIVE SEQUENCE (illus 58)

One of the most complicated sets of features excavated on the site was composed of layers of cobbles, large stones, clay and midden material which together seemed to have formed the base of a simple dump rampart. This substantial structure originally ran across the N end of the trench but survived most clearly in the wedge of ground left between the later ditch (585) and the Inner Traverse (254) and in the sub-floor of the Cartshed. These layers required great physical effort to excavate because of the angularity and density of the stone and clinging quality of the clay. The problems of recording and interpreting such large-scale deposits were aggravated by having to excavate in stages. This was unavoidable, not the least because they constituted part of the foundations for the 18th-century Cartshed. As a result, there exists doubt about the orientation, dimension and purpose of the rampart, but there can be no doubt that these layers were deliberately deposited with the intention of creating a stable earthwork mass.

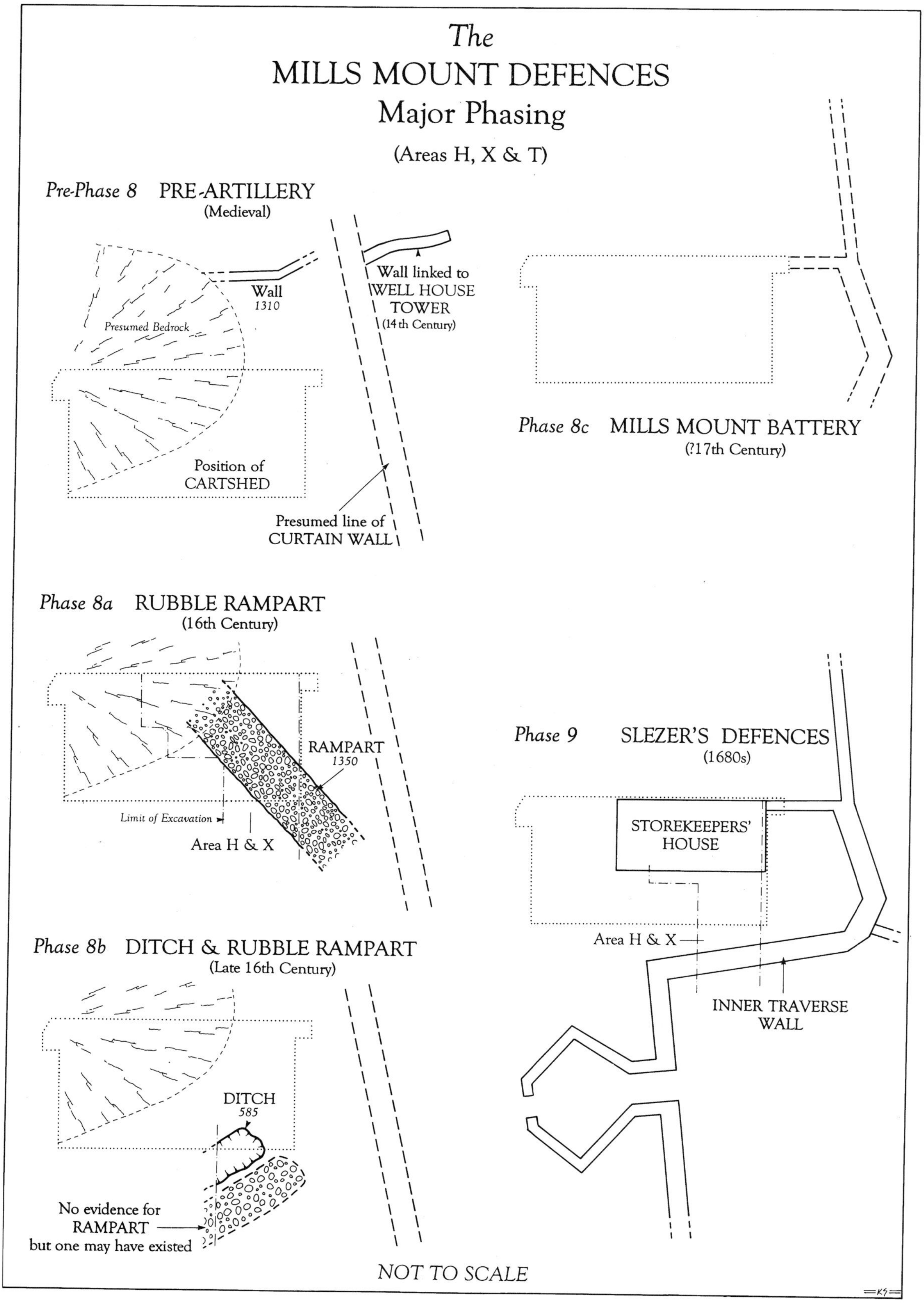

The
MILLS MOUNT DEFENCES
Major Phasing
(Areas H, X & T)

Pre-Phase 8 PRE-ARTILLERY
(Medieval)

Presumed Bedrock

Wall
1310

Wall linked to
WELL HOUSE
TOWER
(14th Century)

Position of
CARTSHED

Presumed line of
CURTAIN WALL

Phase 8a RUBBLE RAMPART
(16th Century)

RAMPART
1350

Limit of Excavation

Area H & X

Phase 8b DITCH & RUBBLE RAMPART
(Late 16th Century)

DITCH
585

No evidence for
RAMPART
but one may have existed

Phase 8c MILLS MOUNT BATTERY
(?17th Century)

Phase 9 SLEZER'S DEFENCES
(1680s)

STOREKEEPERS'
HOUSE

Area H & X

INNER TRAVERSE
WALL

NOT TO SCALE

Illus 58
Mills Mount Phase 8: interpretive plans of defences.

The sequence of deposition was as follows. A mass of large irregular stone fragments, which in places was composed entirely of shattered bedrock (571 and 355), but elsewhere was composed of various stones types, was laid directly on the surface of the Redeposited Midden. In places this was covered by a mixture of stone in a matrix of midden (353). In all cases, this basal layer of stones was capped by clay which varied in colour from grey (1352 & 570) to dark brown (352 & 316). With the exception of 316 which contained a proportion of midden, these layers were almost pure clay which was up to 0.2m deep. The clay was followed by more stones, (1350) which provided the main bulk of the rampart. The rampart core included mortared rubble as well as freshly shattered bedrock (1350) and unworked irregular stones and small boulders (311 & 312). Spreading away from the main concentrations of stones were deposits of stone (290, 347) which seem to have been laid down at this time in the area between the rampart and the site of the former smithy, perhaps as paving.

Overall, the rampart deposits spread some 8m N of the later Inner Traverse wall and survived to a maximum depth of 0.9m. Determining the orientation of a large wall in such a small trench is difficult. The best estimate of the orientation is that it ran diagonally across the trench and this would suggest that the real width of the bank was closer to 6m than to the 8m recorded in the section. However, if the stone deposit S of the Inner Traverse is part of the same rampart, then the overall width could have been nearer 10m.

The rampart was superseded by a massive ditch (585) which was oriented approximately at right angles to the rampart which it cut through. It was approximately 6m wide and 2m deep (illus 57 mid inset). It cut through the layers just described and the layers of Redeposited Midden virtually to the level of the Roman/Iron Age occupation. Its profile was distinctive (illus 24, fold-out section). On its S side the steep face was broken by two, possibly three, steps, while on the N side, as far as it was traced, it showed a more parabolic slope. The bottom of the ditch was very flat. The lowest step may have been created by cleaning it out; certainly very little silt (589) or debris (590) had accumulated before its deliberate infilling. The curious stepped inner face of the ditch may have been fashioned to accept a stone facing or timber revetting. Alternatively, the steps may have been to provide a relatively easy access to the ditch.

The filling of the ditch was clearly deliberate: the first deposit was a concentrated dump of coal, coal ash and smithing waste (587). This was followed by a silty clay (586) with few stones. It seems likely that the shallow angle of the upper part of the ditch profile (375) does not represent a recutting, but is due to erosion of the edge during the infilling process which clearly involved cart-loads of material for the infilling. Some of this infill was midden (294) which was indistinguishable from midden layers deposited elsewhere on Mills Mount but one major layer (291) was pure demolition rubble consisting of mortar, stones and plaster (illus 57 bottom inset). This demolition rubble is probably from Phase 9.

PHASE 8 DATING

Two coins of James II–III copper 'CRUX PELLIT' (SF387 & 388), which were issued in the second half of the 15th century, were recovered from within midden layers (1351) sealed by the rampart. However, pottery from within the make-up of the rampart points to a date in the middle of the 16th century. The line established by the rampart was replaced by the massive ditch.

Dating the ditch is difficult. It looks to have been relatively well-maintained and periodically cleaned or recut. The primary silts produced a 'black farthing' of James III issued between 1466–71 (SF586), but, as indicated, the pottery from levels through which the ditch was cut dates to a century or so later. The major infilling deposit produced a gun flint which has been

dated to *c* 1700 (SF 438), an estimate which is certainly too late since the Inner Barrier had almost certainly been built over the infilled ditch by the 1670s.

PHASE 8 INTERPRETATION

There were no signs of timber framing or facing blocks to indicate how the clay and rubble rampart was finished or whether it carried any superstructure. Therefore it is likely that this rampart was never of any great height, indeed a height of only a few metres would provide sufficient cover for an artillery battery. We can only suppose that the rampart was built to provide protection for a battery on the NW portion of Mills Mount, which prior to the construction of the Cartshed (Phase 10) was a rocky outcrop overlooking Hospital Brae. Certainly simple dump batteries are known from recent excavation elsewhere in Scotland, such as the 16th-century dump for the battery at Dunottar Castle (Alcock & Alcock 1992, 271–4), Dundee Law (Driscoll 1996) and Jedburgh (Lewis & Ewart 1995). They can also recognised as field monuments (Fawcett 1994, 298, 300).

The function of the ditch is likely to have been defensive. If so, it is yet another undocumented defensive measure of the 16th or 17th centuries. It is obviously difficult to suggest how such a short stretch of ditch fitted into an overall defensive scheme, but the fact that the ditch cuts into the previous rampart suggests that it may not have performed an overt defence, but provided shelter for gun crews and their ammunition. Certainly one or both of these features could be associated with the battery illustrated on the W of the Castle in Gordon of Rothiemay's plan of 1647 (illus 73).

PHASE 9

Late 17th-Century Slezer's Works – Inner Traverse Storekeeper's House (1675–1745)

PHASE 9 FEATURES (illus 59)

From this phase onwards there exist plans, illustrations and documents which make the interpretation of the major features relatively straightforward. The dominant features of this phase were the remains of a combined artillery and musket rampart and the basement storey of a three-storey building. These can confidently be identified with the Inner Traverse (marked D in illus 22) and the Storekeeper's House (marked Z in illus 22), both of which were depicted by Slezer (illus 60), probably in the 1690s.

Before the Inner Traverse or the Storekeeper's House were built, the hollow left by the large ditch (585) was filled with masonry rubble (291) and midden material (294). Spreads of soil and a few stones were laid on the area to the S of the where the new wall was to be constructed presumably to serve as levelling. These levelling layers can be conveniently described by two contexts (255, 265), but contained a number of trivial variations in composition. One of the later fills produced a coin of James VI issued in 1588 (SF060).

THE INNER TRAVERSE

The Inner Traverse (254) was built in a flat-bottomed trench (348), dug through this levelling material, the upper fill of the ditch (585) and the make-up of the rampart (eg 311/312) as far down as the Phase 7 Redeposited Midden (346). Only the wall-footing survived, but this was a massive structure, 2.0m wide and 0.9m deep, and composed of rough-hewn sandstone blocks of boulder proportions (illus 61). The bonding was of hot lime which retained all of its original strength. The massive scale of the wall was to provide defences for a mixed artillery and musket

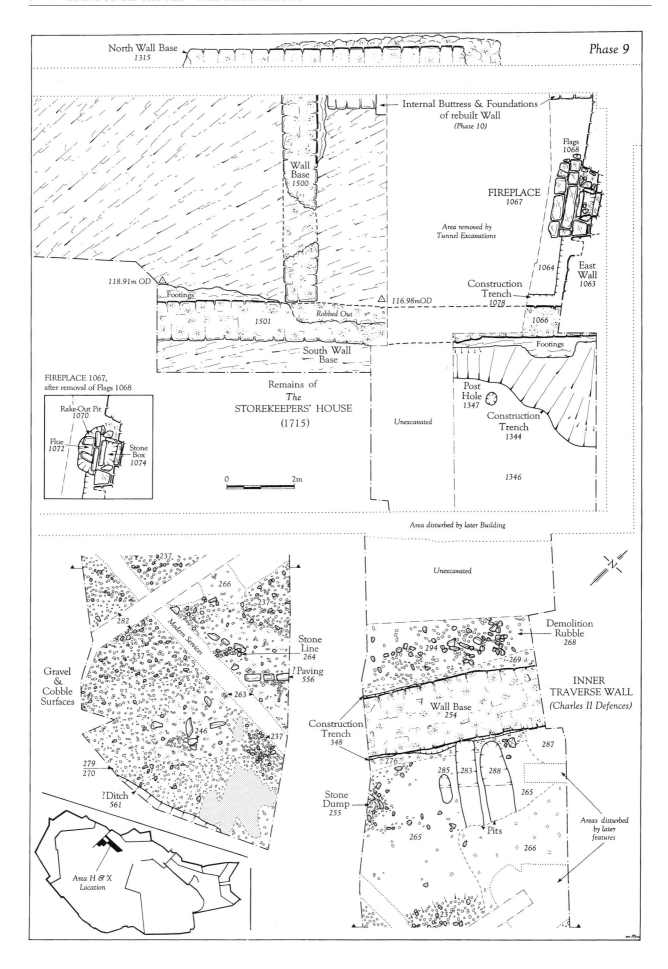

Phase 9

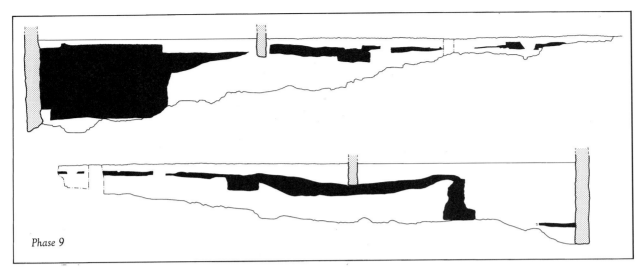

Phase 9

Illus 59 (opp)
Mills Mount (Areas H & X): plan for Phase 9 with (above) key to relevant layers within main section (fold-out illus 24).

battery facing towards the road to the citadel. The missing superstructure can be reconstructed in detail from the surviving stretch on the citadel and from contemporary illustrations (see figure in MacIvor 1993, 83).

The S end of the trench examined an area which was effectively the forecourt for the Inner Traverse, adjacent to the main road through the Castle. Not surprisingly the area showed much evidence of paving and repaving (237, 270, 263). These were cobbled surfaces of varying degrees of fineness, which periodically had been patched or renewed. Here the depth of soil was very shallow and bedrock poked through in several areas. At the S end of the trench, in the area to the S of the Smithy, it was never possible to determine with any confidence the age of these surfaces, not the least because until the tunnel was constructed all of the services were laid under the road. It is nevertheless safe to assume that the most substantial of these surfaces (270) was laid as part of the Slezer works.

THE STOREKEEPER'S HOUSE

The Storekeeper's House was probably built within a few years of the Inner Traverse, but it is not possible to say which was constructed first on the basis of the archaeological evidence. Sharing a common E wall was a casemate which seems to have been built as part of the same project and still survives. (The One O'Clock Gun now stands on the roof of the casemate.) This building was set into the slope of Mills Mount so that the casemate and the basement of the house were below ground level on the S side. On the N-facing side, the bottom storey was completely above ground level. To achieve this cellar level, the archaeological deposits on Mills Mount were excavated down to rock. The early prehistoric (Phase 1 & 2) levels only survived in isolated pockets where the natural level of the bedrock was deeper (eg 1076). At the angle where the casemate projected further S than the front of the Storekeeper's House, a curving edge of the construction excavation survived (1344). This construction excavation was filled in the first instance with a trampled layer (presumably during the construction process (1346)) and then finally filled after the building was complete (1345). Elsewhere along the S wall of the Storekeeper's House (1066) it was extremely difficult to identify the construction trench for the wall because the

masonry had been built hard up against the excavated face. On the inside of the building it was however possible to detect the construction trench (1078) for both the S (1066) and E (1063) walls. One posthole (1347) was cut into the fresh surface of the excavation (1344) for the building and is likely to have been for scaffolding. These features provide little significant information about the building itself. This is largely because the building was so well-documented in the 17th and 18th centuries, in particular by a plan and elevation from 1719 (illus 62) which shows internal partitions not recovered during the excavation.

The excavation did reveal that the walls were built of large rubble boulders, bonded with hot lime and thickly plastered on the inside. None of the exterior masonry survived. The only features of outstanding interest were to be found on the E wall which was a common wall shared with the casemate. Since the casemate was not demolished with the Storekeeper's House the common wall survived. All the other walls were demolished to well below original ground level. However, on the surviving wall the plaster remained almost completely intact and numerous repairs could be seen. Centrally located in the wall was a substantial fireplace (1067) (illus 63), which, in addition to repairs to its plasterwork, had been re-flagged (1068). This obscured an earlier feature of the fireplace which was a flue (1072) which ran under the base and had an opening below floor level, just in front of the hearth (1070). The purpose of this arrangement is not understood and seems to have been abandoned some time before the building was demolished. The only other context of interest was the accumulation of material immediately below the floor level (1069), which may well have contained final occupation debris.

PHASE 9 DATING

The construction of the Inner Traverse and Storekeeper's House can be relatively closely dated to the period between 1677–80, when Slezer was remodelling a number of areas within the Castle (MacIvor 1993, 83). Both structures are certainly accurately depicted in the view of the Castle produced by Slezer at the end of the 17th century (illus 12) and in his earlier plan (illus 22).

Illus 60
Detail from the bird's-eye view of the Castle (1689–1707) attributed to Capt John Slezer (illus 12) which shows the Inner Traverse with the round-headed arch and the Storekeeper's House with twin staircases (by permission of The British Library, Map Library K Top XLIX.74).

Illus 61
Mills Mount Phase 8: view from the N of the Inner Traverse wall foundation in the foreground; the rampart rubble 311/312 (Phase 8) is visible in the bottom left corner; the ends of the retaining walls for the gun ramp 238/241 (Phase 10) are visible in the left section in front of the barrows.

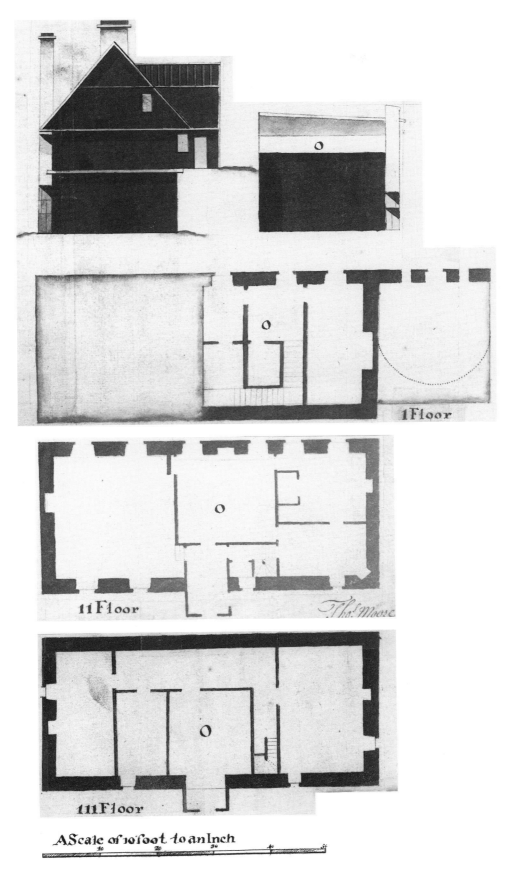

Illus 62
Plan of Storekeeper's House, Ordnance Survey 1719 (National Library of Scotland BO Z2/1b)

Illus 63
Mills Mount Phase 9: detail of fireplace in cellar of Storekeeper's House.

PHASE 10

18th-Century Cartshed (1745–1800)

PHASE 10 FEATURES (illus 64)

The final building events on Mills Mount have created its modern shape. These were the removal of (?part of) the Inner Traverse and the construction of the ramp leading down to the Low Defence in the 1730s and the demolition of the Storekeeper's House and any remaining element of the Inner Barrier followed by the construction of the Cartshed in 1746.

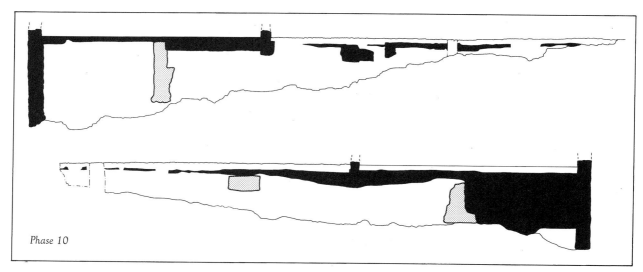

Phase 10

Illus 64 (opp)
Mills Mount (Areas H & X): plan for Phase 10 with (above) key to relevant layers within main section (fold-out illus 24).

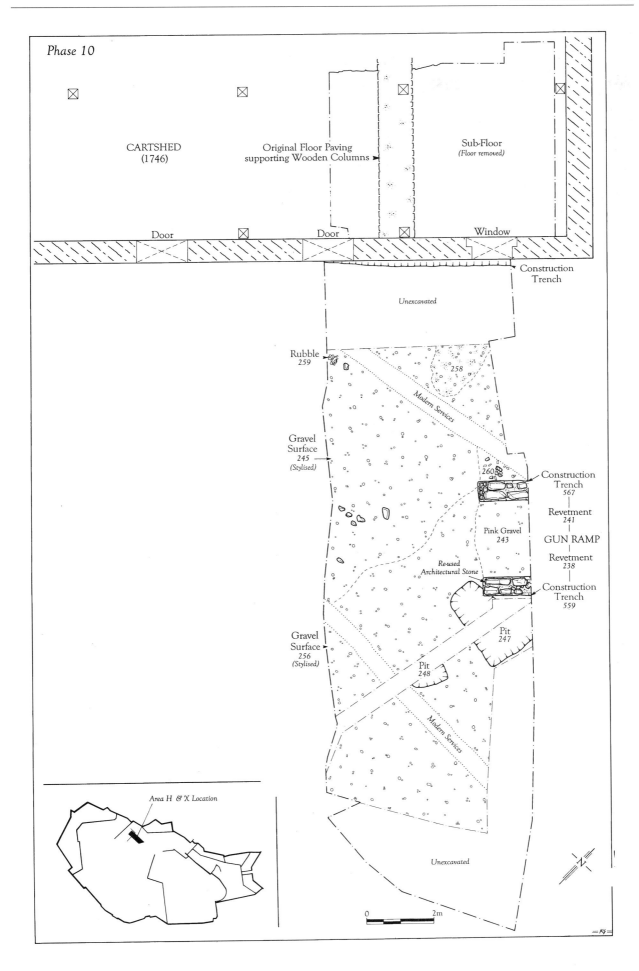

Phase 10

CARTSHED
(1746)

Original Floor Paving
supporting Wooden Columns

Sub-Floor
(Floor removed)

Door

Door

Window

Construction
Trench

Unexcavated

Rubble
259

258

Modern Services

Gravel
Surface
245
(Stylised)

260

Construction
Trench
567

Revetment
241

Pink Gravel
243

GUN RAMP

Revetment
238

*Re-used
Architectural Stone*

Construction
Trench
559

Pit
247

Gravel
Surface
256
(Stylised)

Pit
248

Modern Services

Unexcavated

Area H & X Location

0   2m

Illus 65
Mills Mount: photograph of section showing the primary rubble infill of the cellar of the Storekeeper's House followed by the later soil infill.

THE DEMOLITION OF THE STOREKEEPER'S HOUSE

The demolition of the Storekeeper's house was extremely thorough. Except where the masonry was an integral part of the casemate to the E, the walls were robbed down to the last stone. In the case of the back N wall (1060) (illus 59), which became the foundation of the Cartshed, this was demolished and rebuilt from the ground up. The robber trench (1065), and subsequently the foundation trench for the N wall (1060), was filled with the primary demolition rubble which was used to fill in the cellar level of the Storekeeper's House (illus 65). The creamy sandstone blocks in 1060 were apparently reused, but clearly have been relaid. None of the openings shown on the 1719 plan were visible and the rebuilt wall incorporated buttresses on its inner side. Once this wall had been rebuilt, the rubble, mortar and plaster (1061) from the old Storekeeper's House were placed in the void; this was not sufficient to fill it, so cartloads of soil including building rubbish (1062) were also deposited in the void. Filling up this space, which was approximately 4m deep, allowed the ground-floor of the Cartshed to be located on the same level as the ground surface of Mills Mount.

THE CARTSHED

The Cartshed was in the first instance paved with setts, but later in the 19th century it was transformed into a barracks and the fireplaces were added. So too were wooden floors. The first floor (1340) was the most interesting. It was constructed 'ship lap' style with the joints between the planks being filled with fillets of wood and tar.

The Cartshed (built 1746) was accompanied by a change in the artillery defence. A new battery, the Low Defence was built between 1730–37 on the N side of the castle below the Argyll Battery by Romer (MacIvor 1993, 94). Access to the Low Defence was via a ramp which is now occupied by a flight of stairs. The ramp was built by excavating a trench (559) and constructing parallel retaining walls (238 & 241). One of the stones built into the S retaining wall was a reused piece of a splayed window opening (SF 152, 4.3.6). A variety of gravel surfaces were laid down within the ramp (242, 243, 244). These gravel surfaces were ultimately replaced by a paving of setts, the only traces of which were the mortar stains where they had been bonded to the retaining walls.

Towards the modern road, the surface was a mixture of gravel and fine cobbling (550), but elsewhere the surface (245) was simply of gravel. Two pits containing 18th-century rubbish (247, 248) were excavated. It may be that they represent soakaways for improved drainage, but there is no firm evidence for this.

PHASE 10 DATING

The documentary evidence for the sequence of building is supported by a number of small denomination coins, a few fragments of pottery and clay pipe.

3.4 17TH-CENTURY DEFENCES WEST OF MILLS MOUNT AND THE 19TH-CENTURY POWDER MAGAZINE (Area T)

3.4.1 ABSTRACT SEQUENCE

Six phases of activity were identified, which are shown on plan (illus 66).

PHASE 1 Prehistoric:

Traces of cobbles set in soils similar to those in the Iron Age levels of Areas H & X. No finds.

PHASE 2 Late medieval:

Small area of paving sealed by sherd of medieval pottery.

PHASE 3 Late 17th century:

Series of defensive walls associated with the work of Capt John Slezer (Mills Mount Phase 9).

PHASE 4 Mid 18th century:

Reordering of the Western Defences involving the construction of various walls and a patrolway.

PHASE 5 *c* 1800:

A range of masonry buildings constructed over the former site of the patrolway.

PHASE 6 *c* 1815:

Powder Magazine constructed and modified.

PHASE 7 Late 19th century:

Demolition of the Magazine as part of the conversion of North Ordnance Store into a hospital. Subsequently replaced by a range of workshops including the last Castle smithy.

3.4.2 DETAIL OF AREA T ARCHAEOLOGICAL STRUCTURES (illus 66)

PHASE 1 • PREHISTORIC PAVING

The basalt bedrock, sloping down from Area H, continued at a gentle angle into this area, where a very sharp slope down to the N was recorded. Archaeological remains survived only in the deeper areas beyond this break in slope.

The most ancient remains were found below the base of the E wall of the Magazine (1319). It was only possible at the time to investigate a small area, 0.75m by 1.50m, against the inside face of the E wall. At the base of this sondage was an area of flat, well-worn whin paving stones, almost resting on top of the bedrock. These were of a size and character strongly reminiscent of the Iron Age paving found in Area H (Phases 1 and 2), 30m to the S. The stones measured on average between 0.25m and 0.40m.

PHASE 2 • LATE MEDIEVAL MIDDEN

This ancient paving was directly sealed by an organic-rich layer (1328), which was between 0.50m and 0.75m in thickness, and sloped down from S to N, following the bedrock profile. This grey-brown clayey layer contained much burnt bone and coal flecks, and although only excavated in this limited area produced a number of large sherds of late medieval pottery (see pottery report 4.3.2). This is likely to be contemporary with the levelling deposits of Area H/X (Phases 6–7).

PHASE 3 • LATE 17TH-CENTURY DEFENCES

A multiplicity of walls were revealed during the excavation, the relationships between them often being difficult to understand. These works are contemporary with those discussed in Mills Mount Phase 8. One helpful indicator however is the fact that almost all the pre-19th-century walls have very deep foundations, being built onto or down to bedrock.

The understanding of structures related to this phase is further aided by the existence of a handful of early, but nevertheless accurate, plans of the defences. The earliest of the two plans may date to the 1670s and is attributed to Captain Slezer (illus 22). It depicts upper and lower defences in the NW part of the Castle, the N end of the upper line being clearly revealed in the excavations as walls 1303 and 1314. The former was aligned NE–SW and was an average of 1.20m in width. The W excavated part merged into the outcropping bedrock, whereas to the E the upper part of the foundation was made of partly-dressed rectangular blocks, each about 0.50m in length.

According to the historic plans, the E end of this wall would originally have continued on to join with the NW–SE wall (1314) which formed the S side of a set of steep stone steps. The extant lower part of these steps date from this phase, and gave access to the lower defensive line, as they still do today. The side revetment wall (1314) was of random rubble construction, being 0.80m in width.

PHASE 4 • MID-18TH-CENTURY DEFENCES

The arrangement of the defences was reordered, firstly by the construction of a new E–W wall (1309) at the N end of the upper defensive line (1303). This was located 2m to the S of the steps revetment (1314) and was 0.96m in width. This created an E-W passage between the two walls, probably constructed at the same time as the lower part of the steps were rebuilt, being roofed over and provided with a stronger dog-legged exit passage. The W end of 1309 is extant and equipped with rusted hinges on the N side (see Phase 6 below).

The patrolway created by the construction of 1309 continued to the S where it was enclosed by a new wall (1310), built parallel with and 2.5m to the SE of the inside of the upper defensive line (1303). This wall was of the same width and construction as 1309. Both were well-built and constructed of partly dressed whin

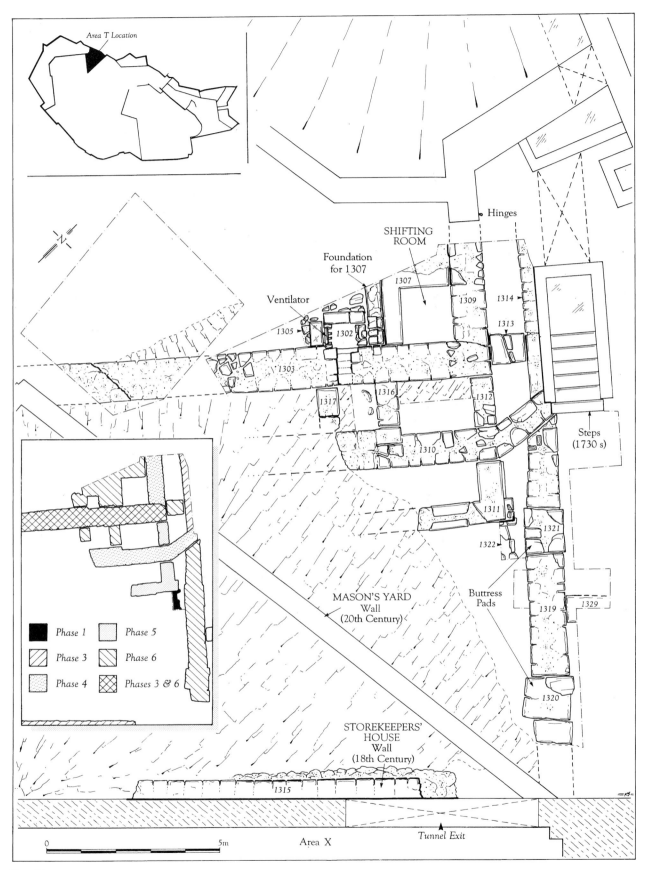

Illus 66
Area T: plan of the 17th-century defences and 19th-century powder magazine.

Illus 67
Area T: view of the excavated
structures looking towards the NW.

and iron-rich sandstone. The patrolway is clearly depicted on a plan of 1746. No evidence was discovered which will allow more precise dating, but it is likely that these works are part of the scheme of changes to the N and W of the Castle designed by Romer between 1730–37 (MacIvor 1993, 94) and which were described in Mills Mount Phase 10.

At some time, possibly in the second half of the 18th-century, wall 1310 was rebuilt with an angled wall at the N end, which would have blocked the access from the patrolway to the steps.

PHASE 5 • *C* 1800 STONE BUILDING

The patrolway was removed and replaced by a range of stone buildings, abutting the inside of the defensive wall (1303). This range is depicted on a plan of 1813 drawn immediately prior to the construction of the Magazine but is of unknown purpose. The archaeological evidence for this was found in the shape of two walls (1311 and 1312) which formed the E corner of the complex, thus continuing the line of 1309 to the S over a length of 4.30m.

This corner, which had an odd projection to the E, 0.30m long, was built from reused, good quality, dressed whinstone, as was much of the S return wall (1311). Some blocks were 1.10m in length by 0.35m in width, and may well have been provided by the demolition of steps and other architectural features originally part of the patrolway.

The 1813 plan shows a 13m long range with two conjoined rectangular buildings abutting the entire length of 1303 up to the point where it turned to the W through an angle of 25 degrees. By this time, the foundations of what had been the W upper defensive wall were incorporated into the N wall of what became the North Ordnance Store and ultimately the hospital.

PHASE 6 • 19TH-CENTURY POWDER MAGAZINE

The excavations have produced a detailed picture of the front of the Magazine known from contemporary plans to have been built here by 1815. The construction was characterised by the economical reuse of existing defensive wall elements. The design was achieved by simply extending the Mills Mount (Phase 10) Cartshed to the N, which by this time had been converted into barracks.

The NW defensive wall (1303) must have still stood to some height, as this was reused as the foundation of the front wall of the Magazine. It was extended to its original length at the NE corner by the construction of a short piece of infill walling (1313), which was shallow and did not rest on bedrock. The latter feature was common to most lengths of the new walls. This wall was only 1.07m long by 0.86m wide; its base being simply constructed from two large slabs. This allowed the N corner of the Magazine to rest upon, and be strengthened by, the existing side wall (1314) on the SE side of the steps. A pilaster buttress existed here at the corner.

The alignment of 1314 was continued to the SE to create the N side wall (1319). This wall was 1.05m in width, and ran SE to be bonded with the rear lower wall of the Cart Sheds adjacent to the entrance into the casemate upon which the One O'Clock Gun now stands. A further two buttresses enlivened this otherwise plain elevation. The bases of these (1320 and 1321) were revealed as stone pads with very deep foundations, both 1.30m in width. The base of 1321 was 0.65m beneath that of the NW part of 1319. The construction of this N wall of the Magazine cut through an earlier wall (1329), located between the stone pads, which was 0.80m in width. It was only possible to observe a short length of this wall, and it is therefore left unphased on the plan (see discussion below).

A plan with elevations from 1827 shows the E buttresses and other details which have also been identified in excavation. Of particular interest is the entrance arrangement abutting the outside of the front wall (1303). The 1827 plan shows a flight of five steps immediately W of a 'shifting room'. This was located just to the SW of a doorway inserted into the standing 17th-century wall (1309). The doorway was probably created around

this time to allow access from the lower Western Defences to the newly created upper Queen's Post. The shifting room (1307) was where the soldiers would change from their boots and uniforms into cotton shifts to avoid sparks, before ascending the steps up to the raised ground floor of the Magazine.

Excavation revealed that the narrow gap of 0.50m between the two outer structures had been paved with small stone slabs. Next to this the bottom tread of the steps (1302) survived as a worn slab 1.15m in length. This was built on a rubble foundation bonded with hard orange-beige mortar. On the W side a ventilator had been built under the steps (illus 68). A rectangular opening, 0.40m wide was created with the top and the S side formed from a single reused L-shaped block of stone. The N side was a single brick, and a tripartite opening was created by the insertion of two vertical, slim slabs of stone. The entire construction was cemented onto a large, flat base stone, which in plan projected some 0.30m to the west. This arrangement created an air passage which then turned a right angle through a 0.40m wide channel made in the foundations of the front wall. There was a groove in the base and sides of the N end of the channel which would have held an iron grille, presumably matched by another in the S end. A flow of air was thus encouraged beneath the raised floor of the Magazine.

The floor inside the entrance was supported on two dwarf walls (1316 and 1317). The 1827 drawings show that wall foundation 1311 was also reused as the base for an internal wall, which created a separate room in the NE corner of the Magazine. This was given a vaulted appearance by the provision of semi-circular ceiling trusses. The rest of the ground floor was further raised above the sloping bedrock on dwarf walls.

This building was demolished by 1897, and was replaced by an enclosing wall aligned E–W to accommodate a mason's yard. A range of service buildings, including the last smithy in the Castle, abutted the N side before being demolished in 1989 to make way for the tunnel portal.

Illus 68
Area T: detail of the vents for the powder magazine.

Illus 69
Area T: view from the E of the wall running to the Well-House Tower in Princes Street Gardens.

DISCUSSION

The excavations here have shone some light on the ancient development of this part of the outer fringe of the Castle, again serving to underscore the suggestion that occupation of much of the Rock was more extensive and intensive than could ever have been appreciated before. It is likely that the Iron Age occupation recorded on Mills Mount also existed here, possibly enclosed by a rampart on the line of the current Western Defences.

No evidence for the Medieval Western Defences was revealed, although it is likely that they did exist. The Medieval cobbled road found on Mills Mount would have run just to the W of this area, to continue down and around the side of the Rock, possibly to terminate at an earlier version of the western sally-port.

The Medieval stone structure which does exist in the vicinity is the stump remains of a substantial wall which runs down the hill (illus 69). This may have been part of an engine for winching water up from the Well House Tower and could date to the 14th century. This wall is approximately in line with the small fragment of wall (1329), deliberately left unphased on the plan, found on the N side of the N wall of the Magazine (1319). Little is known of this structure, only a very small part of which was recorded. It is possible, however, that it formed part of the 14th-century structure, projecting from this area.

Thanks to the full record contained in the drawings of the military engineers, there is no more to add concerning the Magazine.

3.5 THE 1801 MAIN GUARD (Area F)

3.5.1 ABSTRACT SEQUENCE

PHASE 1 ?17th century:

Scant traces of lightly built masonry buildings. No complete plans or firmly associated artefacts recovered.

PHASE 2 1801–1877:

Construction and use of the Main Guard building with little sign of modification or refurbishment.

PHASE 3 1877 – present:

Evidence of landscaping for a lawn or garden following demolition and the erection of two parallel fence lines probably during the First World War.

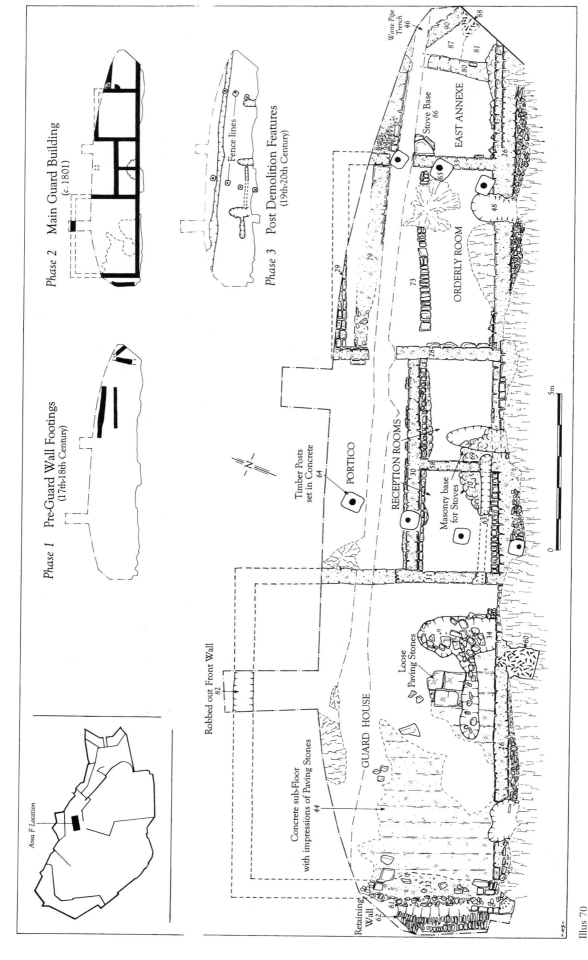

Illus 70
Area F: plan of the 1801 Main Guard.

3.5.2 DETAIL OF AREA F ARCHAEOLOGICAL STRUCTURES (illus 70)

The site of the Main Guard was located opposite the Argyll Battery, W of the Lang Stair at the foot of the cliff upon which St Margaret's Chapel is perched. The excavated remains consisted almost entirely of foundation walls and demolition debris, but they were sufficient to confirm the layout indicated by contemporary plans and to merit consolidation and display. In addition, scant traces of earlier buildings were recovered.

PHASE 1 • THE EARLY STRUCTURES

Three walls, all of which survived only as a single course, were discovered near the base of the Lang Stair. None of the walls was physically related and it is likely that they represent at least two or more building episodes. Adjacent to these walls were spreads of mortar, small rubble and some soil. These produced some sherds of 17th-century pottery (layers 46 and 54), but had clearly been disturbed during the 19th century. No 18th-century material was recovered from this portion of the site, so it may be that these walls belong to 17th-century buildings.

PHASE 2 • THE MAIN GUARD

The construction of the Main Guard involved not only the clearance of the earlier buildings, but also the drastic reworking of the cliff-face below St Margaret's Chapel. The building consisted of a range of rooms which provided office and accommodation space for the soldiers on guard duty. The constituents of the structure, from W to E, were the Guard Room, the porticoed entry and reception office, the Orderly Room and the East Annexe which may have been a detention cell. The entire structure was a single build and there was no sign of any significant alterations.

Illus 71
Area F: view of the Main Guard under excavation; from the E (on the Lang Stair) looking towards the Cartshed.

The Main Guard was constructed entirely of stone, with the exception of the rear wall against the cliff, which appears to have been brick. Few internal features were recovered and no floor levels survived intact. All finds come from either the demolition debris or the sub-floor area. There was no stratified sequence of artefact bearing deposits, so none of the finds can be said to come from a primary context. The finds are completely consistent with its use by a 19th-century garrison. The finds include purely military objects, such as regimental buttons, as well as common domestic articles, such as crockery and the occasional toy. The building was apparently redundant after 1853 and 1877, but there is no archaeological evidence to suggest how it may have been used during this period.

Little can be said about the architectural character of building beyond what can be adduced from the plan, because, with the exception of the SW corner, none of the masonry stood above foundation level and in places even this had been removed. Even doorways could not be located with confidence. Much of the interpretation of the buildings relies upon the 1852 Ordnance Survey plan.

Several features may be commented on in passing. In the Guard House the floor was paved with regular stone slabs. A few of these remain approximately *in situ*, but impressions of most were preserved in the concrete sub-floor. No internal features survived here. Elsewhere, the floors were timber and rested on joists supported on scarcements extending (0.1–0.2m) from the foundations. The sub-floor area was full of chipped stone, presumably from the cutting back of the cliff to accommodate the building.

In the two small reception rooms and the East Annexe there were irregular stone plinths in one corner of the room. Concentrations of chimney pot fragments were recovered from around these features so it is presumed that they served as the bases for stoves. Cast iron stoves are known from similar contemporary structures

at Fort George. No such feature was noted in the Orderly Room, which may have been equipped with a fireplace.

The plan of 1852 indicates the presence of a portico fronting the two small reception rooms and sheltering the doors into the Orderly Room and Guard House. No trace of the base of the central pillar (shown on the 1852 plan) was discovered. It was probably arched in a similar manner to that surviving at Fort George Main Guard.

The irregular five-sided shape of the East Annexe was apparently designed to accommodate the Lang Stair as it stood in 1801. The E wall of this room was subsequently built upon by the slight modification of the Lang Stair following demolition of the Main Guard. Access to the East Annexe appears to have been via the Orderly Rooms and it may be that this small room served as a detention cell.

PHASE 3 • POST-DEMOLITION USE

Before excavation the ground sloped gently downwards from the cliff-face. This slope was caused by the build-up of rubble towards the cliff. There are several features which seem to indicate that the area was used as a lawn or garden. A series of large irregular pits were dug against the cliff face which apparently were to serve as soakaways to help drain the water which pours off the citadel and down the cliff-face.

The only other event of any interest was the erection of two lines of posts set in concrete running across the line of the road. These were substantial timbers and could have supported fences which were six to eight feet high. The erection of the fences is most likely to have taken place during the First World War. The erection of these fences would have had the temporary effect of recreating the check point at the foot of the Lang Stair which had been abandoned when the Main Guard was demolished.

3.6 HISTORICAL BACKGROUND TO THE ENTRANCE DEFENCES
Doreen Grove

The Castle of the early Middle Ages survives only in the scant descriptions in the papers of the English wardens of Edinburgh written between 1335 and 1339 (Cal Docs Scot III). It is clear from their descriptions that Robert I's instructions to slight the Castle had been well-executed. The building work undertaken during the English occupation of the Castle included a gateway with a stone arch. This was presumably on the NE approach to the Rock.

Within thirty years the gate built by the English was either replaced by or incorporated into the Constable's Tower (on the site of the Portcullis Gate). The Lang Stair is first mentioned at this time. Thereafter there are only occasional references in official papers to repair work on the gate and the stone-built porter's lodge. No references have been found describing the gate or lodge in detail prior to 1610, when the Master of Works Accounts refer to an inner porter's house and the rebuilding of an outer porter's house, which was said to be in the sight of everyone that came by (Works Accts 1957, 327).

The earliest documented arrangement of the defences are those drawn during the siege of 1544 for the Earl of Hertford (illus 11; 72). These show the high Medieval configuration of the Castle dominated by David's Tower on the SE which was connected to the round Constable's Tower by a curtain wall (now the Forewall Battery). It is also in this drawing that we catch our first glimpse of an outer defence below the Forewall Battery, which, allowing for the poor perspective, is in the approximate position of the Inner Barrier.

The English campaigns of the 1540s, known as the 'Rough Wooing', shook the establishment in Scotland severely and steps were undertaken to improve the security of the Castle through the introduction of artillery defences (MacIvor 1993, 56–8). An Italian engineer, Migliorino Ubaldini, was invited to address the problem

Illus 72
Detail of the Castle from Earl of Hertford's siege of Edinburgh drawing (illus 11) showing David's Tower on the left connected by the Forewall Battery to the round Constable's Tower with the entrance Flanker in the foreground (by permission of The British Library, Mss Cotton Augustus I, vol. ii ant 56).

of defending Edinburgh Castle. In doing so he was probably responsible for applying to the problem the principles of the new fortifications developed in Europe, resulting in the building of an angle-pointed work, later called the Spur, in the area now occupied by the Esplanade (illus 73). It was an attempt to convert an awkward and unsuitable access site into a fortification which was able to withstand an attack by artillery. Following its construction, approach to the Castle was through the Spur.

The Spur required some repairs in 1560, when the dowager Queen attempted to hold Edinburgh Castle against the Lords of Congregation, who had announced her deposition as regent (Cal State Papers Scot I, 389, no 762). A drawing of the siege of Leith in the same year shows the Spur quite clearly with what would appear to be a cross wall to the rear of it. Two further drawings and a written description of the defences came out of the next siege in 1573. The better known of the two was probably drawn to accompany an engineers' report by Rowland Johnson and John Fleming who were charged with the task of devising a plan of attacking the Castle (BM Mss Cotton Caligula C IV ff 15). The 'platte' which accompanied their report has been lost, but it would appear that a drawing published in 1577, in Holinshed's Chronicle was based on their original (illustrated in MacIvor 1993, 63; British Library Ac. 8248/19). Both drawings are bird's-eye views taken from the S. Their intention was to give an impression of the Castle and the problems associated

Illus 73
View of the Castle by Gordon of Rothiemay (1647) showing the Spur as a prominent projecting structure. The excavation has suggested two new readings of this drawing's details. The ?gallows in the foreground may sit in one of the silted-up medieval ditches and the two cannon battery at the back of the Castle may be the Mills Mount defences which preceded the Inner Traverse (By courtesy of Edinburgh Central Library YDA.1828.647).

with an attack on it; these and the report must have been completed without access to the Castle. Johnson and Fleming's report includes the first detailed description of the Spur:

> 'Also we fynde upon the said este syde a spurre lyke a bulwarke standing befor the foot of the rocke that the said courten stands on, which spurre inclosethe that syde flanked out one bothe sydes; on the sowthe syde is the gaite wher they enter into the castle. Which spur is lyke XX foote high vamyred with turf and basketes set up and furnished with ordinance' (Cal State Papers Scot IV, 475 no 529).

Regent Morton repaired the Castle and rebuilt its defences after the 1573 siege. It was at this time that the Castle received the profile so familiar today, with the construction of the Half Moon Battery and the Portcullis Gate. Despite this, further work was necessary by 1623, when a new outer gate and a section of wall from the new gate to the North postern are recorded as being built (Works Accts 1982, 107). This may have referred to one of the interior gates or an external gate in the Spur.

Our understanding of the development of the entrance defences during the 17th century is confused by uncertainty about the dates of two key drawings. The two undated drawings of proposed works at the Spur

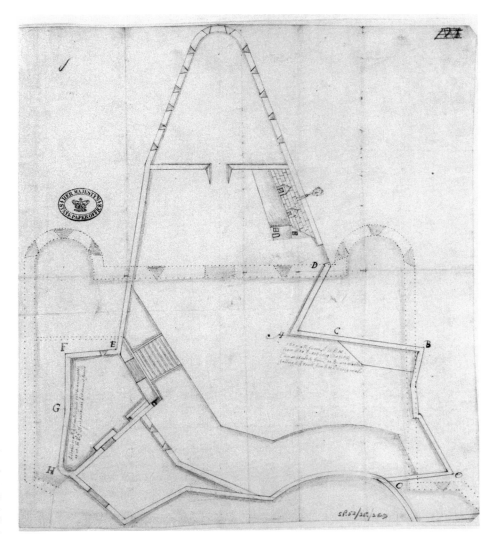

Illus 74
Plan of Spur (*c* 1620–1640)
showing entrance Flanker
(walls annotated E, F, G, H)
probably approached over a
bridge; North is to the left.
(Crown Copyright PRO State
Papers 52/25/2).

are principally important because they show details of the internal arrangements of the Spur and the entry arrangements into the Castle (illus 74; 75; PRO State Papers 52/25/1 and 2). In the drawing, the main outer gate is in the S wall of the Spur, which is defended by a guardhouse or blockhouse. The approach up into the Castle is across a drawbridge and into the SE wall of a quadrangular masonry structure (the North Flanker) and then out through a gate in the SW wall of the Flanker towards the portcullis gate. Two sections of wall, the N wall of the Flanker and the section of the S wall between the main gate and the Half Moon Battery, are described as being of concern structurally.

The undated plans of the Spur illustrate the development of the idea of a new eastward defence. The first shows the repairs already noted and has a new plan superimposed, but not annotated (illus 74). The new design is drawn with a much lighter hand and may have been added to an earlier plan. The superimposed sketch shows round towers flanking a section of wall bisected by a central gate, to be built up across the rear of the Spur. This plan was superseded by the second, also undated, plan (illus 75), which shows a similar arrangement, but with angle-pointed bastions and an outer ditch instead of the round bastions. Dunbar is of the opinion that they date to the 1620s to 1640s, on the basis of other elements of the Castle which are illustrated, and on palaeographic grounds. (1969, 12).

These drawings may relate to the work undertaken in 1623 or may well describe the situation when Sir Patrick Ruthven came to re-arm the Castle in 1640. Then he found the Spur was again in need of repair; indeed, during rebuilding works a section of the wall collapsed:

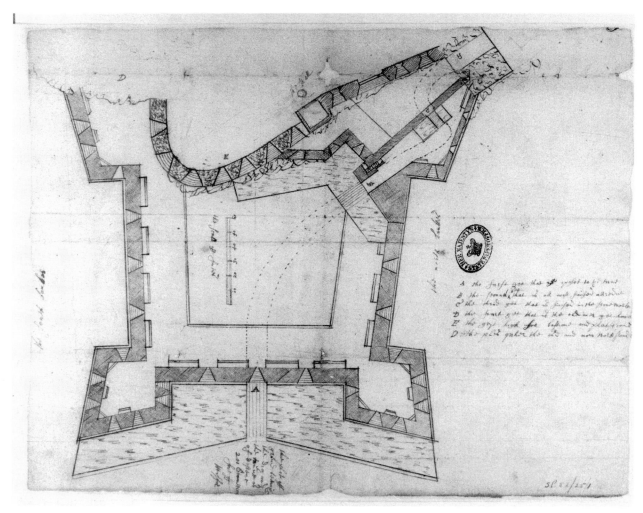

Illus 75
Plan of proposed replacement outworks for the Spur which were never executed. These show the entrance Flanker approached over a bridge crossing a ditch and passing over a second bridge within the Flanker. To the left of the outside entrance to the Flanker is a stair leading to a sally-port in front of the Inner Barrier; North is to the right. (Crown copyright PRO State Papers 52/25/1).

'. . . a parte of the Castel wall, quhilk is toward the entrie on the southe, fell in the nycht, with sik a noise, that all within took it for a myne or a surprise of the Castell' (Cal State papers Scot, Domestic 1639–40, 120–1).

The rigours of the 1640s seem to have been the final blow for the Spur; by 1649 the order was issued for its demolition (Edinburgh Burgh Recs 1642–55, xlvi, 206–9, 237, 241, 248–9). Shortly before the Spur was condemned it was illustrated, by Gordon of Rothiemay (illus 73). Dunbar has suggested that the demolition was completed within a year (1969). This would seem to be a tall order, unless replacement defences had already been designed and implemented. An account of work undertaken by Mr Mylne in 1639 indicates that a drawbridge was being built, presumably at the Inner Barrier, immediately S of the Flanker (Works Accts, 410, 419, 421, 424, 427). That this work was associated with the demolition is confirmed by a reference in the Master of Works Account that a master mason was paid for carrying stones away from the Spur in 1649 (Works Accts, 447). Following the demolition of the Spur, a start was made on the dry ditch, which survives, backed by low artillery batteries, which do not (MacIvor 1993, 81).

The arrival of John Slezer in Edinburgh (at first on private business, then to assist Lord Hatton to complete a report for the treasury on the state of the defences and the accommodation in Edinburgh Castle) marks the beginning of a coordinated policy to turn the Castle from a Royal Palace into an army base. The report submitted to the treasury in 1679 (Mylne 1893, 204–5), makes it clear that the outer defences were not quite complete:

'I find the new fortification very near finished, for it only consists of a dry ditch walled in both sides with a parapett or breastwork within for planting gunns & c and a glasis without, and all this is finished bot some small part of the coping. And concerning this new fortification as to the masone work and materialls, for that Sir Wm. Sharp is under contract with Robert Mille [Mylne]. There is a small addition of two walls both being about 60 foot in length and 4 foot thick and 16 foot high, which are yet to found, which being done will compleat the stone work, etc of the new fortification . . . . There is yet two Imbrasseurs towards the Castle Hill which by the Agreement Robert Mille is obleidged to repair. It is proposed by the Ingineer that for compleating the new fortification the old wall of the Castle may be taken doune, to witt, from the present drawbridge at the 2d gate till the round to the south end of the great halfe round bastion, and that in place therof a low wall of 8 foots in hight may be built to cover the sight of the 2d gate . . . . This, with some other small and inconsiderable reparations, is all that relates to the fortifications, except a new drawbridge and 3 or 4 gates which are ordered to be made.'

This describes the Eastern Defences of the Castle which were to remain for the next 200 years.

The plans made for the Castle defences over the next 50 years make so much more interesting reading than what was in fact built. An unsigned and undated drawing (British Library Map Library K.Top XLIX/74a) which has been attributed (probably correctly) to Slezer (Anderson 1913, 17–21), but may in fact be the work of Theodore Dury, reveals a brilliant mind applied to the problem. The answer it came up with is a star defence system on an outrageous scale (illus 12). This superb drawing is also important because it gives us the first accurate depictions of the Castle and its defences as they existed in the late 17th century.

The construction work on the star defence was begun by Theodore Dury in the early years of the 18th century. When it was barely under way, this scheme was reduced by Dury's successor Captain O'Bryen. Soon after 'A report concerning the fortifying Edinburgh Castle' was commissioned from Talbot Edwards for the Master of the Ordnance. The report assessed the military value of the initial scheme against Capt O'Bryen's and both against his own reduced hornwork.

Despite all the words and drawings none of the schemes seems to have been fully implemented. The casemates approached from the Coal Yard may be part of the Dury scheme to improve the entrance (MacIvor 1993, 89). Of the outworks only one small stretch of wall was completed by Dury to the N of the Castle. It was described on later plans as 'Le Grande Secret' or 'plan of an outwork begun by Mr Dury, never completed, now a ruin'. Some traces of this can still be seen in Princes Street Gardens, and, on the S, stretches of wall visible above Johnston Terrace may also be related.

Thereafter the external arrangements were only altered slightly. Captain Romer strengthened the E face and altered the N wall of the ditch in 1742. But essentially they stayed the same until the late 19th century. The emphasis moved from the development of larger defences to strengthening those that existed. The Inner Barrier had become the second gate, and the main route into the castle. A Port Guard House existed between the first and second gates, in the Inner Barrier forecourt, from at least 1674 until its demolition after 1853.

After the scare caused by the 1715 Jacobite Rising, efforts were made to strengthen the Flanker; embrasures were altered in the wall overlooking Castle Hill and new ones installed overlooking the Nor' Loch. The Flanker remained under-used except for storage; it is described as a coalyard in the early 19th century. It was not until later in the century, under pressure from the size of the army, that it was reused. The open interior of the Flanker was roofed over in 1853 to create a guardroom. In 1866–7 lockup cells for military prisoners were added to the W (SRO RHP 35713). The guardroom had a shelf-bed running along the N wall and an open-grate fireplace and served as a combination workroom and a common room.

Stables for the Commanding Officer were built in the yard to the W of the cells between 1877 and 1893. After the building of the present Gatehouse in 1887, the cells were redundant; they were later converted as store rooms, firstly for the quarter-masters and then for the annual Tattoo.

The new Gatehouse and gateway, designed by an unknown officer in the Royal Engineers, were built in 1886–8. It incorporated the last working drawbridge to be built in Scotland, which was an unusual 'rolling back' bridge.

3.7 THE ENTRANCE FLANKER (Areas G, J, K & R)

3.7.1 ABSTRACT SEQUENCE

An attempt has been made to use the same phasing for the three principal elements of the entrance – the Flanker, the Inner Barrier and the Coal Yard. The Flanker, being the most complex of the structures, provides the master phasing which has been used to structure the discussion of the other areas. For Phases 1 to 5, the correspondence between areas is exact. After this, documentary evidence describing the modern (18th-century and later modifications) allows the events to be more tightly dated and the phases diverge. The evidence for most phases is quite fragmentary so reference to the graphic interpretation of the phasing sequence is provided to act as a guide (illus 76).

PHASE 1 Pre-15th Century:

Prehistoric occupation debris and Roman pottery in lowest levels. Entrance defended by pair of massive ditches (in Area M) possibly with an upcast earthwork rampart and timber or stone entrance. Exact location of entrance unknown.

PHASE 2 Late medieval (mid-16th century):

Construction of first entrance double angle-pointed bastion. This Flanker is shown in drawing of 1544. After 1550 the external ditches were partially replaced by the Spur and the inner ditch was realigned. The road ran along the NE side of the Rock through a series of entrance defences which included the Flanker, an internal gatehouse and finally the gate at Constable's Tower.

PHASE 3 Late 16th century:

Evidence of serious damage to the fabric of the Flanker and internal gatehouse, probably as a result of the 1573 siege. The Flanker was almost completely rebuilt with a single angle-point, while the gatehouse may have been left ruinous. Road line was maintained, but the outer gateway of the Flanker was extended and strengthened.

PHASE 4 1620s–1640s:

This phase saw a drastic reconfiguration of the approach into that which is still in use. This new route bypassed the Flanker which was transformed into a pure artillery battery. A new gateway and gatehouse were established at the Inner Barrier.

PHASE 5 Mid- to late 17th century:

Construction of a purpose-built artillery battery on the site of the Flanker. Includes a sally-port to below the Inner Barrier lifting bridge. Cemetery in Coal Yard (Area M)

PHASE 6 c 1715–1853:

Further dumping of soil within Flanker. Remodelling of E firing platform. Flanker converted into coal store.

PHASE 7 1854 – present day:

Flanker converted to Guard House. Detention Cells added (1866), W yard converted to Commanding Officer's Stable (before 1893). Converted to quartermaster's store after 1887 and later used as general Castle store until 1986.

3.7.2 DETAIL OF ARCHAEOLOGICAL STRUCTURES (illus 77)

These four areas have been grouped together because, for most of their past, they formed part of one structural unit. From the Middle Ages these areas were all contained within the masonry defence which guarded the entrance (illus 77). This Flanker was located on the NE edge of the Castle Rock which from the

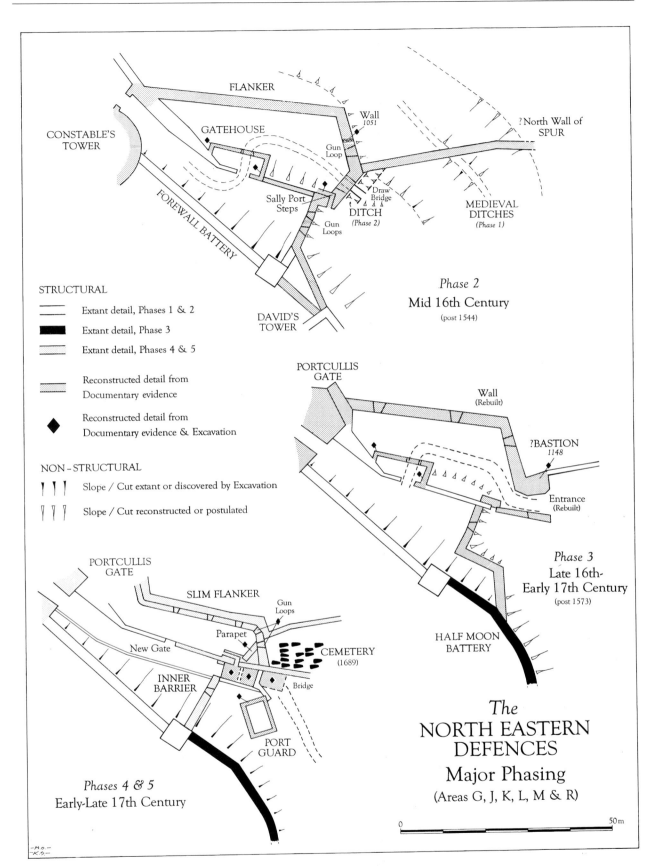

Illus 76
Summary of major phases of development of the entrance Flanker and Eastern defences.

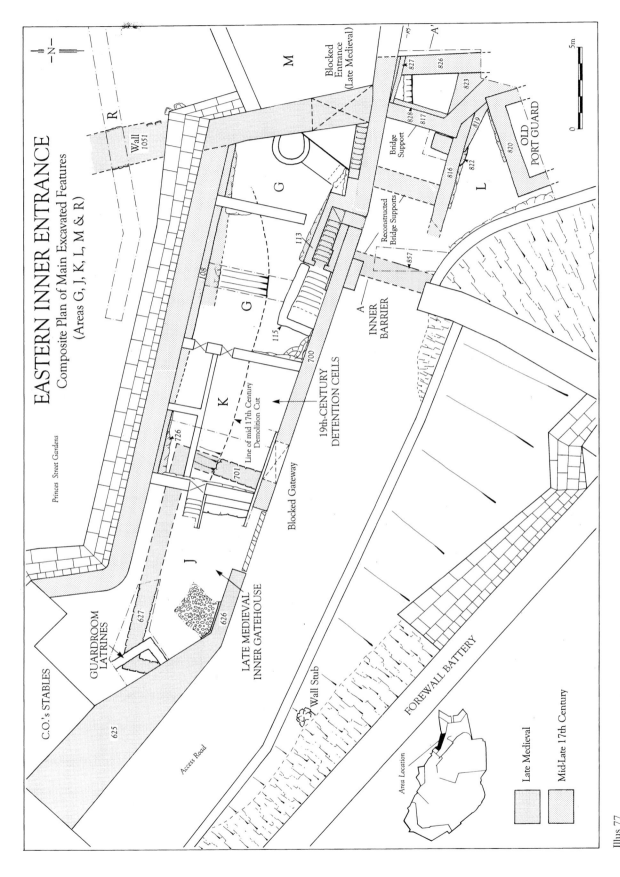

EASTERN INNER ENTRANCE
Composite Plan of Main Excavated Features
(Areas G, J, K, L, M & R)

Illus 77
Composite plan of Flanker (Areas G, J, K, and R) and Inner Barrier (Area L). For section A-A' see illus 94.

medieval period, if not before, appears to have offered the easiest natural access route into the Castle. It was only from the 18th century onwards that the Flanker was divided up into the separate units that gave rise to the various area divisions.

For many centuries, access to the prehistoric and early Medieval fortresses, and to the Medieval Castle, was gained by ascending a steeply inclined path which curved gently around the NE side of the Rock, arriving at what is now the bottom of the Lang Stair.

During the 16th century, the lower part of this path was enclosed within the gated bastion (the Flanker), which projected outwards from the base of the steep part of the Rock, occupying a fairly level natural platform. Much of the original Flanker is now within Princes Street Gardens. These construction phases are likely to have been in response to damage caused by the sieges of 1544, 1573, 1640 and 1650.

The interpretive scheme followed below (illus 76) is based both on excavated evidence and that provided by the early drawings discussed above (especially illus 74; 75). In the past these historic drawings had been dismissed as being unexecuted designs until the excavations in the Coal Yard (Area M) and the Inner Barrier established their reliability and consequently allows their use for the Flanker.

PHASE 1

Pre-16th-Century Bank and Ditch Defences

PHASE 1 FEATURES

Sealing the bedrock, at the lowest level in the three main excavated areas, was a thick deposit of dense, hard, chocolate-brown clay. This had tinges of yellow and red, and contained animal bone and charcoal throughout. It was closely comparable with the earliest deposits at Mills Mount (cf context 536). In the W part (Area K, 769) this was 0.4m thick underneath wall 701; it was also found beneath wall 160 to the E (Area G). Elsewhere it appeared as a less substantial layer on top of bedrock.

PHASE 1 INTERPRETATION

The deep, natural-looking soils contained evidence of pre-medieval occupation, as well as some remnants of a turf-line or topsoil (I Mate pers comm). However, these areas produced no prehistoric structural remains, and the only early artefact, a sherd of Roman pottery, was residual within a 16th-century context. It is likely however that there was prehistoric activity on this part of the Rock, which has been disturbed by medieval building. The natural line of ascent is by traversing the contours of the NE apron of the Rock, and this may have been the site of prehistoric defences. It is not until the medieval period that there was evidence for the Eastern Defences in the form of a pair of massive ditches (below 3.9). These probably date to at least the 13th or 14th centuries, but may have enlarged upon earlier defences. The upcast from the medieval ditches would probably have been used to create earthwork ramparts on either side of the ditches, associated with entrance structures and bridges. No evidence for these earthworks was observed and only slight evidence for pre-Phase 2 construction work was found here. Nothing can be said about the thin mortar layer (163) buried deeply beneath Phase 2 construction levels (161).

PHASE 2

Late Medieval (Mid-16th-Century) Low Flanker and Inner Gatehouse (illus 76; 77; 78)

PHASE 2 FEATURES

Two stretches of wall (627 and 701), thought to belong to a substantial rectangular stone building, were excavated in Areas J and K. In the W, the structure had abutted on to the massive standing wall (625) projecting E from the portcullis gate. This wall survives to a maximum thickness of 3.8m, and contains confused signs of blocked gun-loops. The great thickness may indicate that it was designed to protect the exposed NE base of the Constable's Tower (illus 77). The building abutting the massive wall was constructed of slighter walls (627) 0.9m wide. The construction of 627 appears to have cut the footings for 625. Wall 627 survived at 1.1m below modern ground level and although it was excavated to a further 1.2m the bottom of was not seen. From where it abutted with wall 625, it ran N for a 2.4m before returning to the E and running for a further 5.4m, after which point it had been demolished (illus 79). A fragment of the same wall (701) was located further E where it was possible to excavate it to its base. The top of this E wall (701) survived to the same level as 627. This 2.7m length of wall ran parallel to the W stretch of 627.

Wall (701) was founded on bedrock at its S end but upon a thick clay layer (769) towards its N extent (illus 80). The wall foundations clung to steep natural profile to bedrock here, hence the N end was 2m deeper than the S. At its base this wall was 1.3m wide, and after a height of 1.1m narrowed to 0.9m leaving a marked offset on the E side. Construction debris (757), consisting of mortared rubble, charcoal, shell and sandy clay, was found sealing natural clay on the E side.

This structure composed of walls 627 and 701 was made of rough-hewn blocks of igneous whinstone bedrock with some sandstone, arranged in a roughly checkered fashion with rubble infill. The largest block was 0.95m long. The faces were heavily smeared with yellow-brown lime mortar, but in all cases were well-finished. There were signs of subsequent repointing with grey mortar.

The space enclosed by this rectangular structure measured 12 × 4m. The only possible contemporary internal surfaces were observed against the inner face of the E wall (701) at the deepest level (illus 80). Here a 0.5m thick rubble layer abutted the wall base; roughly mortared cobbles (752) formed the top of this layer. However, this was directly sealed by a 0.35m thick sticky grey-brown clay layer (749) containing charcoal, bones, shells and a sherd of East Coast White Gritty Ware. This layer appeared to have been formed by the compression of a number of deposits, and was matched by similar deposits (755) abutting the exterior face of the wall. These two deposits (749 and 755) were probably laid down immediately after the completion of building 627/701.

At the E end of this area, there was evidence for a contemporary masonry structure. At the base of the surviving E wall of the Flanker, at a depth of 6m below the modern floor level, a 2.2m

Illus 78
View of Flanker from the E after partial demolition of casemates (left). The vertical white line on the Flanker is a surveyor's staff marking the centre of the blocked entrance.

length of wall (160) was observed running approximately N–S (illus 81). This appears to have been bedded upon slightly disturbed natural clay (162) and associated with a 0.04m thick layer of cream-white mortar (163) and a 0.4m thick dark-brown clay layer. The wall (160) survived to a height of 1m, above which it had been demolished and rebuilt by a later wall (158, Phase 3). Wall 160 was built of coursed rectangular blocks in a matrix of cream-white mortar.

This early Flanker wall had been truncated to the S by housing for a 19th-century water main and to the N by the existing North Flanker wall (108, Phase 5). However, excavations on the same line, 7m to the N in Princes Street Gardens (Area R), revealed what appears to be part of the continuation of this wall. Here it was possible to record a section through the wall (1051) where it was found to be 2.5m wide, and survived to a height of over 2m (illus 77; 82). The base of 1051 was not observed. Due to the sloping topography, the wall here was found at a level 6m below that in the Guardroom. The wall construction was very similar in both areas; the largest block observed here was 0.7m in length.

PHASE 2 INTERPRETATION

The archaeological record does not provide evidence to date closely the two structures identified in this phase. They may have been constructed as part of the remodelling which followed the siege of 1544, when the Spur was built. However it is not necessary to see these as new creations of c 1550. Indeed the

rectangular building could be part of the gatehouse outside Constable's Tower noted in the early 17th century. Similarly the early build of the Flanker may be the structure represented in the drawing produced at the time of the siege in 1544 (illus 72). This shows it as a relatively low-walled open enclosure, which is how it has been reconstructed in illustration 83.

Whatever their origins, it is clear that both structures were significant elements in the entrance defences designed about 1550, which featured the new Spur. The archaeological work does help to read with more certainty the version of the Rowland Johnson and John Fleming 'platte' made in 1573 and published in 1577 in Holinshed's Chronicle (MacIvor 1993, 63; British Library Ac. 8248/19).

The Spur must have cut across the Medieval ditches (see below Area M), necessitating their infilling, except on the N and S perimeters, and required modified access arrangements. The Flanker represented in the c 1573 plan is with more certainty a double angle-pointed bastion (160/1051) which closed off access to the Castle through the rear of the Spur. Although only a short section of what appears to have been the interior face of the E angle-point (160) was excavated, it is possible to estimate its original size. The location of the N corner can be reconstructed by projecting the wall-line 1051, seen in the Gardens, and the line of the wall which extends from the NE corner of the Portcullis Gate (illus 76). This defines an area within the Gardens which is relatively flat and could have happily accommodated a bastion which would have measured about 48 × 16m.

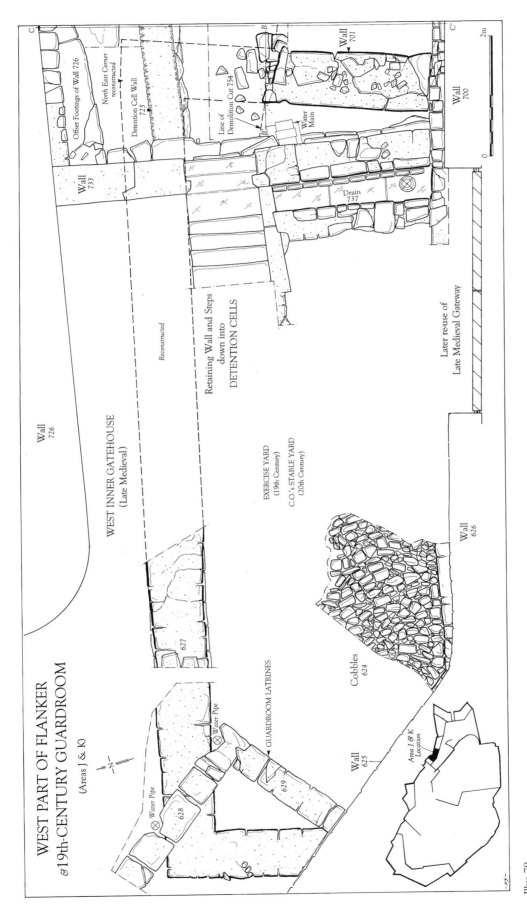

WEST PART OF FLANKER
& 19th-CENTURY GUARDROOM

(Areas J & K)

Wall 726

WEST INNER GATEHOUSE
(Late Medieval)

Reconstructed

Retaining Wall and Steps
down into
DETENTION CELLS

EXERCISE YARD
(19th Century)

C.O.'s STABLE YARD
(20th Century)

GUARDROOM LATRINES

Cobbles
624

Wall
625

Water Pipe

Water Pipe

Water Pipe

628

629

Wall
626

Later re-use of
Late Medieval Gateway

Area J & K
Location

C

Wall
733

Offset Footings of Wall 726

North East Corner
reconstructed

Detention Cell Wall
725

Line of
Demolition Cut 754

Water
Main

B

B'

Wall
701

Wall
700

Drain
737

C'

0   2m

Illus 79
Area K: plan of W part of Flanker including 19th-century features. For section B-B' see illus 80; for section C-C' see illus 86.

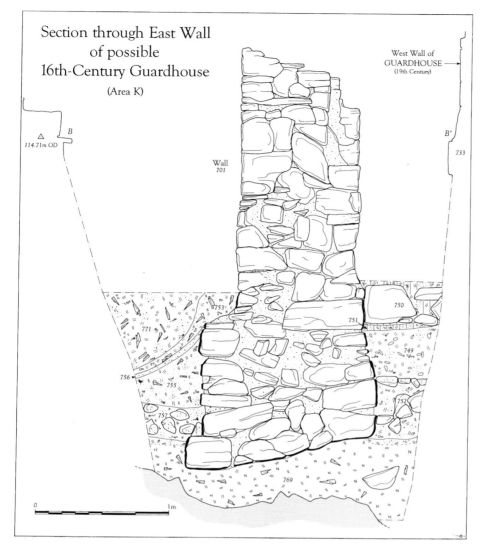

Section through East Wall of possible 16th-Century Guardhouse (Area K)

West Wall of GUARDHOUSE (19th Century)

B
114.71m OD

Wall 701

B'

733

753
771
750
751
756
755
749
757
752
769

0   1m

Illus 80
Area K: section (B-B') through the E wall of possible 16th-century gatehouse. See illus 79 for section location.

The E gate into the Flanker is shown in the plan of *c* 1573 in the SW facing wall of the bastion. Because of later works, such as the Phase 5 parapet (156), it is not expected that this would survive. Indeed work in the Coal Yard (Area M) indicated that the original levels adjacent to the entrance had been considerably reduced, following the mid-17th century.

The natural slope of the bedrock observed during the watching brief indicates that the area enclosed by the Flanker included some steeply sloping ground. The gradient of the path between the E and W portals was approximately 1 in 6: over a horizontal distance of 25m the level rose by 4m. Utilisation of ramps, now destroyed, could have reduced the severity of this grade.

The SE corner of the Inner Gate House was seen to be free-standing and the walls were too slight to form part of an external defensive circuit. Nevertheless, as the Inner Gate House, it was probably equipped with a loop firing onto the E entrance.

The likely position of the W opening through the Gatehouse and the S wall of the Flanker is the same position as that occupied by the W doors to the shop. It is still possible to observe scars in the masonry which supported the notion that the opening had been blocked (Phase 4) and subsequently reopened (end of Phase 6).

Thus after the construction of Phase 2 access to the Castle would

thus have been through the Spur to a gate in the E end wall of the bastion (160/1051). At the W end of the Flanker it would have proceeded to pass through or alongside the Inner Gatehouse (627/701) before continuing on to the Constable's Tower (illus 76; 83).

PHASE 3

Late 16th to Early 17th Centuries Rebuilt Flanker

PHASE 3 FEATURES

The E wall (701) of the building found under the Stables Yard (Area J) saw layers accumulate against either side during this phase. A level deposit, 0.05m thick, of grey-brown, loamy clay (751) was found against the W face, 0.85m above the bottom of the wall. This contained fragments of stone charcoal and mortar, sealing the thick deposit (749) described in Phase 2.

At a similar level on the outside E face of the wall was what appeared to be a thin (0.08m thick) deposit (756) of crumbly

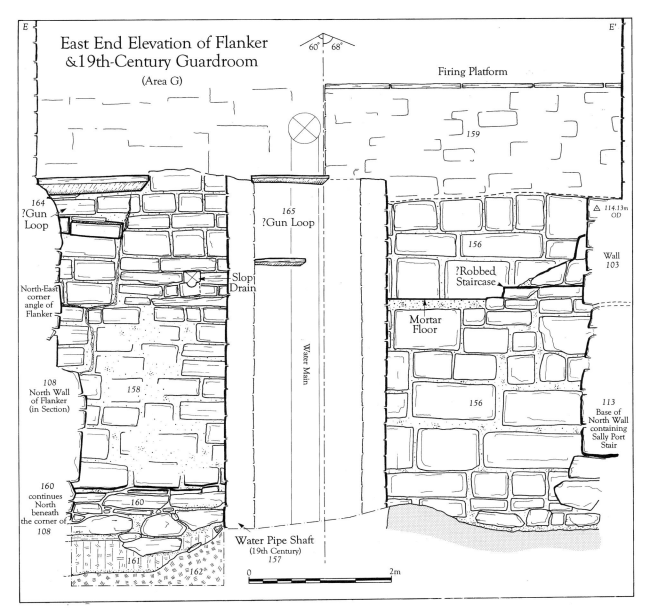

East End Elevation of Flanker &19th-Century Guardroom
(Area G)

60° 68°

Firing Platform

159

164
?Gun Loop

165
?Gun Loop

Slop Drain

114.13m OD

156

?Robbed Staircase

Wall 103

North-East corner angle of Flanker

Mortar Floor

Water Main

108
North Wall of Flanker (in Section)

158

156

113
Base of North Wall containing Sally Port Stair

160
continues North beneath the corner of 108

160

161

162

Water Pipe Shaft (19th Century)
157

0   2m

Illus 81
Area G: elevation of the E interior of the Flanker; see illus 84 for elevation location.

Illus 82
Area R: view of the E wall of the Flanker in Princes Street Gardens, with the corner of the modern Flanker in the background; from the NE.

Illus 83
Reconstruction of the approach to the Castle *c* 1544, showing the medieval ditches overlain by the artillery Spur with the late medieval entrance Flanker to the rear (reconstruction by D Pollock).

cream-pink mortar in a matrix of clay-sand. This construction debris sloped steeply down to the E at an angle of 45°, and was associated with the construction of the earliest phase of the S wall of the Flanker (700). Today this forms the S wall of the gift shop.

The construction of wall 700 truncated the S end of the earlier wall (701); the two were then bonded together at right-angles to the N face of 700. The construction was of small rectangular blocks of Old Red Sandstone which had been patched on numerous occasions. At the junction with 701, the later wall survived to a height of 1.4m. It projected forward 0.15m from the face of the Phase 5 rebuild (741). This formed a scarcement which widened to 0.3m to the E.

Contemporary with this construction, the E wall (160) of the Flanker was substantially rebuilt, (Area G, 158/1154). Only 2m length of this wall survived, but it stands over 6m high (illus 81). The new build was of some large, but mainly smaller part-dressed blocks of mixed whinstone and ORS, in an original matrix of coarse, beige crumbly mortar. The blocked archway (1155) visible in the exterior E face (illus 78), appears to be contemporary (below).

The demolition of wall 160 was matched at the same time by the partial demolition, at least, of the E wall of the W gatehouse

structure (701). A 0.6m thick layer of demolition rubble (750) was found against the inside W face of the wall, at a level 1.5m above bedrock. This layer was full of charcoal, and was in a matrix of brown clay-loam. It was paralleled by a similar demolition layer (767) outside the structure to the E.

PHASE 3 INTERPRETATION

This phase appears to present evidence of the consequences of the disastrous siege of 1573, and the response of the military engineers to the damage. The severity of the damage was recorded in reports made in the aftermath. With respect to the entrance the most dramatic consequence of the siege was the replacement of the Constable's Tower by the Portcullis Gate. As for the Flanker, George Douglas of Parkhead appears to have responded by totally rebuilding the bastion, slightly enlarging it to the E, but reducing it to the W.

The E enlargement involved the construction of a new gateway. The robbed out foundations of the N outer corner were located in excavations in the Coal Yard (Area M 1148, illus 99), which appeared to form a short wall, 5.4m wide. A fragment of the matching S wall was indicated during excavations in the Inner Barrier forecourt, where the existing SE corner wall (Area L, 827) was found to have originally continued to the E (illus 77). The new entrance would have been 6m wide externally, narrowing to 4m. The location of the gate survives today as a shallow pointed arch (Area M, 1155) visible in the Coal Yard (illus 78; 100; 106). This may be the actual opening or a relieving arch for a smaller gateway, details of which have been completely removed.

The pathway within the Flanker appears to have remained unaltered through this phase. But the Inner Gatehouse (701) certainly shows signs of damage or demolition in layers 750/767 (illus 80). Unfortunately, it was not possible to determine whether the Gatehouse was repaired or modified.

After the initial rebuilding work, there is evidence that further improvements took place. The plans of the Spur and gate arrangements (illus 74), loosely dated to the 1620s–1640s (Dunbar 1969, 12), show the bastion reduced to a single angle-point, and equipped with a gun-loop in the E wall and a pair of loops are depicted in the N wall of the bastion. One version of the drawing (illus 75) shows a ditch and bridge at the site of the Inner Gatehouse, but the area investigated was too small to have identified any such ditch.

The undated plan also shows a stair and sally-port into an ditch outside the E end of the Flanker. No evidence was found in the Coal Yard for such a ditch although, if the level here had been considerably reduced in Phase 6, it could have existed.

PHASE 4

1620s–1640s

PHASE 4 FEATURES illus 76

The gateway and road were reconfigured into the approach that is still in use, which bypassed the Flanker on its inner, S side. The gateway in the E wall of the Flanker was blocked. Masses of earth were dumped within the bastion and a new gun-loop inserted into the E wall at a high level. A new doorway was cut through the S wall of the Flanker and the internal Gatehouse was finally demolished.

Few traces of the transformation of the Flanker into an artillery battery have survived later modification. Most of the evidence is to be found in the narrow section of the E wall in the NE corner (158, illus 81) which was altered by the insertion of three architectural features in the N part. These consisted of a pair of lintelled openings, 3m apart centre to centre, and a small slop drain in between. All that survived of the larger, N, one (164) was a finely dressed under-chamfered lintel. The masonry in the wall immediately below the N lintel was a confused mishmash of numerous repairs, including another chamfered lintel fragment at what had become a structural weak point. This was evidenced by an existing crack. The smaller lintel (165) had a corresponding base, but any associated jambs had been destroyed by the insertion of the 19th-century water main (157). It is thought that these represent blocked gun-loops. Unfortunately no corresponding blocked openings could be seen on the much-repaired exterior face of this wall (1154).

Between the two lintels, at a level 1.4m below them, a stone slop drain had been inserted. The drain mouth was 0.24m wide with a shallow base, which sloped down to the E. There had originally been a front basin which had broken off in antiquity. The drain was still open for a length of 1.5m but did not extend through the 2m-thick wall. There was no surviving sign of the exit on the E facade.

These three features point to a significant change in the ground level within the Flanker. Not only would a higher level be required if the guns were to use the loops and for the drain to be of any use, but the interior of the Flanker would have required reorganisation if guns were to be moved around inside. This can only have been achieved by blocking the former E entrance (1155) into the Flanker and importing large quantities of soil. Little evidence for either exercise survives.

Of the gateway it is unfortunate that later construction completely obscures the inner side, while little is to be gleaned from the blocked exterior. Most, if not all, of the soil required to level the interior was removed during the subsequent rebuilding of the Flanker which involved the excavation of a vast foundation trench (754, Phase 5, illus 86). At the W end of the flanker there was some evidence for reorganisation of the interior consisting of the cutting of a new gate through the S wall of the Flanker further E than the original one (illus 77). There was also evidence for the further demolition of the original Inner Gatehouse (701/627). Curiously, however, major parts of these walls were left standing, in places to a height of 2m or more.

Despite this scant evidence there can be little doubt that the level was raised to even out the topography. Simply to compensate for the natural slope will have involved a rise in the ground level of some 5m on the N side, requiring perhaps 640 cubic metres of soil. The position of the gun-loops above all required this higher level surface.

PHASE 4 INTERPRETATION

This work can be interpreted as a relatively brief period of transition between the Flanker Gatehouse and the purpose-built artillery Flanker, built in the next phase. The new gun-loops were located at a level which allowed them to fire over the Spur towards the burgh. There was no dating evidence to establish when this work was done. The earliest that the approach could have been modified was after the drafting of the undated plans (Dunbar 1969), which is to say not much earlier than 1623. Some of these works were undertaken after the Castle was regained from the Covenanters in 1639 (MacIvor 1993, 78) or after the Covenanters' siege of 1640.

PHASE 5

Mid-Late 17th-Century Slimline Flanker

PHASE 5 FEATURES illus 84; 85; 86

The major event was the construction of a purpose-built artillery battery on the site of the Flanker. This involved the demolition of the N Flanker wall and the construction of a new Flanker on a narrower plan. Internal modifications included a new gun platform and sally-port to below the Inner Barrier lifting bridge.

In building the slimline Flanker the most substantial change to the existing structure was the construction of a new N wall, which reduced the enclosed area by half to only 9m wide, but still 45m long. It is essentially this wall with its battered base that rises up from Princes Street Gardens. Not surprisingly, the wall has been founded on bedrock on both sides which required a massive construction trench, which removed the dumped infill (Phase 4) and natural hillwash. This excavation must have coincided with the demolition of the old N Flanker wall.

This trench was recorded in three locations. In the E end (Area G), an archaeological excavation midway across the Guardroom (illus 84) was supplemented by a watching brief during machine excavation of the shop basement. In both places the slope of the foundation trench (148) was a very steep 60–65 degrees (illus 85), cut down to a depth of 3m. The same event was also recorded to the W in Area K (illus 86), where the cut (754) removed part of the remaining N wall of the Inner Gatehouse (701). It widened considerably from E to W, starting off on a modest scale, but increasing to 3.5m in Area J. This increase was governed by the contours of the bedrock.

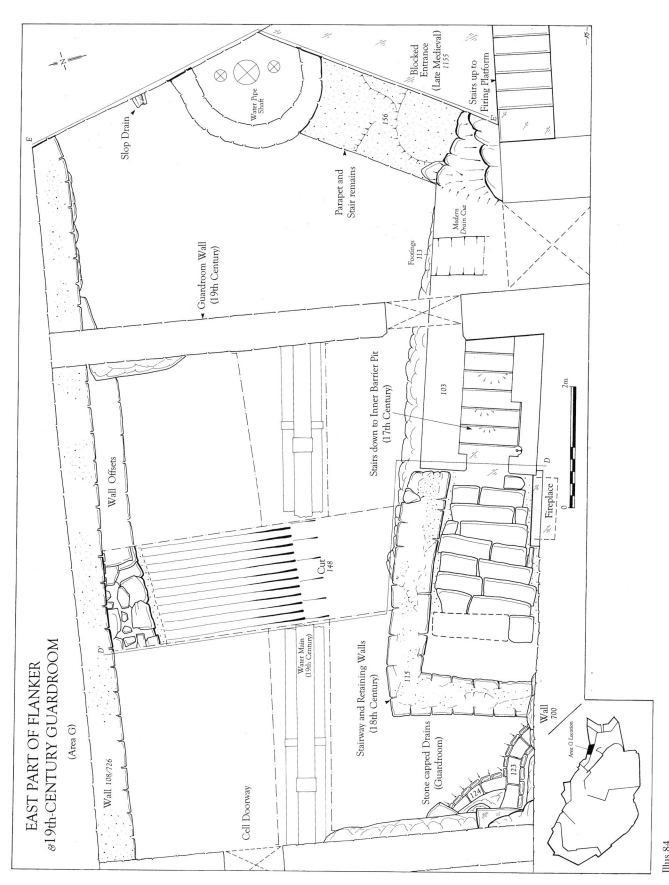

EAST PART OF FLANKER
&19th-CENTURY GUARDROOM
(Area G)

Wall 108/726

Cell Doorway

Wall Offsets

Water Main
(19th Century)

Cut
148

Stairway and Retaining Walls
(18th Century)

Stone capped Drains
(Guardroom)

Wall
700

123

124

115

103

Fireplace

D

Stairs down to Inner Barrier Pit
(17th Century)

Guardroom Wall
(19th Century)

Slop Drain

Water Pipe
Shaft

Parapet and
Stair remains

156

Footings
113

Modern
Drain Cut

Blocked
Entrance
(Late Medieval)
1155

Stairs up to
Firing Platform

E'

E

D'

Area G Location

2m

Illus 84

Area G: the E part of the Flanker and the 19th-century Guardroom. For the section D-D' see illus 85; for the elevation E-E' see illus 81.

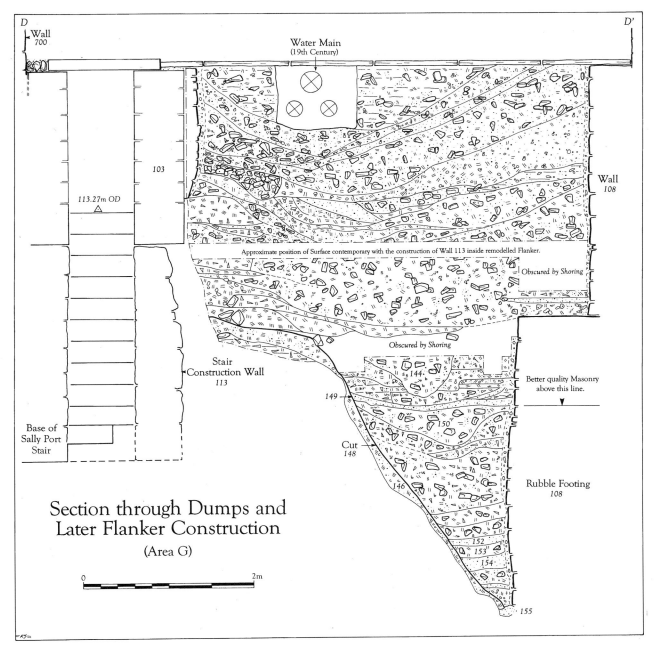

D Wall 700

Water Main (19th Century)

113.27m OD △

103

D'

Wall 108

Approximate position of Surface contemporary with the construction of Wall 113 inside remodelled Flanker.

Obscured by Shoring

Obscured by Shoring

Better quality Masonry above this line. ▼

Stair Construction Wall 113

149

144

150

Base of Sally Port Stair

Cut 148

146

Rubble Footing 108

152
153
154

155

Section through Dumps and Later Flanker Construction
(Area G)

0   2m

Illus 85
Area G: section (D-D') through the Flanker interior showing levelling dumps and backfilled construction trench for Slimline Flanker. See illus 84 for section location.

The widening is also reflected in the construction of the new wall (108/726), which was built of mixed igneous and sandstone dressed blocks, containing much reused material. The exterior base was built with a pronounced batter, but the interior was built in large offset steps which decreased the thickness of the wall as it rose (illus 77; 85; 86).

Contemporary with the new N wall, the S wall was substantially rebuilt (741), and there is evidence to suggest that the original access was reopened. There is some difficulty, however, in interpreting features observed in the S face of this standing wall (741).

This remodelling also saw the modification of the E end of the Flanker. A mass of masonry was inserted into the angle (156) in the SE corner (illus 84; 87). This obscured the blocked E entrance and was originally 6m long by 4.2m wide at its maximum. This feature was built by firstly cutting down into the infill dumped at the end of the last phase, then the whole construction was stepped in at a height of 3.1m above bedrock. The step was 1.4m wide and in places was floored with white mortar over levelling slates. The general construction was of rough-hewn blocks mainly of sandstone in a matrix of hard white mortar with some levelling slates. It was originally associated with what appeared to be the base of a stone stair at its S end. A scar caused by the removal of the steps was recorded on the E and S walls of the Flanker (illus 81).

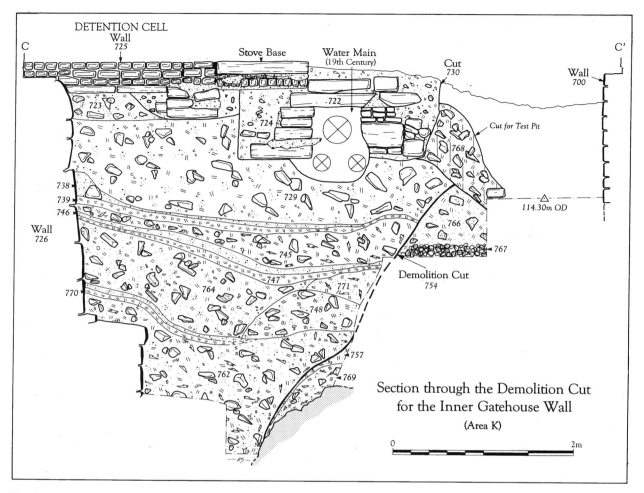

Illus 86
Area K: section (C-C') through the Flanker interior showing levelling dumps and backfilled construction trench for Slimline Flanker and demolition cut for Inner Gatehouse wall. See also illus 79 for section location.

The construction trenches for the new works were filled with massive dumps of clean, homogeneous dark-brown silty clay, which was interspersed with stone rubble and construction debris. Some lenses of crushed mortar and stone rubble were found interleaved between the clay dumps (G 144, 146, 149, 150, 152, 153; K 745, 748, 762, 764, 766, 771). These deposits contained very few finds. 748 was unusual in providing sherds of reduced green-glazed pottery and some clay pipe fragments which could be dated to the early to mid-17th century. As well as infilling the construction cuts, these dumps produced a level interior. At the W end, in Area G, the dumps were sealed by two hard-packed rubble and mortar layers (738, 739) which contained pipes dated to 1610–1640 (see 4.4.5).

Towards the end of this phase, a staircase (103/113) leading to the base of the S wall in the E corner was built (illus 85). This stair lead to a sally-port which was located under the Inner Barrier lifting bridge. This may have replaced an existing sally-port (see 3.8 below). Externally, on the N side, the staircase was bonded to the W face of parapet structure 156. In places the stair had to be cut into the bedrock to a depth of 2m. The lower 2.1m of the external case (113) for the stair was made of irregular undressed stone, which appears to have been trench-built, whereas the upper 2m was of finely-dressed masonry. The change of build was at the same level as that of parapet 156 and must represent the contemporary ground level of the Slim-line Flanker at the time of construction.

The quality of the stonework in the staircase and around the portal was of the highest finished ashlar. The entrance to the stair was 0.66m wide and had been designed to accommodate a door approximately 0.2m thick. The S side of the portal was wider to accommodate the door when open. One hinge survived 0.2m above the threshold but the upper hinge position was only marked by a scar, 1.2m higher. A bolt hole was observed behind the N jamb at 1.02m above threshold. Externally the outer jamb edges had a fine chamfer running vertically; unfortunately the top course or two and the head were missing.

The staircase was roofed with stone slabs, each measuring 0.77m N–S by 0.31m, which were pitched at an angle of 35 degrees. At the foot of nine straight steps, there were three set and angled to turn the stair through 90 degrees. There were a further two steps through a slightly shouldered arch. At the end of the passage was a finely-made round-headed doorway which was secured by a bar sliding from the E side (illus 88; 94). This was the sally-port to the Inner Barrier dry ditch.

PHASE 5 INTERPRETATION

The complete reconstruction of the Flanker was probably stimulated by the need to repair the damage caused by the

Illus 87
View from the N showing detail of the robbed staircase 156 in the SE corner of the Flanker (behind the horizontal scale) and of the staircase retaining wall 113 under the 19th-century doorway right of the vertical scale.

assaults of the mid-17th century. The opportunity was taken to reduce the Flanker in width and design a structure especially for housing artillery. The result was a high, slim Flanker projecting out from the Rock and bristling with guns. This was capable of protecting the N and E sides, as well as monitoring the new road.

This work would appear to have been broadly contemporary with the demolition of the W Spur around 1650, either shortly before, or immediately after Cromwell's siege of that year. This building certainly appeared after Gordon of Rothiemay completed his drawing in 1647. Gordon shows nothing at all on this site and it may have been executed during the period of reconstruction.

The purpose of the new Slim-line Flanker was to provide an up-to-date artillery battery. The triangular masonry mass (156) in the SE corner was aimed at strengthening the blocked gateway, and at the same time provided a gun platform at ground level. The lower platform certainly served the gun-loops constructed in Phase 4 (165 and 164); this would have meant that the SE corner was angled. An existing crack in the masonry under the S end of the top of the loop appears to provide the location of the original rebate. The platform was equipped with steps to the roof of the sally-port stair, and presumably more led to a higher parapet (which no longer survives).

The unusual fineness of the sally-port and stair suggest that they are part of a separate scheme. They certainly post-date the original gun platform in the SE corner (156). The high quality work was probably an integral part of the Inner Barrier lifting-bridge scheme depicted by Slezer (see Area L, Phase 5).

PHASE 6

C 1715–1853

PHASE 6 FEATURES

In the E end wall of the Flanker, the upper firing platform and pair of gun-loops were substantially rebuilt at an unknown time during this phase. This change in build is marked by a levelling course of thin sandstone slabs at the cill level of the gun-loops. The gun-loop in the S wall near the E corner, overlooking the approach to the Inner Barrier, was probably installed as part of these modifications (illus 94). Much of the upper part of the main N wall was rebuilt during this phase (illus 81).

During this period the internal levels were altered. These dumps were up to 1.4m thick and comprised brown clay soils with a high rubble content (729, 606, 610, 608). One of these (610) produced a cache of five musket balls of the Brown Bess type. The result of the dumping was to raise the W end approximately 1m higher than the E end.

Raising the level in the E end of the Flanker required the addition of eight stone steps (115) which were added to the W of the stair (103) to the Inner Barrier sally-port. The late stairs were not nearly as finely constructed as the original ones. They were built of reused masonry and were of irregular heights and widths.

The final deposit from this phase was a 0.25m-thick layer of brown-black loam (605) containing a very high proportion of coal dust. The coal-rich deposits and soil dumps only survived at the W end of the Flanker. This is likely to be the result of site preparation for the construction of the new Guard House (Phase 7)

PHASE 6 INTERPRETATION

There is little to add to the description of the features thanks to the information provided by the contemporary maps and historical accounts.

Illus 88
View of early 17th-century sally-port Doorway.

PHASE 7

1854 to the present day

PHASE 7 FEATURES

The E half of the Flanker interior was roofed for use as a combination Guard House (1854) to which detention cells were added (1866). This involved terracing the site and inserting a doorway and window just E of the Inner Barrier. Area G became the Guardroom, the floor of which covered over the sally-port stair and access via a hatchway. The cells were reached by a short flight of stairs.

Beyond the cells, the W end of the Flanker was an open courtyard (illus 79). A consequence of Guard House construction was that the gate through the S wall was moved back to the site of the late medieval opening, where it stands today. The courtyard contained a small latrine building, which was represented by the rectangular stone base of its E and N walls (628, 629). The open W end of the Flanker was apparently paved with carefully laid, large, worn cobbles (624) set in a layer of dirty yellow-grey sand, which sealed the layer of coal dust (605). This cobbled surface was only 0.15m above the floor of the detention cells. The cobbles in the small area where they were examined were covered with a thin layer of coal dust. This would have been associated with an ash bin located near the E end the latrine (illus 89).

The final modification was the installation of stables at the extreme W end of the Flanker. This involved raising the yard surface by approximately a metre and required the modification of the gateway. The higher level of the Stable Yard necessitated the provision of a set of stone steps down into the cells and a drain to prevent them flooding.

The guardroom and cells were made redundant by the construction of the new Gatehouse in 1887 and thereafter were used as quartermaster's stores.

PHASE 7 INTERPRETATION

As with Phase 6, there is little to add to the phase description, thanks to the information provided by contemporary documents.

Illus 89
View from E of W end of Flanker (Area K) with walls of 19th-century Guardhouse demolished. Stairs lead from the Guard House in to the CO Stables Yard. Open stable doors can be seen at base of Portcullis Gate.

3.8 THE INNER BARRIER FORECOURT (Area L)

A diagonal trench was cut across the road into the Castle from the SE corner of the Flanker (shop) towards the Inner Barrier gateway. Excavations for this area were required in advance of the construction of the E end of the tunnel so all trenches were excavated to the bedrock. Observations were made on the relationships between the masonry features as they were being demolished.

3.8.1 AREA L ABSTRACT ACCOUNT

PHASE 1 Pre-16th century:

In order to make the phase numbers correspond as closely as possible with those used in the Flanker and Coal Yard, Phase 1 has been used, although no pre-16th-century features were identified.

PHASE 2 16th century:

A small area of cobbling at the rear of the defensive works associated with the Spur (corresponds to Flanker Phase 2).

PHASE 3 Late 16th century:

A repaving associated with the rebuilding of the entrance Flanker (corresponds to Flanker Phase 3).

PHASE 4 1620s–1640s:

The realignment of the entrance road onto an elevated bridge and the creation of the Inner Barrier gateway (corresponds to Flanker Phase 4).

PHASE 5 Mid to late 17th century:

Modification of the bridge approach and construction of the Port Guard House in the 1690s S of the bridge complex (corresponds to Flanker Phase 5).

PHASE 6 Mid 18th century:

The gradual infilling of the pits and the replacement of the lifting bridges with permanent road surfaces. Underneath these road surfaces two bombproof casemates were built in the 1740s.

PHASE 7 Late 18th century to present:

No major changes.

3.8.2 AREA L ARCHAEOLOGICAL STRUCTURES (illus 90; 91)

PHASE 1

Pre-16th Century

No physical remains from this period were identified. The sealed natural surfaces were of green lumpy clay, lying above red shattered sedimentary rock.

PHASE 2

16th Century Paving

PHASE 2 FEATURES

This phase followed on directly from the construction of the Spur; all that survived here from this period was one small area of cobbles located at the lowest point in the area below the lifting bridge (illus 94; 95). This cobbled surface (852) was made of closely-packed flat stone which appeared to have been laid on a bedding layer of clean grey clay.

The cobbles were found at a depth of 4.7m below the modern ground level. These levels were waterlogged, and the difficult circumstances of excavation made it impossible to record the wear-pattern, if any, on this surface.

PHASE 2 INTERPRETATION

The understanding of this context is dependent not only on our understanding of the Flanker sequence but also on the interpretation of the two plans of c 1620–40 (illus 74; 75). Both depict variations on a wall with gun-loops on the line of what became the Inner Barrier. The pointed bastion variation shows a ditch in front of the wall and in front of the E entrance to the Flanker. The same drawing also shows that access to the front of this early Inner Barrier was gained by a sally-port from the Flanker in the same location as the later sally-port (Area G 103). The cobbled surface (852) was probably outside this sally-port.

PHASE 3

Late 16th-Century Paving

PHASE 3 FEATURES

The cobbled surface would still have been in use when the main entrance was remodelled after the siege of 1573. This involved the rebuilding of the E wall of the Flanker. Evidence of this rebuilding was found firstly in the form of a vertically-sided construction trench (829), cut more than 1m into the easily shattered sedimentary bedrock. The trench was filled with a very rough footing (827) for the wall. It formed the S side of the re-formed Flanker entrance. Many of the masonry blocks were squared, measuring 0.45m in length on average. The wall survived to a height of 3.4m at which point a ledge was encountered, representing a subsequent rebuild (Flanker Phase 5). Only a 2.5m length of this wall survived for investigation, but in comparison with the footing, the wall proper was well-constructed and was clearly meant to be seen from the first course up.

The construction level of wall 827 was sealed by a new layer of cobbling (818) composed of large angular cobbles set in a clayey matrix. This layer abutted the base course of the wall at a level 0.8m above the cobbling laid down in Phase 2.

The new cobbling was matched by an identical layer (837) located 5m upslope to the W. Later construction destroyed the remains of the cobbling between these two points. The W area of cobbling survived as a patch 1.1m E–W by 0.6m wide, and was located at the same level as the outer threshold of the Inner Barrier sally-port.

PHASE 3 INTERPRETATION

It seems likely that at this time the base of the steep rock-head may have sloped down from the citadel curtain wall to a point close to the S edge of this cobbling (837). This created a very constricted space only 6m wide N–S, forming in plan the narrow neck of the rear part of the Spur, into which any attacker would be funnelled. The rock-head here had subsequently been cut back a further 2m to the S.

PHASE 4

1620s–1640s New Approach and the Inner Barrier

PHASE 4 FEATURES

This phase describes the dramatic realignment of the entrance roadway to the higher level route, still in use today and the creation of the Inner Barrier gateway. The existing wall with gun-loops was replaced by an elevated roadway carried on timber bridges including a lifting bridge. This reading of the excavated remains relies to a significant extent on the Slezer depiction drawn over half a century later (illus 92).

The E end of the complex consisted of an L-shaped wall (823/828) bonded onto the SE corner (827) of the Flanker, which provided the support for a timber-built road surface (illus 93). Although the E wall had been subsequently destroyed in the 18th

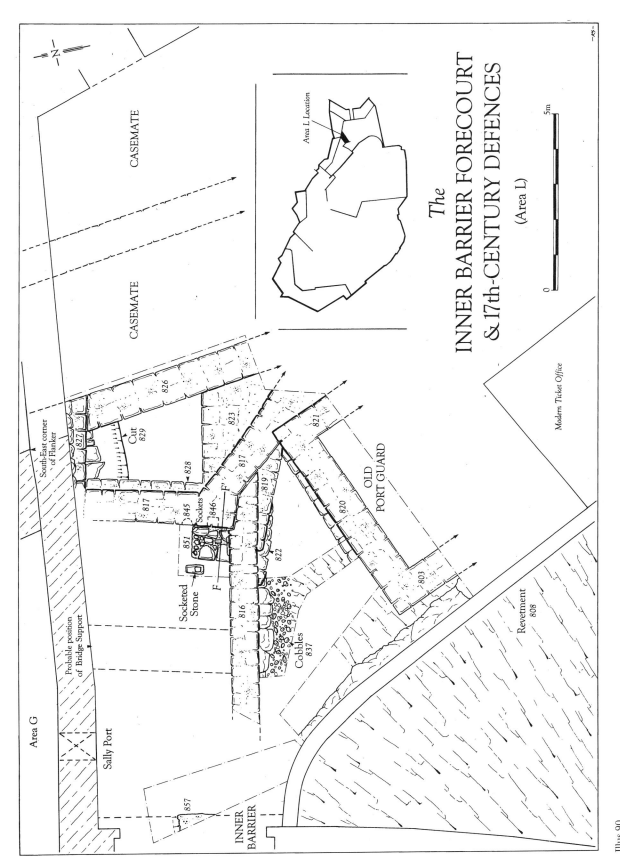

The
INNER BARRIER FORECOURT
& 17th-CENTURY DEFENCES
(Area L)

Area L Location

CASEMATE

CASEMATE

South-East corner
of Flanker

Area G

Probable position
of Bridge Support

Sally Port

826

827

Cut
829

828

817

845

846

851

Sockets

F'

817

823

821

819

822

820

816

OLD
PORT GUARD

803

Cobbles
837

Sockected
Stone

F

857

INNER
BARRIER

Revetment
808

Modern Ticket Office

5m

0

Illus 90
Area L: plan of the Inner Barrier forecourt and the 17th-century defences. For section F-F' see illus 95.

Illus 91
Area L: view of the Inner Barrier after demolition of casemates and installation of the temporary bridge on the left. Lifting bridge support 817 can be seen in the foreground; from the E.

century by the construction of casemates (see below Phase 6), it is thought that it would have in effect created a pit below the road surface.

The S wall (823) and the W wall (828) were built of large random rubble using grey whinstone. Some blocks were as large as 0.8 × 0.6m. These walls survived to a height of 2m, being built up from bedrock and cutting the earlier cobbled layers. Although strong, the finish of the walls was poor, which is not surprising as they were entirely below the contemporary ground level. It is likely that they originally stood to a total height of about 3m.

The W end of this bridge complex was only glimpsed. The top of a short stretch of wall (857) was found at the existing Inner Barrier gateway. The E face of this wall (857) was 0.8m to the E of the pilasters of the Inner Barrier.

The only other excavated remains of this period were found in what would have been the open space between these two walls. Here two tip layers (835 and 836) were recorded, both being of brown sandy-clay with charcoal and oyster shells. Too little of

these was examined to be certain, but they may have represented no more than spillage from the ramping of the road up from the Spur.

PHASE 4 INTERPRETATION

It can be surmised that, as part of the realignment of the road, a substantial soil ramp was formed in the E end of the Spur to allow the roadway to ascend at a gentle gradient before reaching the Inner Barrier area.

Slezer's drawing of the area immediately in front of the Inner Barrier shows an arched wooden bridge spanning the distance between the W supporting wall (857) at the Inner Barrier and another supporting wall about 4–5m to the E. This central support was not observed, because it falls in an area which was not disturbed by the shop and tunnel construction (illus 92; 94). Slezer shows that the missing central wall not only supported the arched bridge but also the W side of a timber lifting-bridge, which, when raised, would have formed a strong vertical barrier with a gaping chasm in front. It seems likely that the E support

Illus 92
Detail from the bird's eye view of the Castle (1689–1707) attributed to Capt John Slezer (illus 12) which shows the lifting bridge arrangement (by permission of The British Library; Map Library K Top XLIX.74).

Illus 93
Area L: working on the E bridge support following demolition of the casemates. The Flanker is to the right, wall 828 is being drawn and the ladder rests on wall 823.

originally supported a static wooden bridge. Whatever its form, it had been swept away by the time Slezer came to illustrate the entry.

The finely-built Flanker sally-port was probably constructed as part of this complex. This portal gave access into the area below the Inner Barrier arched bridge to attack any enemy who might penetrate the defences thus far; also it allowed access for cleaning. These supports created pits which were an ideal sump for the collection of rainwater and other detritus channelled from above, as was found by the modern excavators during their re-excavation.

There are many reasons why the roadway had to be realigned necessitating the construction of the complex set of bridges. Probably the most compelling was to make it easier to get guns and men in and out of the Castle. The earlier approach through the Flanker involved negotiating a much steeper gradient, a bend and perhaps steps. The new approach was more gradual and straighter. The Inner Barrier also represented a new approach to the access and its defence. Bypassing the Flanker and evening out the ascent probably speeded movement and allowed for more traffic, which would be consistent with the increasing military usage. The new route was defended differently, since easier access may have posed a potential threat. Elevating such a long stretch of the road deprived attackers from shelter and exposed assailants to flanking fire from the N (the Flanker) and above (the Forewall Battery and the Portcullis Gate).

PHASE 5

Mid- to Late 17th-Century Rebuilding of the Inner Barrier Bridge and Construction of the Port Guard

PHASE 5 FEATURES

REBUILDING OF THE INNER BARRIER BRIDGE

The approach to the E end of the bridge complex was shifted to the S and parts of the supports strengthened and rebuilt. It is possible that the earlier wall and bridge arrangements had suffered siege damage during the Civil War and required rebuilding. However, the renewal of the masonry apart, there is no direct evidence of any damage.

The key element of the alteration is the new wall (817), which reused and raised the W wall (828) of the E bridge support and defined a new orientation to the E support (illus 90; 95). The new wall (817) was constructed of roughly-shaped sandstone blocks, bonded with pink, hard sandy-mortar. It raised the height of the support by 0.55m and directed the approach further to the S, towards the spine of Castle Hill. The earlier support was probably square in plan, this support seems to have created a triangular area where the route dog-legged as it approached the Inner Barrier.

Suggestions that this was occasioned by damage are supported by signs that the upper parts of the S wall (823) and SE corner of the Flanker were rebuilt at the same time.

A small area was excavated W of the E support in the area below the bridge. Here a number of features were found which appear related to the construction of 817 (illus 95). A pair of sockets had been cut into the exterior of the W side of the E support (828) immediately below the base of the new wall (817) (illus 96). These sockets (844 and 845) were simply formed by chiselling-out a single block of masonry. They were 0.26–0.3m wide and 0.2m deep and spaced 0.7m apart. To know the exact phase of the sockets is difficult to judge, but they clearly were cut at the same time as 817 was built. It seems likely that they served as joist-holes to carry a new bridge structure.

At the foot of the E support a stone-built platform (851) was recorded, abutting the base of wall 828 at a depth of 2.25m below the timber sockets (illus 95; 97). This platform was constructed of small coursed blocks of stone, each about 0.3m in length. It was bonded with a pink-coloured, cream tinged mortar. It was rough, irregular in plan and not level. It was 0.5m thick, varied between 0.75 and 0.95m wide and was not square with wall 828. This feature is interpreted as the base of a timber bridge support.

A single socketed stone (852), found at the same level and adjacent to the stone platform (851), is probably a related bridge support. The socketed stone was formed from what appeared to be a broken voussoir finished with crisp, diagonal tooling. The shallow socket was 0.17 m square and 0.03 m deep. This looks as though it was the base for a timber bridge support. The stone platform and the socketed stone were sealed by a waterlogged deposit (850) at the bottom of which fragments of squared wooden pegs had been preserved.

PORT GUARD

Security was further strengthened in the last decade of the 17th century by the construction of the Port Guard House. This was located on the S side of the approach road, immediately E of the

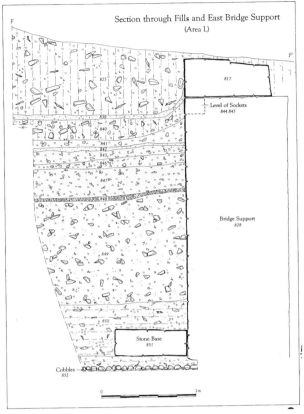

Illus 95
Area L: section through fills to the W of the E bridge support for the lifting bridge. For section location see illus 90.

Illus 96
Area L: detail of the E face of E bridge support 828, showing sockets 844 and 845 and the top added course of masonry 817.

Illus 97
Area L: detail of platform 851 abutting wall 828 of the E bridge support and timber support of reused masonry (SF368).

bridges and is clearly depicted in Slezer's drawing (illus 92). The Port Guard is illustrated as a small, rectangular building with a pitched roof with a doorway in the E side.

Excavation showed the building to be 6.3m wide, but did not expose the full length. No evidence for its internal structure or occupation deposits was observed. The W wall (803/820) was constructed of dressed yellow sandstone facings, bonded with a white lime mortar, and was a total of 0.9m in width. It was built on a wide foundation, which provided a 0.25m-wide offset on the W side. The foundation was 1.0m deep, and was built onto bedrock. The N corner of the building abutted and overlay the new wall (817) of the E support. The space between the Port Guard and the support was filled with rubbish and builders' debris. The main fill layer (833) overlapped foundations of wall 820 and contained a clay pipe dated to 1700.

Following the construction of the Port Guard, the bridge was again modified. This involved the construction of a wall (816) along the S side of the bridge (illus 98). This wall closed off access to the area under the bridge from the S and rendered the Flanker sally-port redundant. The wall does not appear on Slezer's drawing of c 1695 but is likely to immediately post-date it.

The S bridge wall was founded directly onto the Phase 3 cobbled surface (837). Its construction was very similar to that of the Port Guard. Both used yellow sandstone with dressed facings. Diagonal tooling, similar to that recorded on the socketed stone in the middle pit, was observed on the lower portions of the S face. The upper part of the wall was obscured by orange-yellow

harling. The harling began 1.4m above the base foundation course and had been applied at least twice. It seems possible that the harling was a secondary feature, added after tumble and other detritus had been allowed to build-up against this S face. The diagonally-tooled blocks are likely to have been reused from elsewhere.

Illus 98
Area L: excavation in progress under the temporary bridge at the Inner Barrier showing detail of cobbled surface (837) on the S side of wall 816 which blocked off access under the lifting bridge and to the sally-port.

The building of the E end of this wall (816) may have upset the balance of forces within the pre-existing structures, as it was necessary to add a thickening construction (819/822) which bonded together the lower parts of walls 816, 817 and 820 (illus 90).

During this phase, layers of soil accumulated under the bridge pits, a process which was undoubtedly promoted by the construction of the S wall (816). A wet clayey layer (849) could be distinguished from the deepest waterlogged deposits (850). This layer (849) contained quantities of rubbish including fragments of building material, pottery, glass and clay pipe fragments. Amongst the finds was a worn Irish halfpenny of Charles II 1680 (SF367), but the clay pipes probably give a better idea of when this deposit formed; they range between the 1690s and the 1730s. It seems likely that this layer represents accumulation after the construction of the S bridge wall (816).

PHASE 5 INTERPRETATION

The sequence of development observed on the bridge complex is probably partially precipitated by the sequence of assaults experienced by the Castle in the second half of the 17th century. The original bridge system was rebuilt and re-oriented. This may

have been occasioned by the siege of 1650, as there is certainly evidence for the repair to the Flanker which would be consistent with artillery damage. This damage may account for the evidence for timber bridge supports in the form of masonry pads at the foot of the E bridge support and for the joist sockets, which seem best explained as a temporary structure required as the masonry structure was being rebuilt.

The rebuilt bridge with the lifting bridge complex is probably the one recorded by Slezer c 1695. Coming after the rebuilding of the bridge, and certainly present by Slezer's time, was the Port Guard House (illus 92).

The support structure of the bridge was modified by the addition of a S wall which effectively closed off access to underneath the bridge. This is not shown in the Slezer drawing. This made the Flanker sally-port useless and certainly no attempt was made to clear away the material that accumulated under the bridge. It may be speculated that, when this new wall was built, the lifting bridge may have been replaced by a simple static bridge.

PHASE 6

Mid-18th Century

PHASE 6 FEATURES

The Inner Barrier bridge continued in use until at least as late as 1737 when it is shown on a plan. In the middle of the century, a pair of casemates, bomb-proof barracks, were built into the ramped approach to the bridge. These windowless barrel-vaulted rooms were narrow (only 3.6m wide) and must have been unpleasant accommodation. The W wall of the casemates (826) cut away most of the E bridge support. Fragments of masonry from the Phase 3 entrance to the Flanker were incorporated into the N end of the W casemate wall.

The upper layers of soil under the bridge appeared to represent deliberate infilling because they contained material which had been deposited out of sequence. One of the higher layers (847) contained clay pipes dating between c 1685 and 1700, whilst lower deposits produced pipes dating to c 1730 (illus 95). The final layer (825) provides the latest artefact, a clay pipe dated to 1740, from within a mixture including pipes dating back to c 1640. Once the area was filled there was no longer a bridge at the Inner Barrier.

PHASE 6 INTERPRETATION

Dating the construction of the casemates and the removal of the bridge is difficult. The area under the bridge must have been filled in at the same time as the casemates were constructed. Material from the infilling would allow this to have taken place before the 1745 Rising. Part of Capt John Romer's improvements to the N and W perimeters involved finishing the masonry work for the dry ditch (MacIvor 1993, 94). This was completed in 1742 and perhaps such large-scale engineering works provide the best context for the building of the casemates (illus 100). It seems likely that if such works were undertaken in the aftermath of the Jacobite Rising plans would have survived as they have for the Mills Mount Cartshed.

PHASE 7

Late 18th Century to the Present Day

This area then remained essentially untouched until the construction of the existing Gatehouse in 1887, and the ticket office during the early years of the 20th century.

3.9 THE COAL YARD (Area M)

3.9.1 AREA M ABSTRACT SEQUENCE

PHASE 1 Pre-14th century:

Although no features dating to before the 14th century were observed, in order that the phase numbers for the Coal Yard correspond with those used in the Flanker and Inner Barrier as closely as possible, the sequence of features starts with Phase 1.

PHASE 2 Medieval (14th century or earlier):

Two massive ditches (1125 & 1135) built curving around the E side of the castle. Possibly on line of earlier ditches (corresponds to Flanker Phase 2).

PHASE 3 16th century:

Ditches partially filled in and approach to Flanker entry strengthened (corresponds to Flanker Phase 3).

PHASE 4 1620s–1640s:

Ditches completely filled in, entrance via Flanker blocked and new access established (corresponds to Flanker Phase 4).

PHASE 5 Late 17th century:

Area E of Flanker used as burial ground, probably in siege of 1689. N revetting wall overlooking Princes Street Gardens added (corresponds to Flanker Phase 5).

PHASE 6 Early 18th century:

Casemates built under the new road approaching the Inner Barrier.

PHASE 7 19th century – present:

Converted to store yard for coal and then converted to workshops for maintenance of the Castle.

3.9.2 AREA M: DETAIL OF ARCHAEOLOGICAL STRUCTURES

The Coal Yard describes that area to the E of the Entrance Flanker. The name Coal Yard is not particularly old and it was expected that the archaeological deposits would have been similarly recent. Three trial trenches dug within the Coal Yard before the tunnel construction started revealed a build-up of masonry rubble (incorporating post-Medieval artefacts) to a depth of approximately 2.0m below the existing ground level. At the time, this was taken as confirmation that the area of the Coal Yard consisted entirely of made-up ground retained by the 19th-century wall overlooking the Princes Street Gardens. It later turned out that all three of the trial trenches had been placed over the backfilled Medieval ditches, whose latest fills consisted of post-Medieval rubble.

The presence of significant archaeological remains was first revealed at the start of the tunnel construction. Workmen, engaged in temporary pipe-laying operations, disturbed two burials. This discovery of archaeological remains late into the construction programme dictated that archaeological investigations had to be arranged around the building work. As a consequence there are some gaps in the area covered and in the stratigraphy.

PHASE 2

Medieval (14th-Century or earlier) Twin Ditches

PHASE 2 FEATURES (illus 99)

The earliest features in this area were a pair of massive ditches (1125 and 1135), which cut across the E approach to the Castle Rock. From what was seen of the ditches, they apparently curved towards the E from the portion excavated in the Coal Yard and curled to the NW where they approached the rock face. As the geological report makes clear, much of this rockface has subsequently been altered (2.3.2 above).

The general alignment of the ditches cuts off the E approach to the Rock from Castle Hill, but the precise alignment could not be determined with confidence. Only a narrow (2–3m wide) machine-dug trench was excavated through the ditch fills (illus 100). Apart from the machine-dug trench the inner edge of the inner ditch could not be identified with confidence. As the area became available two different possible edges were seen in plan (these are marked ?1125 in illus 99), but could not be excavated to a sufficient depth to confirm the precise line of the ditch. The temporary service trench dug in Princes Street Gardens (Area R) revealed a spread of masonry rubble including post-medieval artefacts, which apparently corresponds to the final fill of the ditch seen in the Coal Yard. No clear edge was observed in the shallow pipetrench and the topography of Princes Street Gardens provides no clue as to the alignment of the ditch.

Only the dimensions of the inner ditch (1125) are known, although with some uncertainty (illus 101). The machine trench showed that it was about 13m wide, although this measurement may be somewhat oblique to the line of the ditch. The ditch was flat-bottomed and about 5m deep, but it was not conclusively bottomed, because the reach of the mechanical digger was limited to 5m.

Only a small portion of the outer ditch (1135) was investigated, because only a small portion of it fell within the Coal Yard. Much of the outer ditch had been removed by the existing dry-ditch, although some of it may remain under the Esplanade. All that can be said of the outer ditch is that it was steep-sided and evidently contemporary with the inner ditch. Between the two was a narrow piece of level ground, metalled (1136) with gravel and small cobbles (illus 102).

The earliest dated pottery from what was apparently a primary silt (1134) can be dated to the 14th century. However, this pottery was mechanically recovered. The pottery did not appear to have been mixed with any later finds and appeared to come from the base of the inner ditch, but safety considerations prevented close examination of the primary silts.

PHASE 2 INTERPRETATION

Logically one might expect these medieval ditches to follow the line of earlier Iron Age or early medieval earthworks defences, for this is the highest position on the approach to the Rock at which earthworks can be constructed. Further up the hill it becomes craggy.

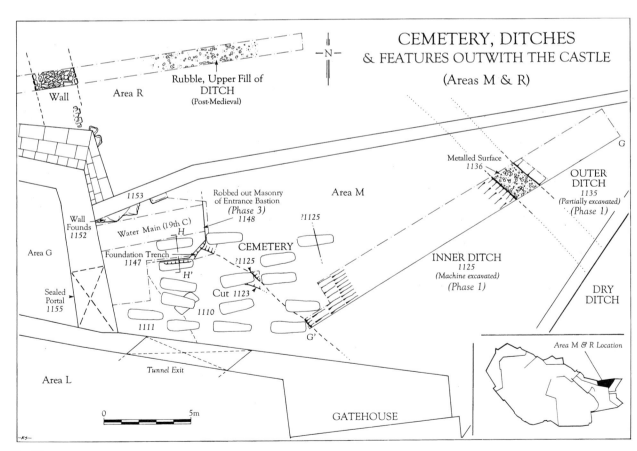

Illus 99
Areas M and R: plan of the Coal Yard cemetery, ditches and features outwith the Castle. For section G-G' see illus 101; for section H-H' see illus 104.

Illus 100
Area M: view along machine-dug trench
through the inner ditch 1125 towards the
casemates under the Inner Barrier and the
Flanker; from the E.

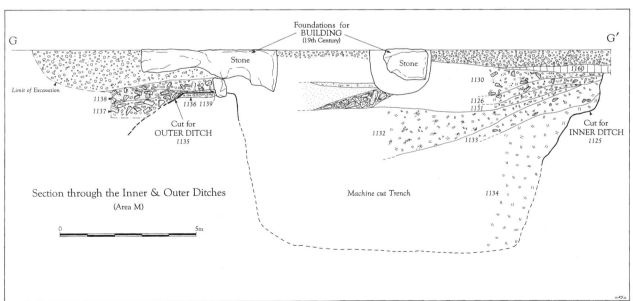

Illus 101
Area M: section (G-G') through the ditches. For location see illus 99.

There was no evidence for how or where the ditches were crossed. Some sort of bridge must have been provided and using the position of the entrance to the Flanker as a guide one may speculate that it was on the N side of what is now the Esplanade.

PHASE 3

Late 16th-Century Entrance to Flanker

PHASE 3 FEATURES

The only ancient masonry structure discovered in the Coal Yard was the robbed out traces of what may have been an angled bastion fitted to the N side of the E entrance to the Flanker. Only the corner of the mortar and rubbled filled robber trench (1147) was examined and this feature was not bottomed (illus 103; 104). No sign of how this may have related to the Flanker was evident in the surviving masonry because of subsequent rebuilding work. The full form of the structure at foundation level is unknown, but the remains of the wall on the S side of the entrance (Area L, 827), which may have formed the corresponding defence to the entrance, stood over 3.4m high (see illus 76; 90).

No sign of any metalling or paving for the road leading to the entrance of the Flanker was noted, but given that the area was dug

in stages and that the later burials cut into the subsoil, it could have gone undetected.

PHASE 3 INTERPRETATION

On available evidence there is no way of knowing how long the ditches were maintained. It may be supposed that they continued to be part of the defensive circuit when the first Flanker was built. However, already by the mid-16th century, that stretch of the ditches occupied by the Spur would have been filled in and by the time the entrance of the rebuilt Flanker was constructed the ditch was probably also partially filled (illus 83). It was probably not completely filled because, as late as Gordon of Rothiemay's drawing of 1647, it is possible to recognise the ditches (illus 73).

PHASE 4

1620s–1640s Abandonment of Approach to Flanker

The closure of the entrance through the Flanker left few, if any, traces in the Coal Yard. This is perhaps the most logical time to suggest that the ditches were finally filled in and the ground levelled, but the finds from the upper fills of the ditch were not chronologically precise enough to confirm this.

Illus 102
Area M: view of the edge of the outer ditch 1135 showing the metalled surface 1136 between the ditches (under the horizontal scale); from the W.

Illus 103
Area M: view of possible robbed-out foundations to a bastion for the entrance Flanker represented by loose mortar and rubble (under the scale); after the removal of the later graves; from the E.

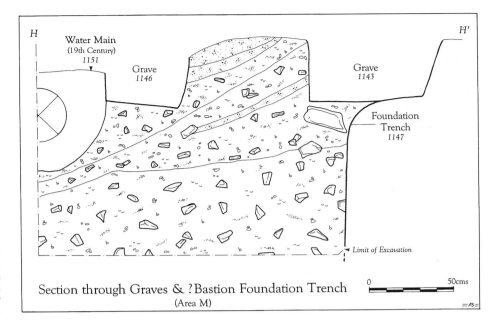

Illus 104
Area M: section (H-H')
through the bastion
foundation trench which had
been cut by graves. For
location see illus 99.

Section through Graves & ? Bastion Foundation Trench
(Area M)

PHASE 5

Late 17th-Century Cemetery

PHASE 5 FEATURES (illus 105)

The angled bastion at the blocked entrance to the Flanker was completely demolished and robbed of its stone to foundation level leaving only a rubble-filled pit. Within the demolition rubble (1149), a forged Charles II/James II halfpenny (SF 493), c 1686, was recovered.

Following the demolition of the bastion, a small cemetery was laid out in front of the blocked gate and over the infilled ditches. Two of the graves (1141 and 1144) were dug into the upper rubble fill (1148) of the robber trench for the Bastion (illus 104; 106).

The cemetery consisted of four ragged rows of graves and comprised at least 15 individuals (illus 107). The graves were relatively orderly, with no overlapping of grave cuts but did not appear to have been dug in a single event. The cemetery appeared to have had an extended period of use with graves having been dug on five or six separate occasions. No sign of grave markers was noted. Two additional burials are known from just outside the Coal Yard in Princes Street Gardens (illus 108) and, although it is impossible to determine if they were on the same alignment, it seems likely that they were. If so, more of the cemetery probably awaits discovery in the Gardens.

The dead were placed in shallow graves, only about 0.75m below the presumed original ground surface, with their heads to the W. All were buried in wooden coffins, which were probably no more than boxes held together with a few nails (illus 105). No coffin fittings were discovered. The presence of three or four small wire pins with most of the bodies probably indicates that they were placed in shrouds. There were no traces of clothing.

The analysis of the skeletal remains suggests that all of the individuals were male (see Report on Human Remains below 6). Most were relatively young (18–25), with only one which could be as old as 35–45 years. Several of the skeletons exhibited signs of trauma, but none was the cause of death.

PHASE 5 INTERPRETATION

The forged coin (c 1686) gives the best guidance to the date for the formation of this cemetery which was laid out within unconsecrated ground in the Castle. No physical evidence of the cause of death was noted amongst the 15 skeletons, which suggests that some at least died from disease. The layout of the cemetery with several groups of aligned burials also suggested that several bodies were buried at the same time. The use of simple boxes as coffins may also suggest that the burials were made under duress with a minimum of ceremony.

The siege mounted by the supporters of William and Mary in 1689 against the Castle held by those loyal to James VII and II provides the most likely circumstances for the cemetery. The siege lasted from March to June and the garrison was not well prepared for such an ordeal. During its course, food and water ran short and epidemics are reported (MacIvor 1993, 84).

PHASE 6

Early 18th Century: Casemates

The entrances for the two casemates built to the E of the Inner Barrier were in the Coal Yard. No evidence of any contemporary activity in the Coal Yard was noted, but circumstances were not ideal for picking up minor changes in the surfaces. It is likely that some levelling took place at this time, but the upper levels of the Yard had been churned up by later use of the area. If, as seems likely, the casemates were built as part of the improvements to the dry ditch, then it seems equally likely that the existing N wall to Princes Street Gardens was erected at this time to create a forecourt for the casemates.

PHASE 7

19th Century to the Present Day

The space was converted to a storeyard for coal and later workshops were built on the E side of the yard which were used by the Castle maintenance squad until the construction of the tunnel.

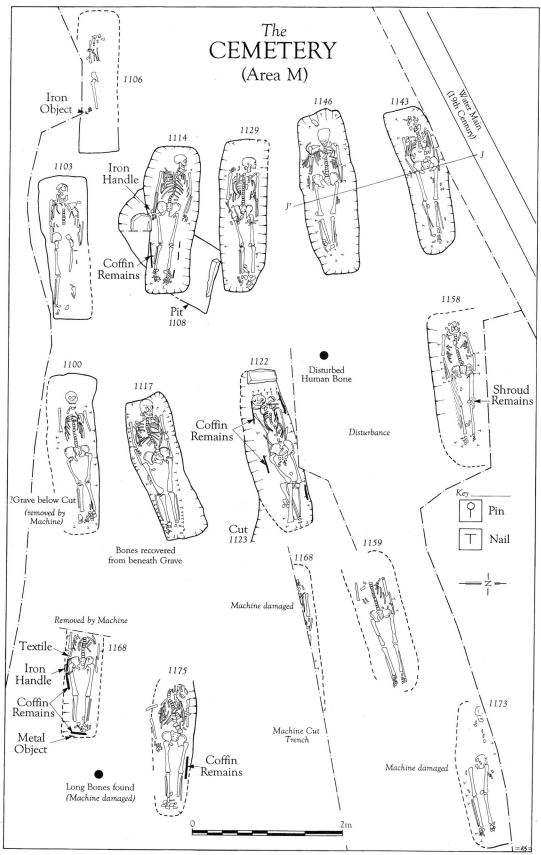

The
CEMETERY
(Area M)

Water Main
(19th Century)

1106

Iron
Object

1103

1114

Iron
Handle

Coffin
Remains

Pit
1108

1129

1146

1143

J

J'

1158

Shroud
Remains

1100

?Grave below Cut
(removed by
Machine)

1117

Bones recovered
from beneath Grave

Coffin
Remains

1122

Disturbed
Human Bone

Disturbance

Cut
1123

Key

⊘ Pin

⊤ Nail

N

1168

Machine damaged

1159

Removed by Machine

Textile

Iron
Handle

Coffin
Remains

Metal
Object

1168

Long Bones found
(Machine damaged)

1175

Coffin
Remains

Machine Cut
Trench

Machine damaged

1173

0   2m

Illus 105
Area M: detailed plan of the Coal Yard cemetery.

Illus 106
Area M: view of possible entrance bastion foundation (lighter mortar between the burials) showing its relationship to the blocked entrance and the casemates; from the N.

Illus 107
Area M: view of the Coal Yard cemetery under excavation; from the S.

Illus 108
Two skeletons excavated in the 1960s in Princes Street Gardens which may be part of the Coal Yard cemetery (Copyright: Royal Commission of the Ancient and Historical Monuments of Scotland; NMRS neg B 13829.)

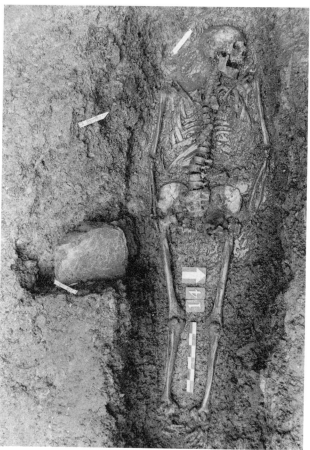

Illus 109
Area M: Skeleton 1114 from the Coal Yard cemetery fully excavated.

THE FINDS

In this section we bring together the catalogues and discussions of artefacts, as well as the analytical work done on the industrial residues and fabrics. Overall, the most important aspect of this collection is the time span it represents. In Scotland it must be one of the longest stratified sequences of material from a single site, extending as it does over the last three millennia. The material has been grouped into four broad chronological assemblages: prehistoric, Roman, medieval and post-medieval, so that comparisons within and between periods can be made. However, it is recognised that in doing so, objects have been amalgamated which could well have been used centuries apart. Much of the grouping is a reflection of the analytical process and the academic specialisation within the discipline. These are thus not true assemblages but represent total assemblages of object types from the site. For instance in the case of the coins, the report has not been broken into separate fragments for each period assemblage but has been left so that the reader can have all of the evidence in one place.

Within the catalogues a standard form of entry is used:

Catalogue No Area (Phase) Context Small Find No
Description/dimensions

The catalogue numbers refer to the series pertaining to each separate report, thus there are several pots with the number 22: a prehistoric sherd, a Roman coarse ware sherd, a medieval sherd and so on. Occasionally the specialists have subdivided catalogue numbers by adding letters, eg 22a, 22b, 22c, in order to illustrate some relationship or for administrative convenience, such as distinguishing between two fragments which were originally thought to belong to the same object. In addition to the printed catalogue, there are tables and lists of the more ubiquitous small finds such as the nails and potsherds in the fiche which accompanies the text (1:B5–2:A14).

In the course of the discussion we have tried to draw attention to the artefacts of particular chronological significance. Where appropriate, we take those dating considerations further here in the catalogue and the discussions prepared by the various specialists who have analysed the material. This is also the place where the consideration of use, function, decorative style and manufacture are most fully explored.

4.1 THE PREHISTORIC ASSEMBLAGE

4.1.1 INTRODUCTION

The assemblage from the earliest levels of Edinburgh Castle (illus 110) is in many respects typical of those found in hillforts of the later prehistoric period in SE Scotland. However it is exceptional in several respects. With the exception of Traprain Law, it is the only substantial assemblage to form part of a sequence which continues into the Roman era and beyond. The fact that the material comes from a stratified sequence that covers much of the last three millennia sets it apart from all other collections on mainland Scotland. There may be pockets of early deposits preserved elsewhere on the rock (eg in Hospital Square) or in the Coal Yard (Area M), but all of the material discussed here relates to the Mills Mount trenches.

The individual categories are not particularly large, but they are comprehensive in that they include most types of artefacts and represent a wide range of activities which touch upon most aspects of Iron Age life.

Illus 110
A selection of the prehistoric finds.

The pottery assemblage appears to span the period from before Roman contact to the early historic era. However, it is not large and some of the contexts from which the earliest pots come from are not tightly sealed. Thus the chronology of the sequence is based in part on conjecture. The group includes a number of distinct vessel types, displays differences in manufacturing processes and hints of changes in food preparation. The most distinctive early pots are massive earthenware buckets with very heavy gritting and extremely thick walls. These have been interpreted as cooking pots which where placed directly in the fire and used as 'slow cookers'. The large pots are supplemented by other less massive bucket-like forms, all of which rely on stone tempering. This tradition is typical of the later 1st millennium BC and the early centuries AD.

The first discernible alteration in the manufacturing tradition is the change to tempers of grass or sand or the absence of a tempering element. These lighter tempered pots are also slighter in scale although they retained similar basic forms. It has been suggested elsewhere (based on the unpublished Broxmouth and Dryburn Bridge excavations) that these slightly finer vessels were contemporary with the massive cooking pots (Cool 1982). However it would seem that the finer forms are also contemporary with the Roman wares found on the site and that they do not include the slow cooker. The stratigraphic sequence is too imprecise to do more that suggest this, but it may reflect a change in cooking and dietary practices in the early centuries AD.

The most interesting possibility raised by this assemblage is that there may also be a post-Roman coarseware tradition present. Because of the small size of the collection and the chronological uncertainty of the stratigraphic contexts, this can only be a suggestion. The absolute numbers of sherds from the later levels (Mills Mount Phases 4 & 5) only amounts to five, of which three are from pots with an angled base. There is only one other angled base from an earlier phase, so the suggestion is that this is a new form which developed during the post-Roman centuries. Unfortunately, at the time of writing, the pottery assemblage from Traprain Law could not be located in the Royal Museum of Scotland, so close comparisons with the only other excavated site to span this period could not be made.

The prehistoric ironwork contains a good range of material if nothing spectacular. There is a single leaf-shaped spearhead and a square-sectioned socketed implement which may be a unique form of a spear-butt. Other tools include a knife (discussed with all the knives in the medieval section below 4.3.5) and small tools for working materials such as leather, bone or possibly metal.

There was only scant evidence for the working of iron or bronze in the earliest phases. Nor was there much evidence for other industrial activity. All of the antler artefacts were complete, there was no scrap. The antler rings were both well worked and worn. Similarly there was relatively little manufactured animal bone waste, although none of the possible textile working tools of bone was complete.

Textile working was certainly taking place as indicated by the few spindle whorls and the possible bronze netting needle. The other aspect of domestic industry which is surely present is the processing of cereals. Both saddle and rotary querns were found in various states of completeness. Apart from the querns and spindle whorls, stone was little used for artefacts. Only a handful of worked flints was recovered.

When dealing with some of the more undiagnostic material certain, categories of objects are discussed as groups even though it is likely that prehistoric and medieval artefacts are being grouped together as with the knives, nails and bone objects.

4.1.2 THE COARSE POTTERY

Ann MacSween

The coarse pottery assemblage from Edinburgh Castle comprises 38 sherds representing as many vessels, plus the greater part of three vessels (*2, 11, 12*). The majority of fragments (representing 34 vessels) were recovered from Phases 1–3 with five sherds being recovered from Phase 4, one from Phase 5 and two from Phase 6.

Given the disturbed nature of the Phase 1 and 2 deposits and the fact that the Phase 4 contexts are from midden deposits, it is not surprising that most vessels are represented by only one or two sherds. As a consequence, however, the reconstruction of vessel size and shape was, in most cases, not possible. The following is a summary of the information contained in the catalogue. In this discussion individual vessels are referred to by their catalogue number.

PHASE 1 • THE EARLY IRON AGE ASSEMBLAGE

(illus 111)

Two rim sherds, one basal sherd and eight body sherds, as well as numerous sherds from three vessels (*2, 11, 12*) were recovered from the Phase 1 deposits.

The only decorated sherd (vessel *1*) in the assemblage was recovered from context 592, the earliest occupation surface identified. It is a body sherd with incised decoration comprising two horizontal parallel lines with a diagonal line between. The sherd appears to widen to a maximum at the lower edge of the decoration and was possibly carinated at this point. Unfortunately the exterior of the sherd has spalled below the decoration so its profile cannot be determined. The nature of the decoration suggests a Bronze Age date.

The two vessels for which the majority of sherds were recovered could be partially reconstructed, although complete profiles could not be obtained because of the fragmentary nature of the sherds. One vessel (*11*) appears to have been flat-based, with walls 18 mm thick. The vessel has a flat rim. The coil-construction method had been used, diagonal coil-junctions being noted on some sherds. The fabric is a sandy clay, tempered with around 60% of angular rock inclusions, and the exterior and interior surfaces are slipped.

A second vessel (*12*) also has a flat rim, and thick walls (16mm thick). As with vessel *11*, the fabric is sandy clay, tempered with angular rock fragments (40%).

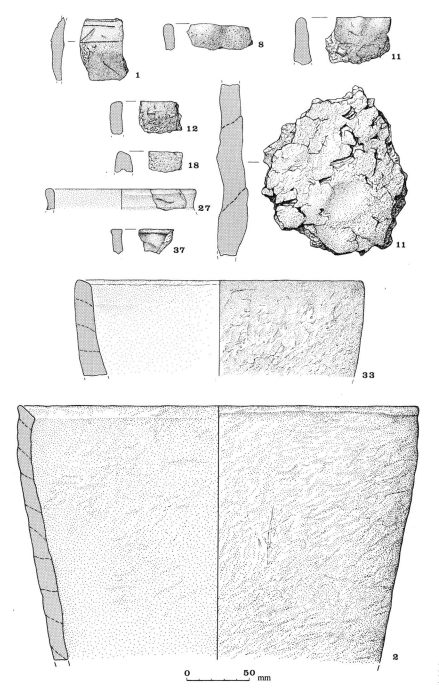

0   50 mm

Illus 111
Prehistoric pottery.

The other rim sherds from Phase 1 contexts comprise a further flat rim (*8*), a plain rim (*3*) and an internally bevelled rim (*2*). A range of vessel sizes was indicated, both from rim diameter (the plain rim is 130mm in diameter while the bevelled rim is 300mm in diameter), and from wall thickness (body sherd *13* is 13mm thick, while rim sherd *8* is only 7mm thick). Surface treatment was not common, only two sherds being slipped (*2* and *13*) in addition to vessel *11*. Only one basal sherd (*10*) was recovered from Phase 1, a plain angled base with walls 5mm thick.

The dominant fabric type of Phase 2 is rock-tempered (nine out of the 14 vessels), with only five sherds having been being formed from untempered clay.

PHASE 2 & 3 • ROMAN IRON AGE (1ST TO 3RD CENTURY)

(illus 111)

Twenty vessels are represented in the Phase 2 and 3 assemblage: all are represented by single sherds.

Five rims were recovered from Phase 2 contexts – a slightly inverted plain rim (*26*), two flat rims (*27* and *34*) and two internally bevelled rims (*18* and *33*). The diameter of only two of these sherds, *33* and *34*, 260mm and 180mm respectively, could be determined. Wall thickness varied a great deal, from 3mm (*33*) to 12mm (*18*). As with Phase 1, only one basal fragment (*24*) was recovered, a plain angled (flat) base with a diameter of 80mm.

A variety of shapes is suggested: *33*, for example, is likely to have been from a near vertical-sided vessel, whereas the basal sherd (*24*) suggests angled walls.

None of the vessels in this phase is decorated but sherds from four vessels are slipped (*19, 31, 33, 34*) and one other sherd (*23*) is burnished.

Several fabrics were used – ten vessels were made from untempered clay while five were tempered with rock fragments, five with grass.

PHASE 4 • POST-ROMAN

(illus 112)

No body sherds were recovered from the Phase 4 levels, the assemblage comprising three plain angled bases, one plain rounded base, and a flattened, slightly splayed rim. The profile of the angled bases suggests that they came from open vessels. Again a range of vessel sizes is represented. The plain angled bases (*35, 36, 39*) have diameters of 200mm, 80mm and 200mm respectively, while the rounded base (*38*) has a diameter of 200mm and the rim sherd (*37*)

has a diameter of 80mm, again indicating a range of vessel sizes.

None of the vessels are decorated, nor do they have any surface treatment apart from a general smoothing.

The five sherds from Phase 4 are all untempered apart from the angled base (*35*) which was tempered with chopped grass or straw.

RESIDUAL SHERDS

Only three coarse ware sherds were found in Phases 5 and 6: a rim sherd (*41*) and an abraded body sherd (*42*) from Phase 6; and a rim sherd (*40*) from Phase 5. Given the small quantity of coarse pottery from the later phases of the site, and the associated medieval pottery, it is probable that these sherds are derived from the previous four phases.

Vessel *40* is an everted rim sherd, which probably sloped out to a globular or shouldered body. It is very abraded and the only sherd to have been shell-tempered. It compares well with the globular Roman coarseware jar (catalogue number *29*) and may also be Roman.

Rim *41* is a plain rim, apparently from a straight-sided vessel with an angled base. In thickness and angle it is similar to vessel *35* and may be residual from Phase 4.

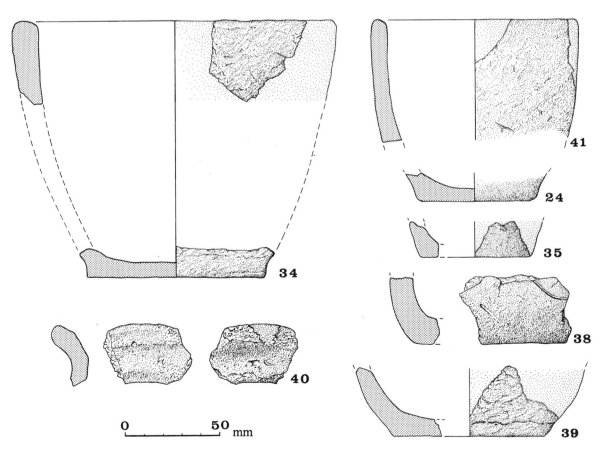

Illus 112
Prehistoric and possible early medieval pottery.

DISCUSSION

As has been stated above, the coarse pottery assemblage from the Edinburgh Castle excavations comprises only a small number of sherds and few reconstructible vessels. In dealing with assemblages without recognisable decoration or morphological attributes, detection of points of change in the sequence must rely more on technological attributes such as fabric types and surface finishing. Serious analysis of this type requires a minimum of several hundred sherds. Unfortunately, the assemblage from Edinburgh Castle, and indeed from most small-scale excavations of hillforts in the region, is too small for technological analysis. The summary points below are provided in the hope that, as more sites are excavated, regional patterns may emerge.

In all phases, coil-construction was the favoured method of manufacture. Some of the larger vessels may have been built up by adding short coils around the circumference rather than one continuous coil. Surface finishing is uncommon, with burnished sherds only being recovered from Phase 2 and 3 contexts. It is possible that grass-tempering is also characteristic of the 1st to 3rd centuries (see table 5). The only indication of a new vessel type is in Phase 4; sharply angled bases were not recovered from contexts of the preceding phases.

PHASE 1

The Phase 1, pre-Roman Iron Age, contexts produced several sherds with inverted rims (eg *12*). These rims are commonly found on hillfort sites of SE Scotland including Hownam Rings, Roxburghshire (Piggott 1948, 213, fig 10, A.1 & A.2), Clatchard Craig, Fife (Close-Brooks 1986, 152, illus 21), Kaimes, Midlothian (Simpson 1969, 21, fig 8) and Broxmouth (Cool 1982, 95). The only other distinctive rim form from Phase 1 is the slightly everted rim with an internal bevel (*2*) which can be paralleled with a rim from the lower occupation deposits at Traprain Law (Cruden 1940, fig 7a) and at the unenclosed settlement at St Germains (J Close-Brooks pers comm).

PHASES 2 & 3

From Phase 2 and 3 there were no diagnostic sherds, but the presence of grass-tempered fabrics seems new. There is very little recorded grass-tempered pottery of comparable date to the Phase 2 sherds from Edinburgh Castle, but it is possible that a grass-tempered, barrel-shaped vessel from the primary phase of the recent Dunbar Castle Park excavations, may be of similar age (P Holdsworth pers comm).

There may be an overlap with the Roman pottery tradition as demonstrated by two vessels from Phase 3 which contain shell tempering (catalogued with the Roman coarseware nos 28 and 29). In his discussion of the 1975–8 excavations at Crammond, Holmes (forthcoming) suggests that some of the shell-tempered vessels from that site were made by local potters in imitation of the types of pottery being used by the fort garrison. One Crammond vessel, very similar in both profile and fabric to Roman pot no 29, Holmes would regard as an imitation of Black Burnished ware.

PHASE 4

The presence of angular bases contrasts with the earlier straight-sided vessels and may be an indication of a local coarse pottery tradition in existence after the end of the Roman era. The number of sherds is far too small to be conclusive on this point and this may only be resolved by further excavation here or elsewhere.

Table 5 Number of vessels in each phase by fabric types

Phase	untempered	rock-tempered	grass-tempered	shell-tempered
1	3	11	–	–
2 & 3	9	6	5	–
4	4	–	1	–
Residual	1	1	–	1

POTTERY CATALOGUE

★ = illustrated (illus 111; 112)

1 H (1) 592 SF192★
1 body sherd; T = 9mm, Wt = 22g. Brown with a grey core. Exterior is spalled – above the spalling is incised decoration on a possible carination. The decoration comprises two horizontal parallel lines and a diagonal line between them, incised when the vessel was in the 'leather-hard' state. Fabric – hard; clay matrix has quartz, black igneous inclusions and mica. Interior sooted.

2 H (1) 1443 SF419A★
Large part of one vessel; T = 13mm, Diam = 300mm. Internally bevelled rim. Grey with red surfaces. Exterior slipped. Fabric – hard; clay matrix has quartz; added crushed igneous rock – up to 5mm – 40%. Coil constructed. Exterior and interior sooted.

3 H (1) 1433 SF419B
1 rim sherd; T = 8mm, Wt = 3g. Plain rim. Red with a grey core. Fabric – hard; clay matrix has quartz; some voids, possibly from firing rather than from organic additions.

4 H (1) 1433 SF419C
1 body sherd; T = 8mm, Wt = 3g. Red exterior, grey interior. Fabric – hard; fine matrix; added igneous inclusions up to 2mm, 10%.

5 H (1) 1433 SF419D
1 body sherd; T = 8mm, Wt = 11g. Grey with red margins. Fabric – hard; fine matrix; added mixed rock inclusions up to 6mm, 10%.

6 H (1) 1433 SF419E
3 fragments of burnt clay; Wt = 32g. Red. Fabric – soft; fine clay.

7 H (1) 536 SF320
1 body sherd; T = 11mm, Wt = 4g. Brown. Fabric – hard; clay matrix has quartz and black igneous inclusions; added rock fragments – up to 3mm – 40%.

8 X (1) 1427 SF964a★
Flattened rim; T = 7mm, Diam = 130mm, Wt = 13g. Black with red surfaces. Fabric – hard; quartz/igneous matrix with additional larger inclusions up to 5mm, 20%.

9 X (1) 1427 SF964b
1 body sherd; T = 7mm, Wt = 8g. Red. Fabric – hard; matrix contains quartz and black igneous inclusions; larger rock fragments up to 2mm, 10%.

10 X (1) 1427 SF964C
1 basal sherd, plain angled base; T = 5mm, Wt = 5g. Red. Fabric – hard; matrix has quartz sand with occasional black igneous inclusions; possible shell inclusions.

11 X (1) 1431 SF417a★
Numerous fragments from one vessel; T = 18mm, Wt = 4kg. Plain rim, flattened. Some sherds from the flat part of the base. Grey with buff surfaces. Exterior and interior slipped. Fabric – hard; matrix has quartz; added mixed rock inclusions up to 17mm – 60%. Exterior and interior sooted.

12 X (1) 1431 SF417b★
Numerous fragments from one vessel; T = 16mm, Wt = 2.5kg. Flat rim. Grey with buff surfaces. Fabric – hard; matrix has quartz; added mixed rock inclusions up to 10mm – 40%.

13 H (1) 592
1 body sherd; T = 13mm, Wt = 46g. Grey exterior, red interior. The exterior is possibly slipped. Fabric – hard; fine clay matrix with quartz and igneous inclusions; igneous rock fragments up to 5mm, 20%.

14 H (1) 592
1 body sherd; T = 5mm, Wt = 3g. Red. Fabric – hard; clay matrix contains quartz sand and mixed rock inclusions up to 3mm – natural.

15 H (2) 531 SF328
1 body sherd; abraded, Wt = 8g. Grey with brown exterior surface. Fabric – hard; clay matrix has quartz and black igneous inclusions; some black igneous rock fragments up to 5mm, 5%.

16 H (2) 531 SF329
1 spall, abraded; Wt = 1g. Fabric – hard; clay matrix has quartz, opaques and mica.

17 H (2) 535 SF334
1 body sherd, abraded; Wt = 17g. Grey with red exterior surface. Fabric – clay matrix has quartz and black igneous inclusions; added mixed angular fragments of rock up to 3mm, 5%.

18 H (2) 535 SF336★
1 rim sherd; T = 12mm, Wt = 7g. Internally bevelled rim. Coil constructed - U-shaped coil junction. Fabric – hard; clay matrix with quartz and black igneous inclusions; added mixed rock fragments – up to 5mm, 5–10%. Exterior surface sooted.

19 H (2) 1392
1 body sherd; T = 8mm, Wt = 4g. Red with a grey core. Possible black slip. Fabric – hard; clay matrix has quartz, mica and small rock inclusions, up to 1mm.

20 H (3) 516
2 body sherds; T = 10mm, Wt = 21g. Red/grey. Fabric – hard; clay matrix contains quartz, black igneous inclusions and mica. One sherd may be vitrified.

21 H (3) 516
1 body sherd; T = 9mm, Wt = 7g. Grey with buff exterior surface. Fabric – hard; clay matrix contains quartz, mica and opaques; grass temper.

22 H (3) 520 SF323
1 body sherd; T = 6mm, Wt = 2g. Grey with buff exterior margin. Fabric – hard; clay matrix contains quartz and opaques and occasional mica. Interior sooted.

23 H (3) 520 SF346
1 body sherd; T = 11mm, Wt = 12g. Red. Exterior has been burnished. Fabric – hard; clay matrix has abundant quartz; occasional larger inclusions (natural) of mixed rocks, up to 3mm. Interior sooted.

24 H (3) 520 SF962★
1 basal sherd; T = 8mm, Diam = 80mm, Wt = 12g. Plain angled base. Black with grey exterior surface. Fabric – hard; clay matrix has quartz and mica; and organics have been added.

25 H (3) 522 SF333
1 body sherd; T = 5mm, Wt = 2g. Grey with red surfaces. Fabric – hard; clay matrix has quartz, black igneous inclusions and occasional mica.

26 H (3) 522
1 rim sherd; T = 11mm, Wt = 23g. Plain rim, possibly from a barrel-shaped vessel. Grey with red margins. Coil-constructed U-shaped junctions. Fabric – hard; clay matrix has quartz, black igneous inclusions and mica; added grass temper. Exterior and interior sooted.

27 H (3) 522 SF961★
1 rim sherd; T = 6mm, Wt = 4g. Flattened/slightly splayed rim. Red. Fabric – hard; clay matrix has quartz and black igneous inclusions; larger rock inclusions up to 5mm – natural.

28 H (3) 522
1 body sherd; T = 6mm, Wt = 5g. Exterior grey, interior red. Exterior smoothed. Fabric – soft; clay matrix contains frequent quartz and occasional black igneous inclusions and mica. Exterior sooted.

29 H (3) 522
1 body sherd; T = 10mm, Wt = 5g. Red. Fabric – hard; clay matrix has quartz and black igneous inclusions; angular rock fragments up to 5mm, 50% – mixed rocks.

30 H (3) 522
1 body sherd; T = 13mm, Wt = 6g. Red with grey core. Fabric – hard; clay matrix has quartz and black igneous inclusions; mixed angular rock fragments to 4mm – 20%.

31 X (3) 1387
1 abraded body sherd; Wt = 31g. Grey with a red exterior margin. Exterior slipped. Fabric – hard; clay matrix has quartz and black igneous inclusions; additional larger rock inclusions up to 5mm, and organics, evidenced by their impressions.

32 X (3)   1387
1 abraded body sherd; Wt = 4g. Grey. Fabric – hard; clay matrix has quartz and black igneous inclusions; occasional larger black igneous fragments up to 4mm, and organics, evidenced by their impressions.

33 H (3)   1402   SF958*
1 rim (958); T = 4mm, Wt = 233g. Internally bevelled rim. Brown. Probably slipped. Fabric – hard; quartz/black igneous matrix; larger mixed inclusions up to 1mm, 10%. Interior sooted. Broken off along an H-shaped coil-junction.

34 H (3)   1402   SF960*
Flattened rim (960); T = 3mm, Diam = 180mm. Flat part of base (959); T = 3mm, Diam = 90mm. Wt = 90g. Grey with brown surfaces. Probably slipped in the exterior and interior. Fabric – hard; fine clay containing occasional quartz and black igneous inclusions; occasional larger mixed inclusions up to 5mm, 5%. Possibly vitrified. Interior sooted.

35 H (4)   461   SF165*
1 basal sherd; T = 11mm, Diam = 20cm, Wt = 46g. Plain angled base. Grey. Coil constructed. Fabric – hard; clay matrix containing quartz, black igneous inclusions and occasional mica; larger angular rock inclusions up to 15mm, 5%; organics – chopped grass/straw. Exterior and interior sooted.

36 H (4)   493   SF185
1 basal sherd; abraded. Diam = 80mm, Wt = 6g. Plain angled base. Grey with brown exterior surface. Exterior smoothed. Fabric – hard; clay matrix has quartz and black igneous inclusions and occasional mica. Exterior sooted.

37 H (4)   493   SF354*
1 rim sherd; T = 70m, Diam = 80mm, Wt = 5g. Flattened rim, splayed to the exterior. Grey/brown. Fabric – hard; clay matrix contains frequent quartz and mica and occasional opaques. Exterior and interior sooted.

38 H (4)   493   SF965*
1 basal sherd; T = 12mm, Diam = 200mm, Wt = 36g. Plain rounded base from a barrel-shaped vessel. Black with brown exterior surface. Coil constructed – N-shaped coil junctions. Exterior and interior smoothed. Fabric - hard; clay matrix contains quartz and mica. Exterior and interior sooted.

39 H (4)   1382   SF 963*
1 basal sherd; sharply angled (c 45°). T = 10mm, Wt = 30g. Brown interior, grey exterior. Exterior burnished. Fabric – hard; clay matrix contains quartz, mica and black igneous inclusions up to 1mm. Exterior sooted.

40 H (5)   496   SF182*
1 rim sherd; T = 10mm, Diam = 140mm, Wt = 18g. Everted rim, sloping out to a globular or shouldered body. Black. Fabric – hard; clay matrix contains quartz and black igneous inclusions; additional shell and black igneous rock fragments – up to 4mm, angular, 20%. Exterior and interior sooted.

41 H (6)   381   SF176*
1 rim sherd; T = 11mm, Diam = 160mm, Wt = 48g. Plain rim, probably from a barrel-shaped vessel. Grey with a brown exterior surface. Coil constructed. Exterior probably slipped. Fabric – hard; clay matrix containing quartz (1mm), some organics, probably natural. Exterior sooted, internal residue.

42 H (6)   391   SF348
1 abraded body sherd; Wt = 5g. Grey with red exterior margin. Fabric – hard; clay matrix containing quartz and black igneous inclusions – natural.

4.1.3 THE COARSE STONE ARTEFACTS

Ann Clarke

The coarse stone assemblage (illus 113, 114 & 115) comprises 35 objects including three medieval 'cannon balls' discussed elsewhere (below 4.3.6). Over half of the objects come from Phase 3 Roman/Iron Age contexts whilst the rest are present in small quantities in all phases where they are likely to be residual. Details for each artefact are given in the catalogue below and only a few objects will be commented on here.

DISCUSSION OF SELECTED PIECES

The two saddle querns and the quern rubber (1, 4, 2; illus 113) are all made of dolerite, a material that weathers naturally into slab forms. It was probably extracted from a source local to the Castle Rock. Both of the querns are shallow and have been worn right up to the perimeter. This form of saddle quern is often associated with later prehistoric contexts (Close-Brooks 1983, 288). The inclusion of a quern (1) and a rubber (2) in the same pit is of interest although the rubber is quite large in relation to the quern and it is possible that they were not actually used together.

There are three fragments of rotary querns: one upper stone (12) and two lower stones (9, 19; illus 114). The upper stone is of dolerite and has a raised moulding around the central hole, which is similar in nature to two querns from Dunadd (Christison 1905, fig 29). The two lower quern stones are of sedimentary rocks. Their bases are flat and the outer faces have been only partially dressed. On both, the central holes are smooth and worn inside and neither are completely perforated.

Four pieces have been classified as whetstones of which two (16, 25; illus 115) are only probable whetstones. These are simple, regular-shaped pebbles of micaceous siltstone and a fine-grained sandstone. On one (16), the surface is quite weathered and no wear can be detected whilst on the other, light traces of abrasion are present on one face. More fully developed wear patterns are present on piece 24 and this, of basalt, has worn concave faces and in addition the narrower end has been lightly flaked and a high polish has developed on the flaked edges. Piece 30 is a developed haunch hone of micaceous siltstone.

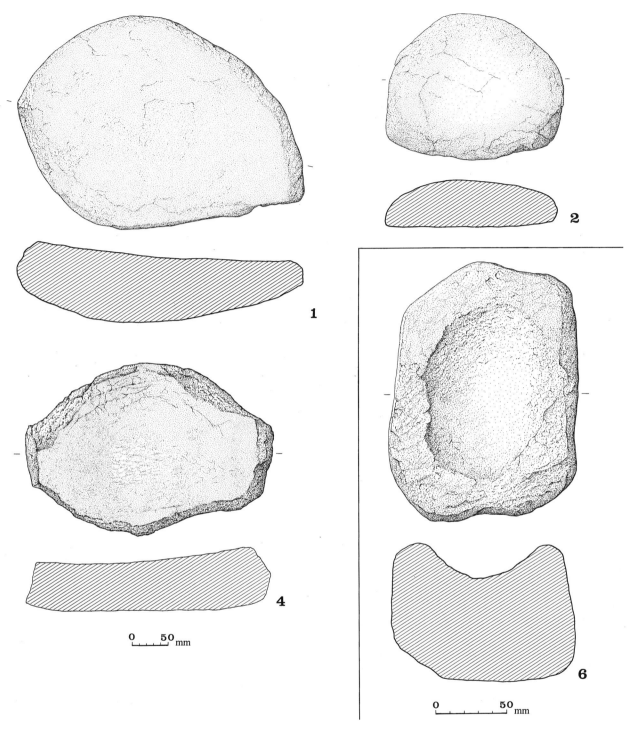

Illus 113
Saddle querns and rubbers.

There are four stone discs and one possible rough-out for a disc (27). These all vary in size, shape and material and the most interesting is the disc of pink sandstone (15; illus 115). This has been finely ground all over to form a very thin disc with rounded edges. The most likely derivation for the raw material is the Torridonian sandstones of the north of Scotland although it is possible that it is associated with the New Red Sandstones of south west Scotland and Fife (Livingstone pers comm). This is the only stone artefact that has been made from a stone occurring outwith the Edinburgh area. Such finely ground discs are common to

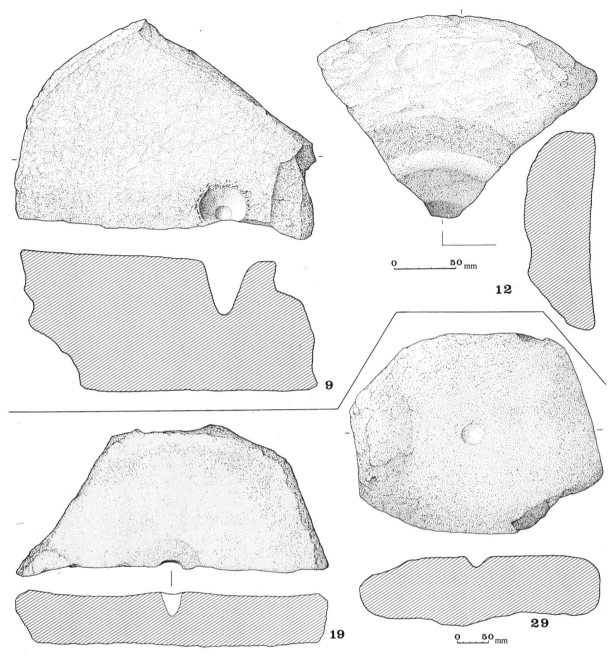

Illus 114
Rotary querns.

many Iron Age sites in Scotland (Henshall 1982, 235) but these discs are normally thicker than this example and their edges tend to be square in section.

The eight cobble tools are made of a variety of materials: sandstone, greywacke, basalt and quartzite. One piece, of sandstone (8), has been flaked around the edge and over one face to form an oval shape which narrows at the break. This edge shaping may have been in order to facilitate some form of hafting. The wear on the rest of the cobbles of sedimentary rock (21, 26, 32) is generally light and lacks uniformity. The other three cobble tools (3, 17 (illus 115), 31) have been selected for the hardness and fine grain of the material. On these, the areas of wear are very smooth and have a light polish.

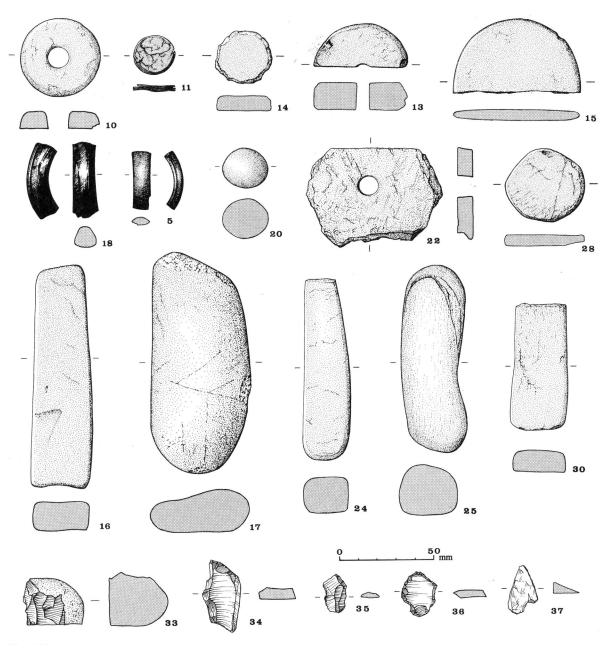

Illus 115
Assorted small prehistoric coarse stone artefacts.

COARSE STONE CATALOGUE

*= illustrated (illus 113; 114; 115)

Catalogue entries are by phase, area and context. All measurements are in order length × width × thickness (L × W × T) unless otherwise noted.

1   X (1)   1431   SF418*
   Saddle quern made on a dolerite slab. Oval in plan and partially fragmented. The base is gently rounded and the wear on the upper face extends right to the edges to form a shallow concave surface, slightly asymmetrical in long section. This was found in the same pit as the quern rubber (catalogue number 2). 440 × 310 × 35mm.

2   X (1)   1431   SF441*
   Quern rubber of dolerite. The worn face is convex in section and small parts of its edges are particularly flat and smooth. This was found in the same pit as the saddle quern (catalogue number 1). 250 × 220 × 65mm.

3   H (2)   514   SF209
   Sub-rectangular pebble of basalt. One end has a pronounced convex face which is very smooth and polished. Probably rubbing stone/polisher. 46 × 27 × 23mm.

4   H (2)   531   SF206*
   Saddle quern made on a dolerite slab. It is oval in plan with a gently rounded base. The upper face is concave and

asymmetrical in long section and the wear extends right to the edges. 350 × 255 × 50mm.

5   H (2)   535   SF210*
Fragment of a shale bracelet. Ellipse-shaped section. Inner Diam = 42mm; T = 10mm.

6   H (2)   535   SF403*
Sub-rectangular block of sandstone. The base is irregularly curved and lightly pecked. The upper face has had a large oval-shaped hollow with a round base pecked out of the centre. The inner face of the hollow is rough. Block 195 × 130 × 100mm.

7   H (2)   535
Tabular fragment of basalt. One flat face is natural and the opposite face appears to have been pecked all over. Possible quern fragment. T = 49mm.

8   X (2)   1422/1433
Cobble of sandstone, broken across the width and very abraded. The cobble has been flaked from the edges and over one face to form an oval shape which tapers towards the break. This tapering may indicate possible shaping for hafting. Broken L 195 × 105 × 50mm.

9   X (2)   1447   SF444*
Fragment of a lower stone of a rotary quern made of greywacke. The base is flat and the surviving curved edge has been partially dressed. The upper face is flat and has been pecked. The central hole has been worked to a depth of 45mm and is U-shaped in section. Probable Diam = 335mm; T = 110mm; Diam of central hole at the top = 35mm.

10   X (10)   1342   SF389*
Spindle whorl made of white 'trap rock'. It has been ground all over leaving one face flat and the other face and edges slightly convex in section. The perforation is straight sided and smooth inside with striations around the circumference. Diam = 42mm; T = 100mm; diam of hole = 11mm.

11   H unstratified *
Shale gaming piece. Diam = 21mm; T = 3mm.

12   H (3)   516*
Rotary quern fragment of dolerite. The upper face has a raised moulding around the central hole and the base is concave in section and very smooth and worn, particularly around the outer edge. Radius 164mm; T at moulding 47mm.

13   H (3)   522   SF365*
Spindle whorl made of sandstone. Broken across the width truncating the perforation. Both faces have been ground flat and the sides are slightly convex. The perforation is straight sided. Diam = 53mm; T = 15mm; Diam of hole = 10mm.

14   H (3)   522*
Small disc of basalt. Both faces are flat and smooth and the edge has been bifacially chipped. Diam = 30mm; T = 8mm.

15   H (3)   522   SF362*
Disc made of a pink micaceous sandstone, either Torridonian or New Red Sandstone. Broken across width. Both faces have been ground to a very smooth finish and the edge is finely rounded. Diam = 70mm; T = 6mm.

16   H (3)   522   SF363*
Sub-rectangular pebble of fine micaceous siltstone. The surface is quite weathered. Probable whetstone. 122 × 32 × 16mm.

17   H (3)   522*
Flat, sub-oval pebble of a fine grained metamorphic rock. At one end the pebble appears to have been bevelled on both faces. The bevelling is smooth and shiny. Possible undeveloped bevel on opposite end. 121 × 53 × 26mm.

18   H (3)   529 S   F321*
Fragment of a shale bracelet. D-shaped section. Inner diam = 55mm; T = 11mm.

19   H (3)   529 S   F204*
Fragment of a lower stone from a rotary quern, made on sandstone. The outer edge of the quern has been dressed although the original plan of the stone does not appear to have been a regular circle. The central hole has been truncated by breakage and its surviving inner face is very smooth. The upper face of the stone is smooth and concave in section with a slight raised collar around the central hole. Diam = 480mm; T = 75mm.

20   X (3)   1387   SF400*
Stone ball, material unidentifiable. In shape it is a slightly flattened sphere and it appears to have been smoothed all over. 24 × 24 × 22mm.

21   X (3)   1387   SF440
Flat oval cobble of greywacke. There is light pecking on the ends and one side. On the opposite side a large flake has been detached. 124 × 72 × 33mm.

22   X (3)   1387   SF424*
Broken tabular fragment of slate with a straight-sided perforation made towards the centre. Broken L = 72mm; broken W = 51mm; T = 9mm; Diam of hole = 11mm.

23   X (3)   1402
Irregular shaped block of sandstone. Three/four shallow U-shaped grooves made on one face running almost parallel to each other at right angles to the length. 200 × 95 × 78mm; grooves c 3mm wide.

24   X (3)   1382   SF401*
Sub-rectangular pebble of basalt. Both faces are worn and concave in section. The narrower end has been flaked and is highly polished on protruding edges. Whetstone. 98 × 25 × 21mm.

25   X (3)   1382   SF402*
Narrow oval-shaped pebble of fine-grained sandstone. Possible light wear on one face. Probable whetstone. 110 × 33 × 30mm.

26   X (3)   1406   SF408
Flat oval cobble of greywacke. Part of one edge has been bifacially flaked through use. 107 × 68 × 25mm.

27   X (4)   1382
Tabular piece of unidentified rock with light chipping around parts of the edge. Probable rough-out for stone disc. 95 × 90 × 17mm.

28   H (5)   418*
Sub-circular disc of slate. Both faces are flat and the edge has been ground to a square section. 42 × 39 × 6mm.

29   X (6)   1356   SF442*
Possible pivot stone. Large, slightly irregular boulder of dolerite. A small, round based hollow which has signs of pecking and smoothing has been worked in the centre of the upper face. 390 × 340 × 115mm. Diam of hollow = 35mm; depth 15mm.

30   X (6)   1356   SF394*
Haunch hone of micaceous siltstone. Broken across the width. Both faces and the sides are smooth and concave in section. Broken L 69 × 29 × 17mm.

31   X (7)   1353
Pebble of very fine grained quartzite. One very flat face has been worked at right angles to the bedding planes and is very smooth and shiny, no striations are visible. ? Polishing stone. 52 × 44 × 41mm; flat face 46 × 32mm.

4.1.4 THE WORKED FLINT

William F Finlayson

The total number of flints recovered from the excavations was only ten pieces, a surprisingly low count. Other than the gun-flints (which are discussed below with the post-medieval finds 4.4.4) little can be said about the collection other than providing a piece-by-piece description.

CATALOGUE

*= illustrated (illus 115)

33 H (8)   589*
Black flint, rounded battered cortex indicates beach pebble origin. 1/4 pebble, possibly originally used as a core, with the ventral surface used as a striking platform. The heavy rippling on the piece suggests the use of a hard hammer technique. 33 × 32 × 26mm.

34 H (6)   593*
Brown mottled flint. Flake with heavy secondary modification round all edges. Some of this is probably the result of accidental crushing rather than deliberate working. 38 × 19 × 7mm.

35 H (3)   522*
Grey flint. Badly burnt flake. 22 × 13 × 4mm.

36 H (7)   344   SF208*
Brown flint. Flake with abrupt inverse retouch round edges truncating original shape. 24 × 18 × 5mm (drawing shows ventral surface).

37 H (6)   435   SF 161*
Black flint, flat, soft, chalky cortex indicates nodular origin. Simple unmodified flake. 27 × 16 × 8mm.

38 X (1)   1427   SF414
Grey flint, badly burnt, hard hammer flake with large platform. Burning obscures detail, but on lateral margin is blunted by fine abrupt retouch. 34 × 27 × 10mm.

39 X (1)   1463   SF439
Black with grey mottled flint, with cortex. Regular blade with the bulb of percussion removed by a single flake. Fine retouch and edge damage around the edges. A gloss along one edge, visible to the naked eye, suggests that some of this damage is the result of use. A cursory microscopic examination of the polish confirms this diagnosis. The large notch on the same margin is however almost certainly accidental damage. Note that the removal of the bulb facilitates hafting (for example, in this case, as a knife). 50 × 18 × 5mm.

40 H (2)   535   SF406
Grey flint. Secondary flake with battered (pebble) cortex, also red stained patination on an old fracture surface, suggesting that this piece may be reworked. 28 × 22 × 5mm.

4.1.5 PREHISTORIC WORKED BONE ARTEFACTS

Jane Clark

DESCRIPTION OF THE PIECES

BONE HANDLES

Five antler handles were recovered from Phase 3, 4 and 5 contexts. They are all of a plain design, and slightly bulbous, tapering shape, with straight cut ends (illus 116). Four are of almost uniform dimensions. Antler is a common material used in handles for blades and other tools, as it provides solid tissue for the insertion of a longitudinal tang. Of the Castle handles, only one (*1*, SF356) retains its iron implement (illus 110; 116). None of the other handles shows the remains of a tang, with no trace of iron staining, or evidence for force having been used to break or wrench out the metal. Rather, they appear to be unfinished and/or unused, although they are all well-shaped, with smooth, polished surfaces.

BONE RINGS

Seven cut and hollowed rings of red deer antler, from Phases 2, 3 and 4, form a small group of objects for which there are several alternative interpretations. They are of cut lengths of between 20 and 29 mm. Four (SF489, SF488 (illus 116, 9), SF399 and SF190) are abraded, and worn around both inner and outer surfaces to form a globular shape. The other three (SF217, SF189 and SF178) are less worn, with straight-cut edges and less rounded outline. The unworn antler lengths may be off-cuts, but the worn examples have been subject to some use. Similar lengths of bone and antler have been interpreted as toggles (Millett & Russell 1982, 85, fig 7: 7 & 8), or beads (Ritchie 1971, 103, fig 2:19). A more certain interpretation can be given to other examples, with single transverse perforations, which were used as pin heads (MacGregor 1974, 76, fig 8: 114–7).

BONE PIN

Only one bone pin was recovered from a prehistoric context.

BONE TOOLS

The fragmentary and abraded condition of many of the Castle bone and antler artefacts makes functional

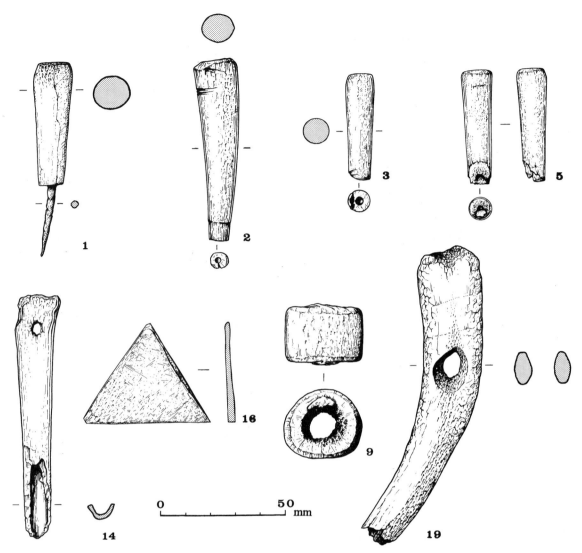

Illus 116
Assorted small prehistoric worked bone artefacts.

interpretation difficult. The majority come from Phase 3 contexts, and, in general, two broad groups emerge: textile working tools and objects used as a means of fastening and attachment.

PERFORATED ANTLER TINES

Both *19* (SF474; illus 116) and *20* (SF368) are possible cheek pieces for bridle bits. Antler cheek pieces are known from late Bronze Age through to early medieval contexts (Roes 1963, 44). Bulleid & Gray classified six different forms of cheek pieces and other perforated tines from Glastonbury, two forms with single perforations, and four types with two or three holes, or a single hole with a central notch on the inner curve (Bulleid & Gray 1917, 440–3, fig 155). The fact that SF474 is worn flat along one face, and slightly faceted on the other, would fit with an interpretation as a cheek piece. As the lower part of the tine is broken, any evidence of a second perforation at the tip is lost. The identification of SF368 is less certain, although a similar worked tine from an Iron Age burial at Viables Farm, Hampshire, has been interpreted as an unfinished cheek piece (Millett & Russell 1982, 82, fig 5: 2). The cut marks around the eye of SF368 are more likely to be wear marks than finishing cuts, in which case SF368 is a used, not unfinished, artefact. It may, alternatively, have been used as a coarse needle, for example in thatch or straw work.

BONE AND ANTLER CATALOGUE

* = illustrated (illus 116)

1   H (3)   522   SF356*
    Antler handle with a tanged iron awl of rectangular cross-section. L of antler handle = 50mm; Diam = 12mm. Total L of awl = 78mm.

2   H (4)   431   SF179*
    Antler handle, tapering over its full length, with shallow holes at either end, and chipped damage around the wider end. L = 75mm; Diam = 17mm.

3   H (4)   493   SF177*
    Antler handle, with a shallow tang hole in the narrower end, which is crossed by irregular cutmarks, and cut on a slight diagonal. L = 44mm; Diam = 11mm.

4   H (4)   1382   SF428
    Shaped antler form, with no beginnings of a socket hole. L = 46mm; Diam = 11mm.

5   H (5)   433   SF361*
    Antler handle, broken diagonally across a shallow tang hole in the narrower end. L = 45mm; Diam 11mm.

6   H (2)   531   SF217
    Antler ring, L = 20mm; Diam = 37mm.

7   H (3)   516   SF190
    Antler ring, L = 24mm; Diam = 20mm.

8   H (3)   522   SF189
    Antler ring; L = 23mm; Diam = 27mm.

9   H (3)   1387   SF399*
    Antler ring; L = 22mm; Diam = 32mm.

10 H (3)   1387   SF488
    Antler ring; L = 21mm; Diam = 31mm

11 H (3)   1387   SF489
    Antler ring; L = 29mm; Diam = 33mm

12 H (4)   431   SF178
    Antler ring; L = 20mm; Diam = 27mm

13 H (3)   520   SF371
    A broken, headless pin shaft, tapering over its length to a rounded point. L = 82mm.

14 H (3)   520   SF369*
    A broken shaft of sheep/goat metatarsal, pierced transversely at the epiphysal end. The smooth, polished surface of the shaft is typical of textile working tools. It may have been used as a needle for coarse textile, netting, thatch or straw work, although the rough finish around the eye suggests that it was not subject to the frictional wear expected in a needle. Alternatively, it may have been used as a peg, for example to hold the edge/selvedge of the cloth to the upright of a warp-weighted loom (Rogerson and Dallas 1984, 167, fig 189–90). L = 100mm

15 H (3)   520   SF370
    Sheep/goat metatarsal broken just above a transverse hole through the shaft. Similar objects, using the complete bone, with a central perforation, have been interpreted as bobbins (Wild 1970, 34; Wardle 1990, 158, fig 141: 971). L = 82mm

16 H (3)   520   SF347*
    A triangular plate of horn. It is cut to give straight edges, and polished to give smooth surfaces, with linear scratch marks. The size and shape of this object suggest that it may be an unfinished weaving tablet. If complete, it would have had a thread hole in each corner. Triangular weaving tablets were popular during the Roman period, both in Britain (Wild 1970, 140-1; MacGregor 1985, 191–2; fig 101, 20), and on the Continent (Roes 1963, 49–50; pl LIX, 2). L of edges = 47, 48, 50mm

17 H (3)   1406   SF434
    An unfinished spindle whorl of cattle femur: prox articulation. Central holes have been drilled from both sides, two from the outer rounded surface (5 & 3mm deep) and one from the cut surface (8mm deep). W = 39mm; H = 25mm.

18 H (2)   1422   SF435
    SF 435 (red deer antler) is a bobbin or toggle, with a single transverse perforation, in three adjoining fragments. One end is rounded and blunt, the other is broken. L = 68mm.

19 H (3)   1387   SF474*
    SF474 (red deer antler) is a tine, broken at both ends, and pierced transversely towards the broader end. The aperture is worn on both faces, narrowing in the middle (9mm min diam). One side of the tine is worked and worn flat and smooth along the complete length. The opposite side is slightly faceted above the hole, to form a small stepped notch. Shallow cut marks cross the squared end above the hole, possibly made by a cord or wire wrapped tightly around, cutting into the antler. L = 127mm.

20 H (4)   493   SF368
    SF368 (red deer antler) is a perforated tine. The broader end is cut square, and is chipped and abraded above the transverse hole (8mm diam). Shallow cut marks cross both apertures. L = 114mm.

4.1.6 IRONWORK

Jane Clark

There is little metalwork which is not iron. All of the possible prehistoric bronzes are discussed with the Roman bronze work below (4.2.5). Several key categories include material from the early phases but are discussed as a group elsewhere. All knives are discussed below (4.3.5), as are the nails (4.3.5 and 4.3.5mf, 1: F1–4).

There are two items which might be regarded as weapons, a spear blade (illus 117, 2) and possible spear-butt (3). There are in addition two ferrules and four objects which have been tentatively categorised as tools. Four tools came from Phases 1 to 4. The functional interpretations given here are tentative, with only the leather-working awl, SF356 (illus 110, 116, 1), having good parallels (MacGregor 1978, 43, fig 26:4).

IRONWORK CATALOGUE

* = illustrated (illus 117)

1   H (3)   516   SF183*
    A pointed tool with an unusually shaped socket. Two narrow bar tangs extend from diagonally opposite corners of the square-sectioned shaft. The socket is shallow, and there are no rivet holes through the tangs; further binding would have been necessary to secure a handle, unless it was held solely by vertical pressure exerted during use. There is little evidence for burring or wear at the tip. The original presence of a

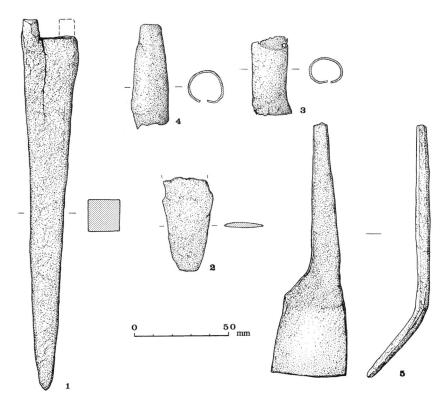

Illus 117
Assorted prehistoric ironwork.

handle argues against this being a metal working tool; it probably had an offensive, rather than craft, function and is likely to have been a spear-butt. L = 172mm.

2   H (3)   534   SF860*
A spearhead, broken at the shoulder. It has a small, leaf-shaped blade, of diamond cross-section, and can be compared with the more complete spearheads of Manning's Group 1A, with their well-made, leaf-shaped, blades and welded sockets (Manning 1985, 163–5 figs V38–V69), all dated to the mid-1st century, such as an example from Maiden Castle (Wheeler 1943, 278, fig 91:5). L = 51mm.

3   H (2)   534   SF954*
An open-seamed sheet ferrule, to fit an object of oval cross-section. The longitudinal edges are partially folded back, revealing an internal cross-bar plate. The section behind the cross plate (about one third of the total length) is hammered flat to close the end. The other end is open. L = 44mm.

4   H (4)   562   SF461*
A sheet ferrule, of oval, slightly bulbous, cross-section. It is broken along the length of the seam and at tip. However, a small inturned lip survives at the tip, suggesting that it was originally flat ended, rather than pointed. It may have served as a scabbard chape (Goodall 1983, 248, 251, fig 9, 201–4). L = 55mm

5   X (1)   1470   SF422*
A bent, tanged tool. It apparently served two sequential functions: firstly as a blade, possibly of agricultural form, such as a coulter (Rees 1979, fig 69). Later, after vertical breakage through the tip, the break was reworked to a straight, wedged, cutting edge, and the tang bent to an angle of c 140˚ to the blade. The resulting tool, a scraper rather than a cutting blade, may have served a similar function to later, medieval coulters' knives, or slickers, used to scrape dirt and excess grease from hides (Goodall 1991, 132 fig.102, 319–21). L = 142mm; W = 41mm.

6   H (3)   516   SF564
A tool, possibly a file, of rectangular cross-section, with a slightly bulbous shaft. L = 116mm; W = 8mm.

7   H (3) 522 SF356 (illus 110, 116)
An awl of square cross-section, held in an antler handle (see above Worked Bone Report 4.1.5, no1). L = 78mm.

8   X (4)   1382   SF397
SF397 is a ring-handled tool, of rectangular cross-section, with a flat, wedged tip, and broken shaft. The two fragments recovered may not represent the full length of this object. Tools of similar shape, but of considerably longer length (c 300mm), from Romano-British contexts, have been interpreted as smiths' pokers (Rodwell 1976, 46–8, fig 3:11; Manning 1985, 12, fig A40). Total L = 99mm.

4.2 THE ROMAN PERIOD ASSEMBLAGE

4.2.1 INTRODUCTION

Although grouped under a Roman period heading (illus 118), not all of the finds discussed here are necessarily Roman in origin or cultural attribution. However, it has been convenient to use groupings which reflected, if nothing else, the research interests of the specialists who studied the various categories of material. For the same practical reason, a number of the less chronologically distinctive artefacts (of stone, bone, bronze and iron) have been described above in the Prehistoric Section, which might be attributed to the Roman period.

Illus 118
Pottery, metalwork and glass of the Roman period.

Only one Roman coin was recovered, a denarius of Hadrian (4.3.8 Coin Catalogue *1*) and only two sherds of glass, but there are several examples of Romano-British bronzework and substantial quantities of both coarse and fine wares. The pottery provides the best guide to the length and significance of the contacts with the wider world. The range of Roman pottery recovered from the site is striking. The most numerous vessels are from the 2nd century and they clearly reflect the enlarged military presence at that time. However, there is a significant amount of 1st-century material and some from the 3rd–4th century. Collectively this body of material suggests that for the first few centuries AD Edinburgh was one of the most important centres in SE Scotland.

The glass and ceramic vessels have been catalogued with a continuous set of numbers.

4.2.2 THE ROMAN GLASS

Denise Allen

Two fragments of Roman period glass were recovered. The first (illus 118; 119, *1*) a rim fragment of a flask or jug of greenish colour with a trail of dark blue beneath the rim and the second a small fragment of blue-green.

The addition of a short applied spiral trail beneath the rim (fragment *1*) was a favourite decorative device used on a variety of flask and jug forms, particularly during the mid to later Roman period. The trail is most often colourless, using the same metal as that of the glass itself (eg Harden *et al* 1987, nos 59–62, 70–72).

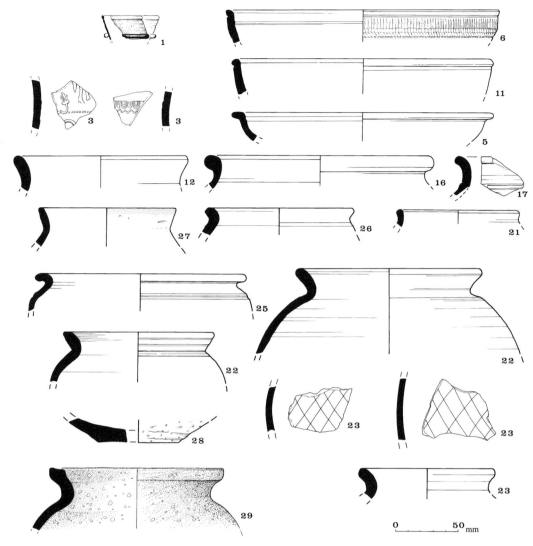

Illus 119
Roman period glass, fine and coarse wares.

Coloured trails occur most often on the snake-thread glasses of the later 2nd and early 3rd centuries, but these are almost invariably opaque blue, opaque yellow or opaque white (cf Fremersdorf 1959). Dark blue applied to colourless glass, as on this piece is more unusual, and is found most often at a later date. During the 4th century, greenish or colourless vessels were decorated with applied blobs of coloured glass, most commonly dark blue, on its own or combined with other colours (Harden et al 1987, 102–3, nos 46–49). Applied trails of dark blue glass occasionally occur at the same period on vessels of both western and eastern provenance (Harden *et al* 1987, nos 47 and 73). The fairly poor quality of the vessel glass itself, with its pinhead bubbles, is also most typical of the late Roman period, although not exclusive to that date.

In summary, the rim fragment is suggestive of a fairly fine piece of decorated tableware, probably a jug or flask, of 4th-century date. However, in the absence of dated parallel British finds, and with such a small fragment surviving, this identification cannot be made with certainty.

Apparently featureless body fragments of glass are never easy to identify with certainty. However, there are clues on the second piece, such as the flat profile, and the indications that it had been blown into a mould, that it is part of a flat-sided (prismatic) bottle. By far the commonest variant of these is the square (Charlesworth 1966), but hexagonal, rectangular and octagonal vessels also occur. They were used as containers for a wide variety of liquids, and fragments are found on almost every site in Britain where there was occupation during the 1st and 2nd centuries. Manufacture of square bottles continued from the mid-1st century to probably the end of the 2nd, but their large numbers mean that they are not uncommon as residual finds in later contexts. The less common bottle shapes had a more restricted period of use within this broad span.

1   H (8)   257   SF68*
    Rim fragment of a flask or jug of greenish-colourless glass; surfaces pitted, and many pinhead bubbles within the metal. Rim outflared, and folded inward and downward, beneath which part of a horizontal applied trail of dark blue glass still adheres. Rim diam = 45mm.

2   X (3)   1387   SF415
    Small, flat fragment of blue-green glass, both surfaces gloss, but one showing very slight pitting, as though from contact with a mould. Small elongated bubbles within the metal, indicating that it had been blown. c 4mm thick.

4.2.3 SAMIAN WARE AND OTHER ROMAN FINE WARES

Brian Hartley

There are 14 vessels represented in the Edinburgh Castle assemblage, which span the later 1st to the later 2nd centuries AD. The material can be linked to the various phases of Roman military occupation of North Britain, but the range of material hints at the possibility that supply of the fine pottery was not exclusively via the military. This is particularly true for the post-Severan objects, and may well have been true of some of the other material.

Although one or two pieces of the Samian are likely to have been made in the late Neronian or early Flavian period at La Graufesenque (c AD 54–80), a phenomenon paralleled at Camelon, there is nothing in the early part of the Samian range which could not have come from the same sources as the supply to the Flavian or Flavian-Trajanic military sites of Scotland (c AD 80–117). The only slightly unusual feature is the presence of two sherds from different 1st-century Lezoux pots (4 and 5). But, as is noted below, similar pieces are now known from Camelon and Strageath, and the Edinburgh Castle sample is, of course, far too small to make significant statistical deductions from the presence of two such vessels.

There is nothing among the Samian which must fall in the Trajanic or Hadrianic periods (c AD 98–138) and it seems that the supply of Samian to Edinburgh picked up again with the Antonine occupation of Scotland (AD 139–45). The mixture of Central Gaulish (Lezoux) sherds with single vessels (8 and 13) from Montans and La Madeleine is typical of forts on the Antonine Wall. A single vessel (4) of Curle 15 or 23 is the only piece which seems at all likely to be later than the occupation of the Antonine Wall (ie post AD 164), but it would almost certainly belong to the period when Newstead and sites on the Dere Street to the S were still held. There is nothing assignable to the Severan (early 3rd century) period, when Cramond and Carpow were held.

There is a slight hint that the use of this pottery may extend beyond the time of its manufacture and distribution. A number of the vessels come from relatively late in the sequence of activity represented at Mills Mount. In addition two sherds (9 and 11b) indicate that the broken pots were put to additional use after they were broken.

The very small sample of non-Samian Roman sherds adds little to what the Samian tells us. The only pieces which would be out of place in the Flavian or Antonine military occupations of Scotland are the Nene Valley sherd (16) and the one suggested for the Vale of York (21).

FINE POTTERY CATALOGUE

* = illustrated (illus 119)

SAMIAN

3   H (8)   313   SF85 and SF106*
    Two fragments of the same form 37 with diagnostic features, such as an ovolo (Rogers B97), squarish beads in the vertical border combined with a wavy-line border under the ovolo (Stanfield & Simpson 1958, p 142, 33) and leaf (Rogers J144). These allow it to be assigned firmly to Cettus of Les Martres-de-Veyre whose work was common in Scotland during the Antonine occupation. Cettus's dates are now securely established as c AD 135–160 (Hartley 1972, p 34).

4   H (3)   497
    Form Curle 15 or 23 in Central Gaulish fabric, almost

certainly from Lezoux and presumably the first form, as Curle 23 is not known from Scotland. This is certainly an Antonine sherd, but closer dating is difficult, though the piece is relatively thick and crude and perhaps unlikely to have been made early in the period.

5 H (5)   409   SF148*
A sherd of form Curle 15, Central Gaulish. Although certainly Antonine, in contrast to the other presumed example of the form (497), this is relatively delicate, and is unlikely to be later than AD 160. The degree of wear on the rim is unusual and suggests either some secondary use, or possibly that the dish had served as a lid.

6 H (3)   520   SF345*
A sherd from the rim of a decorated bowl of form 29, South Gaulish. This will have been made before AD 85, but probably not long before, as it has the strongly out turned profile of Flavian examples, though the quality of the glaze is akin to Neronian-Flavian pieces. c AD 70–85.

7 H (5)   495   SF174
A small flake from a decorated bowl, probably form 37 rather than form 30, Central Gaulish. The surviving decoration is too slight to suggest a potter, though one of the motifs is probably part of the head of a lioness (D793). Antonine.

8 H (3)   534   SF203
A slightly burnt fragment from the footring and base of a dish of form 18 etc. This is unusual in two ways, it has a strong groove around the footring, reminiscent of that used on form 27, and the fabric is very pale. Both features suggest origin at Montans. A precise parallel has recently been found at Bosfield Farm, Hertfordshire in a 2nd-century context, and as it is now well known that Montans ware was reaching Scotland in the earlier part of the Antonine period (Hartley 1972, 42 with Hartley 1989, 216, D34).

9 H (7)   393
A small strip from a large dish or bowl in Central Gaulish fabric typical of the earlier Antonine period. For whatever reason this piece has been deliberately rubbed down to its present shape, as the facets show.

10 H (4)   431   SF175
A burnt fragment from a dish, probably of form 18/31R. Both the details of the form and the fabric, despite the burning, are typical of Flavian-Trajanic products of La Graufesenque, such as appear at Newstead (Hartley 1972, 9).

11a X (7)   1353*
Part of the rim and wall of a dish of form 31 in Central Gaulish fabric. The details of form and fabric suggest early or mid-Antonine date.

11b X (7)   1353
A fragment from the centre of the base of a dish of form 15/17 or 18 in the fabric of La Graufesenque. A poorly-impressed, fragmentary stamp may read SS or CS. There is no secure identification, though there are considerable similarities to one stamp of the Bassus-Coelus association, which would suggest early Flavian date at the latest, and the details of the form would accord with such a date. The dish was worn on the central cone, perhaps after fracture. (Such wear is not uncommon on the cones of complete bases with the walls trimmed off, as if they had been used as tops by children).

12 H (5)   418*
A flake from the wall of a large vessel (form 31 etc), Central Gaulish, Antonine.

13 H (7)   344   SF138
A slightly burnt flake (or one buried in hot ashes?) from an uncertain form. The unusually soapy feel of the surface suggests that this may be from La Madeleine, near Nancy, as such fabrics are there typical. La Madeleine ware was the only East Gaulish Samian to reach sites on the Antonine Wall, so this could be derived from normal supplies to Antonine Scotland, though Hadrianic importation would theoretically be possible.

14 X (6)   1356
A similar flake to 344, very possibly from the same vessel.

15 X (2)   1392
A tiny flake of Samian in La Graufesenque fabric of the kind normal in Neronian and early-Flavian contexts.

OTHER FINE WARES

16 X (9)   1346   SF499*
A jar rim in colour-coated ware. The form, fabric and the slaty blue-grey coat are characteristic of Nene Valley products of the mid-3rd to early 4th century. This is close to pots made at Stibbington in the late 3rd or early 4th century. A slightly earlier date, after about AD 240 however, could not be excluded, as some similar pieces were found in the filling of a kiln at Sibson which went out of use at that time.

17 G (-)   161*
The rim of a narrow-mouthed jar in pinkish buff, micaceous fabric. The form is akin to Gillam 30, and has a Belgic ancestry, but the fabric, in northern military contexts, is typically Flavian-Trajanic, and it seems likely that the same dating applies here.

18 H (3)   522
Although a very small fragment, and almost certainly with its surface discoloured by burning, the reddish fabric and grey core is reminiscent of some northern imitations of Black-Burnished Category 1 current in the Antonine period and reaching military sites in Scotland.

19 H (3)   522   SF186
Probably a fragment from a flagon with its outer surface discoloured by burning. While Antonine date could not be excluded, the nature of the fabric and the relatively high firing temperature are best paralleled in Flavian-Trajanic groups.

20 H (5)   418
A fragment from a large vessel, possibly a *lagena*, in reddish-buff oxidized fabric, somewhat micaceous. Almost certainly 1st or 2nd century.

21 H (4)   493*
The rim of a medium-mouthed jar in granular reddish brown fabric with patchy red-brown, brownish grey and black surface. Both the fabric and the rather square-cut end of the rim are like jars made somewhere in the northern part of the Vale of York, or its immediate vicinity in the late 2nd and 3rd century, and this suggests that the Edinburgh piece is Roman in origin and probably of similar date.

4.2.4 ROMAN COARSE POTTERY

John N Dore

Approximately 120 sherds of pottery were examined. A reasonable estimation of the number of vessels represented would be 37. There seems to be no material present of a date later than the 2nd century AD and all the pieces could fall within the range AD 90–160, with the possible exception of two locally manufactured vessels (*28, 29*).

COARSE POTTERY CATALOGUE

★ = illustrated (illus 119)

DATABLE VESSELS

22 H (3)   522   SF184, 351–3★
A total of 3 rim sherds and 28 wall sherds representing 2 jars. The vessels are of similar form (though one has a somewhat shorter rim than the other), and are of the same fabric: Dark red brown with mid-grey core and black burnished outer surface; inclusions: common, quartz (mainly 0.2–0.5mm, max 1mm), and a little red iron ore, (0.2–0.5mm). The outer surface is burnished in narrow (c 2mm wide) horizontal strips. There are sufficient wall sherds from the girth and lower wall to suggest that one, if not both, of the vessels had an unburnished zone around the girth, divided in two by a single horizontal burnished line. The form of the rim and the style of the burnishing all suggest affinities with jars in Black Burnished Ware Category 1 (BB1) dating to the early and middle part of the 2nd century AD. However, recently I have noted a very close parallel at Vindolanda (unpublished) in a level of period II (c 90–105 AD). A fairly wide date bracket of c 90–160 AD would therefore seem appropriate.
Wall sherds from these two vessels occur in a number of other contexts:

22a	H (3)	516	SF194	3 wall sherds
22b	H (2)	531	SF330	1 wall sherd
22c	H (6)	391		1 wall sherd
22d	H (5)	418		1 rim sherd
22e	H (3)	516		1 wall sherd
22f	H (3)	520/522		1 wall sherd
22g	X (2)	1392		1 wall sherd
22h	X (3)	1387		1 wall sherd

23   X (2)   1400
1 rim sherd from a jar in BB1. There are very faint indications of a burnished wavy line on the neck, c AD 120–160. There are wall sherds which are quite likely to come from this vessel in a number of contexts:

23a   H (3)   516   SF195★
1 wall sherd showing acute angle cross hatching.
23b   H (5)   496   SF181
1 wall sherd which joins with the sherd from H 516 (22).
23c   H (3)   520   SF324   1 tiny scrap.
23d   X (3)   1387★
3 wall sherds, 2 of which show acute angle cross hatching.
23e   X (2)   1392   1 base sherd.

24   H (3)   516
1 small wall sherd, probably from a bowl or dish, showing decoration of parallel, diagonal, burnished lines; probably BB2, in which case post c AD 140.

25   X (4)   1382★
1 rim sherd from a jar. Mid-grey with burnished surface; inclusions: common, sub-round quartz (0.2–0.5mm); c AD 100–150.

26   X (3)   1402★
1 rim sherd from a jar. Dark grey-brown with burnished surface; inclusions: common, quartz (up to 0.1mm); c AD 100–150.

27   X (3)   1410★
1 rim sherd from a small hand-made jar. Pale orange with dark grey core; inclusions: common, rounded quartz (mainly 0.1–0.2mm, max 0.5mm) and red iron (mainly 0.1–0.2mm, max 0.5mm); the date of this vessel need not be confined to the Roman period.

28   X (3)   1387★
1 base sherd from a jar or bowl. Black with dull red-brown inner surface; inclusions: common, sub-round limestone (up to 2mm), angular calcite (1–2mm) some of which are recognisable as fragments of shell, rounded quartz (0.2–0.5mm). This resembles a ware which occurs at Cramond and was possibly produced in that area. Many of the forms occurring at Cramond seem to be copying imported Roman forms. The ware cannot be more closely dated at Cramond within the overall limits of the military occupation, ie Antonine to Severan (pers comm N Holmes).

29   H (3)   522   SF360★
29 body sherds, 1 rim sherd, T = 7mm, Diam = 140mm, Wt = 297g. Everted rim with an interior bevel, from a hand-made vessel. Form was probably a globular body with a rounded base. Hard grey fabric, clay matrix has abundant quartz tempered with 10% crushed shell. Interior and exterior sooted. Also likely to have been made locally as vessel no 28 above.

OTHER (UNDATABLE) ROMAN SHERDS

30   H (7)   395
1 base sherd from a jar in oxidised ware; 2 wall sherds oxidised ware.

31   H (3)   520
3 wall sherds oxidised ware

32   X (6)   1356
1 wall sherd in orange ware

33   X (4)   1382
1 wall sherd in orange burnished ware, probably from the same vessel as the sherd in vessel no 35.

34   X (3)   1387
1 wall sherd grey burnished ware;
3 wall sherds in pale orange ware, all possibly from the same vessel;
3 wall sherds in grey ware, probably from different vessels.

35   X (3)   1387
2 wall sherds in grey ware with black surface; acute angle cross hatching;
4 wall sherds grey ware, possibly all from different vessels;
3 wall sherds orange ware, probably all from the same vessel.

36   X (9)   1344
1 wall sherd in grey ware

37   X (4)   1382
1 wall sherd in grey ware

38   X (3)   1387
2 wall sherds from a large jar or bowl in grey ware; possibly from the same vessel as the sherd from vessel no 39;
1 small wall sherd in grey ware;
1 wall sherd in orange burnished ware; probably from the same vessel as the sherd from vessel no 33;
2 small wall sherds in oxidised ware.

39   X (2)   1447
1 wall sherd from a large jar or bowl in grey ware; possibly from the same vessel as the two sherds in no 38.
Two sherds were submitted as questionably Roman; both could quite easily be so:

40   X (2)   1447
1 wall sherd in very pale yellow fabric with pale yellow surface.

41   X (3)   1387
1 wall sherd in very pale yellow fabric.

4.2.5 ROMAN PERIOD BROOCHES AND OTHER BRONZEWORK

D F Mackreth

with entries by Jane Clark (JC) and ST Driscoll (STD)

DISCUSSION

THE TRUMPET BROOCH (SF133) (illus 110; 120, *1*)

A recent review of the dating of Trumpets (Mackreth (forthcoming) concluded that the floruit ran from before AD 75 to the quarter century AD 150–175 although there are enough to suggest that a few may have survived to *c* AD 200. In general, it is hard to detect which types of Trumpet should be early in the series. The only probable indicator of an early date is the continuation of the general curve of the profile of the upper bow into that of the lower bow. This certainly applies to the two earliest dated Trumpets which came from The Lunt, Baginton (Hobley 1969, 110, fig 19,9; 1973, 66, fig 19,8). How soon the straight lower bow or the recurve were developed is beyond knowing at present. Similarly, the replacement of the standard petalled knop by other ones is ill understood and it would be a mistake to assume that the presence here of a variant is a mark of lateness. Two features, however, in the present brooch call for comment: the hole in the catch-plate and the decoration on the catch-plate return. Pierced catch-plates in general seem to disappear in the later 1st century when the separate loop and collar, or the cast-on version of that, begins to appear. However, there is a great number of brooches with neither and this shows that a loop or piercing was not a necessary feature. To find a catch-plate piercing on a brooch which was automatically provided with a loop and collar is unusual. Decoration on the return of the catch-plate is uncommon and tends to occur on Colchester Derivatives dating to the later 1st and possibly the early 2nd century. Both features may suggest a date no later than AD 125 and the lack of a curve in the lower bow could show that it is not as early as *c* AD 75.

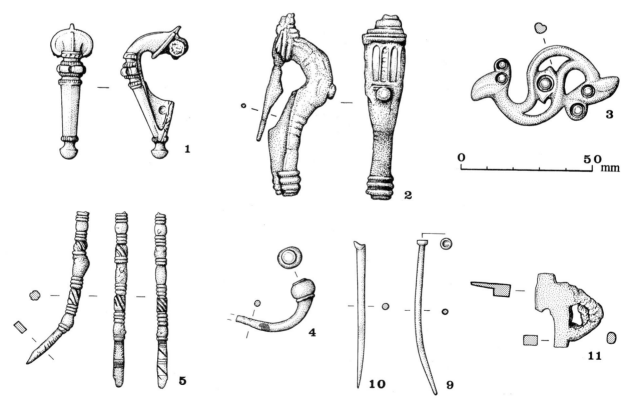

Illus 120
Roman period bronze brooches and assorted artefacts.

THE FIBULA (illus 120, *2*)

The design of fibula *2* (SF420), with its marked curve at the top of the profile and the strong recurve below, is distinctive and belongs to a particular group in a fairly eclectic series whose full details have yet to be worked out. The chronology of the whole is also not well established. Fortunately, the present brooch is a member of the most common group and its dating is: Silchester, *c* AD 100–120 (Cotton 1947, 145, fig 8,3); Derby, AD 115–140 (Mackreth 1985, 213–214, fig 128,33); Biglands, AD 125–180/197 (Potter 1977, 171, fig 11,16). Although meagre, the evidence points firmly to the 2nd century and, as for other bow brooches, suggests a terminal date for manufacture in the third quarter.

THE DRAGONESQUE BROOCH (SF407) (illus 120, *3*)

The earliest known Dragonesque, also with a bowed profile, is one from Longthorpe, Cambridgeshire: Claudian–Neronian (Dannell & Wild 1987, 87, fig 21,9). A similarly plain iron example from Maiden Castle, although found in the late levels of the circular hut, may also be early (Wheeler 1943, 262, fig 85, 32). This distinctive pattern was recognised by R G Collingwood as being the earliest form of Dragonesque although the example he gave has not been independently published with the dating evidence: Braughing, associated with Rosette brooches and other objects hardly later than the Conquest itself (Collingwood 1930, 53, fig 11a). The quality of design shown by the present example finds a good parallel in one from Lakenheath, Suffolk, unfortunately with no dating (Fox 1958, pl 41b). The only other plain specimen to have a date comes from Rudston where its context was placed around AD 90–100 (Stead 1980, 95, fig 61,17) and the same site produced another plain brooch whose context was dated AD 140–160 (*ibid*, 95, fig 61,16). Turning now to the enamelled series, the dating evidence is: Old Winteringham, Neronian–early Flavian (Stead 1976, 198, fig 99,11); Newstead, two examples, AD 80–*c* 200 (Curle 1911, 398, fig 1; 320, pl LXXXV,7); Milking Gap, Northumberland, Trajanic? (Daniels 1978, 168); Wroxeter, up to AD 130 (Bushe-Fox 1916, 24, pl XVI, 9); Watercrook, *c* AD 110–140 (Potter 1979, 210–211, fig 84,14); Scole, Norfolk, two examples, Trajanic-mid-Antonine (Rogerson 1977, 107–109, 133–134, fig 55,10,11). The conclusion is that the type almost certainly originated in southern England and the overall date-range is from the middle of the 1st century AD to *c* AD 150 and the enamelled series may have ceased to be made before then. The absence of enamel, coupled with the openwork design, may suggest that the present brooch is earlier than AD 100–125.

THE PENANNULAR BROOCH (SF366) (illus 120, *4*)

The penannular brooch is relatively common type; the distribution covers the whole of Roman Britain and the only distinction which can be made is that, in the Pennines and to the north, the pin is more often arched than not, straight pins being more prevalent to the south. Most examples have only one moulding next to the boss, as here, and it is probable that the presence of two or three has no chronological significance. The dating for those with only one moulding next to the boss is: Maiden Castle, 150–100 BC, (Wheeler 1943, 264, fig 86, 2); Hod Hill, before AD 50 (Brailsford 1962, 12, fig 11, E, 2; Richmond 1968, 117–119); Waddon Hill, Dorset, *c* AD 50–60/65 (Webster 1981, 62, fig 25, 12); Colchester, *c* AD 75/80–80/85 (Crummy 1983, 18, fig 15,95); Prestatyn, AD 70s–160 (Mackreth 1989, 98, fig 40,25); Newstead, AD 80–*c* 200 (Curle 1911, pl LXXXVIII, 3); Ilchester, early 2nd century (Leach 1982, 247, fig 117, 28); Rudston, AD *c* 140-160 (Stead 1980, 95, fig 62, 21); Mumrills, AD 140–*c* 163 (Macdonald & Curle 1929, 555, fig 115–116); Vindolanda, c AD 223-225 (Bidwell 1985, fig 39,12); Rudston, 3rd century AD (Stead 1980, 95, fig 62, 23). The one from Maiden Castle has a small diameter in relation to the section of the ring. The example from Mumrills also has the flat, raised face next to the opening found on the present specimen. The indicated date-range is from the 2nd century BC to, perhaps, the early 3rd century AD, although a cut-off date in the 2nd century may be more appropriate.

POSSIBLE BRACELET OR HAIR PIN (SF 357) (illus 120, *5*)

A good parallel for the decorative scheme seen on object *5* is found on bracelets, and these are mainly late Roman. A similar bracelet fragment is known from the hillfort at Clogher, Co Tyrone and has been dated to the 4th century (Young, S 1989, 186, no 172). Southern British parallels for hair pins are discussed by Cool (1990).

BROOCHES & BRONZEWORK CATALOGUE

★ = illustrated (illus 120)

1 H (6)   381   SF133★
Trumpet Brooch. The spring is a repair held to the body of the brooch by an axis bar with burred ends passing through the coils and a loop behind the head of the bow. The new pin appears to have been on the left, instead of on the right as is usual. Originally, the spring had an internal chord held in place by the ends of a wire loop, rising above the head, seated in a rolled sheet tube. The waist of the loop would have been held by a collar. The nib on the head was intended to prevent this arrangement from being pushed forward over the head. The trumpet is plain, apart from a ridge down the middle and is slightly waisted. The knob has a central moulding, with a scalloped plan, between two thinner beaded mouldings. Above and below these is a flute and then a double moulding, the larger one of which was beaded. The lower bow is plain with a median arris. The foot-knob, projecting below the catch-plate, consists of a rounded boss under a waist and topped by a beaded moulding. The catch-plate has a small circular hole and the return has the remains of a chevron made of paired grooves along it, possibly with another pair across the top. The brooch shows signs of considerable wear.

2 X (3)   1387   SF420★
Unclassified fibula. The poor condition of this brooch obscures some of the detail. The axis bar of the hinged pin is housed in a semi-circular projection behind the head-plate. This is made up of three cross-mouldings above a base which has two more. There may have been a cast-on loop on the top. The underside of the head-plate is semi-circular and has a groove along it. The upper bow is rounded underneath, curved in profile and has a flat front face ending below in either a point or a curve. The main face has a raised centre with three enamelled strips running down it. The colours have almost completely disappeared, but there appears to have been a chequered pattern of orange-red alternating with another colour. The plain lower bow has an arris down the front. The foot-knob, of four cross-mouldings, lies under the catch-plate.

3 X (3)   1406   SF407★
Dragonesque brooch. The pin is missing. The form of the brooch is that of an S with a zoomorphic head at each end. Each head has an eye in the form of a boss with a groove around it. The snout finishes in a similar boss. The surface of each head is modelled in curvilinear relief to give a trumpet between the bosses and with a lobe running up the back of the ear. The central element of the S is broad and has openwork ornament. In the centre is a boss lying in a hollow between two crude trumpet shapes. The containing frame has a rounded upper surface, the two arms joining to form the necks of the heads. The earliest Dragonesques appear to have been plain, solid plates, furnished with the characteristic terminals. One from Wetwang, in iron and not yet published in detail, is also bowed in profile (Hull & Hawkes 1987, 168, 73 pl 50, 2D).

4 H (3)   522   SF366★
Penannular Brooch. Only a distorted fragment survives. The extant terminal consists of a boss with a basal moulding next to the ring, and a flat, raised face next to the opening.

5 H (4)   493   SF357★
Possible Bracelet or Hair Pin. Two fragments both originally part of the same object. One fragment consists of strip metal one side of which is decorated: down the middle is a groove showing signs of dying out suggesting that what survives is near the end of an object. Along each edge is a series of small nicks. The second fragment is also part of a decorated rod. Closer inspection shows that it does not have a uniform section. Most of the object has a circular section and moulded with bead-and-reel ornament: three reels between the five beads, and three more at the end. One bead is a cylinder with spiral grooving. The remaining part has a thin rectangular section, widening towards the broken end, and decorated with a kind of repeat of the bead-and-reel being divided into panels by cross-grooves. On one side, the panels have diagonal lines in them, on the other they seem to be plain but the borders have small nicks. The end face of the circular-sectioned part is squared and seems to have had a very narrow projection rising from the centre.

6 H (3)   522   SF364
Mount; L = 8mm; W = 3mm (JC)

7 X (3)   1387   SF768
Mount; L = 9mm; W = 6mm (JC)
Objects no 6 (SF364) and 7 (SF768) are small, broken, corrugated, sheet mount fragments, without rivet holes. Corrugation is a well recognised means of stiffening thin sheet metal (Shell & Robinson 1988, 256).

8 X (3)   1387   SF775
A headless copper-alloy tack/nail, with a slightly faceted shank. L = 34mm (JC)

9 X (3)   1402   SF404★
A pin, with a straight shaft, slightly splayed at the top to form a grip for a small circular ahead. The head is broken, and it is therefore unclear whether it is formed from a wound strip of metal, or from separate soldered parts. L = 61mm; shaft diam = 2mm; head diam = 3mm (JC)

10 X (6)   1356   SF822★
A pin with a straight evenly tapering shaft, and an irregular globular head. The head is broken making the original form unclear. L = 56 mm, shaft diam = 2 mm. Although this comes from a medieval context such form as is preserved suggests that it is likely to be of later prehistoric or early medieval date (Foster 1990) (STD).

11 H (3)   516   SF197★
An eyed fitting, or possibly a small handle, formed in two pieces, probably soldered together. The main section is cast and is stepped in both outline and cross-section to give a square-ended projection, possibly for a cord etc to be wrapped around and caught. The eye is formed from a bent length of rod, considerably more corroded than the cast part, and attached to the broader length of the base. L = 28mm; H = 25mm; max W = 5mm. (JC)

Off-cuts of sheet bronze. There are five fragments of bronze sheeting which were apparently discarded during some manufacturing process. The largest of the off-cuts is 20 by 15mm. All of the sheets are listed together in the medieval copper-alloy artefacts 4.3.4.

4.3 THE MEDIEVAL PERIOD ASSEMBLAGE

4.3.1 INTRODUCTION

The small finds provide some evidence for the continued occupation of the rock in the post-Roman period. These early Medieval or Dark Age finds are few (illus 121) and are not closely datable, but they hint at occupation in the period of the Gododdin even if they can shed little light on the nature of that occupation.

Illus 121
A selection of medieval finds.

There are few artefacts which reflect the military character of the Castle and even fewer which might be regarded as royal in character. The shortage of the former type of artefact might be explained by the efficiency of the smiths, who probably recycled most of the scrap which might have been expected from a castle smithy. Only two Medieval weapons were recovered, a spearhead and an arrowhead (illus 130). No armour was recovered.

The almost complete absence of high status artefacts such as might have been expected from a royal residence probably testifies to the origins of the materials deposited on the Mills Mount in the years before and after the smithy was active. In particular the great mass of soil deposited on Mills Mount as levelling in the 16th century (Phase 8) seems likely to have been brought in from outside, so that the artefacts found (such as the wide range of medieval pottery types, illus 122–6) are perhaps, in the main, indicative of life in the burgh rather than of the Castle itself.

Certainly the most interesting aspect of the Medieval assemblage concerns the smithy and its products. The relative absence of weaponry may be a sign that the armourers were working elsewhere and that this workshop catered for the mundane domestic needs. It certainly seems as though the industrial area was relatively extensive judging from the spread of industrial features. The objects turned out by the excavated smithy workshop (or at least brought into it as scrap) include quantities of building hardware (especially nails), some horse gear, a few tools and a number of more complex items such as locks (illus 130–3). Of the small number of tools recovered, few appear to have been for smithing. It does seem likely that tools, including knives, were made, repaired and provided with handles here.

Apart from the handles, there are very few bone artefacts and few traces of bone-working (which in any case is likely to reflect activity outside of the Castle). Among the artefacts which were recovered were a tuning peg from a stringed musical instrument (illus 121; 127, 5) and two well-made, but enigmatic handles (illus 121; 127, 6, 7).

The bronzework included various buckles, belt plates and lace-ends, but there were also a couple of nice pieces of horse gear: a heraldic pendant (illus 121; 127, 2) and a bell (1). The off-cut scraps suggest that sheet copper was being commonly worked in the smithy.

4.3.2 THE MEDIEVAL POTTERY

Robert S Will

This report deals mainly with the pottery from Mills Mount (Area H) where the main excavation was concentrated and the most securely stratified pottery was found, although the material from all areas was examined. All of the Medieval, Post-Medieval and modern sherds recovered from the Castle are included in the archive catalogue together with fabric descriptions (see 4.3.2mf, 1: B5–D12). The assemblage contains some 5000 Medieval sherds. The Post-Medieval and modern pottery are discussed below (4.4.2).

Initially the assemblage was extensively examined for joins: this was largely unsuccessful as only one full reconstruction for the locally produced material was possible, although some profiles for imported vessels were obtained (illus 122). The Medieval sherds came from a large midden deposit and were often quite small and badly abraded. This midden appears to have been in use over a long period of time and subject to constant disturbance. As a result the sherds were often scattered and re-deposited within the midden (see above Phases 6 and 7, 3.3.3). There was little chronologically significant stratigraphy in the midden due to this disturbance, although the lower levels suffered less. Some of the earlier pottery came from these less disturbed levels, including a group of 14th-century cooking pot rims (illus 123, 24). In one instance, large groups of sherds from the same vessel were recovered but these failed to provide a full profile, although partial reconstructions were possible (illus 123, 30).

Most of the Medieval sherds seem to date from the 15th century with residual or disturbed 14th-century sherds mixed through the deposit. The earlier sherds are generally thinner-walled and of a better quality than the later sherds. The pottery belongs to two main traditions: Scottish East Coast White Gritty Ware and Scottish Post-Medieval Reduced Ware. These probably share the same production areas and show considerable similarities in style and technique. The work already published on White Gritty and its problems (Haggarty G 1980a, 1984; Brooks 1980; Cox et al 1984; Crowdy 1986) suggested that there was little point in dividing the sherds into fabric groups and similarly no geological analysis was pursued.

DESCRIPTION AND DISCUSSION

The sherds represent mainly cooking/storage jars and jugs. These vessels share the same characteristics: flat or sagging bases, knife trimming of the base and walls, and applied or stamped decoration. The jugs tend to be highly decorated and glazed compared to the storage vessels which tend to be unglazed or only partially glazed. Both straight-sided and globular storage jars are present although sherd size and the lack of complete profiles make it difficult to establish quantities or a typology. The jugs have either grooved or combed strap handles, the unglazed handles tend to be grooved.

THE IMPORTED POTTERY (illus 122)

The 15th-century date for the midden deposit is supported by the sherds of imported pottery, although some of these imports could be earlier; the content of the midden as a whole supports deposition in the 15th century. The largest group of imported sherds represent Seigburg and Langerwehe stoneware vessels. One sherd (illus 122, 2) represents a Siegburg drinking bowl; these were popular in the period 1450–1550 and are quite rare in Britain, although one has already been found in Edinburgh (Schofield 1976). Three conjoining sherds, including the base, were found and are

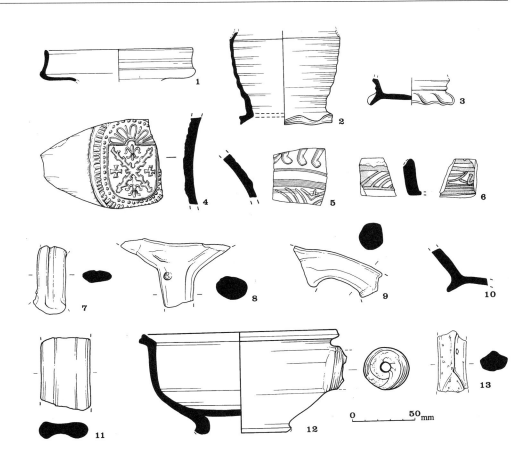

Illus 122
Imported medieval
pottery.

probably from a beaker or flask, although without the upper portion it is impossible to say. Unfortunately, little can be said about the remaining Siegburg and Langerwehe sherds as only four base sherds and 34 body sherds were found, making detailed identification of vessel type impossible. The lack of rim sherds hinders closer dating as it is the rims that are most chronologically sensitive not the characteristic frilled bases. Nevertheless the base sherds and body sherds represent at least four, or possibly five, different stoneware vessels that can be paralleled with the stoneware found at the Edinburgh High Street excavation (Schofield 1978).

One Spanish sherd was found within the midden and appears to be Late Andalusian or Early Valencian lustreware, dating to the late 14th or early 15th century (illus 122, 6). The sherd is from the rim of a flanged dish and is decorated with inter-lacing foliage in a metallic copper-coloured lustre. These vessels are relatively rare in Britain and only three sherds have been found in Scotland. These represent a limited trade in the vessels themselves as opposed to their use as containers (Hurst 1977).

A sherd of Beauvais Sgraffito ware (illus 122, 5) was also found within the midden and would again date to the first half of the 16th century. The sherd has a red/brown slip that has been scored to leave a yellow-white design of foliage and gothic script; unfortunately the sherd is not large enough for the letter or motto to be legible. The underside is unglazed but has an impressed semi-circle on it.

Several sherds of Dutch Redware (illus 122, 7–10) were found from the midden and were unglazed apart from splashes of clear glaze. This would suggest a late 14th- to 15th-century date. Although uncommon in Britain, these vessels were imported into Newcastle in large numbers from the 14th century.

Several conjoining sherds of Saintonge ware were found and would appear to represent a small bowl with a spout or handle (illus 122, 12). Whether this was part of a more elaborate vessel is hard to say and more research is required. Again this would date to the 15th or 16th centuries.

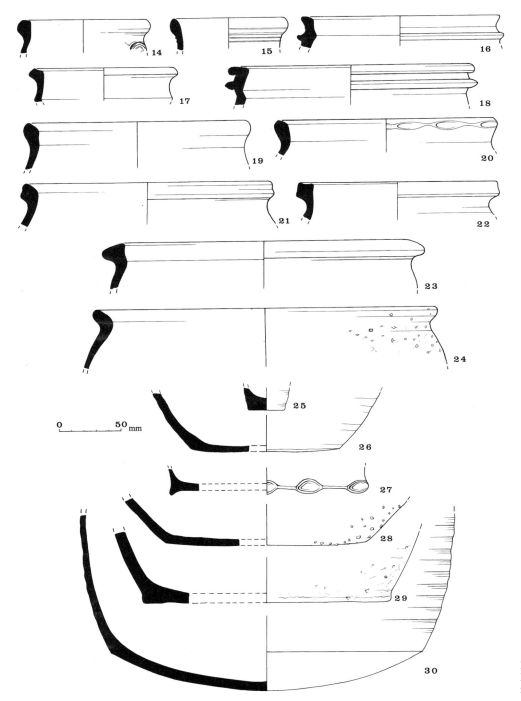

Illus 123
Local medieval wares
rims and bases.

The main medieval deposit (illus 122, *13*) produced a handle that may be from a Loire Jug which could date to the 14th century (Cruden 1956).

The medallion from a Frechen Bellarmine (illus 122, *4*) was found from the upper layers of Area H/X and would appear to be from the late 16th century. Unfortunately no other sherds from the vessel were recovered.

INDUSTRIAL VESSELS

The medieval deposits in Area H produced sherds from two presumably industrial or medical vessels. The most complete was a group of 15 conjoining sherds that represent about 50% percent of a bell-shaped

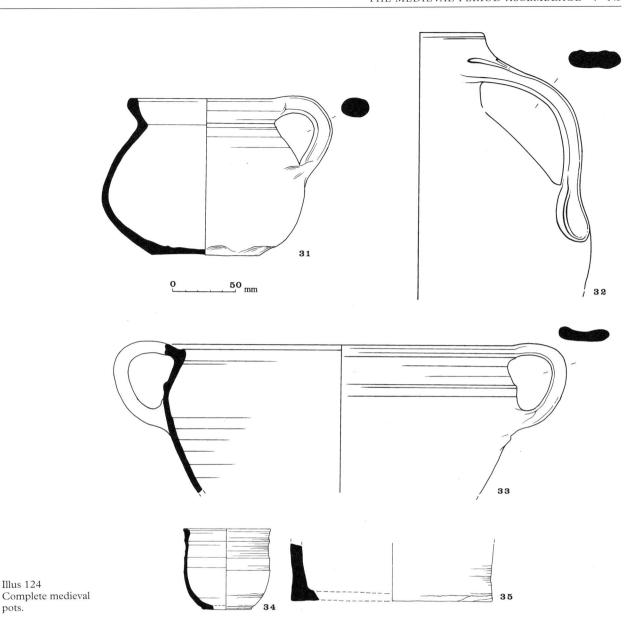

Illus 124
Complete medieval
pots.

crucible (illus 124, *34*). The fabric is grey and reduced to the point of vitrification, presumably as a result of repeated firing or heating. The vessel is well made, wheel-thrown with pronounced rilling on the outside. The crucible has a flattened rim with a slight cordon. The rim has yellow staining on both sides, presumably a residue from the industrial/medical process that the crucible was used for.

The other sherd of possible industrial origin is a base angle sherd in a pink gritty fabric (illus 124, *35*). The vessel has a flat base and the walls seem to slope inwards; unfortunately the sherd is not big enough to be sure of this. There is pronounced rilling on both the inner and outer wall surfaces and the vessel seems to be coated with a black polished slip.

The complete base of a small drug pot was also recovered (illus 123, *25*). Only the base and the beginnings of the walls survive. The pot is made from a white gritty fabric and seems to be undecorated.

Surprisingly there was very little Yorkshire (Scarborough type) ware recovered, only four sherds, all of which came from modern deposits. The sherds consist of two sherds of 'scales' from a Knight's jug (illus 125, *42*) and two sherds of a flat rim. These would date to the period 1290–1330 (Farmer 1979).

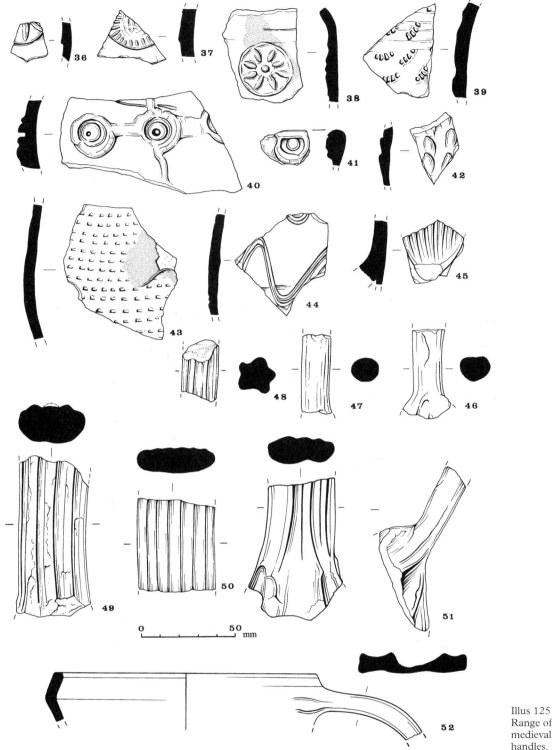

Illus 125
Range of domestic medieval decoration and handles.

SUMMARY

In sum this assemblage represents a collection of largely domestic vessels of local manufacture, dating from the 14th–17th centuries. In addition there are a few exotic imports from Germany and the Low Countries and several interesting local vessels of industrial or medical function. As a collection this is not as distinguished as might be expected from a Royal castle.

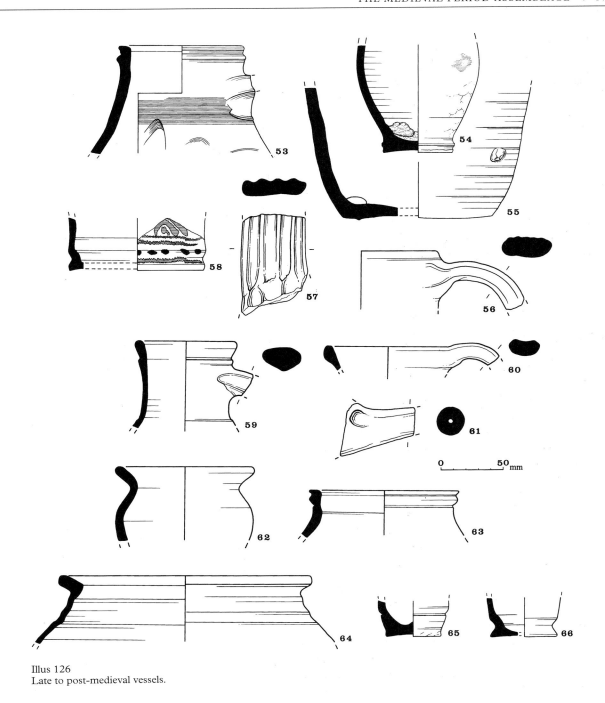

Illus 126
Late to post-medieval vessels.

SELECT MEDIEVAL POTTERY CATALOGUE

The following is a select catalogue of the pottery from Edinburgh Castle. It includes only those vessels which are illustrated. A full catalogue is published in microfiche (4.3.2.1mf, 1: B5–D12, 1: E1–13).

Cat No	Area	(Phase)	Context	Description
				IMPORTS (illus 122)
1	H/X	(9)	1346	German (Langerwehe) Stoneware Cup
2	X	(9)	1344	German (Siegburg) Stoneware frilled beaker
3	H	(7)	344	German (Siegburg) Stoneware frilled beaker
4	X	(9)	1344	Frechen Bellarmine medallion
5	X	(8)	1351	Beauvais Sgraffito
6	X	(7)	1353	Late Andalusian or Early Valensian Lustreware
7	X	(10)	1361	Dutch Redware handle

8	X	(7)	1353	Dutch Redware handle
9	X	(9)	1069	Dutch Redware handle
10	X	(8)	1351	Dutch Redware
11	H/X	(9)	1346	Saintonge jug handle
12	H/X	(8)	586	Saintonge bowl
13	H	(7)	344	Loire jug handle

LOCAL WARES – RIMS AND BASES (illus 123)

14	H	(7)	366	Jug rim
15	H	(6)	391	Jug rim
16	H	(7)	332	Cooking pot rim
17	H	(9)	294	Jug rim
18	H	(8)	586	Cooking pot rim
19	H	(6)	381	Cooking pot rim
20	H	unstratified		Cooking pot rim
21	H	(6)	596	Cooking pot rim
22	H	(9)	294	Cooking pot rim
23	H	(9)	298	Cooking pot rim
24	H	(5)	433	Cooking pot rim
25	H	(7)	344 (SF167)	Ointment pot base
26	H	(7)	399	Pot/Jug base
27	O		1022	Jug Base?
28	H	(7)	440	Cooking pot base?
29	H	(7)	344	Cooking pot base?
30	H	(6)	390 (SF139)	Cooking pot base

COMPLETE AND RECONSTRUCTED POTS (illus 124)

31	H/X	(8)	586	Chamber pot
32	X	(7)	1353	White Grittyware jug profile
33	H	(7)	346	Handled bowl
34	H	(7)	366	Crucible
35	H	(7)	344	Industrial vessel

RANGE OF DOMESTIC DECORATION AND HANDLES (illus 125)

| 36 | H | (7) | 344 | Applied rosette |

37	H	(7)	344	Applied rosette
38	H	(7)	344	Complete rosette
39	H	(9)	294	Stamped decoration
40	H	(6)	381	Dot and eye decoration
41	H	(7)	344	Dot and eye decoration
42	H	(9)	294	Scale-Aquamanile Scarborough
43	H	(6)	575	Rouletting incised
44	H	(8)	330	Incised line decoration
45	H	(7)	340	Incised, possible Scarborough
46	H	(8)	298	Rod handle
47	H	(7)	344	Rod handle
48	H		?302	Ribbed handle
49	H	(7)	346	Strap handle
50	H	(9)	349	Strap handle
51	H	(7)	344	Spout, ? puzzle jug
52	H	(7)	366	Rim and handle

LATE TO POST-MEDIEVAL POTS (illus 126)

53	L		811	Reduced green-glazed jug neck
54	L		814	Unglazed jug containing pigment
55	L		814	Reduced green-glazed jug base
56	X	(7)	1353	Jug handle
57	X	(7)	1353	Strap handle
58	L		825	Tin-glazed ? jug
59	K		720	Jug
60	K		729	Jug
61	G		111	Pipkin leg – ?Dutch
62	O		1020	Jar
63	F		54	Jar
64	X	(6)	1442	Jar
65	X	(10)	1342	Small jar
66	X	(10)	1062	Small jar

4.3.3 MEDIEVAL BONEWORK

Jane Clark, with contributions from Sally M Foster (SF)

DISCUSSION

Of the two combs recovered, the form of the more complete example (illus 127, *1*) suggests it is an early Medieval type, although there are unfortunately very few later medieval Scottish combs (cf Alcock and Alcock 1992) with which to compare it. In the absence of complete dimensions and the form of the end plate, the main features of the comb are the shape of its connecting plate, the decoration, the teeth of differing thicknesses, and a general impression that the comb was long and thin rather than short and squat. Scottish Medieval combs are mainly known from the Atlantic Province and the Southwest, double-sided composite examples falling broadly into three categories (Foster 1990):

The 'Roman type' with one set of teeth markedly coarser than the other set; whilst this is a feature of some later combs, this variety tends to be short by comparison to depth when compared to the later varieties. Decorative profiling of the end plate is common on these combs. Specifically Roman type combs are rare in Scotland, all examples being from the south, and recognition is mainly on the basis of form rather than context. Most notable are the examples from Keil Cave (Ritchie 1967) where there was intermittent activity from the 3rd century onwards.

The 'Dark Age type A' group: double-sided combs which are distinguished from Anglo-Saxon double-sided combs in their form and distribution. In form they are closer to a Roman original: that is, short in comparison to height (Curle 1982 type A; overlap with Dunlevy 1988 Irish class B; MacGregor 1985, 94). The connecting plate is usually deep and flat in cross-section and sometimes a narrow area is left in reserve at the extremities of the end plate. The teeth graduate becoming progressively shorter over the last 30mm

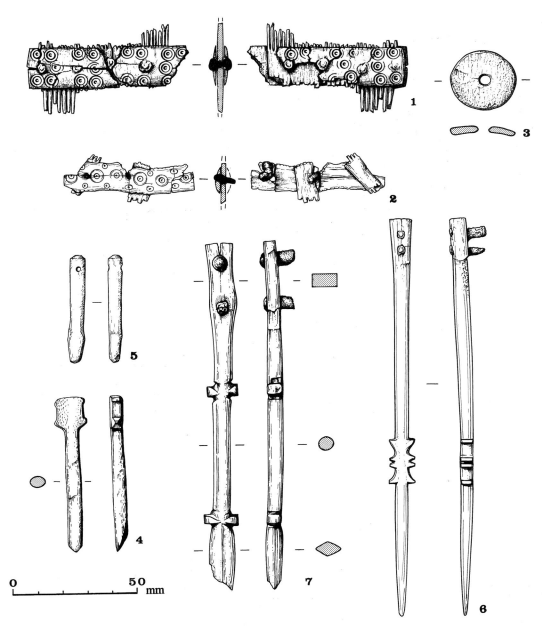

Illus 127
Medieval bone combs and assorted small artefacts.

or so of each end-plate, resulting in triangular or D-shaped solid zones which are generally decorated. None of the Scottish examples are from contexts which can be dated to earlier than the 7th century.

The 'Dark Age type B' (Curle 1982, 156) group: combs which share some similarities with Irish classes D1–2 (Dunlevy 1988): the teeth are not graduated (or are only very slightly graduated), and the connecting plates do not usually extend to the end of the comb where there is a narrow vertical band for an end space. The connecting plates are usually not bevelled, but shallow and semi-elliptical in form, and overall decoration is less ornate. There are few examples of this type in Scotland. This form is found mainly in Orkney, Caithness and rarely in the Western Isles, but there is an example from St Ford's Links, Fife (Munro 1901, fig 2). With one exception (Curle 1982, no 204) all dated examples come from Norse contexts (eg Buckquoy, Ritchie 1977, nos 53 & 55). But on the basis of the representation of these combs on Pictish Class II stones (Curle 1982, 57) and the existence of Anglo-Saxon and 4th- to 10th-century

Irish parallels (Dunlevy 1988, 359) at the latest an 8th-century date can be suggested for the Scottish examples.

The profile of the connecting plates on comb *1* is not typical for combs of either of the first two groups. Similarly it cannot be definitely ascribed to either of the first two types in the absence of end plates. There is also a general impression that the well-preserved comb is not short or squat enough to belong to either of these categories. Although ornate decoration is more typical of these groups than of the Dark Age type B group, on balance it is most likely that the combs are of Dark Age type B, despite the fact that it is not so common for such combs to have teeth of differing thickness. The possibility that the combs are Anglo-Saxon in origin, rather than a local interpretation of an Anglo-Saxon form, cannot be excluded. In which case it would form part of a very small quantity of Anglian material of any date to have been discovered in Scotland. To conclude, the well-preserved comb (1) is probably of 7th- or 8th-century date. (SF)

The tuning peg (illus 127, 5) comes from a stringed instrument with an open structure, tuned from the back, and falls into Lawson's type A IV (Lawson, 1990, fig 201). There are no grooves or stain marks around the string hole, implying the use of an organic string, such as animal gut or horse hair, rather than a metal string. Bone tuning pegs are increasingly recognised finds on medieval sites, the earliest stratified example being dated to the late 12th century (Lawson, 1978, 139, fig 7e), although they are more common from early 14th- through to 17th-century contexts (Lawson, 1990, 711–3; Lawson, 1991, 188–9).

The two riveted bone pins/pointers (SF412 and SF134; illus 127, 6, 7) exhibit the same essential features, but in differing proportions. They are not a pair, although their design implies a common specific function, most probably as some form of pointer, possibly as the decorative tip of a longer shaft. There is no trace of the material to which they were originally riveted, presumably an organic, most probably wood. The lack of known parallels makes any definite interpretation impossible. The features common to both include a flat head with two iron rivets, and a hand-trimmed shaft of roughly circular cross-section, the line of which is broken by expanded, notched zones, which are possibly functional as well as decorative, although there is no wear between the notches or across the shaft. They differ in that SF412 is the more delicate, with a narrower head and shaft, and smaller, more closely set, rivets.

MEDIEVAL BONEWORK CATALOGUE

★= illustrated (illus 127)

BONE COMBS

1   H (4)   493   SF191★

An incomplete bone, possibly antler, double-sided composite comb which includes at one end the original terminals of both connecting plates. The extant comb consists of two teeth plates (of differing width: 28 and 20mm) secured by four iron rivets at their centres and edges to two connecting plates. These are shallow and convex in section with a slightly curved end. The teeth are coarse on both sides, but average about 7 per 10mm on one side and 5 per 10mm on the other. The original full dimensions of the comb cannot be estimated, although it may never have been much wider or longer. The presence of a rivet at the end of the most extreme tooth plate would suggest that there was formerly an end plate here, which may have extended the comb for a further 20mm. Since teeth are cut into the comb after the plates have been riveted together, and there is no sign here of teeth having been cut into the connecting plate (as invariably happens), full-length teeth cannot have been cut into this end plate. Teeth, if they existed, must therefore have been graduated.

Each side of the connecting plate is similarly decorated with dot-in-double-circle ornament. This is arranged in three parallel rows but grouped together in balanced groups of five, if not four, often in combination with a rivet.

Overall dimensions: L = 64mm, W = 38mm, T = 9mm. Connecting plate: 17mm wide, max T = 2mm.(SF)

2   H (6)   440   SF191★

A burnt and incomplete example of a double-sided composite bone comb, similar to the previous entry. The surviving comb has been much distorted by fire but consists of one surviving connecting plate and two portions of teeth plates held together with three iron rivets. The connecting plate is convex in section and decorated with ring-and-dot and dot-in-double circle ornament. A central row of dots surrounded by double rings is aligned with the rivets. Smaller ring-and-dot ornaments run down each edge and are spaced between the central decorations. The teeth of the comb only survive as stumps, but evidently one side was finer than the other. The comb is clearly incomplete so the original size and form cannot be determined.

Overall dimensions: L = 52mm, W = 17mm, T = 8mm. Connecting plate: W = 12mm, T = 2 mm.

BONE PIECES

3   H (5)   409   SF492★

A thin, circular disc of bone, smooth on one face and rough on the other, with a central hole of 5mm diameter. Such discs were used as buttons, either on their own with a central stud, or as formers, covered in thread or cloth. Diam = 26mm.

4   X (6)   1442   SF426★

A rectangular-headed pin with an untapering shank, broken before the point. The corners of the head are rounded and slightly projected. L = 64mm.

5   M (-)   1176   SF383★

A tuning peg for a stringed instrument. The shaft is cylindrical (diam 5mm) and is hand-finished, with longitudinal trim marks. The head is squared, with a rectangular cross-section. The chipped marks around the head suggest that a metal key or wrench was used to turn it. The drilled string hole is at the opposite end of the shaft to the tuning head. L = 43mm.

BONE HANDLES OR POINTERS

6 X (6)   1356   SF412★
A pin/pointer with a shaft of circular cross-section, tapering from a diameter of 7mm to a point. It is decorated with a zone of small, triangular teeth, in a symmetrical design, aligned at right angles to the rivets in the head. The head is of rectangular cross-section (9 × 7mm) with a squared end. The rivets extend 4mm beyond the back face of the head. L = 163mm.

7 H (7)   361   SF134★
A pin/pointer with a shaft of oval cross-section, of diam 6 × 5mm, expanding into a wedged tip of diamond cross-section (10 × 6mm), which is broken across the tapering point. There are two areas of square-toothed design, forming small cross bars to the shaft, and marked with small, diagonally cut lines crossing the shaft. These cuts are very regular, and are decorative rather than wear marks. The cross bar nearer the riveted end is further defined by rounded notches cut into the shaft. The head is of rectangular cross-section (10 × 5mm), with a slightly wavy outline and squared, split end. The rivets extend 6mm beyond the back face of the head. L = 143mm

8 H (7)   332   SF108
A broken tine of red deer antler with a single transverse perforation (7mm diam); c 45mm from the tip. It was probably a coarse needle. L = 85mm

There are three cut antler tines, and one cut cattle horn core, all from medieval contexts.

Area (phase)	context	SF	Description
H (7)	395 373	tine	L = 87mm
X (7)	1353 436	tine	L = 77mm
H (8)	586 430	tine	L = 62mm
H (7)	336 446	horn core	L = 81mm

4.3.4 MEDIEVAL COPPER-ALLOY ARTEFACTS

Jane Clark

CATALOGUE AND DISCUSSION

★= illustrated (illus 128;129)

BELL

1 X (7)   1353   SF392★
The copper-alloy bell (SF392; illus 128, 1) is of conical body, broken around the open-mouthed rim, with a flat, expanded, suspension loop. No trace of a clapper remains. Bells of this size were used as mass bells from the 13th century (Biddle & Hinton, 1990, 725). However, similar bells, from earlier 9th-/10th-century contexts (Goodall 1980, 504, fig 264, 55), suggest further, non-ecclesiastical functions. One bell from Norwich for example, found in an 11th-/12th-century context in association with a large iron buckle, is interpreted as a possible harness bell (Williams, 1988, 67, fig 57, 16). H = 30mm; mouth diam = 32mm.

HORSE HARNESS PENDANT

2 H (9)   279   SF58★
The horse harness pendant (SF058; illus 128, 2) is of cast copper-alloy with gilt and enamel decoration. It is of a typical circular shape (LMMC 1967, 118), with a broken suspension loop. The design, a triple chevron within a shield frame, is a conventional heraldic device (Wilmott 1987, 45–47, fig 12:13). The raised lines of the chevrons and shield are picked out in gilt, with an enamel infill. The bluish-green colour of the surviving traces of enamel may be misleading, resulting from the post-depositional oxidation of, for example, a red enamel (Cronyn, 1990, 133). Harness pendants may have originated in the 12th century, or even earlier (Griffiths 1986b, 1; Hinton 1990, 1047–8), although they can be dated most commonly to the 14th century. As a type form, they were usually more ornamental than strictly heraldic, and their decorative effect is well shown in the details of contemporary manuscript illustrations and aquamaniles (Griffiths 1986, 1, fig 1; illus 128). H = 35mm; W = 23mm

BUCKLES AND BUCKLE PINS

The copper-alloy buckles include a D-shaped buckle (SF355; illus 128, 3), an annular buckle or brooch (SF139; illus 128, 5), a double buckle (SF758; illus 128, 7), and two possible buckle pins (SF396 and SF123).

3 H (4)   493   SF355★
D-shaped buckles have a long chronological sequence. Early medieval examples are known from 6th-/7th-century Anglo-Saxon burial contexts (White 1990, 135–6, fig 6), and from 7th-/8th-century Irish occupation contexts (Hencken 1950, 66; fig 11, 323). The broad-bowed frame of the Castle buckle, stepped above and below the bulbous pin stem, is a common 13th-/ 14th-century form (Hinton 1990, 514; fig 130, 1124, 1126; Goodall 1991, 148–9; fig 114, 586). The iron pin is most probably a repair. L = 37mm; W = 56mm

4 X (4)   1382   SF396
SF396 is a possible buckle pin, now badly corroded and bent. L = 53mm.

5 H (6)   390   SF139★
The annular frame of SF139 is common to both brooches and buckles found in late 13th- to 15th-century contexts. Such forms functioned as brooches, at the necks of garments (Goodall 1980, fiche 2 B13), or as buckles, to secure the hose or breche (Russell-Smith 1956, 218–21). Distinction between the two may rely on stylistic criteria, for example between plain buckles and decorated brooches (Hinton 1990, 511). A plain example from Leicester, for example, found with fragments of leather attached to the frame and pin, may confidently be described as a buckle (Clay 1981, 133; fig 48, 24). Diam = 44mm.

6 H (7)   346   SF123
A possible buckle pin, made from a small, thin strip of copper-alloy, with a down-turned, rounded end. L = 19mm.

7 X (9)   1344   SF758★
A wide, double buckle, of a type first seen in 14th-century contexts, but more common from the 15th century (Hinton 1990a, 521; fig 132, 1206) and later, post-Medieval, contexts (Goodall 1983, 231; fig 1:9). The frame is of bevelled profile, with finishing file marks on the back face. L = 45mm; W = 44mm.

BELT PLATES, STRAP ENDS AND BUCKLE PLATES

Belt plates, in the form of strap ends, buckle plates, or belt hasps, were riveted to leather straps to provide reinforcement, protection, decoration and linkage. The three Castle belt plates exhibit a

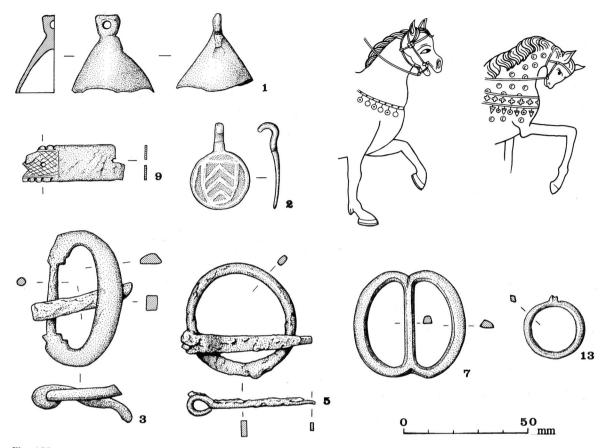

Illus 128
Medieval copper-alloy buckles and decorative objects including a horse harness pendant, with representations of how it would have appeared.

range of quality, from the basic design of the strap end (SF482), to the decorative effect of the buckle plate (SF155; illus 128, 9).

8   H (6)   435   SF482
A strap end, made from a trapezoidal plate, pierced at both ends, and folded double, with the holes aligned for a single rivet. The wider back face is indented with punched chisel marks, made when the object was folded and flattened. L = 19mm; W = 21mm

9   H (7)   344   SF155*
A rectangular buckle plate, broken at the tubular indentation for the buckle pin. The end away from the buckle is cut with a trifid edge, and the front face is decorated with a panel of incised cross-hatched lines, framing a single rivet hole. A buckle plate from Winchester, with similar decoration, is dated to the late 15th-/16th-centuries (Hinton 1990a, 522; fig 133, 1215). L = 40mm; W = 14mm

10   H (8)   306   SF089
A broken belt plate, either a strap end or buckle plate, with three or four torn. rivet holes. L = 45mm; W = 14mm.

11   H (7)   344   SF131
An incomplete ring of diamond cross-section, narrowing at the break. It may be the frame for an annular brooch or buckle, broken at the constriction for the pin. Alternatively, such small rings, of penannular form with tapering ends, have been interpreted as possible earrings (Goodall 1984, 69; fig 110, 17–21; Margeson 1985, 204; fig 35, 1) Diam = 23mm

12   H (7)   344   SF141
A large ring of oval cross-section. It may have been the frame for a large buckle, although there is no constriction for, or wear from, a pin. Alternatively, it may have been a simple ring, used, for example, as a belt link or as a ring hook for hanging textiles. Diam = 49mm

13   H (8)   328   SF092*
A small ring of diamond cross-section, with a notched projection, probably for use as a link ring with a small catch, rather than as a (broken) finger ring. Diam = 25mm

MOUNTS AND APPLIQUÉ

Copper-alloy mounts and appliques were attached to leather, textile and wooden artefacts, both as decoration and as local points of reinforcement. Tacks were generally used to secure mounts to wooded objects, while rivets were used on leather and textiles. Of the Castle mounts, only one (SF129; illus 129, 19) retains any of its original rivets. Belt fittings, such as strap-ends and buckle plates, are discussed separately. The mounts from medieval and post-Medieval contexts display a range of forms.

14   X (6)   1356   SF411
Stud appliqué. Diam = 15mm.

15   H (8)   586   SF820
Stud appliqué. Diam = 9mm

SF411 and SF820 are small bosses, with single, central holes. They are probably the broken heads of hollow, domed tacks or studs, for use on leather or textile furnishings. As a type form, such tacks have long-lived parallels from the 12th century (Groves 1990, 1106, fig 361, 4261) through to the post-medieval period.

16   H (8)   297   SF110*
A small rectangular sheet mount, with a central single rivet hole. The shorter sides are cut to form a triple petalled edge, reminiscent of rosette bosses of 13th- to 15th-century date (Harvey 1975, 255; fig 240, 1731; Caldwell 1981, 107; fig 10, 17). The central panel is decorated with four lines, parallel to the shorter edge. L = 10mm; W = 14mm

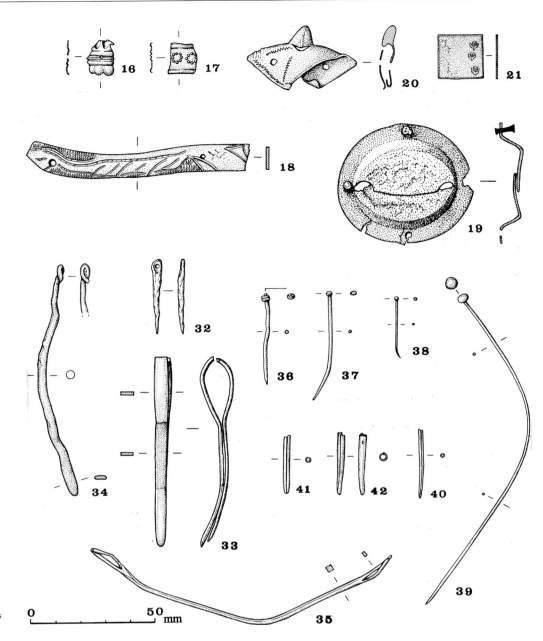

Illus 129
Assorted medieval
copper-alloy objects
including pins.

0   50
|___|___|___|___|___| mm

17 H (9)   294   SF479*
A torn fragment from a strip mount, bent back along its straight edges to clasp its backing material. It is decorated with two small circles, each made up of eight raised dots. L = 13mm; W = 11mm.

18 H (8)   257   SF069*
A strip mount, with two rivet holes, cut to give a slightly angled and wedged end. It is decorated with two uneven, longitudinal lines, infilled with wavy diagonal lines, and bordered with rocker tracer pattern, a design common from the 13/14th centuries. Faint punch marks are visible on the reverse side. L = 90mm; W =10mm

19 H (7)   344   SF129*
A circular bossed mount, at present torn and squashed into a misshapen oval. The boss was originally either flat or slightly domed across the top. The rim is pierced by four, evenly placed, rivet holes, two of which are torn. The other two holes retain their rivets, each 7mm long and burred at both ends. L = 53mm; W = 48mm.

20 H (8)   317   SF319*
A rectangular mount, with a small, central, square-based, pyramidal boss. There are two rivet holes, mid-way along each of the shorter edges. Lines of rocker tracer pattern border the shorter edges and run diagonally from each corner to the base of the boss. In its present condition, it is twisted and flattened. L = 43mm; W = 28mm

21 X (10)   1061   SF757*
A square sheet (c 0.5mm thick) of copper-alloy, stamped with three small thistles, all from the same die. The size and regular shape of the plate suggest that it may have been cut for use as a weight, although the rough alignment of the thistles down the right hand side of one face suggests fairly careless execution, possibly as a trial stamping. A slightly smaller square plate (13 × 13mm), of similar thickness to SF57, and with no stamped or incised markings, was recovered from a 10th- to 11th-century context in Thetford, and has been interpreted as a possible weight (Goodall 1984, 75; fig 114, 66). More definite identification can be given to weights with die stamps of particular date and origin, such as a coin-weight from Southampton, of similar size (square 17 × 17mm), but of thicker sheet metal (c 1.5mm), dated to the late 16th century and sourced to Antwerp (Dolley 1975, 250–2; Harvey 1975, 264; fig 244, 1816). L = 18mm; W = 18mm

SHEET COPPER ARTEFACTS (NOT ILLUSTRATED)

The miscellaneous sheet copper-alloy artefacts include two ring collars, a staple, and fragments of strip and sheet objects.

22 H (5)   433   SF173
A plain ring collar. Diam = 23mm; H = 8mm.

23 X (9)   1064   SF754
A ring collar, with a slightly inturned lip (W 1.5mm). Diam = 19mm; H = 8mm.

24 X (6)   1356   SF761
A staple/clip of strip sheet. The strip is bent so that the ends meet centrally and turn outwards. L = 22mm; W = 5mm.

25 H (7)   344   SF135
A strip fragment, decorated with rocker tracer pattern along the length of one face. L = 30mm; W = 5mm

26 H (8)   290   SF111
A curved binding/framing strip, with three, unevenly spaced, rivet holes along its length. L = 46mm; W = 9mm

27 H (6)   575   SF342
A torn, folded fragment of thin sheet, with two converging, cut sides. L = 87mm; W = 40mm

28 H (7)   336   SF125
A torn sheet, with a single rivet hole in the angled corner of two converging, cut sides, and a rounded notch cut into one edge. L = 47mm; W = 24mm

29 H (8)   334   SF122
A very fragmentary sheet fitting/binding. Two fragments retain lozenge-shaped sheet rivets, which are now folded flat, but which would have originally been the means of attachment to a backing material, probably organic. Largest fragment. L = 31mm; W = 20mm.

COPPER-ALLOY TOOLS

The copper-alloy tools include three needles, a netting needle, a pair of tweezers and a possible ear scoop. All are from Medieval and post-Medieval contexts, although the netting needle is probably residual. Two of the needles (SF064 (illus 129, *32*) and SF822) are of wire; the third (SF473) is of tightly rolled sheet. The heads of all three are flattened for the eye. SF064 is complete, with a drilled eye; SF822 and SF473 are broken across the eye.

30 X (6)   1356   SF822
Needle; L = 54mm

31 H (7)   346   SF473
Needle; L = 56mm

32 H (8)   257   SF064
Needle; L = 30mm★

33 H (7)   346   SF124★
These tweezers are made from two strips of copper alloy, joined by a single copper-alloy rivet. The arms are bent apart to form the pincer action, and are cut straight to form a squared grip end. The handle tapers slightly to a rounded end. Tweezers are common finds on Romano-British and Medieval sites. The Castle tweezers are unusual in that they are made from two separate strips of metal, riveted together, rather than from a single strip folded over, as is typical of Romano-British and Medieval examples; nor do they have either of the features associated with many Medieval examples, namely decoration or a slide. L = 79mm

34 H (8)   586   SF410★
A badly corroded length of copper-alloy rod, expanded into a small spatula at one end, and tapering to a point at the other. The point is bent back in a closed loop. This object may have been used as a toilet implement in the same way as the more elaborate, twisted-stemmed examples with small, spooned ends that have been interpreted as unguent spoons or ear-scoops (Margeson 1985, 58; fig 39, 22 & 211; fig 36, 21).

35 X (8)   1350   SF777★
A wire tool, with bifurcated ends. The prongs are flattened, and one of each pair is bent to cross over its partner. Several parallel examples, in both iron and copper-alloy, have been found in Romano-British contexts (Bushe-Fox 1915, 63, fig 22), and are usually interpreted as netting needles. Manning suggests that the iron examples were netting spacers, used to give a uniform mesh size, while those of copper-alloy may have been used as surgical instruments (Manning 1985, 37). However, the fact that the prongs of SF777 are deliberately bent at both ends to close the forks favours Wild's interpretation of such tools as forked shuttles, for use in band or tablet weaving (Wild 1970, 73). L = 124mm

SHORT PINS

The Medieval pins fall into two groups of short pins (max L = 66mm) and long dress/hair pins (L = c 150mm). A number of short pins were used to fasten shrouds in the Coalyard Cemetery (Area M) these are catalogued elsewhere with the post-Medieval artefacts (below 4.4.4).

Short wire-drawn pins would have had a wide range of uses, in fixing garments, upholstery, etc, and have been found in contexts dating back to the 13th century in Winchester (Biddle & Barclay 1990, 560). Wire-drawing is a technique mentioned by Theophilus, writing in the early 12th century, while references to pinners' guilds in York date back to the mid-14th century (Biddle & Barclay 1990, 561–3). The majority of the Castle pins are spiral wound, with heads formed from lengths of wire, sometimes of a thinner diameter than that used for the shank, wound two or three times round the shank, and probably held with a solder such as niello (Caple 1983, 269.). The heads of many have been left as wire-wound (Type 1), but several have been wire-wound and then drop c-stamped, to fix the head more firmly to the shaft, and to form a more rounded shape (Type 2). A third group of pins (Type 3) have small rounded heads of solid metal, probably soldered on.

TYPE 1: WIRE WOUND

Cat no	Area (Phase)	context	SF no	dimensions
-	X (5)	1360	767	L = 10mm
-	X (6)	1377	817	L = 39mm
-	H (7)	368	146	L = 43mm
-	H (7)	368	147	L = 37mm
36	X (7)	1353	764	L = 38mm★
-	H (8)	257	76	L = 21mm
-	H (8)	297	109	L = 36mm
-	H (8)	586	769a	L = 38mm
-	H (8)	586	769b	L = 30mm
-	H (8)	586	769c	L = 30mm
-	X (9)	1346	751	L = 34mm
-	X (9)	1349	753	L = 20mm

TYPE 2: WIRE WOUND AND STAMPED

Cat no	Area (Phase)	context	SF no	dimensions
-	X (6)	1076	755a	L = 26mm
-	X (6)	1076	776	L = 26mm
-	H (8)	353	116	L = 41mm
-	H (9)	270	67	L = 39mm
-	H (10)	256	56a	L = 32mm
-	H (10)	256	56b	L = 25mm

TYPE 3: SOLID HEAD

Cat no	Area (Phase)	context	SF no	dimensions
37	H (8)	298	74	L = 45mm★
38	H (9)	279	59	L = 26mm★
-	X (9)	1346	760	L = 26mm
-	X (10)	1061	763	L = 28mm

SHAFT ONLY

Cat no	Area (Phase)	context	SF no	dimensions
-	X (6)	1076	755b	L = 14mm
-	X (6)	1354	762	L = 42mm
-	H (8)	586	769d	L = 66mm
-	H (8)	586	769e	L = 26mm
-	X (8)	1351	771a	L = 36mm
-	X (8)	1351	771b	L = 20mm
-	X (8)	1351	771c	L = 10mm

LONG PINS

Two long dress or hair pins came from the same context. Both have shafts of drawn wire, and similar globular, mushroom-shaped heads, soldered to the shaft.

Cat no	Area (phase)	context	SF no	dimensions
39	H (7)	344	118	L = 151mm★
-	H (7)	344	130	L = 147mm

POINTS OR TAG ENDS

Copper-alloy points or tag ends were fastened to the ends of leather and textile thongs and laces to stop them fraying or tearing. They are common finds in Medieval contexts from the 16th century, with some examples known from late 14th-century contexts (Biddle & Hinton 1990a, 581–3).

The Castle points do not fall easily into the divisions recognised elsewhere, based on whether they gripped the lace along an inturned seam, or were fastened with a rivet (Oakley 1979, 262–3; Margeson 1985, 204, 211, fig 36; 16–8.). None retains a rivet, although one (SF168) has a single rivet hole, and two (SF057 and SF824) have possible broken rivet holes. The main division is in the shape of the cut metal sheet before it was rolled:

Type 1 points are formed from a rectangular sheet, which, when rolled, gave a straight seam with no overlap between the edges;

Type 2 points are formed from a slightly tapering sheet, so that, when rolled, the edges overlap, often with the finer edge being inturned at the broader end, to grip into the lace.

TYPE 1

Cat no	Area (Phase)	context	SF no	dimensions
-	X (6)	1377	819	L = 25mm
-	H (7)	346	168	L = 22mm
	H (7)	346	781	L = 36mm
40	H (8)	297	485	L = 28mm★
-	H (8)	317	91	L = 23mm
-	H (9)	268	62	L = 20mm
	H (9)	269	63	L = 18mm
41	H (9)	270	66	L = 24mm★
-	H (9)	294	83	L = 24mm
-	H (10)	233	55	L = 30mm
-	H (10)	256	57	L = 31mm

TYPE 2

Cat no	Area (Phase)	context	SF no	dimensions
-	H (6)	163	435	L = 27mm
-	H (6)	481	435	L = 17mm
42	X (6)	824	1076	L = 25mm★
-	H (7)	120	344	L = 21mm
-	H (8)	71	257	L = 13mm

CORRODED

Cat no	Area (Phase)	context	SF no	dimensions
-	H (6)	406	145	L = 30mm
-	H (8)	95	306	L = 20mm
-	H (8)	103	330	L = 36mm
43	H (8)	330	SF096f	

A ferrule made of two sheet tubes, one within the other. The inner tube is tightly rolled and held by the outer tube. The outer tube is closed at one end, with a pinched, open seam along its length. L = 14mm; diam = 6mm

OFF-CUTS AND SHEET FRAGMENTS

The copper-alloy off-cuts include irregularly shaped, cut sheet fragments, and cut lengths of rod and wire. The sheet off-cuts are of a range of shapes, sizes and thicknesses, and include several thin slithers, possibly waste from the manufacture of tag ends. Torn and broken sheet fragments that are too small and misshapen to allow any artefactual description are catalogued as sheet fragments.

SHEET OFF-CUTS

	Area (Phase)	context	SF no	dimensions
-	X (6)	772	1377	72 × 12mm
-	H (7)	115	344	15 × 2mm
-	H (8)	70	257	30 × 1mm
-	H (8)	72	257	20 × 2mm
-	H (8)	78	257	35 × 20mm
-	H (8)	80	257	40 × 8mm
-	H (8)	73	298	10 × 10mm
-	H (8)	88	306	53 × 18mm
-	H (8)	97	335	21 × 7mm
-	H (8)	102	335	63 × 3mm

ROD OFF-CUTS

	Area (phase)	context	SF no	dimensions
-	H (6)	778	575	L = 68mm; D = 2mm
-	H (7)	816	344	L = 45mm; D = 2.5mm

WIRE OFF-CUTS

	Area (phase)	context	SF no	dimensions
-	H (7)	14	343	L = 38mm; D = 1mm
-	H (8)	100	330	L = 26mm; D = 1mm

SHEET FRAGMENTS

Prehistoric or Roman (Phases 2 and 3)

	Area (phase)	context	SF no	dimensions
-	H (2)	327	531	4 × 5mm
-	H (3)	196	516	20 × 15mm
-	H (3)	782	522	6 × 8mm
-	H (3)	201	534	17 × 7m
-	X (3)	774	1402	15 × 12mm

Phases 5 to 9

	Area (phase)	context	SF no	dimensions
-	H (5)	156	409	11 × 4mm
-	H (6)	170	391	18 × 8mm
-	H (6)	483	435	11 × 21mm
-	H (6)	484	435	49 × 6mm
-	X (6)	818	1377	18 × 15mm
-	H (7)	112	344	17 × 12mm
-	H (7)	113	344	21 × 7mm
-	H (7)	119	344	17 × 13mm
-	H (7)	153	344	5 × 3mm
-	H (7)	154	344	32 × 7mm
-	H (7)	136	344	39 × 31mm
-	H (7)	157	344	33 × 22mm
-	H (7)	472	399	32 × 31mm
-	H (8)	77	298	49 × 30mm
-	H (8)	90	306	35 × 8mm
-	H (8)	101	328	15 × 13mm
-	H (8)	107	330	18 × 11mm
-	H (8)	104	337	23 × 20mm
-	H (8)	821	586	15 × 12mm
-	H (9)	75	294	56 × 15mm
44	H (7)	344	SF132	

A body fragment from a cast copper-alloy vessel. Its curvature is very shallow, suggesting a large vessel. There are shallow, horizontal file marks on the outer surface. L = 38mm; H = 47mm.

| 45 | H (8) | 308 | SF84 | |

A fragment of a cast copper-alloy vessel. Its profile is angled, and is probably part of a rim. L = 24mm; H = 20mm

4.3.5 MEDIEVAL IRONWORK

Jane Clark

CATALOGUE WITH DISCUSSION

★ = illustrated (illus 130–133)

KNIFE BLADES AND HANDLE

(illus 130)

The collection of blades and blade fragments includes several complete, or near complete, whittle-tang knives, and one incomplete scale-tang knife. They are of a range of shapes and sizes, reflecting both the general, functionally insignificant, variation noted in many collections of Romano–British (Manning 1985, 108–23) and medieval date (Goodall 1990, a835–60), and

the increasing use of functionally specialised forms, noted from the 12th century, and of growing importance from the 14th century (de Neergaard 1987, 51–57).

The Castle blades fall into four main categories, all common type forms: three forms of whittle-tang blade, none of which are chronologically distinctive, and one of scale-tang. Scale-tangs are unknown in the archaeological record before the 13th century, and did not supplant whittle-tangs in great numbers until the 14th and 15th centuries (Goodall 1990, 838–839; Cowgill 1987, 26).

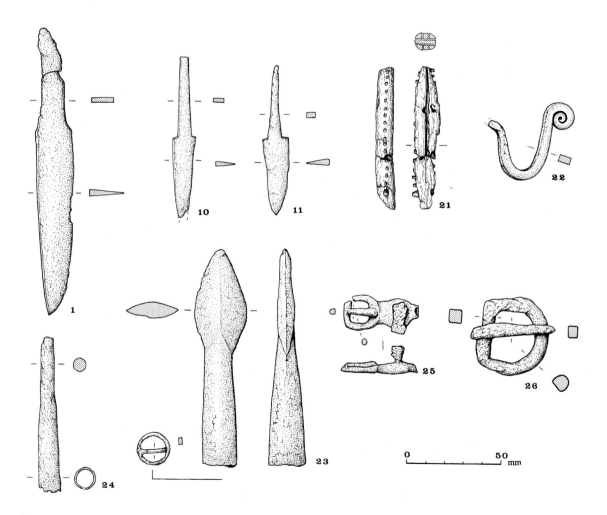

Illus 130
Medieval knives, weapons, iron buckles and fire steel.

The four main categories adopted for the Castle blades are based on shape, and, considering the fragmentary condition of most of the blades, on the angle of the blade edge and back at the juncture with the tang in particular. Even when preservation and completeness is good, the original blade shape and size may have been disguised by frequent whetting during use. A fifth category includes blade fragments, recognised by their triangular cross-section, narrowing either to a cutting point, or to a tang juncture.

The Castle blade types are all of utilitarian form, suitable for everyday, personal use. However, particular features of individual blades may indicate specialised use, and may be compared with manuscript illustrations of the 12th to 15th centuries, depicting the use of knives in a variety of situations, albeit stylized, and on an exaggerated scale (de Neergaard 1987, 57). Some idea of function is reflected in the relative thickness and depth of the blade, an indication of the pressure likely to be applied on the knife when in use. For example, the narrowness of one blade (SF 956), relative to its length, would restrict its use to delicate tasks. The back of this blade is also slightly curved at the tip, emphasizing the fine, long point. Two blades are distinctive for their curved tips. SF144 expands slightly just before the tip, and then curves up into a flattened, rounded point. This has parallels in 14th-century blades from London (Cowgill *et al* 1987, fig 57, 46; fig 60, 86 & 87). SF794 has a curved notch in the tip of the cutting edge, turning down, into a rounded point.

CATEGORIES 1–3: WHITTLE-TANG BLADES

CATEGORY 1

Blades with a straight, or slightly curved, back, continuing the line of the tang, and with a straight, or slightly curved, cutting edge, rising from a curved or sloping shoulder to the tang. This category includes the earliest blade (SF 350, illus 130, 1) from a Phase 3 context. SF350 is also the longest knife in the collection, with a blade length of 105mm, and broken whittle tang of 29mm. It falls into Manning's Type 18b, current throughout the Romano–British period (Manning 1985, 117, figs Q 57 & Q 58).

Cat no	Area (phase)	context	SF no	dimensions
1	H (3)	516	350	L = 134mm; blade depth = 19mm★
2	H (7)	332	955	L = 71mm; blade depth = 11mm
3	H (7)	332	956	L = 9 8mm; blade depth = 11mm
4	H (8)	298	794	L = 71mm; blade depth = 15mm
5	H (8)	306	797	L = 73mm; blade depth = 16mm

CATEGORY 2

Blades with slight, sloping shoulders at the juncture of the tang to a straight back. The straight, or slightly sinuous, cutting edge either rises from the sloping shoulder with the tang, or runs parallel to the back of the blade.

6	H (7)	344	912	L = 53mm; blade depth = 17mm
7	H (7)	361	144	L = 81mm; blade depth = 13mm
8	H (8)	335	854	L = 80mm; blade depth = 28mm
9	X (9)	1064	865	L = 86mm; blade depth = 14mm

CATEGORY 3

This group includes two blades: SF166, from a Phase 4 context, and SF793, from a Phase 8 context. Both have a straight, vertical shoulder either side of a centrally placed whittle tang, with a straight back and cutting edge, tapering from the shoulder to the tip. The two blades differ slightly in width and length.

10	H (4)	461	166	L = 92mm; blade depth = 1mm★
11	H (8)	306	793	L = 82mm; blade depth = 13mm★

CATEGORY 4 SCALE-TANG BLADES

One scale-tang blade (SF800) came from a Phase 7 context, and one possible scale tang fragment (SF811) from a Phase 8 context. SF800 is broken at the juncture of the tang to the cutting edge, but still retains one tubular iron rivet. The back is straight, and the cutting edge rises from the shoulder. Both the back and edge are steeply angled at the tip.

12	H (7)	346	800	L = 120mm; blade depth = 16mm
13	H (8)	295	811	L = 40mm; tang depth = 18mm

CATEGORY 5 BLADE FRAGMENTS

14	H (6)	391	551	L = 78mm; blade depth = 11mm
15	H (6)	435	851	L = 66mm; blade depth = 12mm
16	H (7)	350	801	L = 52mm; blade depth = 25mm
17	H (7)	344	898	L = 86mm; blade depth = 18mm
18	H (7)	344	748	L = 130mm; blade depth = 22mm
19	H (8)	306	798	L = 79mm; blade depth = 20mm
20	H (8)	586	799	L = 120mm; blade depth = 18mm

KNIFE HANDLE

21	H (7)	344	SF859★

A highly decorative handle of elm wood (identification courtesy of Rod McCullough), for a scale-tanged blade. The two pieces of wood, each of semi-spherical section, are riveted to a broken iron tang, and to each other, by tubular copper-alloy rivets. A line of 17, slightly unevenly spaced, copper-alloy tubes is visible running the length of the less corroded side. Not all serve as rivets, with several, which do not extend the depth of the handle, being purely decorative. This handle is closely paralleled by an example from London, dated to the late 14th century (Cowgill *et al* 1987, 95, fig 64: 125). L = 77mm; cross-section of arm = 11 × 8mm.

FIRE STEEL

Sally M Foster

(illus 130)

22	H (3)	516	SF193★

Just under half of a pelta-shaped fire-steel (Arwidsson 1984 type 1a). It consists of a rectangular-sectioned strip of iron originally bent around into an oval with the ends scrolled with two turns. It is broken, with a clean transverse break and bent out of line and axis, just at the point where the inside striking edge starts to expand. A clean break such as this might be expected when tiny slivers of metal are being shaved by a sharp flint or hard flinty stone. Overall dimensions: L = 44mm, W = 47mm. Width of strip = 1-8mm, depth 2–4mm.

Scottish fire-steels are unknown in prehistoric contexts and rare in early Medieval north Britain. The presence in this early level is therefore unusual. Fire-steels similar to this example are best known in Scandinavia where the form has a wide distribution. The oldest examples are found in Vendel contexts (cf Rygh 1885, type 426; Peterson 1951, 433 ff; Arwidsson 1984, 155–6) where they are commonly found in male graves (eg at Birka, Arbman 1943, pl 144). Scottish early Norse examples are known only from 9th-century domestic contexts at Jarlshof (Hamilton 1956, 128, pl XXIXa). This type was the commonest type of fire steel in the 10th and 11th century at Novgorod (Thompson 1967, 76) and similar forms have been found in Scandinavian towns in Medieval and post-Medieval contexts suggesting that they were in use as late as the 19th century (Anderson et al 1971, 141; Grieg 1933, 211). Variations on this form are certainly known from post-medieval Scotland (cf Catalogue of the National Museum of Antiquities of Scotland 1892, 336; Christy 1926, 27 cat nos 300, 27, 197).

Given the possibility of a relatively late (9th-century) date for this example some question about the exact provenance of this find must exist. Alternatively, if the Phase 3 dating is correct, this would become the oldest example from Scotland.

WEAPONS

(illus 130)

23 H (5)   433   SF172*
A small spearhead. It has a short, leaf-shaped blade, and closed shaft of circular cross-section, expanding slightly from the blade, and retaining a single rivet. Typologically, it can be closely compared with Swanton's Anglo-Saxon type F1 spearheads. This type classification has a general Southern distribution, between the Humber and Thames, and is not found in contexts of later than mid-6th-century date (Swanton 1974, 14–16, fig 5a). It can also be paralleled with a blade, of similar size, from Lagore crannog, occupied from the 7th to 10th centuries (Hencken 1950, 97, fig 31:B; Scott 1990, fig 5.3.17a). L = 117mm.

24 H (5)   433   SF558*
A socketed arrowhead, with a broken blade shaft. The circular cross-section of the shaft argues against it being a barbless arrowhead, a form designed to pierce armour, and typified by a square or diamond cross-section. It may be classified as LMMC type 11, of 14th-/15th-century date, an armour-piercing form, with a short blade (LMMC 1967, fig 16, 11), and illustrated by an example from Threave (Caldwell 1981, 112; fig 11, 72). An earlier, 13th-century crossbow bolt from Winchester has a similar long shaft, with a four-sided blade (Biddle 1990, 1077-9; fig 346, 4025). L = 83mm

BUCKLES

(illus 130)

The iron buckles are all of a basic, plain design, for use on a wide range of leather and textile articles, such as belts and harness fittings. Plain rings, some of which may be annular buckle frames, are catalogued with the household ironwork.

25 H (5)   433   SF849*
A small, D-shaped buckle with an integral plate and raised attachment bar. It is unusual in that the pin appears to be wrapped around the free end of the frame, rather than through a hole in the plate. In this feature, it is paralleled by a Medieval buckle, with socketed plate, from Capel Maelog, Powys (Jones & Courtney 1990, 72; fig 16, 73). The raised attachment bar resembles the raised stud on a small, copper-alloy buckle, also Medieval, from Lurk Lane, Beverley (Goodall 1991, 148–9; fig 114, 585). L = 40mm; W = 19mm.

26 H (7)   344   SF143*
Buckle. L = 44mm; W = 42mm

27 H (7)   344   SF858
Buckle. L = 28mm; W = 38mm

SF143 and SF858 are both plain D-shaped buckles, of a common all-purpose type, found throughout the Medieval period in a wide range of sizes. SF143 retains its pin, rolled round the pin bar, and curved up at its tip, to rest on the frame. SF858 is a buckle frame only.

28 H (7)   395   SF603
A small, plain buckle. It is badly corroded, and lacks its pin bar. The extant frame is semi-circular, and the pin, found with, but unattached from, the frame, is of curved profile, with a flat, spatulate end. L = 24mm; W = 23mm

29 H (9)   294   SF908
A corroded pin of curved profile. L = 48mm

TOOLS

(illus 131)

SF427 and SF792 are heckle or woolcomb teeth. They would have been mounted in wooden blocks to form combs (Goodall 1990, 214), sometimes bound with iron (Goodall 1984, 79; fig 119, 20 & 21), and used to separate flax or wool fibres prior to spinning. They are of an equal complete length of c 97mm (the head of SF427 is broken). Teeth within this range came from wool combs, with the rarer, larger examples, such as a 14th-/15th-century tooth of 246mm, from Threave (Caldwell 1981, 112; fig 11, 78), being from flax combs.

30 X (6)   1356   SF427*
Heckle tooth. L = 94mm

31 X (6)   1356   SF792
Heckle tooth. L = 97mm

Despite the structural evidence for the Medieval smithy, the artefact assemblage lacks the basic tools of the Medieval smith, such as cold sets, hammers and tongs. The waste products of metalworking (both copper-alloy and iron) are discussed elsewhere (below 4.3.7). A considerable proportion of the raw material brought into the smithy may have been in the form of scrap ironwork, including broken nails, and bar and strip fragments, reused both in repairs and new forgings. The tools most directly associated with the smithy were found within the Phase 6 collapsed base of the furnace structure:

32 H (6)   314   SF81*
A punch, with square cross-section, burred head and pointed end, used to drive holes in the iron (Goodall 1981, 51; fig 50, 7). L = 178mm; W = 19mm

33 H (6)   314   SF966
A tanged fragment of a tool with a lozenge cross-section. L = 50mm.

34 H (6)   314   SF967
A thin, wedged tool of square cross-section, tapering to a wedged tip. L = 100mm.

35 H (6)   314   SF968*
A possible file, of triangular cross-section, tapering over its length. L = 272mm.

36 H (7)   332   SF957*
A smaller punch than SF081, with a round cross-section,

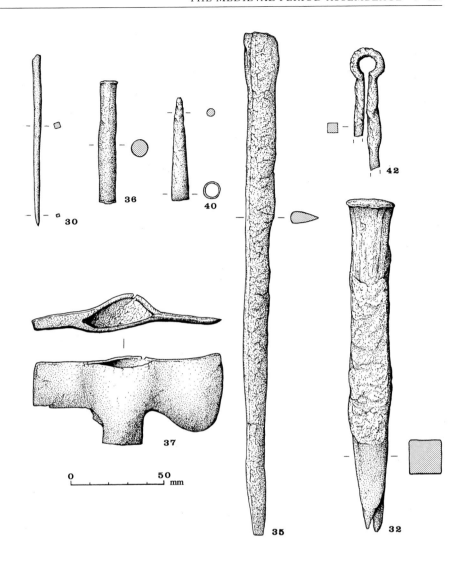

Illus 131
Medieval iron tools.

burred head and slightly widened, flat end (Goodall 1983, 240; fig 4, 28). L = 66mm

37   H (7)   344   SF945★
A centrally-socketed woodworking axe, with a flattened shaft hole, typical of the 15th century (Thompson 1967, 74, fig 72). The hammer head is more pronounced than common on Medieval axes (Goodall 1981, 53; fig 51, 2–5). L = 100mm; W = 48mm

38   H (7)   366   SF887
A bar length, of rectangular cross-section, broken at one end, and expanded to a flattened, rounded tip at the other. It may be the broken arm of a small pair of tongs or tweezers. L = 40mm; W = 7mm.

39   X (9)   1344   SF692
A possible stoneworking tool, such as a slaters' pick or mill pick (Goodall 1990, 299, 302; fig 67, 416–20). L = 107mm; W = 23mm

40   H (6)   575   SF802★
A sheet cone ferrule, of circular cross-section, with mineralised wood fragments adhering internally. It has a closed seam, and tapers throughout its length to a point. L = 56mm

41   H (4)   461   SF562
A sheet ferrule, of oval, slightly bulbous, cross-section. It is broken along the length of the seam and at tip. However, a small inturned lip survives at the tip, suggesting that it was originally flat ended, rather than pointed. It may have served as a scabbard chape (Goodall 1983, 248, 251; fig 9, 201–4). L = 55mm

42   H (7)   332   SF529★
Shears were manufactured in a wide range of sizes, for use in many tasks, from small shears for personal use, such as cutting hair, and larger shears for cutting cloth, or shearing sheep (de Neergaard 1987, 58–61). The basic form remained unchanged from the Iron Age through to the 16th century, when scissors became more common. The handle (SF529) is typical of shears of average length, broken centrally at the point of greatest strain: the catalogue of blades from recent Medieval excavations in London includes 57 shears, of mid-12th- to mid-15th-century date, of 74–318mm total length, 23 of which were broken exactly in half (de Neergaard 1987, 60). L = 66mm

NAILS

(illus 132)

Nails constitute by far the largest category of find (except for pottery), with over 1000 examples, from small shank fragments to complete headed nails.

Over 90% of the nails are from Areas H and X, Phases 6, 7 and 8. A quantity of fragmentary bar band strip iron, of roughly equal

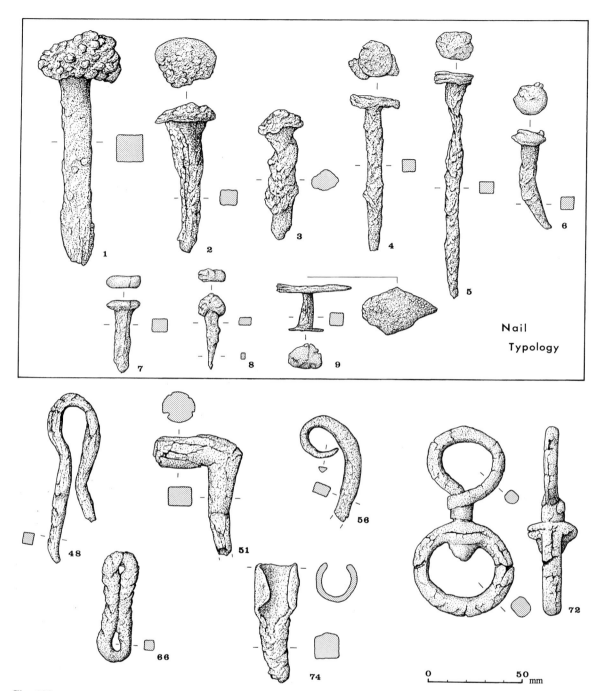

Illus 132
Medieval iron nails and structural ironwork.

bulk, was recovered from the same contexts. Many of these nails, and other fragments, may have served as scrap for the smithy, brought in from other areas of the Castle. This may account for the fact that nails of heavier types, which would be more worthwhile recycling, form a proportionally larger group than might be expected.

The forging of nails would have been a common job at the Castle smithy, as at most smithies until the 17th century. The nails were formed from iron rods, which were heated and hammered to shape the shank, and then cut, reheated, and placed in a nail-

heading tool to shape the head from the shank (Long & Long 1983, 279).

Many typologies have been developed for nails, such as Manning's inter-site classification for Romano–British nails (1985, 134–7), and, for Medieval nails, the within-site classification for Sandal Castle (Long & Long 1983, 279–80). The principal divisions recurrent in these classifications aim to reflect the functional differences determining the nail form. Reference to contemporary usage can be sought through Salzman's compilation and discussion of documentary sources, including order lists detailing amounts and prices (Salzman 1952, 286 317). However, Salzman warns against taking documented, generic terms as standard, with one nail form having a range of names, and one name referring to a range of nail types.

The Castle nails were classified into broad groups on the basis of a visual examination of the nails themselves, in their generally very corroded state, and with reference to the X-rays. Detail, such as faceting on the heads, could only be noted for particular examples.

Nine groups of headed nails, including horseshoe nails and clench nails, were defined (see 4.3.5 mf for details of measurements):

TYPES 1 AND 2

These are large, heavy nails, that would have been used for load-bearing timbers. Type 1 heads are chunky and irregular, while type 2 heads are more standard: flat, wide and rectangular. The heads of both types would have been clearly visible, for example in doors and hinges, and may have had some display, as well as functional, value.

TYPES 3, 4 AND 5

These are less heavy, but are of sufficient length to be used in structural joints and frames. Type 3 have typical 'knob' heads, while types 4 and 5 have more slender shanks with large and flat, or small and rounded heads respectively. A noticeable number of type 5 nails are bent at 90 degrees, 60–70mm along the shank.

TYPES 6 AND 7

These are smaller, general carpentry nails. Type 6 includes flat-headed 'clouts' used in attaching metal sheeting and fittings to timber, while type 7 includes 'brads', with no heads, or small lipped heads, that would lie flush with the timber, for example in planking.

TYPE 8

These are horseshoe nails, of fiddle-key type for countersunk nail-holes.

TYPE 9

These are clench nails. Nails were clenched over lozenge-shaped, or elongated roves, to prevent them pulling back through the wood. The presence of clench nails in occupation deposits may be partially explained as the result of boat timber being brought in as firewood, or for reworking (Goodall & Carter 1977, 297). However, clench nails were also employed on other timber features, in particular those with rear ledging, such as doors or hatches, as shown on the 12th-century well-cover from Lydford, Devon (Geddes 1980, 165, fig 17).

In addition to the headed nail types, four types of shank fragment were defined, to correspond with the general length and stoutness of the shanks of the headed nail types:

Type A: shank for type 1
Type B: shank for types 2 and 3
Type C: shank for types 4 and 5
Type D: shank for types 6, 7 and 8
Type UN: nail fragments too small to be further defined.

The nails are catalogued by type, per context, and summarised by type, per phase; in the text tables summary totals are given, (in the fiche there is a context by context catalogue 4.3.5.1mf, 1:F2–4). Table 6 shows totals for all nails with heads (ie types 1 to 9): a minimum number per context or per phase. Table 7 shows a total of all headed nails plus and shank fragments (ie types 1 to 9, types A to D, and type Un) to provide a maximum number per context or per phase.

Table 6 Headed nails

Total of headed nails by type (T1–T9) and phase.

Phase	T1	T2	T3	T4	T5	T6	T7	T8	T9	Total
3						3				3
5		4	1	1	5	7				18
6		9	8	13	16	11	1			58
7	8	43	24	31	81	51	7		4	249
8	3	14	12	20	39	26	9	2	1	126
9	4	7	1	6	20	5	2			45
10	1		3		35	11				50
mod						3				3

Table 7 Unheaded Nails

Total of unheaded nails by type (TA–TD) and phase and overall total nails by phase.

Phase	TA	TB	TC	TD	Un	Unheaded	Maximum
3	2	1	1			4	7
5	10	3	4	4		21	39
6	8	30	15	7	8	68	126
7	6	54	62	33	12	167	416
8	6	43	34	26	36	145	271
9	-	16	8	12	12	48	93
10	-	5		2	3	10	60
mod							3

STRUCTURAL HARDWARE

(illus 132)

The catalogue of structural ironwork includes fittings used both in architectural construction and in furniture making. A functional form, such as the hinge pivot or hasp, is found in a wide range of sizes in the archaeological record, reflecting the adaptability of such utilitarian forms to many uses. The design of such forms remained fairly constant from the Roman Iron Age through to the early modern period, changing only in response to developments in use and technology.

The Castle structural ironwork includes a range of fittings used to fasten timber to timber, such as the cranked tie, or to fix other iron fittings to timber, such as the U-shaped staples, used with chains, hasps, rings, handles, etc. Hasps were used with hinges, staples and/or chains to hold moving elements, such as doors, gates or lids, and could be secured with padlocks and/or chains. The Castle hasp (SF948; illus 132, *48*) is bent sharply, possibly the result of having been fixed to the lid of a chest, and bent to pass over a staple on the front face. The stake (SF666) is catalogued separately from the nails, as it is unique in its size and heaviness.

Both pivot hinges and pinned hinges are represented. None of the hinge pivots shows any trace of the lead caulking often found coating masonry hinges. Rather, all have the short, tapering shank associated with use in timber. Except for one small example (SF796), possibly from a chest, they are of a fairly standard size, for use in shutters, doors and gates.

SF942 is a broken scroll terminal from a hinge strap (illus 132, *56*). Shaped terminals, usually bifurcated, but sometimes more elaborate (Goodall 1990, 347; fig 85, 678), were a common decorative feature on Medieval doors and coverings, as displayed, for example, on the 12th-century well-cover from Lydford (Geddes 1980, 165, fig 17).

Hinges with pinned eyes were far less common during the Medieval period than pivoted hinges, and were probably used mostly on furniture. The wings of pinned hinges took a variety of shapes: strap, butterfly or more decorative, such as a late 15th-/early 16th-century leaf-shaped hinge wing from Winchester (Goodall 1990, 975; fig 303, 3459). With the exception of the strap hinge from Phase 10 (SF862), the Castle pinned hinges are broken too close to the pin to give detail of their wing form.

Cat no	Area (phase)	context	SF no	object	dimensions
43	H (5)	418	617	tie	L = 58mm
44	X (5)	1360	429	cranked tie	L = 67mm
45	H (7)	344	943	staple	L = 57mm; W = 32mm
46	H (7)	346	833	staple	L = 47mm; W = 31mm
47	H (7)	366	736	staple	L = 63mm; W = 37mm
48	X (7)	1353	948	hasp	L = 96mm*
49	H (8)	335	666	stake	L = 80mm
50	H (6)	381	733	hinge pivot	L = 80mm; H = 47mm
51	X (6)	1076	863	hinge pivot	L = 67mm; H = 45mm*
52	H (7)	344	896	hinge pivot	L = 64mm; H = 62mm
53	H (8)	298	796	hinge pivot	L = 26mm; H = 33mm
54	H (9)	278	734	hinge pivot	L = 87mm; H = 51mm
55	N (-)	905	827	hinge pivot	L = 64mm; H = 50mm
56	H (7)	344	942	hinge strap	L = 60mm; W = 28mm*
57	H (6)	314	903	pinned hinge	L = 62mm; W = 42mm
58	X (10)	1061	815	pinned hinge	L = 52mm; W = 40mm
59	X (10)	1342	862	pinned hinge	L = 145mm; W = 46mm

HOUSEHOLD HARDWARE

(illus 132; 133)

The household ironwork, from Phases 6 to 10, includes fittings and bindings that would have been suitable for use in a wide range of circumstances: ring and chain links, ring collars and binding strips.

Objects of a more particular use are the swivel rings, usually associated with tethering (Samson 1982, 466, fig 1: 3–6), and the candle holders. Of the two Castle candle holders, one (SF935) has a closed grip socket and right-angled stem, that would have been inserted horizontally into a wooden stand, while the other (SF879; illus 132, *74*) has an open socket and straight stem.

Cat no	Area (phase)	context	SF no	object	dimensions
60	H (7)	344	727	ring	D = 34mm
61	H (7)	344	749	ring	D = 31mm
62	L (-)	850	726	ring	D = 53mm
63	H (6)	578	568	ring fragments	D = c 25mm
64	N (-)	931	893	ring collar	D = 22mm
65	H (6)	391	616	figure-of-eight chain link	L = 70mm
66	H (8)	335	853	figure-of-eight chain link	L = 61mm*
67	H (7)	344	582	broken link/staple	L = 40mm
68	H (7)	399	728	bent strip	L = 77mm
69	H (8)	328	808	riveted strip	L = 36mm
70	X (10)	1061	929	bent riveted strip	L = 43mm
71	X (6)	1356	413	swivel ring & loop	L = 110mm
72	H (7)	344	142	swivel ring & loop	L = 105mm*
73	H (6)	381	935	candle holder	H = 50mm
74	H (7)	344	897	candle holder	H = 65mm*

There are three iron mounts, from Phase 7 and 8 contexts, for which a specific function is not known, although the design of SF846, in particular, would suggest a particular setting. SF950 (illus 133, *76*) and SF846 were originally fixed to, or mounted on, other objects, while SF847 (illus 133, *75*) was suspended, possibly from a ring or chain, through its eyed head.

75 H (7) 336 SF847*
A bar mount of roughly rectangular cross-section, recessed longitudinally along three faces, and along the two intervening corner edges. The fourth face is faceted. The recesses are straight sided, and are deepest (3.5 to 5mm), and widest (6.5 to 7mm), along the two opposing side faces. There are no traces of any original inlay or adhesive agents, nor does the metal lip over the recessed areas, to hold an inlay in place. L = 62mm

76 X (7) 1353 SF950*
A rolled sheet, socketed fitting, of oval cross-section, tapering to a solid bar shank with split ends. One end is curled, and the other is broken. L = 76mm.

77 H (8) 316 SF846*
A plate casing, of rectangular box shape, with broken faces on four sides. Two faces are formed from a bent strip, over which the side sheet plates are rolled, to form a shallow, curved ridge. A narrow strip runs centrally along the length of the top plate, terminating in a raised, rolled curl. L = 48mm; W = 24mm; H = 21mm

LOCKS AND KEYS

(illus 133)

The lock components are all from Phase 6 and 7 contexts, and include a barrel padlock bolt (SF807; illus 133, *78*), two possible padlock keys (SF949 and SF791), a key for a mounted lock (SF093; illus 133, *81*) and a keyhole escutcheon (SF923; illus 133, *82*).

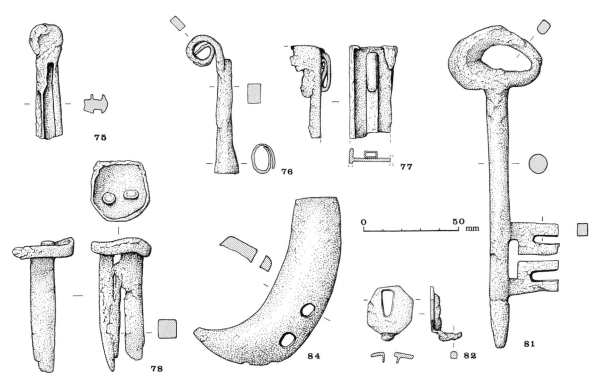

Illus 133
Medieval iron locks and fittings.

Barrel padlocks, with their accompanying keys, are a type form with a long chronological span, from the 11th century (Goodall 1987, 183; fig 158, 105–10) throughout the Medieval and post-Medieval period (Goodall 1990, 1001).

78 X (6)   1356   SF807*
A barrel padlock bolt. It has two spines, each with a double spring, set at right angles to each other, and riveted through the oval closing plate. Parallel examples are known with two, or three, double-spring spines (Goodall 1991, 141; fig 109, 479). L = 70mm.

79 X (6)   1442   SF949
A slightly bulbous, broken stem, with a looped handle. Its identification as a padlock key is tentative. L = 56mm

80 H (6)   435   SF791
Badly corroded: identification as a possible padlock key was made from the X-ray. It is unclear whether or not the ward cuts project out from the stem. A similar padlock, from Castlehill of Strachan, is dated to the 14th century (Duncan & Spearman 1984, 354–6; fig 25, 4). L = 115mm.

81 H (7)   329   SF093*
A key with a symmetrically-shaped bit, of a type designed for use on either side of a mounted lock. It has a solid stem, projecting beyond the end of the bit, and a D-shaped bow. This form of key is common in Medieval and post-Medieval contexts (Harvey 1975, 287; figs 256, 2085 & 6; Goodall 1990, 1032–3; fig 3328). L = 176mm.

82 H (7)   344   SF923*
An escutcheon of hexagonal outline, with a slightly off-centre triangular keyhole, and a non-ferrous plating. It was held in the lock by a small, angled tang at the top of the plate, and by a raised lip around the back rim of the hole. H = 29mm; W = 24mm

HORSESHOES

(illus 133)

The diagnostic features commonly used to classify horseshoes include the width of the webs, the outline form of the shoe, and the shape of nail-holes, whether rectangular or countersunk (Goodall 1990, 1054–6).

Except for one modern find (SF105), all the Castle horseshoes come from Phases 6, 7 and 8. All have the rectangular nail-holes and smooth outline of the Medieval form typical from the 13th–14th centuries (Macdonald & Laing 1974–5, 146–7; fig 10, 9–10; Samson 1982, 466; fig 1, 8 & 9), replacing the earlier, late 11th-/12th-century, type with countersunk nail-holes and wavy outline (Goodall 1982, 230; fig 41, 126–30). None are fullered, a post-Medieval development (Goodall 1983, 251).

The majority of the horseshoes are small fragments of arms and heels, and, with the exception of the modern shoe, not complete enough to give a full outline. Two (SF622 and SF725) are arm sections with three nail-holes. Several of the remainder are broken at the first or second hole.

Variation is shown in the shape of the heel. Three fragments have upturned calkins: SF738, SF742 and SF622. Four are thickened at the heel: SF725 and SF900 narrowing gradually, SF857 narrowing more sharply, and SF569 (illus 133, *84*) not narrowing.

One shoe (SF622) retains a nail with expanded head and flat top, of a type found at Perth in contexts of 16th-century date (Ford & Walsh 1987, 137; fig 70).

The modern shoe has a complete diameter of 70mm, to fit a small pony or donkey.

Additional finds of horse gear are catalogued elsewhere in the metalwork report: two loose horseshoe nails, catalogued in the nail report (4.3.5 above), are of fiddle-key type for countersunk nail-holes; a gilded harness pendant (SF058) is in the copper alloy catalogue (4.3.4); two swivel rings (SF413 and SF142), probably used in tethering, are catalogued under household ironwork (4.3.5).

Cat	area (phase)	context	SF no	dimensions
83	H (6)	381	724	L = 57mm; W = 30mm
84	H (6)	575	569	L = 105mm; W = 22mm*
85	X (6)	1356	803	L = 91mm; W = 24mm
86	H (7)	305	738	L = 57mm; W = 28mm
87	H (7)	344	899	L = 70mm; W = 30mm
88	H (7)	344	900	L = 70mm; W = 29mm
89	H (7)	346	725	L = 123mm; W = 35mm
90	H (7)	366	742	L = 70mm; W = 26mm
91	H (8)	298	857	L = 68mm; W = 25mm
92	H (8)	295	622	L = 110mm; W = 28mm
93	H (mod)	234	105	L = 68mm; W = 13mm

IRON SHEETING

94   X (9) 1344 SF866
Five fragments of riveted sheet iron were found in a Phase 9 context. The separate fragments do not join, but were all part of the same flat, circular object, possibly a lid or cover. The curved edge of each of the fragments is bound by a folded iron strip (16–25mm wide on either face), attached by a series of rivets, unevenly spaced at intervals of 11–40mm. Largest fragment: L = 110mm; W = 75mm.

4.3.6 STONE: ARCHITECTURAL FRAGMENTS AND MISSILES

(illus 134)

The surprisingly small number of excavated architectural stone fragments are listed below. Few were found in Medieval contexts simply because available stone tended to be reused, in most cases more than once. So when a building was remodelled or destroyed by siege, the masons literally picked up the pieces.

Of particular interest is the hood moulding found on Mills Mount (Area X, context 1378). This was reused in an 11th- to 13th-century context, thus indicating the existence of stone buildings in this early period. Also of note is the 17th-century voussoir fragment (Area L, context 850; illus 134, 2). This must have started life in a strong-looking arch forming part of the entrance defences, which was then probably damaged by siege, only to end up a few years after it was first cut as a bridge support of the mid-17th century.

Two complete and one fragment of what are interpreted as stone cannonballs were recovered from Medieval and post-Medieval contexts (illus 134, 6, 8). There is no sign that they were ever fired from guns and may represent missiles hurled by siege engines such as the trebuchet. There is also a slight chance that they were ornamental and not intended for military purposes.

STONE CATALOGUE

* = illustrated (illus 134)

1   H (8)   432   SF152*
Jambstone, from a door or window. 340 × 145 × 370mm. Chamfer 70mm across. Red sandstone. May be 15th-century, due to narrowness of the chamfer. Found thrown into the Phase 6 quenching trough. May previously have been reused in the blacksmith's furnace (above 3.3.3).

2   L (5)   850   SF368*
Voussoir. 490 × 270 × 200mm, with a later slot cut into the top. Slot: 160mm square × 30mm deep. Attempt at simple rustication by means of diagonal droving on arch face. Grey sandstone. 17th-century. Found at the base of the Inner Barrier E bridge support. The slot is presumed to be a socket for an temporary timber bridge support(above 3.8.2).

3   M (-) Unstratified
Attic column base. Very good quality classical work. 130 × 140mm fragment. Grey sandstone. 18th-/19th-century.

4   X (10)   1061   SF460*
Cill or lintel, with a deep-cut rebate for a shutter check. 480 × 180 × 180mm deep, with 50mm deep rebate. Grey sandstone. Found in an 18th-century context and may relate to the demolition of the 17th-century Storekeeper's House.

5   X (5)   1378   SF468
Hood mould from a door or window. A simple moulding with diagonal pecked tooling. Split underneath and roughly redressed. Burnt. 500 × 10mm wide. Flat face 60mm deep, above a concave roll 50mm across. Red sandstone. Medieval – this form common to entire Medieval period. Found reused as drain cap, in what may be an 11th- to 13th-century context.

6   H (6)   594   SF343*
Cannonball or missile made from very coarse grit. Pecked all over to form a slightly irregular flattened sphere. Diam = 205–220mm.

7   H (8)   347   SF318
Fragment of a cannonball or missile made of coarse grit and roughly pecked to shape.

8   X (10)   1061   SF443*
Missile made of very coarse grit. Pecked all over to form a slightly flattened sphere. Diam = 230–250mm.

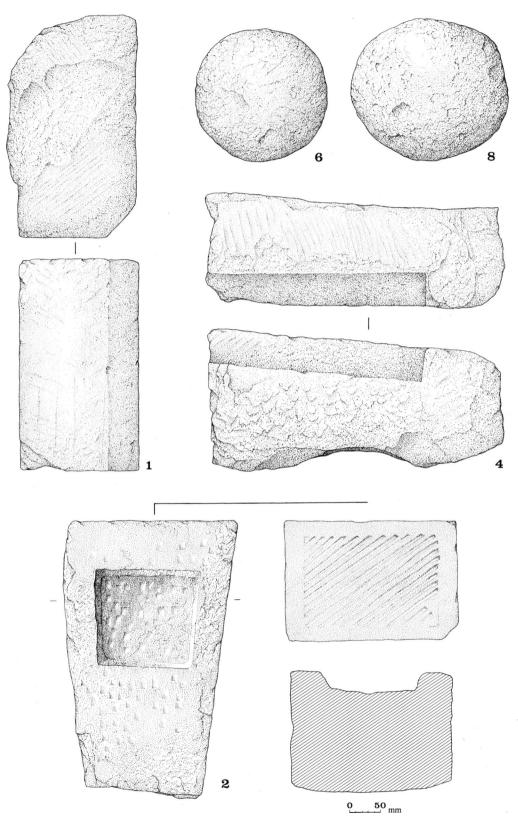

Illus 134
Medieval architectural stone and stone missiles.

4.3.7 THE SMITHY AND METALWORKING DEBRIS FROM MILLS MOUNT

R Michael Spearman

The excavations produced a range of evidence for Medieval metalworking. The overwhelming majority of these industrial features and their related debris came from the trenches at Mills Mount. This report therefore concentrates on the evidence from the Mills Mount area and provides an interpretation of the industrial features and debris found there. All of the industrial debris from the Mills Mount was examined visually at ×10 magnification and checked for magnetic attraction. The majority of the material relates to ironworking but there was also limited evidence of non-ferrous metalworking having taken place in the vicinity. A fragment of crucible from the area was kindly examined using standard X-ray fluorescence techniques by Mr Wilthew of the National Museums of Scotland's Conservation and Analytical Research Department. The result of the visual and X-ray fluorescence analysis of debris from the Mills Mount are presented in Tables 8–15 in fiche (4.3.7.1mf, 1:F5–12) and summarised in the text.

Smaller quantities of residual industrial debris were also found in the forecourt outside the Inner Battery (Area L) and the Coal Yard Cemetery (Area M). Debris from these areas and other parts of the Castle was examined in the same way as that from the Mills Mount, and a classified catalogue of the results of this work is provided in fiche, Table 16 (4.3.7.1mf, 1:F13–14). The range of debris from elsewhere in the Castle was essentially the same as that from the Mills Mount. No discussion of the wider significance of industrial debris from these other areas has been undertaken.

THE MILLS MOUNT DEBRIS

A total of 156 samples of possible industrial debris from the Mills Mount area were examined. During excavation the major part of this debris had been treated as part of the general finds from the area. Some pieces of debris were, however, distinguished either as industrial samples or as small finds. Of the 81 contexts which produced industrial debris six were singled out by the excavator for bulk soil sampling. These samples were first checked with a magnet for the presence of hammer-scale and were then wet-sieved using 10mm and then 1mm meshes. The various categories of debris identified from these sievings have been classified in the same way as the rest of the industrial debris. However, as the quality and quantity of the debris recovered is potentially different from the other Mills Mount contexts these sieved samples are identified as such in the appended tables (see 4.3.7.1mf, 1:F5–12).

THE IRON-WORKING DEBRIS

Prior to the introduction of blast furnaces, and therefore the availability of cast-iron artefacts, the production of iron objects depended upon a series of industrial processes. Once the ore had been won it was crushed, sorted and smelted to produce blooms of more concentrated iron. These blooms, spongy masses of iron mixed with slag, fuel and cinder, were then repeatedly heated and hammered to squeeze out trapped slag and cinder. The resulting billets of purer, more compact, iron were then formed by blacksmiths into serviceable wrought-iron artefacts. The vast majority of the metalworking debris from the Mills Mount relates only this last phase of smithing: the manufacture and repair of wrought-iron artefacts.

The ironworking debris has been described and catalogued under the following headings:

a) Bloom-working and cinder waste
b) Coal-based waste
c) Charcoal-based waste
d) Hammer-scale and prill
e) Waste wrought iron
f) Furnace lining

A) BLOOM-WORKING AND CINDER WASTE

This debris has a matt grey pimply exterior with a porous interior, and may be mixed with charcoal, coal cinder, and more vitreous slag. The pieces of debris have very varied iron content and shape. The majority of this material would have been extruded and discarded during the repeated forging of iron blooms to produce serviceable wrought iron.

B) COAL-BASED WASTE

This waste consists of fused masses of coal, cinder, furnace lining and vitreous clinker. The latter has a russet surface and a dark porous interior. Small pieces of dark grey bloom-working debris, hammer-scale and comminuted coal are frequently fused within the general matrix of this debris. A proportion of this debris has a layered appearance suggesting that it had built up from debris which had settled down within the smithy hearth. The major part, however, consisted of unstructured fragments, apparently broken from larger masses of the debris.

C) CHARCOAL-BASED WASTE

This waste consists of fused masses of hammer-scale, small pieces of dark grey bloom-working debris and fragments of charcoal. This debris often has a layered appearance and, as with some of the charcoal-based waste, it is likely to have formed from debris and unburnt fuel settling within the hearth.

D) HAMMER-SCALE AND *PRILL*

Hammer-scale waste consists of small scale flakes of iron produced by the impact of hammers on hot iron during either the refining of iron blooms or the working of wrought iron. The fine hammer-scales are consequently easily corroded and where they survive they often appear as little more than iron filings. A slightly more robust indication of the same process are the tiny droplets of grey iron slag extruded during smithing and known as *prill*.

E) WASTE IRONWORK

A number of small pieces of wrought iron, concreted with soil, comminuted coal and hammer-scale were recovered. Most of this artefactual waste consisted of short lengths of iron rod, rectangular in cross section. Larger billets of iron and several pieces of iron sheet were also noted. It seems likely that this class of debris represents the raw materials and waste products of the smithy. The high proportion of short iron rods and nail fragments would suggest that carpentry nails were a staple product of the smithy. A more complete picture of the smithy's produce may be gained from the report on the medieval ironwork (4.3.5 above).

F) FURNACE LINING

Clay cladding was used to line and protect furnace structures from heat and chemical damage. In the case of metalworking furnaces these linings frequently became vitrified and fused with cinders and other metalworking debris such that the clay had to be regularly repaired or replaced. Many of the pieces of furnace lining from this site are fused with a substantial build up of coal smithing debris.

OTHER TYPES OF DEBRIS

Debris not directly connected with iron-working includes:

g)   Fuel remains
h)   Baked daub
i)   Crucible fragment
j)   Possible mould fragments
k)   Tile and brick fragments
l)   Clinker
m)   Cintered sand and clay
n)   Baked hearth soil

G) FUEL REMAINS

The vast majority of the unburnt fuel recovered was coal, which survived either as individual pieces or fragments mixed with smithy debris (see item c) above). A small quantity of wood charcoal was also recovered from the sieved samples and smithy debris (see item d above). Coal cinders were likewise found on their own and with smithy debris.

Much of the coal was recovered in the form of small granules (ie less than 5mm across). It would have been extremely difficult to force a draught through such a fine coal and it seems likely that what has been recovered is largely unusable dross. Some of this fine coal was, however, fused in a mass with smithy debris, which would suggest that an attempt had been made to use this dross, and the hearth had consequently become clogged with a mass of clinker, slag and coal, all fused to the furnace lining.

H) BAKED DAUB

The baked daub and clay from the site had been tempered with vegetable material and sand. Very little of the daub retains any trace of wattle impressions, although in one instance it is apparent that a withy of more that 20mm diameter had been used. Numerous pieces did, however, have flat surfaces, and it is possible that some of this material had been used to line and bond the furnace structure. Much of the daub was fairly heavily crushed and it may also have been subsequently incorporated in the smithy floor.

I) CRUCIBLE FRAGMENT

A rim and wall fragment of a crucible was recovered from the Mills Mount smithy. Although the fragment is too small to reconstruct the profile of the crucible, the curvature of the body as compared to that of the rim, suggests that it comes from a small sub-triangular crucible. Such crucibles were used during the Early Historic and medieval periods in the casting of pieces of jewellery and other small pieces of metalwork. X-ray fluorescence analysis has indicated that the crucible had been used to melt a tin bronze.

J) POSSIBLE MOULD FRAGMENTS

Some five small pieces of daub retained fine but irregular impressions. These may have been part of a mould or moulds, but none of the pieces show the characteristic discolouration caused by reduction of the mould fabric during casting. If these are in fact mould fragments, and not daub, it would appear that they had not been used.

K) TILE AND BRICK FRAGMENTS

A small number of fragments of tile or brick were recovered from the Mills Mount site. These all have a red sandy fabric and are too small for their form to be determined.

L) CLINKER

Various droplets of a light vitreous material with a porous interior and a streaked brown and milky white surface were recovered from the area. While this debris must have been produced in a relatively hot fire, it is not a direct by-product of metalworking. A more likely explanation is that it was the result of a mixture of organic material, clay and/or sand being roasted in a substantial fire.

M) CINTERED SAND AND CLAY

Of potentially similar origin to the clinker (item l above) are a number of small pieces of more lightly vitrified sandy clay. In the case of this material, however, the individual particles of sand and other debris are discernable within their vitreous matrix. Nor is this cintered material as porous as the clinker, and this may in part reflect a lower fire temperature and/or lower organic content in the original mixture.

N) BAKED HEARTH SOIL

Amongst the samples from hearths and their surroundings, were a number of small lumps of dark red-brown iron rich soil. Their discoloration and bonding is likely to be the result of heat damage from fires set at ground level.

DISTRIBUTION OF METALWORKING DEBRIS

A full statement of the distribution of debris by phase and context appears in table in fiche (4.3.7.1mf, 1:F5–12). The phases with industrial features and debris are discussed here in chronological order.

PHASE 1

Residual Metalworking Debris (Table 8mf, 1:F5–6)

There were no significant quantities of debris from this phase and it is possible that the small fragments that were recovered represent redeposited material from other parts of the Castle (or perhaps contamination from later metalworking levels). Context 592 produced very small quantities of hammer-scale debris and some fine droplets of clinker. Small fragments of baked daub and what appear to be pieces of red brick/tile were also recovered.

PHASE 2

Residual Metalworking Debris (Table 9mf, 1:F5–6)

The types of debris recovered from Phase 2 were similar to those of the previous phase, although the quantity and range of ironworking debris is somewhat increased. In particular there were pieces of both coal-and charcoal-based smithy waste as well as a marked increase in the amount of hammer-scale present. There was a small quantity of cintered sand and clay from this phase. The quantities of debris were still not particularly large and, as with Phase 1, the most likely explanation is that a smithy had been worked in the vicinity.

PHASE 3

Residual Metalworking Debris

Fine clinker droplets were present in context 532, but very little diagnostic metalworking debris was recovered from this phase.

PHASE 4

Residual Metalworking Debris (Table 10mf, 1:F5–6)

Pieces of iron waste concreted with soil and hammer-scale were present in the tilled soil contexts 431 and 493 (illus 44). In addition 141.6g of coal-fired smithy waste were recovered from context 461. It is likely therefore that smithing was again taking place within the vicinity of the Mills Mount trench. A fragment of bronze working crucible was also recovered from context 461, but, as no other bronze working debris was recovered from the phase, it is likely that this crucible had come from elsewhere in the Castle.

PHASE 5

Ground Hearths and Smithy (Table 11mf, 1:F7–8)

A range of bloom-working and smithy debris was recovered from this phase. The major part of the fuel used appears to have been charcoal although a small quantity of coal, some of it fused with smithy waste, was also recovered. Much of this debris was associated with two circular ground-hearths, the fills of which are 417 and 495 (illus 45 inset; 47). Additional smithing debris was also recovered from the surrounding packed clay floors, 409 & 415, and cobbles 363 & 398 (illus 45). Both hearths appear to have been inserted into a slightly earlier flagstone and cobble path, which may have provided a firm floor for the smiths to work on. The larger of these two hearths, 495, sits at the N end of a sub-rectangular cut, 499. The burnt bowl of the earth-fast hearth appears to have been cleaned out several times during its use, while the rectangular cut, 499, may have been made to remove an associated superstructure, such as a retaining wall. The other hearth, 417, appears to have been more ephemeral, although there are pieces of baked daub in the hearth fill which may suggest that the bowl of the hearth had been lined, or that there had been a retaining ring of daub around the fire.

The sequence of these two hearths is not certain although it is stratigraphically likely that the smaller hearth, 417, is slightly later than hearth 495. Both hearths would seem to have been fired directly on the ground and it is probable that any associated superstructures were to retain the fuel and protect the bellows, rather than to lift the fire up off the ground. Such hearths were perfectly acceptable for smithing purposes. The construction of such hearths in which a low wall was used to retain the fire and protect the bellows is described by the 12th-century monk Theophilus (Dodwell 1961) and a mid-15th-century Scottish example of such a hearth has been excavated off Castle Street in Inverness (Spearman 1982, 351, 357). Regrettably both of the Edinburgh Castle hearths are located at the edge of their trench and have suffered from latter levelling and robbing. Were it not for their associated floor levels, 409 & 415, and 363 & 398, the extent of the smithy workshop would not be at all clear.

PHASE 6

Main Smithy Complex (Table 12mf, 1:F7–8)

The types of metalworking debris from this phase are similar to those recovered from Phase 5. The over all quantity of debris is, however, considerably greater and there is a marked increase in the proportion of coal-fuelled smithy waste. The amount and range of smithing debris recovered suggests that a coal-fired smithy had existed in the immediate vicinity of Mills Mount and this was confirmed by the association of much of this debris with a stone-built furnace, other structural remains and floor levels at the S end of the trench.

The central feature of the smithy was a sub-rectangular furnace, 296 (illus 51 a & b). Two or three courses of the furnace's clay-bonded stonework remained in position, the furnace having been largely dismantled in Phase 7. Enclosed within the base of this structure was a dump of burnt clay, 314, but neither this material nor the actual stonework with its bonded clay were sufficiently heat damaged to suggest that the smithy fire had been set at ground level. A far more likely explanation is that the smithy fire had been raised up on a platform or iron grid to about waist height, and that the observed baking of the lower part of the furnace structure was the result of indirect heating. There may have been a raised hearth grid. If so, then access to below the hearth, which would have been necessary to rake out ashes falling through the grid, must have been by means of a vault above ground level – for there is no break in the circuit of the furnace foundations.

The area of the smithy is defined to the S and W by a patchy clay floor, 435, and the wall lines indicated by Phase 7 robber cuts, 331 356 (illus 50). There is no clear definition of a N wall to the smithy and the cobbles and drain found there may have been part of a yard onto which the smithy opened. The eastern side of this yard is however, clearly defined by an area of much more closely packed cobbles, 363, and it is possible that there was a physical boundary between the smithy and at least these eastern cobbles. The smithy floor extended east outwith the area of excavation.

A number of features were excavated within the smithy area which are likely to have related to the working of the smithy. Much of the smithy waste from this phase came from a rock-cut sub-rectangular trough, 438, which lies just to the W of the smithy furnace (illus 50). The smithy debris from this trough includes a high proportion of furnace lining, fused with coal and coal-fired smithy waste. It would appear therefore that the fill in question, 451, represents a deliberate infilling of the trough with debris cleared out of the smithy furnace. The original function of the rock-cut trough was almost certainly to contain liquid for quenching the iron worked in the smithy. It does not appear that the trough was lined, and the rock-cut feature may have been sufficiently water-tight to make lining unnecessary.

A very similar fill of coal-fired smithy waste, 301, was recovered from the later, Phase 8, robber slot, 313, which ran along the N face of the smithy furnace. It seems likely that the source of both these fills (301 & 451) was the same and that the demolition of the superstructure of the furnace should be placed in Phase 8. There is only circumstantial evidence as to what had been removed with this robber slot. The alignment of the furnace and the compact cobbles in the NE part of the trench strongly suggests that there had been a structural division between the smithy and the cobbled yard. Cut 313 is likely, therefore, to have been for the removal of part of that division. Moreover, as the cut is contiguous with the N wall of the furnace it may also be fair to deduce that any roof support or wall had been reinforced at this point to support part of the furnace structure – such as a chimney hood over the hearth.

Against the E face of the smithy furnace, and contemporary with it, was a semi-circular hollow, 557. Smithing debris, coal and charcoal were also recovered from the fill, 578, of this feature, the function of the feature is however uncertain. As has been noted, the continuous wall of the furnace makes it unlikely that the hollow was caused by raking out ashes from below the furnace. Nor is there anything about the feature itself, such as scorching, a high ash content or repeated lensing of the fill, to suggest that this was its function. An alternative explanation may be that this feature contained part of a footing of the timber frame by which the furnace bellows were worked and played onto the raised smithy hearth.

Contemporary with the construction of the smithy is a posthole, 572. This is located off the SE corner of the furnace on what appears to be the mid-line of the building. The post it originally held may therefore have been a roof support rather than part of the smithy furniture.

The smith's anvil would normally have been placed within easy reach of the forge and as such might be reasonably be expected to have fallen within the area of excavation. Most early illustrations of smithies (Treue et al 1965, pl 81) show the anvil set in a substantial section of tree trunk which provided both a stable base for the anvil as well as a large enough mass to deaden the smiths blows. Although there would have been little need for such large blocks of wood to be set into the ground, archaeological evidence suggests that a timber-set anvil was set in feature 572 (illus 49; 51).

The most enigmatic of all of the features relating to the smithy is a long rectangular box, 421, set into the ground to the W of the rock-cut trough, 438. The box was of nailed timber, lined on its sides and base with pieces of thin iron sheet (see illus 52 a & b, conservation report 4.3.7mf, 1:F7–8). There was no indication from the contents of the box as to what its function might have been. Further fragments of iron sheet were found amongst the artefactual iron waste from a range of Phase 6 and 7 contexts. One possible suggestion for its use would be to contain and protect hot metalwork which was to be allowed to cool gradually without coming into contact with, and therefore being marked by, other materials. Gradual cooling in such a safe environment would, for instance, have been required by smiths involved in steeling and tempering weapons and tools. A secure clean box would also have been useful to hold the cooling ironwork which had been coated either for decoration, or against corrosion. For instance, Theophilus describes iron fittings being heated and then rubbed with ox horn or goose feathers to give the objects a black sealing layer of sooty protein (Dodwell 1961, 165).

PHASE 7

Reuse of Smithy (Table 13, 4.3.7mf, 1:F9–10)

The main feature of the smithy were levelled at the start of this phase, although the smithy building appears to have continued to stand until the end of the phase. While there is no change in the range of debris being recovered, the quantity is somewhat reduced.

PHASE 8

Demolition and Sealing Middens (Table 14, 4.3.7mf, 1:F11–12)

The volume of smithy debris continues to decline with this phase, although individual features do contain a high concentration of coal-fired smithy waste. Two features are particularly noticeable in this respect, the robber cut, 313 (with fill 301) (illus 51a), to the N of the furnace site, and a shallow pit, 333 (with fills 337 & 328), over the rock-cut trough (illus 57).

PHASE 9

17th Century (Table 15, 4.3.7mf, 1:F11–12)

Small quantities of metalworking debris continue to occur in this phase, along with a few fragments of brick or tile. The industrial debris appears to be entirely residual from earlier phases on the site.

CONCLUSION

The artefacts, waste and structural remains from the Mills Mount area clearly indicate that a series of smithies had been built and worked on the site during Phases 5 and 6, and that the last and most elaborate of these was run down and gradually demolished in Phases 7 and 8. Although a piece of bronze-working crucible, together with possible mould fragments, was recovered from Phase 5, the quantity of non-ferrous debris is far too slight to suggest anything more than that bronze casting had taken place somewhere in the vicinity.

Two groups of ironworking debris were noticeable by their absence. Tap-slags, which would have been produced in, and drained from, the hotter parts of bloomery furnaces during the smelting of ores, were not present amongst the debris (although a few pieces were found from other sites in the Castle, for which see Table 16, 4.3.7m, 1:F13–14). There was also relatively little debris from the refining of crude blooms of iron (see type a, above) especially when compared to the overall amount of smithing waste recovered (types b–e, above).

The range of debris recovered, plus the lack of these two specific types of debris, indicates that:

1 The Mills Mount smiths were primarily involved in the repair and manufacture of wrought iron.

2 They did not involve themselves with the conversion of bloomery iron into wrought iron.

3 They were not directly involved in the smelting of iron ore.

Archaeological investigation of rural bloomeries and burgh smiddies has established that it was common practice for iron ore to be smelted near sources of ore and fuel and for blooms of iron to be transported to the towns for further refining and working into artefacts (Aitken 1970, 188–204; Spearman 1982, 346–55; forthcoming a).

It is entirely in keeping, therefore, with the normal trading pattern of the industry that the Mills Mount smiths should have avoided the cost of transporting large quantities of heavy ore and bulky fuel to the Castle in order to conduct their own smeltings. What is surprising, however, is that the Castle smiths worked almost exclusively with wrought iron (and presumably steel). Excavated Smithies, and even those in smaller rural fortifications, have invariably produced a far higher proportion of iron blooms than was found at the Castle (Spearman 1984, 349–50). For either economic or artefactual reasons, the Mills Mount smiths did not prepare their own iron for smithing. This could conceivably be a result of the Castle being supplied with its raw materials from the town, or indeed the Mills Mount smithy being mainly for the repair of existing ironwork. The iron being worked at the Castle could therefore have been of local origin, prepared by burgh smiths, or part of the international trade in iron and steel (Thorkander 1975, 68–70; Martens 1981, 39–43; Spearman 1988, 143–44;).

4.3.8 THE COINS

Nicholas Holmes

DISCUSSION

The coins are discussed by area and a complete catalogue follows.

AREAS H AND X : MILLS MOUNT

This area was the most prolific in terms of numismatic finds, with the coin series spanning a period of some 1750 years. The earliest was a Roman silver denarius (*1*) of the emperor Hadrian (AD 117–38), found in a Roman Iron Age floor deposit (illus 31). Unfortunately the high level of corrosion on this coin prevented both a more accurate establishment of its date of minting and any assessment of the degree of wear from circulation. Denarii of this period would have formed a substantial part of the volume of coinage brought into Scotland by the army of Antoninus Pius in the early 140s, however, and it would not be stretching credibility to suggest that this coin reached Edinburgh Castle as a result of contact between the local Votadinian people and the Roman garrison based at Cramond or Inveresk.

Two English silver pennies of Edward II may be associated with 14th-century activity on the site. The later of the two was recovered from the earlier context (Phase 6 industrial activity, illus 49) – this being a penny of class 15b, dated to around 1321–2 (*3*). The coin is rather weakly struck in places, but has certainly suffered a fair amount of wear and may have been lost around the middle of the 14th century. A slightly earlier coin (*2*), of class 11b (*c* 1310–14) was recovered from a midden/make-up deposit of Phase 7 (illus 56 inset). This coin also shows considerable wear, particularly on the obverse, and probably ceased to circulate at much the same general period as the 15b. It is impossible to be precise about the length of circulation of these pennies.

15th-century occupation is attested by the presence of three Scottish copper coins in contexts belonging to Phases 8 and 9. From the primary silt of ditch 585 (illus 57 mid inset) came a 'black farthing' of James III's second issue (*6*), struck between 1466 and 1471. These coins were generally struck so poorly that no conclusions can be drawn from their condition when found. They were extremely unpopular, however, and did not circulate for very long anyway. A date of loss of *c* 1470–80 may be postulated for this example. Two coins (*4* and *5*) of the 'CRVX PELLIT' issue were recovered from a late medieval dump of made-up ground (illus 59). These are the coins formerly attributed to a mint of Bishop Kennedy of St Andrews, but now considered to have been part of the regal coinage. The period of their issue has not yet been accurately established, but must fall within the second half of the 15th century. Like the 'black farthings', these coins were generally unpopular, and they were probably devalued considerably in 1482 (Murray 1977). Occasional examples are found in early 16th-century contexts, but this appears to represent the end of their period of circulation.

Two much later coins were recovered from deposits also assigned to Phase 9, and cut by the Charles II period wall. A billon hardhead of James VI (7), struck in 1588, was probably lost around 1600–30, although poor striking may be exaggerating the apparent degree of wear. A French double tournois of Louis XIII (21), struck in 1640, is unlikely to have been lost before 1660 and could have circulated much longer.

18th-century gravel paving layers of Phase 10 (illus 64) yielded a worn bawbee of Charles II of 1677–9 (8) and an Irish halfpenny of George II (11). The latter, although struck during the period 1747–55, is so worn that a date of loss earlier than 1800 seems extremely unlikely, unless its use involved more than just normal circulation. A Victorian halfpenny of 1893 (18) was found in topsoil.

AREA F : 1801 MAIN GUARD

Seven coins were recovered from this site, these being divisible into two clearly-defined groups. Four coins found in deposits (illus 71) considered to date from the period of occupation of the building comprised one penny and two halfpennies of George III's 1806–7 issue (13–15) and a half-crown of 1817 (16). The presence of the latter piece is of some interest, as it was a fairly high-value coin in the early 19th century. There is a suggestion, however, that this specimen may be a forgery. Where the coin is worn, on the highest points of the design, it appears that a silver wash may be flaking off to reveal a baser white metal core. If this were the case, it would be easier to understand why it may have been discarded.

Three coins found associated with the demolition of the building comprise a farthing of Victoria (1864), a halfpenny of Edward VII (1902) and a penny of George V (1913) (17, 19–20). Curiously, the latest of these shows the greatest degree of wear, and it had probably circulated for 40 years or more before loss. The condition of the two earlier coins suggests dates of loss of c 1875–1900 and c 1905–15 respectively, and these were presumably redeposited in the demolition rubble.

AREA G : FLANKER

No coins were found in this area, but one Nuremberg jeton (22) was found associated with the construction of the Sally Port staircase (illus 87). It belongs to an anonymous group of jetons, dated to around the 1550s and bearing designs which reflect their original purpose of export to France. The moderate amount of wear on this jeton suggests by itself a date of loss of around 1570–1600, but the fact that it has been pierced also suggests a secondary use as part of an item of jewellery, and this date may therefore be too early.

AREA L : INNER BARRIER

From the early deposit below the lifting bridge (illus 94) came an Irish halfpenny of Charles II, dated 1680 (9). This coin was in worn condition and was probably lost during the period c 1720–50. Irish coins were not officially recognised as legal tender in Scotland, but the frequency with which they are found indicates that they must nonetheless have found their way into circulation.

AREA M : COAL YARD – CEMETERY

An unusual find from this site was a poor quality forgery of an Irish halfpenny of Charles II (10). It is unlikely to have found much acceptance in circulation, as it differs markedly from genuine issues. The flan is unusually small and thick, and marking around the rim indicates that it was cast in a two-piece mould. The obverse displays the large lettering characteristic of the 1680–2 issue, with the portrait and titles of Charles II, whereas the reverse is dated 1686, ie to the period of the coinage of James VII/II. Despite this, and the fact that the designs appear to have been somewhat lacking in detail, the coin is undeniably very worn and must therefore have been subjected to prolonged use for some purpose. It may have served as an unofficial token or gambling counter. Reliance on an estimation of its period of circulation before loss would be very unwise under these circumstances, which is unfortunate given its stratified context in the backfill of a robbed-out masonry bastion (illus 103), and all that can really be established is that this deposit is unlikely to date from earlier than about 1700.

The only other coin recovered from this site was again Irish – a halfpenny of George II, dated 1760 (12). This was in very worn condition and was probably lost between 1810 and 1850.

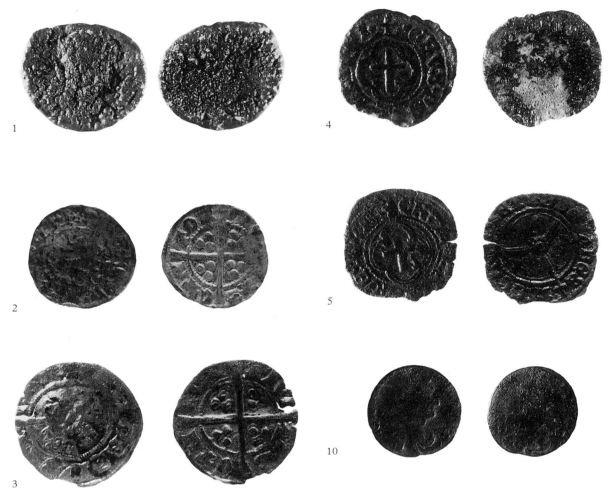

Illus 135
Selected coins (obverse on L, reverse on R): 1 (SF409) Hadrian denarius; 2 (SF344) penny of Edward II; 3 (SF151) penny of
Edward II; 4 (SF387) James II–III copper 'CRVX PELLIT'; 5 (SF388) James II–III copper 'CRVX PELLIT'; 10 (SF493)
forgery of Charles II Irish halfpenny. (Not to a standard scale)

COIN CATALOGUE

★ = illustrated (illus 135)

1   X (2)   1406   SF409★
HADRIAN: denarius (20 × 17.5mm, 3.13g, die axis 6.0):
AD117–38
obv: illegible : bust laureate right
rev: illegible : standing figure
surfaces highly corroded

2   H (7)   346   SF344★
EDWARD II: penny of Canterbury, class 11b (17.5mm,
1.21g, die axis 11.5): 1310–14
obv: +EDWARANGLDN [ShY] B
rev: CIV [I]/[T] AS/CAN/TOR
obverse worn, reverse fairly worn

3   H (6)   381   SF151★
EDWARD II: penny of Canterbury class 15b (17mm, 0.62g,
die axis 7.5): 1321–2
obv: +EDWARRANGLDNShYB
rev: CIVI/TAS/CAN/TOR
fairly worn; slightly off-centre to right; rather weakly struck
to right of bust

4   H (9)   1351   SF387★
JAMES II–III: copper 'CRVX PELLIT' issue, type IIIa (20
× 19.5mm, 2.01g, die axis 11.5): c 2nd half of 15th cent

obv.: +IACOBVS [   ]EX :orb tilted upwards and to left;
rosette in centre: ?saltire stops
rev.: +CRVX★PE [LLIT O] IE★CI★ : 5-pointed star stops: 5-
pointed stars on cusps: nothing in spandrels: edge ragged;
fairly worn; some surface corrosion, especially on obverse;
reverse off centre

5   H (9)   1351   SF388★
JAMES II–III: copper 'CRVX PELLIT' issue, type IIIa
(20.5mm, 1.44g, die axis 5.0): c 2nd half of 15th cent
obv: +IACOBV [S] DEI GRACIA REX : orb tilted upwards
and to left: rosette in centre: no stops
rev: CRVX : [P] E [LLIT] : OE : CRI : saltire stops: trefoils
on cusps: nothing in spandrels:
moderate wear: some flattening and surface corrosion: small
flan crack at 4.5 (obv)

6   H (8)   586   SF405
JAMES III: copper 'black farthing', 2nd. issue (13.5mm,
0.51g, die axis 6.5): c 1466–71
obv: +IACOB [   ] I GRA : crowned IR, saltire stops
rev: [   ] VRG [ ] : crown superimposed on saltire: small
saltire to each side and below
reverse slightly off-centre: uneven striking: moderate wear

7   H (9)   268   SF060
JAMES VI: billon hardhead, 2nd issue (18.5 × 18mm, 1.36g, die axis 5.0): November 1588 : Stewart 200 very slightly buckled: appears worn: much flattening, but possibly poorly struck, as some parts are quite sharp

8   H (10)   244   SF315
CHARLES II: copper bawbee (24.5 × 24mm, 6.49g, die axis 6.0): 1677–9 : Stewart 244; worn: date worn flat

9   L (5) 849 SF367
CHARLES II: Irish copper halfpenny (26.5 × 26mm, 6.12g, die axis 11.0): 1680; obverse very worn, reverse worn: surfaces corroded

10   M (5)   1149   SF493*
CHARLES II: forgery of an Irish copper halfpenny (24mm, 6.01g, die axis 6.0); obverse as of 1680–2 issue, with large lettering; reverse dated 1686, as of James II issue; unusually small, thick flan, with marking around rim indicating the joining of two separate moulds: coin is very worn, but there is a suggestion that the designs were, in any case, rather lacking in detail

11   H (10)   244   SF314
GEORGE II: Irish copper halfpenny (27.5 × 27mm, 7.12g, die axis 6.0): 1747–55; obverse: GEORGIVS; obverse very worn, reverse extremely worn: some surface corrosion

12   M (6)   1110   SF338
GEORGE II: Irish copper halfpenny (27mm, 7.51g, die axis 6.0): 1760; very worn: legends flat

13   F (-)   040   SF020
GEORGE III: copper penny (17.55g): 1806–7; worn: some surface corrosion

14   F (-)   040   SF016
GEORGE III: copper halfpenny (9.36g): 1806; slight to moderate wear: some surface corrosion

15   F (-)   040   SF012
GEORGE III: copper halfpenny (8.80g): 1806–7; fairly worn: much surface corrosion on reverse

16   F (-)   040   SF019
GEORGE III: silver half-crown (13.44g) : 1817; generally moderate wear: where coin is worn on highest points, there is a suggestion of a silver wash flaking off to reveal a baser white metal core: coin may therefore be a forgery

17   F (-)   019   SF001
VICTORIA: bronze farthing (2.67g): 1864; moderate wear: some surface corrosion

18   H (mod)   221   SF317
VICTORIA: bronze halfpenny (5.59g): 1893; apparently slight to moderate wear: some surface corrosion

19   F (-)   024   SF007
EDWARD VII: bronze halfpenny (5.48g): 1902; slight to moderate wear

20   F (-)   024   SF006
GEORGE V: bronze penny (9.05g): 1913; fairly worn

21   H (9)   284   SF053
French, LOUIS XIII: copper double tournois (19.5mm, 1.83g, die axis 6.0); 1640; uneven striking: fairly worn, especially bust on obverse

22   G (5)   113   SF386
Anonymous brass jeton of Nuremberg (27mm, 2.36g, die axis 10.5): probably struck c 1550s;
obv: crown initial mark, fictitious legend: ship sailing to left; arcuate yard-arm; no letter G above; stern-flag to right
rev: four lis in a lozenge; trefoils and pellets outside; fictitious legend; trefoil at end cf Mitchener 1177–82: ?cross in yard-arm; moderate wear: slight corrosion and flattening: pierced at 1.0 (obverse)

4.4 THE POST-MEDIEVAL ASSEMBLAGE

4.4.1 GENERAL INTRODUCTION

The majority of the finds were post-medieval in date (illus 136) and a large proportion of them are directly associated with the use of the Castle as a garrison from the 17th century onwards. Thus although most of the material is domestic in terms of its function, it frequently has a military aspect. Buttons are often from uniforms and some of the clay pipes may have been designed with the soldier in mind.

We have published the post-medieval pottery in some detail so that it might be compared with the medieval sequence. This helps to illustrate the transformation of the late medieval manufacturing traditions and consumption patterns, with their local focus, into a particular modern situation in which centralised industries were supplying a state-run organisation.

The clay pipes, too, form an important group because many are reasonably well dated. They help to flesh out the early history of tobacco consumption in the capital.

A final point of interest are the toys. It is very easy to forget that in the Castle the soldiers were often accompanied by their families.

4.4.2 THE POST-MEDIEVAL TO MODERN CERAMICS (16TH–20TH CENTURY)

Robert S Will

The post-Medieval to modern pottery can be divided into two main groups: that belonging to the medieval tradition and that belonging to the industrial factory system of the late 18th to 20th centuries. During the 16th and 17th centuries the reduced green glaze vessels of the medieval period continued to be produced

Illus 136
A selection of post-medieval finds.

although there seem to be a much wider range of vessels, including chamber pots, skillets and platters although mugs and cups in the English tradition of the time seem to be missing in Scotland (Caldwell, Haggarty, pers comm). Alongside the reduced green glaze there is an oxidised version most commonly identified with the site at Throsk on the upper Forth where jugs, platters and chamber pots similar to those found at the Castle have been found.

Most of the assemblage consists of vessels from the various industrial potteries that were established throughout Britain in the 18th and 19th centuries. Of particular interest are vessels from the potteries of the Forth basin and the rest of Scotland. These potteries tended to produce the same sort of product, although each had its own speciality line. As a result of the rapid industrialisation of the potteries and the competitive nature of the business, many patents were lodged in respect of methods of manufacture, design and decoration. As these patents still exist some designs and vessels can be dated to specific years especially if a maker's mark is on the sherd.

Although many of the sherds recovered from the Castle were white earthenware with little decoration, a number of different decorative styles were identified. By far the commonest was the use of transfer-printed designs in a variety of styles and colours unfortunately, due to the small size of most of the sherds, the designs and actual factories could not be identified. A wide range of sponge-printed designs were noted on sherds, this was a Scottish speciality associated with factories in Glasgow and Kirkcaldy. Even with the introduction of these quicker and cheaper methods, hand-painting was still used, often combined with the other styles (none illustrated).

A large amount of industrial stoneware and redware was recovered from the Castle and represents the everyday ceramics in use throughout Scotland from *c* 1830 which continued to be made into the 20th century. The redware vessels were usually storage jars, often globular in shape, with a dark brown or black manganese glaze and occasionally decorated with slip-trailed designs. Several complete profiles of slip-lined redware 'dairy bowls' were also recovered and would date to the late 19th century. These bowls were made throughout Scotland in most local potteries and it would seem likely that these were made at Prestonpans outside Edinburgh. There were historical references to hawkers selling such wares from Prestonpans in Edinburgh (Edinburgh City Archive, Haggarty pers comm).The profiles from the Castle help to show the size and range of these vessels.

The assemblage also produced some surprise sherds, in particular a marked base from the Dunmore pottery at Bo'ness. This pottery produced highly decorative ornamental pieces which were much sought after at the time and are very collectable today. The presence of such a vessel at the Castle must relate to the Officers' Mess or family quarters. Another such surprise was a base sherd from a blue and white hand-painted tin-glazed mug or posset pot which may date to the 18th century. An unglazed red earthenware vase was recovered which although broken still contained a deposit of yellow paint or pigment on the inside. This vessel could again date to the 17th or 18th century.

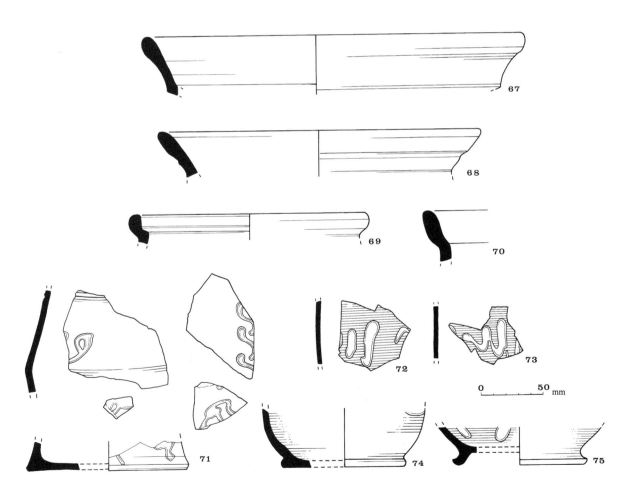

Illus 137
Post-medieval pottery Throsk-types and Slip-decorated Redware.

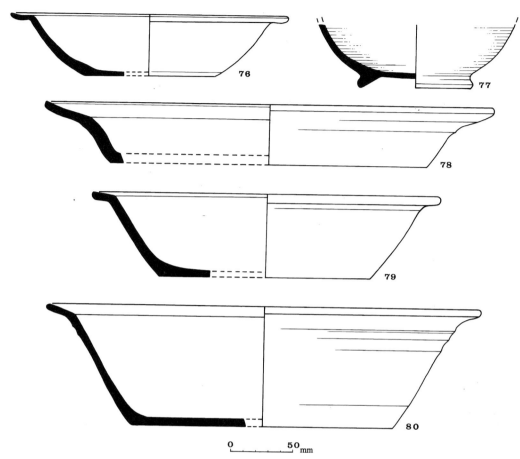

Illus 138
Post-medieval Slip-lined Redware and industrial pottery.

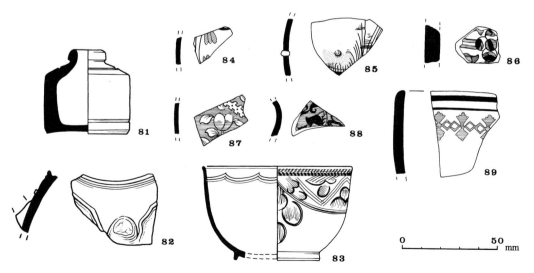

Illus 139
Industrial pottery and transfer-printed wares.

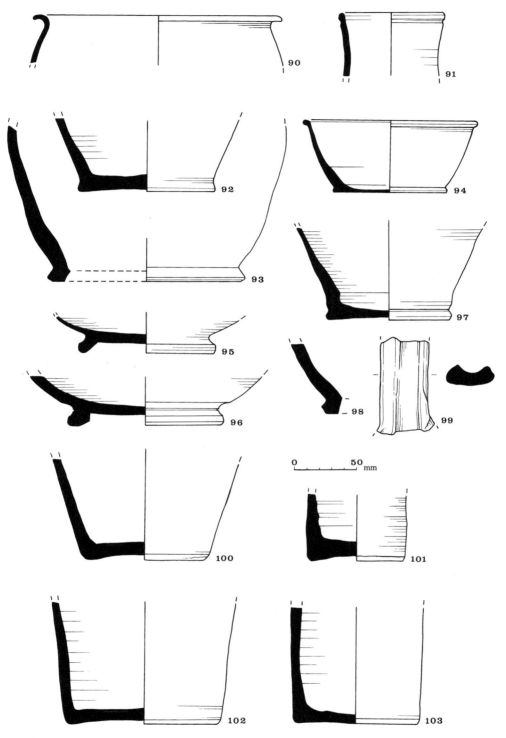

Illus 140
Modern pottery.

CATALOGUE OF ILLUSTRATED POTTERY

The following catalogue contains the selection of post-Medieval pottery which has been illustrated (the numbers continue on from those used in the medieval catalogue).

Cat No	Area (Phase)	Context	Description
	POST-MEDIEVAL (illus 137)		
67	X (6)	1359	Throsk jar rim
68	X (10)	1062	Throsk jar rim
69	G (5)	144	Throsk jar rim
70	K (6)	125	Throsk jar rim
71	L (6)	809	Slip-decorated Redware
72	L (6)	811	Slip-decorated Redware
73	L (6)	?811	Slip-decorated Redware
74	L (6)	811	Slip-decorated Redware
75	L (6)	813	Slip-decorated Redware

SLIP-LINED REDWARE AND INDUSTRIAL POTTERY (ILLUS 138; 139)

76	L (6)	809	Slip-lined dairy bowl
77	L (7)	802	Slip-lined dairy bowl
78	L (6)	811	Slip-lined dairy bowl
79	L (6)	809/813	Slip-lined dairy bowl
80	L (7)	804	Slip-lined dairy bowl
81	F (-)	024	19th-century stoneware inkwell
82	L (7)	802	Teapot tortoise shell decoration

83	L (7)	803	Hand-painted teacup
84	F (-)	089	Hand-painted teacup
85	L (7)	802	Hand-painted with iron stud
86	unstrat		Delft-type
87	L (7)	802	Transfer print
88	L (7)	802	Transfer print
89	L (7)	802	Sponge-decorated

MODERN POTTERY (ILLUS 140)

90	L (6)	813	Bowl/ chamber pot
91	L (6)	809	Jug
92	H (10)	244	Jar
93	unstrat		Jar
94	L (6)	809	Bowl
95	unstrat		Bowl
96	unstrat		Bowl
97	L (7)	804	Bowl
98	L (6)	809	Bowl
99	L (6)	833	Strap handle
100	H (mod)	221	Stoneware
101	unstrat		Stoneware
102	J (7)	624	Stoneware
103	F (-)	088	Stoneware

4.4.3 THE POST-MEDIEVAL GLASS

D B Gallagher

The most important artefacts are presented below; a full catalogue of post-Medieval glass is to be found in fiche (4.4.3.1mf, 1:G3–4; Tables 17–19, 1:G5–7).

VESSEL GLASS

WINE GLASSES

1   H (mod) 221
Fragment of an eight-sided moulded stem of a wine glass, c 1715–1765 (Haynes 1959, 219).

2   H (mod) 210
Fragment of moulded pedestal stem in green glass; 18th century.

3   H (mod) 211
Fragment of a wine glass with a collared top to the stem; mid-18th century (cf Haynes 1959, fig 78e).

4   F (-) 59
Fragment of a ?conical foot of a wine glass, in white glass, broken across the welded junction of foot and stem.

5   F (-) 74
Rim fragment of a saucer-topped wine glass in white glass.

6   H (8) 330
Small fragment of the bowl of a wine glass.

7   H (4) 461
Two small fragments, possibly of the knob of a wine glass.

DECANTERS

8   K (-) 724
Small decanter stopper with spherical top and ground glass sides, this example would be too small for an ordinary decanter and may have belonged to a pint or half-pint decanter, or a cruet (cf Thompson et al 1984, 89).

BEER GLASSES

9   F (-) 34
Beer glass rim in clear white glass.

10   L (-) 824
Three fragments of a ?beer glass in pale green glass.

MISCELLANEOUS VESSEL GLASS

11   F (-) 37
Strap handle, almost straight, in dull green glass. L = 75mm.

12   K (-) 769
Wall sherd of vessel in pale green glass.

BOTTLE GLASS

PHARMACEUTICAL BOTTLES (illus 141)

13   X (10) 1061
Phial in pale blue metal, cloudy with swirl marks and some iridescent decay. Pointed kick and everted rim; H 54mm, capacity 17.5ml; similar examples from a group from a c 1670–1740 context from Temple Balsall, West Midlands (Gooder 1984, 221), whilst finds of pipe and bottle glass from the same context indicate a date towards the end of that bracket.

14   L (-) 802*
Pharmaceutical bottle in pale blue glass, rectangular section; H = 123mm; 19th century.

WINE BOTTLES

15 X (10) 1061
Neck and fragment of shoulder in olive green glass, with a splayed mouth and string rim tooled downwards; c 1720–40 (cf Hume 1970, 64–5).

16 X (10) 1061
Body of a bottle, olive green, with a straight, inward-sloping wall, diam = 115mm; c 1730–45; possibly part of no 3 above.

17 X (10) 1061
Base similar to no 4 above, diam = 125mm.

18 X (10) 1062
Neck fragment, in olive-green glass, with splayed mouth; 18th century.

19 B (-) 201
Neck fragment in green glass with thin string band near rim; early 18th century (cf Hume 1970, 64).

20 F (-) 54
Neck fragment with a bead rim and single string band, in olive green glass; 18th century.

21 B (-) 201
Wine bottle neck in dark green glass, with a single thin string band; 18th century.

22 L (-) 824
Neck of a wine bottle with a double string band, in green glass; late 18th to early 19th century.

23 F (-) 40
Neck of wine bottle in dark green glass with double string band; early 19th century (cf Hume 1970, 68).

24 F (-) 39
Straight-sided bottle in dark green glass, complete except for the neck; mid to late 19th century.

26 F (-) 47
Straight-sided bottle in olive green glass, rim missing; 19th century.

27 H (mod) 221
Lower half of a straight-sided bottle in white clear glass; 19th century.

28 H (mod) 221
Wall sherd in green glass with 'McE(wan)' in relief, late 19th century.

29 F (-) 50
Plain applied seal from the shoulder of a wine bottle, oval, in dull olive green glass; L = 28mm.

SPIRIT BOTTLE

30 unstrat
Base of hip flask, in white glass, with '. . 5/28' in relief on the bottom.

OTHER BOTTLES

31 J (-) 624
Egg bottle for carbonated drink, in pale green glass, neck ring missing; present length 225mm. This length of egg bottle is datable to c 1860–1900 (Talbot 1974, 40).

BEADS

32 F (-) 19
Blue glass globular bead, moulded; diam = 9mm, L = 9mm.

33 F (-) 19
Globular bead in pale blue paste; diam = 7mm, L = 5mm.

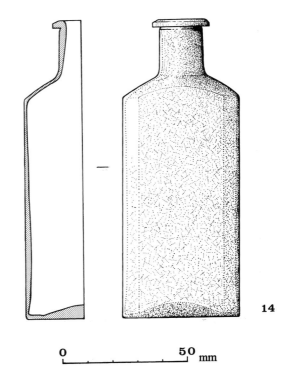

Illus 141
Post-medieval glass bottle.

34 F (-) 19
Globular bead in pale blue paste; diam = 7mm, L = 7mm.

35 F (-) 19
Globular bead in pale blue paste; diam = 7mm, L = 4mm.

36 F (-) 19
Half a globular bead in pale blue paste; diam = 7mm, L = 6mm.

MISCELLANEOUS GLASS

37 X (mod) 1061
Disc of slightly opaque glass, ground edge, diam = 33mm and max T = 2mm. Purpose uncertain, possibly from a locket.

38 H (9) 277
Fragment of glass tubing, in clear glass; L = 16mm and W = 3mm.

WINDOW GLASS

PAINTED WINDOW GLASS

39 H (mod) 221
Fragment of a quarry in pale greenish-blue soda glass, 1mm in thickness, having part of two sides surviving with an angle at the tip of 155°. The fragment is painted with a leaf spray, in red-brown, between two fields of solid red.
Possibly from a 16th- or 17th-century window, cf Basing House (Moorhouse 1970, 71, fig 30.72) and Northampton (Oakley & Hunter 1979, 296)

4.4.4 CLAY PIPES

Dennis B Gallagher

The following is an account of 670 fragments of clay tobacco pipe which were excavated from various areas within Edinburgh Castle. The pipes (illus 142; 143) have been recorded and studied according to the guidelines laid down by Davey (1981). The report is divided into four parts, two in the printed text and two in fiche. First the evidence provided by the pipes for the main excavated areas is considered; secondly, an abstract catalogue of the main diagnostic fragments is presented. In the fiche (4.4.5.1mf) a complete catalogue is presented (2:A3–9) where the pipes are discussed in relation to their manufacture and supply and a summary of the evidence from all excavated contexts is given in tabulated form (2:A10–14).

PIPES IN THEIR CONTEXTS

AREAS H AND X • MILLS MOUNT

40 fragments were excavated from the S side of the Cartshed. Diagnostic forms included a heel fragment of a bowl by Patrick Crawford, who is recorded active as a pipemaker in Edinburgh 1671–c 1700. This was recovered from context 237, associated with the construction of defences of c 1670–90.

A bowl of mid-17th-century form was recovered from context 233, which is associated with the construction of a ramp in the late 17th or early 18th century. This may be either residual or the product of a maker using an old mould.

Area X (under the Cartshed) contained groups of pipes from several closely dated deposits. Context 1344 is the construction trench of the Storekeeper's House which was dated by documentary sources to 1680–95. The pipes from this context are all of a c 1640–60 date, indicating a redeposition of early material. They are mainly of a low quality and contain a number of Dutch imports.

Context 1342 is a levelling deposit of 1746. All the pipes may be dated stylistically to the mid-17th century, but given their poor quality the date bracket must be extended into the latter part of the century. Again, the pipes from this context are redeposited. The context also contained a wig curler. These are difficult to date closely, but the present example is similar to one from Oxford found in a 1700–40 context. It is certainly later than the pipe group and may be contemporary with the deposition.

Context 1061 is a deposit sealed by the erection of the building of 1746. The one bowl from this context is a London-type product whose form can be compared with those from a kiln at Brentford, dated c 1740–80 (Oswald 1981). Other finds from this context include a pharmaceutical bottle of c 1670–1740 and fragments of wine bottles of a c 1720–45 date.

AREA G • THE ENTRANCE FLANKER

33 Fragments of clay pipe were recovered from Area G. Judging from the wide stem bore diameters, all of the fragments from this area are of 17th- or early 18th-century date. The exception was 122 which included six fragments of probable 19th-century date, including a bowl by Peter Wilson of Edinburgh, who was active as a maker 1847–1902.

AREA J • THE ENTRANCE FLANKER

57 fragments were recovered from this area. Context 621 may be dated to immediately prior to the construction of the Detention Block in 1866. This contained a bowl stamped 'CUNNINGHAM 135 FRANCIS St.' Two bowls of c 1690–1740, from context 628 are probably residual from the construction of a 19th-century wall footing. Other residual fragments include a Gateshead stem and a Dutch fleur-de-lis roller stamp.

AREA K • THE ENTRANCE FLANKER

55 fragments were recovered from this area. This area included 17th-century dump deposits: 748 had two bowls of c 1620–40 and c 1640–60 and the stratigraphically later 739 included a bowl of 1610–40. This may represent dumping of c 1640–60.

Context 716 may be identified with the construction phase of the Guard House in the 1860s. The finds include a pipe bowl in a style known in the later 19th century as a 'Beaconsfield'. This name dates from after 1876 when Disraeli was created Lord Beaconsfield, but the pipe form may predate its present title.

AREA L • THE INNER BARRIER FORECOURT

Finds from this area included 141 clay pipe fragments. This included a group from the drawbridge pit, which was infilled in the mid-18th century. Six bowls from this group spanned the dates c 1650–c 1730. Sealed contexts within the pit included a late 17th-century bowl and a roller stamp of the same date from 840. A Gateshead stem stamp of c 1685–1700 came from context 849, stratigraphically earlier than the two above, included two bowls of c 1700–30 indicating that the finds from contexts 840 and 849 were residual. A group of 32 pipe fragments came from 825, a context at the top of the pit fill but not necessarily part of it. This group included two bowls of c 1640–60 and four from c 1680–c 1730.

Context 833 was a deposit abutting a structure which was recorded standing in 1695. The pipe fragments included an Edinburgh bowl of c 1700.

AREA M • THE COAL YARD

28 clay pipe fragments were recovered from this area. This included a bowl from the fill of a grave, feature 1121 and another bowl fragment from the fill of ditch feature 1124.

AREA F • THE 1800 MAIN GUARD

61 Fragments were excavated from this area. Context 40 contained a number of marked fragments, including stems by Duncan of Leith and Thomas White of Edinburgh, of early to mid-19th-century date. This is compatible with the occupation of the Main Guard House, which was demolished in 1854. Post-demolition contexts included a McDougall of Glasgow stem (post-1847), from 19.

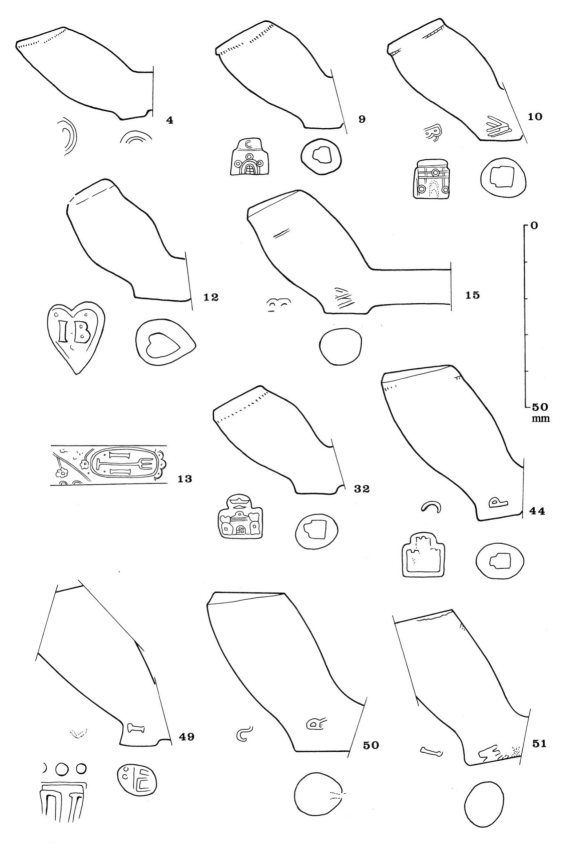

Illus 142
Selected early clay pipes.

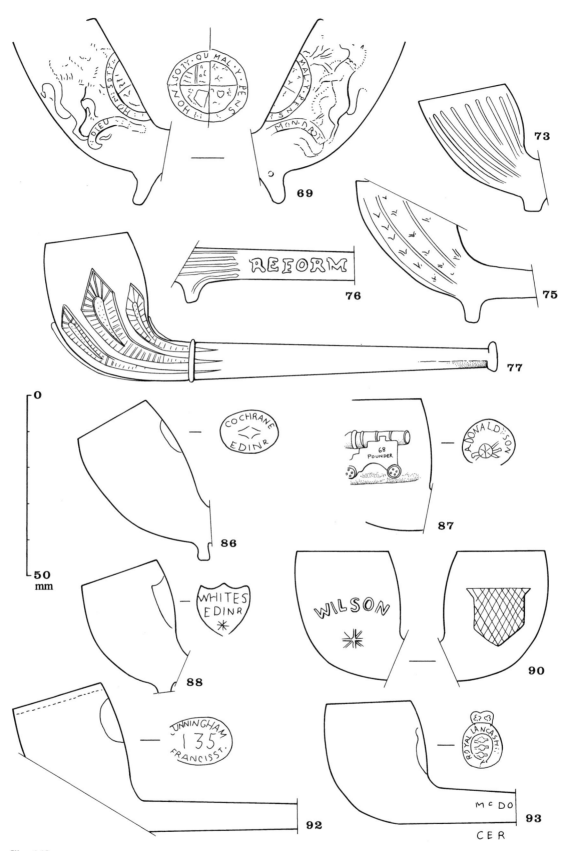

Illus 143
Selected late clay pipes.

DISCUSSION

The marking of Edinburgh pipes during the 17th century is unusual in that they often carry two forms of marking. One is the maker's initials, mould-imparted on each side of the heel. The second form is a basal stamp which is always based on the triple-towered castle: the arms of the City of Edinburgh. This usage is similar to the makings of the Edinburgh pewterers and silversmiths and suggests that the maker was working with civic approval within the guild framework.

Edinburgh pipemaking in the period 1620–60 was dominated by the work of William Banks, who held a Royal Patent granting him a monopoly in pipemaking in Scotland (Gallagher 1987a, 5–8). Four pipes from the excavations (illus 142, *10, 15* & *39–40*) are identifiable as his products, each being marked with a mould-imparted W/B. Other pipes from this period, without the W/B but with the castle basal stamp may be tentatively linked with Banks. This low number of Banks pipes is atypical of 17th-century pipe groups from the Edinburgh area and indicates that the excavated areas do not contain major rubbish deposits of mid-17th-century date.

Eight bowls may be attributed to Patrick Crawford, another major Edinburgh pipe manufacturer (illus 142, *41–6*) Crawford was active 1671–*c* 1700 and after his death his widow, Jean Wemyss, continued to produce pipes marked PC. She is well-documented as a supplier of pipes to the Company of Scotland in their venture to found a colony at Darien, in Central America. Jean Wemyss supplied some 235,600 pipes for this venture (Horton *et al* 1987, 248) and the number of PC marked bowls found on excavations throughout southern and central Scotland testify to this huge output. Several of the bowls from the present group exhibit evidence of the recutting of the maker's initials on worn moulds, resulting in a double impression on the pipe where the earlier letter had not been completely erased.

There is one, or possibly two, bowls with the mould-imparted initials I/A (illus 142, *48–9*). The identification of the source of manufacture of these I/A bowls is problematic. They have been previously assigned to a John Aiken family of Glasgow by the present writer (Gallagher 1987b, 51) but the portcullis basal stamp is a variant of the Edinburgh Castle stamp. An Alexander Aiken is described as a pipemaker in the 1690 Hearth Tax lists for Leith and Canongate (SRO E69/16/3,16) and this may be the same Alexander Aiken who appears in the Glasgow records from the mid 1690s, following his marriage to the daughter of a Glasgow weaver.

A number of stems bear maker's marks of 17th and 18th-century date. These included a roller stamped stem (illus 142, *47*) of James Colquhoun, a major Glasgow maker (cf Gallagher 1987b, 53, fig 7.1). A similar Colquhoun stem was found in the Back Well of Edinburgh Castle. Two stems and one bowl (illus 142, *12* & *53–4*) bear marks of Tyneside makers. The bowl has an IB stamp, possibly a product of John Bowman of Gateshead. The stems have stamps of Thomas Parke, *c* 1667–87 (Edwards 1988, 52, no 5) and Michael Parke, *c* 1692–1737 (Edwards 1988, 48, no 1). Tyneside products are unusual in Edinburgh but not unknown. The export of English pipes to Scotland is recorded in this period but in this case they are more likely to have been carried by soldiers passing through Newcastle on their way to Edinburgh.

The Dutch pipes (*4, 5, 13–4, 27–8* and *55–65*) are of very varied quality, many being low quality products with the occasional mould-imparted decoration. This form of decoration, although it produced a rich effect, was cheap to produce as it required no finishing once the pipe was out of the mould. Examples of this mould-imparted decoration from the excavations include a stem fragment (illus 142, *13*) incorporating the initials of the Gouda I/I maker (Duco 1987, 39–42, who illustrates an example with complete decoration and bowl).

Another stem fragment from this same mould was recovered from the excavations at St. Mary's Street, Edinburgh (Lawson 1980, 172, fig 8P), although it was not identified as a Dutch product in the site report. Some of the other Dutch pipes are of a much higher level of manufacture, some having stems impressed with roller stamps (*61–65*) whilst one is also painted (*61*). Painted pipes of this date are highly unusual; no other example of such decoration has been recorded in Scotland. One bowl fragment has splashes of brown glaze, demonstrating the close relationship between the Dutch pipemaker and the potter who glazed and fired the pipes (Duco 1981, 385). Area X (Phase 10) contexts 1342 and 1344 contained a large quantity of poor quality pipes, mostly Dutch in origin. With one of these bowls (*25*) a misplaced stopper had created an over-thin wall which had collapsed during manufacture forming a hole. This pipe was, nevertheless, sold. On another pipe the maker has slashed two parallel grooves on the wall of the bowl with a milling knife; possibly a deliberate indication of the low quality of the product.

Several of the Scottish pipes are dated to the early 18th century (66–7) but exact dating suffers from a fall in the number of pipes produced, following the growing popularity of snuff, with the subsequent lack of documentary evidence for makers, and also a lack of dated groups. The group from Area X 1342, a context dated to 1746, may be an indication of the rarity of pipe smoking in the castle by the mid-18th century, for whilst a wig curler from the group (29) was possibly contemporary with the 1746 deposition, all the pipes were redeposited 17th-century material. The pipe with the Hanoverian arms (illus 143, 69) is highly unusual in a Scottish context and must be seen in the context of an English garrison in the Castle. The absence of any decoration on the front mould and the shape of the spur ally it with an example from an excavated kiln at Brentford, with a closing date of c 1770 (Laws & Oswald 1981, 51, fig 12.43).

The early 19th century is represented by the thin-walled spurred forms typical of that period. These are often decorated with fluting and occasionally with lettering, either makers' names or slogans (illus 143, 73–6). Some of the later pipes display decoration aimed at a military market. The pipe by Donaldson of Edinburgh (illus 143, 87) has a detailed depiction of a 68 pounder cannon, the largest in the British army. This is an excellent example the work of skilled mould engraving. The rear of the bowl bears a stamp containing the maker's name and a field gun. A McDougall pipe (illus 143, 93), in contrast, only has a stamp applied to the rear of the bowl after moulding. Some of the pipes have decoration in high relief in forms that were common to all the major Scottish pipemakers, eg the basket design (79).

A number of the pipes of 19th- and 20th-century date can be attributed to makers. These are mainly from Edinburgh and Leith and include Thomas White (88), Cochrane (86), Alexander Donaldson (87), J Mackenzie (108–9), P B Wilson (90, 113–14), Duncan (105–6) and William Christie (104). In addition there are pipes by McDougall of Glasgow (93), Tennant of Berwick (111), and Posener (110) and Balme of London (85). Many Scottish makers produced pipes modelled on those of London makers, eg the 'Small Mile End' of William White of Glasgow (Gallagher 1987c, 148) but the Balme bowl in the present group is likely to be a London product for it includes not only the much copied Balme stamp on the rear of the bowl but also the initials P/B on the spur, an uncommon feature of Scottish pipes after the early 19th century.

ABSTRACT CATALOGUE OF CLAY PIPES

A full catalogue is published in microfiche (4.4.5.1mf, 2:A3–9). This abstract list of clay pipes describes those pipes illustrated (illus 142; 143). Like the full catalogue it firstly lists those pipes in stratigraphically significant contexts and then lists pipes in general chronological order.

4   X (9) 1344
Narrow bowl with damaged base, polished, milled and bottered, traces of a circular basal stamp; 8/64"; possibly an Amsterdam product, c 1630–50 (cf Haan & Krook 1988, 23).

9   X (9) 1344
Bowl, burnished, bottered and with almost complete milling, portcullis type basal stamp, no mould-imparted maker's mark; 6/64"; an Edinburgh product.

10   X (9) 1344
Highly burnished bowl, bottered and with coarse milling forming a continuous groove. Mould-imparted W/B, with double impression from recutting of the mould. The letter B has been very crudely cut on the mould, the metal from the centres of the letter having been left in place. Basal stamp of the portcullis type. 7/64". A product of William Banks of Edinburgh, c 1640–60.

12   X (9) 1344
Bowl, bottered but carelessly finished, heart-shaped base with IB stamp having pellets over and between the letters and an indecipherable shape below; 7 /64"; John Bowman of Gateshead, c 1650–75. A Tyneside bowl type 3b (Edwards 1988, 8) and possibly a type A5 stamp. Type A stamps are associated with the bowls of John Bowman, among other, but

Edwards (1988, 19) has not identified this particular sub-category with Bowman.

13   X (9) 1344
A moulded stem fragment with foliate decoration surrounding a cartouche enclosing a dotted I/I and a fork/trident; 6/64"; Dutch, Gouda mid-17th century. This is a product of the Gouda I/I maker. The complete pipe, 230mm in length, is illustrated by Duco (1987, 40).

15   M (-) 1121
Bowl with mould-imparted W/B, the B showing signs of mould wear, bottered; 7/64"; 1650-60; Area M (1121). A late product of William Banks. The lack of milling, burnishing and basal stamp indicates a low quality product.

32   J (-) 602
Burnished bowl, finely milled and bottered, with castle basal stamp; 6/64"; 1640–60.

44   T (-) 1324
Large bowl, bottered, burnished and milled, with mould imparted P/C and castle basal stamp; 7/64"; Patrick Crawford of Edinburgh, c 1680–1720. Also two others bowls produced from the same mould, from context Area T 1318 and Area X (10) 1061.

49   L (-) 849
Fragment of a burnished bowl, bottered, with a mould-imparted I/?A, the second letter being obscured by the finishing, basal stamp of portcullis type; Edinburgh, 1690–1730.

51   T (-) 1325
Bowl fragment, lightly bottered, no milling but with a double indentation on the rear 5mm below the rim, mould imparted W/(?)I; 7/64"; an Edinburgh product, c 1680–1720.

69   L (-) 805

Bowl with forward-projecting pointed spur, bearing the Hanoverian Arms with rose and thistle on either side of the crown, in relief, upper part of bowl missing, front seam undecorated, dot on spur; 1760–80 (Atkinson & Oswald 1980, 373) 6/64". The crowded lettering of DROIT, in comparison with the rest of the motto, suggests a spelling mistake corrected by the insertion of a letter into the design on the mould (cf Le Cheminant 1981, 124, no 20 for a similar pipe with a misspelt motto). Distribution of this type of pipe is mainly concentrated on London (Oswald 1975, 107; Atkinson & Oswald 1980, 390). Its presence in Edinburgh must reflect the presence of an English garrison in the post-1745 period.

77   G (-) 122

Complete pipe, length 120mm, bowl decorated with leaf motifs in relief springing from a collar on stem, no maker's marks; variants on this design are common throughout the 19th century, f4/64".

Cochrane, Edinburgh

86   M (-) 1109

Spurred bowl with 'COCHRANE/ EDINr' and lozenge in oval; 4/64". Possibly the product of Thomas Cochrane, active 1869–1902, or George Cochrane, 1878–86.

Donaldson, Alexander 1858–66

87   L (-) 802

Bowl fragment decorated with a cannon, in high relief,

having '68 POUNDER' in relief lettering on its carriage; a stamp on the rear of the bowl with 'A.DONALDSON' and a field gun in circle. Stamp shows evidence of recutting: double impression of gun and part of DONALDSON; 5/64". The smooth-bore 68 pounder gun was the most powerful gun of the 19th-century British army. It was normally used on fixed mountings in coastal defence. The pipe shows it mounted on a wooden 'garrison standing carriage' (Hughes 1969, 114).

White, Thomas, Edinburgh 1825–51

88   L (-) 802

Spurred bowl with 'WHITES EDINr' and a star in a shield-shaped frame; /64".

Wilson, P B 1847–1902

90   G (-) 122

Bowl with 'WILSON' over a star/hatched shield on sides, in relief; 5/64".

92   J (-) 621

Three adjoining fragments of a bowl and part of stem, the bowl having mould-imparted milling around the rim and CUNNINGHAM 135 FRANCIS St, in an oval stamp, on the rear. 5/64".

93   K (-) 730

Bowl and part of stem, bowl stamped with military badge: 'ROYAL LANCA . .' with three cannon; stem with mould-imparted 'McDO . . / . .CER'; 4/64". This pipe is probably the 'Lancer' design which was no 151 of McDougall's of Glasgow in the 1900 list of moulds (Gallagher 1987c, 145).

4.4.5 THE OTHER POST-MEDIEVAL SMALL FINDS

DB Gallagher

DISCUSSION

The catalogue is preceded by a discussion of the more significant categories of material.

ARMS

Two examples of friction tubes were found in Area L 802, Hume (1991, 423–25) has noted one from Fort George. These copper alloy tubes, used to ignite cannon charges, were introduced into the British Army by 1853 (Hughes 1969, 49). Identical examples were excavated from 1800–60 contexts at Signal Hill, Newfoundland; they are discussed by Jelks (1973, 89) who includes the following explanation of their working:

> The primer is a small tube filled with rifle powder and inserted in the vent at the moment of firing. It is ignited by the friction produced in drawing a rough wire through a friction composition, consisting of one part of chlorate of potassa and two parts of sulphuret of antimony, moistened with a weak solution of gum arabic, and mixed together in a wet state. This composition is contained in a smaller tube which is inserted at right angles, near the top . . . A lanyard, with a hook attached, is used to pull out the wire (Board of Artillery Officers 1864, 14).

One of the two examples from Edinburgh Castle was split and bent outwards at its shorter tube, a result of the misfiring of the cannon.

Other finds included a wide range of ammunition from musket balls and primitive lead shot to more recent bullets and cartridge cases. The cartridge cases are unlikely to have been fired in the Castle itself, they are more likely spent ammunition from ranges, brought back to the Castle to be recycled as scrap metal.

GUN-FLINTS (illus 144) • William Finlayson

The well made gun-flint comes from a surprisingly early context. Flint-lock weapons appear to have only come into general use by the beginning of the 18th century, and were only introduced into the English army in 1686. The regular manufacture of gun-flints only began in France by about 1719 (Skertchley 1879). The regularity of the piece suggests that it was not made near the beginning of flint-lock use as:

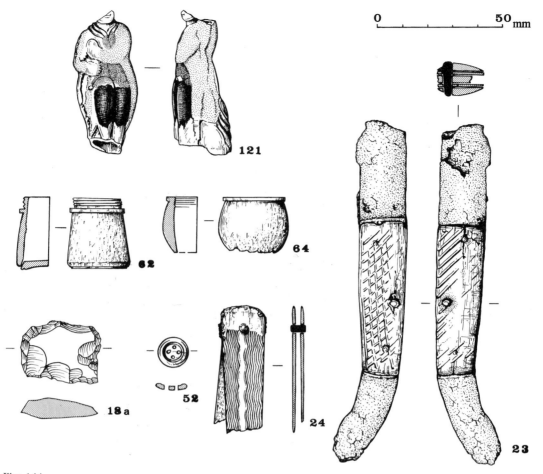

Illus 144
Assorted post-medieval small finds.

At first rough pieces of convenient size were fitted in flint-locks, then with the general use of this fire-arm by the beginning of the 18th century a demand arose for more precise and durable flints . . . in 1727 we find the Hanover War Chancery sending workers to England to learn the trade Rainbird Clarke 1935, 40).

It appears that soldiers were initially responsible for the rough shaping and repair of their gun-flints, and the crude gun-flint found is probably more representative of that type of working. The regular gun-flint does not have the two marked dorsal ridges of classic late 19th-century gun flints from Brandon, so is possibly not very recent in manufacture.

By repute, gun-flints were probably made in Glasgow at some time, using imported flint, although it seems unlikely that this industry would have developed at the beginning of flint-lock use. It is remarkable how few gun-flints have been found. Gun-flints had a fairly short working life, and stores could well have been very large.

THE PLUMB-BOB

This may be simply a tool of the building trade, but given its military context another usage most be considered. Plumb-lines were used by 19th-century British Artillerymen to position, or lay, a mortar. The 'layer' sighted through a plumb-line to the target whilst the mortar was positioned so that the cord was aligned with a chalk line along the top surface of the piece (Hughes 1969, 62–3).

PERSONAL ITEMS

The Buttons

Buttons were an important feature on uniforms during the late 18th and early 19th centuries, many being used for purely decorative purposes, and a wide variety is represented in the finds. Forms include flat one-piece buttons with four holes from shirts breeches and trousers. Materials include copper-alloy, mother-of-pearl and bone. Late 18th-century military buttons often displayed the number of the regiment within a border (*36*). Later buttons have a more elaborate regimental insignia (*32*), whilst a standard General Service button bearing the Royal Arms, was introduced in 1876 (*29–31* and *33*). Makers include Firmin & Sons and Smith & Wright, both of Birmingham, a main centre of the button industry. Smith & Wright were the main manufacturers of buttons for other ranks during the period 1855–71 (Parkyn 1956, 5).

Bone Boxes (illus 144)

All have had screw fitting lids (*61–5*) and at least one (*62*), and possibly two, had their bases fitted with a screw thread. The care taken to make the vessels airtight suggests that they may have held ointments. It is possible that the two bulbous boxes were part of a more elaborate, composite construction, such as the example from HMS 'Dartmouth', which was wrecked in 1690. All the boxes under discussion, however, are from 19th-century contexts.

Comb

This is a double-sided comb of the most common early post-medieval type. For similar combs cf Fox & Barton 1986, 242, fig 154.3 & 4, and Thompson *et al* 1984, 110, fig 55.78.

Pins

The pins range in size from a long 'hair' pin, length 113mm to small 'dressmaking' pins of a 20–25mm length. Several of the smaller pins are from grave contexts; some which were found adhering to skeletons and would have been used for fastening shrouds.

Toys

Miniature household items, implements and weapons, such as the tiny axe (*67*) made of cast copper alloy and dating from the late 16th or 17th century, are recorded from a number of sites (Baart 1977, 466–9; Fox & Barton 1986, 238). They are usually identified as toys. The miniature clay soldier (illus 144, *121*) may also have been a toy. Clay soldiers of this type were manufactured at the Newbigging Pottery in Musselburgh (Haggarty & McIntyre forthcoming).

CATALOGUE OF FINDS

STRUCTURAL IRONWORK AND HARDWARE

NAILS

1   H (-) 566
    Nail of copper alloy, head missing; L = 37mm.
2   L (-) 802
    Nail, L = 38mm, with round flat head; diam = 10mm.
3   H (mod) 221
    Fragment of lead window came, L = 75mm.
4   K (-) 749
    Fragment of lead window came, folded, present L = 75mm.
5   F (-) 34
    Mass of molten lead solidified on a surface of small stones; max L = 120mm.

TOOLS

6   F (-) 34
    Plumb-bob of lead, hemispherical; H = 40mm, diam = 50mm.

ARMS

7   L (-) 802
    Friction tube, for igniting a cannon charge, consisting of a tube of rolled copper-alloy sheeting, 79mm in length and 5mm in diameter, with a short tube, L = 10mm, attached to one end.
8   L (-) 802
    Friction tube; L = 78mm. As above except that the shorter tube is split and bent outwards and the longer tube is opening at the seam.

9   J (-) 610
Five lead musket balls, each 17mm in diameter and weighing *c* 30g.

10   J (-) 602
Lead plug, roughly square in section, W = 6mm, and swelling at one end, L = 29mm; possibly a small shot pellet (cf Baart 1977, 444.837).

11   F (-) 19
Lead bullet; L = 32mm.

12   F (-) 19
Lead bullet, L = 32mm.

13   F (-) 19
Copper-alloy cartridge case, with 'R^L', L = 56mm.

14   F (-) 19
Cartridge case in copper alloy with '765' stamped on exterior, L = 51mm, diam = 18mm.

15   F (-) 19
Cartridge case in copper-alloy, bent; L = 55mm, diam = 17mm.

16   F (-) 19
Cartridge case in copper alloy, compressed; L = 57mm, diam = 18mm.

17   H (-) 295
Chape, made of thin copper alloy sheet; L = 27mm.

18   K (-) 701
Two adjoining fragments of an early wedge gunflint, L = 37mm; *c* 1650–1750 (cf Hume 1972, 219–21; de Lotbiniere 1984, 206).

18a   M (-) 1121 SF341
Dark grey flint. Thick inner flake, secondary removals round all edges, some normal, some inverse and some bifacial. This modification produces a rectilinear flint tablet, probably a gun-flint, although not so regularly made as those from the well known Brandon workshops, and probably made on a flake, rather than on a blade segment. Dimensions 32 × 25 × 10mm.

18b   H/X (8) 586 SF438
Black flint. Inner blade segment, secondary removals all round edge, mostly normal except for one edge with bifacial retouch. This example is extremely regular, on a blade segment made of very fine flint. It is without doubt from one of the major gun-flint workshops, as at Brandon. The sides and heel are very slightly hollowed, noted by Skertchly as a 'point of beauty' (1879). Dimensions 30 × 32 × 8mm. This compares with Skertchly's figures of 33 × 28 × 10mm for best musket, 30 × 25 × 6mm for best carbine, 28 × 23 × 7mm for best horse pistol (original dimensions in inches).

CUTLERY

19   L (-) 802
Fragment of a tapering angular handle of a ?knife, with squared end, in polished ivory, probably sub-rectangular in original section; L = 29mm; cf Hume 1972, 182, fig 63, for a similar example dated to the late 17th century.

20   K (-) 711
Fork, iron tines, shaft and tang with remains of iron rivet for securing a two-piece handle. For a similar example from early to mid-19th century contexts cf Fox & Barton 1986, 241.10.

21   F (-) 44
Small fork, iron tines, shaft and tang with remains of an iron rivet for securing a two-piece handle.

22   F (-) 27
Spoon bowl in copper alloy.

OTHER KNIVES

23   M (-) 1110
Razor or folding knife, L = 140mm, with 'pistol grip' handle consisting of bone scales decorated with incised diagonal lines. secured by iron rivets.

24   L (-) 802
Fragment of a blade handle with scale tang. Flat scales of ?horn expanding to one end, secured by an iron rivet and decorated by 'combed' lines. As only one end of the handle survives the type of implement is uncertain. The flat scales may indicate a razor or penknife rather than a knife.

DRESS ACCESSORIES

25   L (-) 802
Plume holder, in copper alloy, tubular with serrated upper edge and remains of a rivet near the base; L = 65mm, diam = 10mm.

26   L (-) 809
Square belt buckle with central bar, in copper alloy (brass); L = 36mm; probably of mid-18th-century date.

BUTTONS

TWO-PIECE COPPER-ALLOY BUTTONS

27   F (-) 55
Bone back from an officer's button, with traces of a gilt metal front, diam = 18mm; late 18th century.

28   F (-) 59
Shell of copper-alloy coat button, diam = 18mm, with crown above an illegible cipher, possibly 'RV' (Royal Veterans), within a circular frame.

29   F (-) 19
Other ranks' general service button with Royal arms on the shell and 'FIRMIN & SONS Ltd BIRMINGHAM' on bottom, diam = 25mm; post 1902.

30   F (-) 19
Other ranks' small General Service domed button. Royal arms with pre-1902 crown on shell and 'SMITH & WRIGHT BIRMINGHAM' on bottom, diam = 16mm; late 19th century.

31   F (-) 19
Other ranks' small General Service domed button with Royal arms with post-1902 crown on shell and 'SMITH & (WRIGHT) BIRMINGHAM on bottom', flattened; diam = 18mm.

32   F (-) 25
Other ranks' tunic button of the Royal Artillery. Two piece, the shell having a gun with St Edward's crown above, 'SMITH & WRIGHT BIRMINGHAM' on bottom; diam = 22mm; 1855–1902.

33   H (mod)
Other ranks' large General Service button decorated with the Royal Arms with post 1902 crown; diam = 24mm.

34   F (-) 60
Flat face of two-piece button; diam = 26mm.

35   F (-) 59
Bottom of two-piece button; diam = 32mm.

ONE-PIECE BUTTONS

36   H (mod)
Other ranks' pewter coat button of the 19th Regiment of Foot. Flat with 19 in a pellet and spray border; diam = 23mm; mid 18th century. The 19th Regiment of Foot were stationed in the castle in 1754.

37   G (-) 117
Unmarked convex one-piece button in copper-alloy; diam = 23mm.

38   F (-) 40
Flat disc 'blazer' type of button with design of radiating lines within border of concentric circles, broken; diam = 28mm.

39   F (-) 59
Flat button of 'blazer' type or back of button, with shank; diam = 15mm.

40   F (-) 19
Flat button of 'blazer' type with chamfered edge; diam = 18mm.

41 F (-) 37
Flat button of 'blazer' type; diam = 15mm. Four hole copper-alloy.

42 F (-) 37
Flat four-hole trouser button with '. . . RRANTED ★ . . .' on front; diam = 18mm; 19th century.

43 L (-) 802
Slightly concave four-hole trouser button decorated with a pellet ring, diam = 16mm; 19th century.

44 F (-) 40
Four-hole trouser button with '. . . . FOUR HOLES' in raised lettering; diam = 17mm; 19th century.

MOTHER-OF-PEARL BUTTONS

45 F (-) 72
Four-hole shirt button; diam = 13mm.

46 H (-) 234
Four-hole shirt button, diam = ??mm.

BONE BUTTONS

47 A 1
Four-hole breeches button; diam = 29mm; Area A(1).

48 K (-) 723
Four-hole breeches button; diam = 17mm.

49 L (-) 802
Four-hole breeches button; diam = 19mm.

50 K (-) 731
Four-hole breeches button; diam = 18mm.

51 G (-) 122
Four-hole shirt button; diam = 12mm.

52 L (-) 805
Four-hole shirt button; diam = 12mm.

53 H (-) 200
Four-hole shirt button; diam = 12mm.

54 F (-) 59
Disc with one hole, probably the bottom of a two-piece button; diam = 13mm; an 18th-century type (Hume 1972, 90–1).

LACE TAGS

55 H (-) 344
Lace tag of copper alloy; L = 29mm.

56 H (-) 295
Lace tag of copper alloy; L = 33mm.

57 H (-) 317
Lace tag of copper alloy; L = 47mm.

58 H (-) 317
Lace tag of copper alloy; L = 26mm.

59 K (-) 717
Lace tag of copper alloy; L = 38mm.

PERSONAL POSSESSIONS

COMB

60 L (-) 814
Three adjoining fragments of a double-sided hair comb, in polished bone, with equal sized teeth on each side; max L = 34mm, max H = 29mm; 17th century.

BONE BOXES

61 K (unstrat)
Wall and base of a turned bone box with straight, tapering side and screw fitting for lid; diam at base = 16mm, H = 28mm.

62 K (-) 714
Half of the wall of a turned bone box with straight, tapering side and screw fittings for lid and base; diam at base = 25mm, H = 29mm.

63 K (unstrat)
Three adjoining fragments of the walls of a turned bone box with bulbous sides and internal screw fitting for a lid; max diam = 24mm, H = 21mm.

64 K (-) 714
Half of the wall of a turned bone box with bulbous sides and screw fitting for lid; max diam = 26mm, H = 23mm.

65 F (-) 25
Lathe-turned bone box with screw fitting lid, half of the latter missing; diam = 15mm, H = 13mm.

66 L (-) 802
Polished bone terminal in the form of two skull faces, with a separate closure plate pierced by a central perforation; H = 15mm, max diam = 21mm.

TOYS

67 F (-) 50
Miniature long-handled axe in copper alloy; L = 52mm.

UTENSILS AND HOUSEHOLD GOODS

68 K (-) 731
Curtain hook in copper alloy; L = 46mm; Area K(731/733).

69 F (-) 51
Turned bone handle with tang of an iron pin or hook; L = 51mm. Possibly a needlework tool, such as a crochet hook (cf Rogers 1983, 185).

PINS AND NEEDLES

70 M (-) 1110
Pin of copper alloy with solid globular head; L = 25mm.

71 M (-) 1105
Pin of copper alloy, head missing; L = 22mm.

72 M (-) 1116
Pin of copper alloy, head missing; L = 24mm.

73 M (-) 1119
Pin of copper alloy, broken in two parts, with solid globular head; L = 34mm. Found adhering to a skull.

74 M (-) 1119
Pin of copper alloy, broken in two parts, with solid globular head; L = 44mm. Found adhering to a skull.

75 M (-) 1128
Shroud pin of copper alloy with spiral wound globular head; L = 28mm.

76 M (-) 1128
Shroud pin of copper alloy with spiral wound globular head, point missing; L = 28mm.

77 M (-) 1128
Shroud pin of copper alloy with globular head; L = 19mm.

78 M (-) 1128
Shroud pin of copper alloy with globular head, point missing; L = 16mm.

79 M (-) 1128
Shroud pin of copper alloy with globular head; L = 34mm.

80 M (-) 1128
Shroud pin of copper alloy with globular head; L = 28mm.

81 M (-) 1128
Shroud pin of copper alloy with globular head; L = 28mm.

82 H 344
Pin of copper alloy with spiral wound globular head; L = 39mm.

83 G (-) 120
Pin of copper alloy with spiral wound globular head; L = 35mm.

84 G (-) 117
Pin of copper alloy with spiral wound globular head; L = 39mm.

85 G (-) 144
Pin of copper alloy with spiral wound globular head; L = 54mm.

86   J (-) 610
     Pin of copper alloy with spiral wound globular head; L = 57mm.
87   H (-) 350
     Pin of copper alloy, bent, with spiral wound globular head; L = 43mm.
88   H (-) 268
     Pin of copper alloy, with spiral wound globular head; L = 28mm.
89   H (-) 270
     Pin of copper alloy, bent, with spiral wound globular head; L = 35mm.
90   H (-) 294
     Long 'hair' pin with spiral wound globular head; L = 113mm.
91   H (-) 294
     Long pin of copper alloy, bent and with missing head; L = 90mm.
92   H (-) 237
     Small 'dressmaker' pin of copper alloy with spiral wound globular head; L = 26mm.
93   H (-) 270
     Small 'dressmaker' pin of copper alloy with spiral wound globular head; L = 23mm.
94   H (-) 339
     Pin of copper alloy with solid globular head; L = 40mm.
95   H (-) 346
     Needle or pin of copper alloy; L = 53mm, head missing.
96   H (-) 294
     Pin of copper alloy, head missing; L = 40mm.
97   F (-) 19
     Blue paste disc, possibly a gaming counter, with chipped edge; diam = 17mm.

MISCELLANEOUS

MARBLES

98   F (-) 19
     Marble of pipeclay; diam = 21mm.
99   F (-) 19
     Marble of pipeclay; diam = 19mm.
100 F (-) 19
     Marble of stoneware; diam = 21mm.
101 F (-) 19
     Marble of stoneware; diam = 20mm.
102 K (unstrat)
     Marble of stoneware; diam = 21mm.
103 F (-) 25
     Marble of stoneware with white salt glaze; diam = 20mm.

SLATE PENCILS

104 F (-) 24
     Slate pencil in hard dark grey slate roughly circular section, pointed end missing; L = 45mm.

105 L (-) 802
     Slate pencil in hard dark grey slate; L = 46mm.

HORN

106 M (-) 1110
     Fragment of horn with an incised line on one face, possibly a wall sherd of a vessel; max L = 24mm.

MISCELLANEOUS COPPER-ALLOY FRAGMENTS

107 F (-) 19
     Tubular casing, bound together with a ring binding; L = 68mm and diam = 10mm.
108 F (-) 37
     Spring clip in copper-alloy wire; L = 57mm.
109 F (-) 54
     Fragment of a strip, impressed with the numbers '81'; W = 18mm, present L = 26mm.
110 H (-) 270
     Rod, of circular section; L = 31mm.
111 H (-) 566
     Rod, broken at one end; L = 19mm.
112 H (-) 298
     Strip; L = 52mm, W = 3mm.
113 H (-) 566
     Strip, bent; L = 65mm, W = 4mm.
114 H (-) 270
     Fragment of copper-alloy wire, possibly a pin; L = 40mm.
115 F (-) 40
     Tubular casing; L = 28mm and diam = 16mm; open at one end and with 4mm hole at the other. Interior with rod across diameter.
116 F (-) 27
     Slightly curved rod; L = 27mm; diam = 3mm.
117 F (-) 59
     Fragment of sheeting, curved, with two grooves on the concave face; L = 15mm, W = 13mm.

LEATHER

118 H (-) 255
     Strap handle; L = 190mm, with traces of stitching along its folded length and each end pierced by a buttonhole.
119 H (-) 255
     Fragment of a shoe insole with a double line of stitching along the surviving edge; L = 28mm, max W = 25mm.
120 G (-) 122
     Eyelet in copper alloy, sandwiching traces of leather; diam = 8mm.
121 F (-) 74 SF32
     Clay figure of a soldier made in Musselburgh (Haggarty & McIntyre forthcoming).

4.4.6 THE TEXTILES

Thea Gabra-Sanders

Two textile samples were recovered from the fill of a construction trench (1085) Phase 9 for the Storekeeper's House

DESCRIPTION

The material comprised two samples of 'carbonized cloth':

a)   a small fragment

b)   five very small fragments and two short non-carbonized yarns

The fibres which are altered by carbonizing are black, very fragile and beyond recognition by straightforward light microscopy.

One basic weave is represented, tabby (plain weave) and sample A is woven from ?-spun single yarn in both systems whereas two fragments of sample B are woven from slightly Z-spun single yarn in system 1 and ?-spun single yarn in system 2.

The number of threads per 10mm in sample A is 40 in system 1 and 2. Sample B has 50 in system 1 and about 30 in system 2. The fineness (high thread-count) of the cloth would suggest that the material is silk.

The two samples are different in appearance. Owing to the smallness of the samples there is no way of establishing their use. Microscopic examination showed that the fibres of the two very small non-carbonized yarns were wool with a light brown colour. One is 3mm long and S-plied and the other is 5mm long and is S-spun single yarn.

TEXTILE CATALOGUE

The systems are designated 1 and 2 as the warp and weft cannot be identified. The direction of the spin of the yarn is indicated by Z (for clockwise, if a yarn is held vertically, the twisted fibres slope in the same direction as the centre portion of the letter Z). The number of threads per 10mm has been recorded (in general a higher thread count can be taken to indicate a finer fabric).

1   H (9)   1085   sample 113
Fragment of blackened cloth 4 × 2mm. The weave is tabby (plain). System 1, ?-spun single yarn, 40 threads per 10mm. System 2, ?-spun single yarn, 40 threads per 10mm.

2   H (9)   1085   sample 113
Five fragments of blackened cloth:
1)   5 × 2mm. The weave is tabby (plain). System 1, ?-spun single yarn, 50 threads per 10mm. System 2, ?-spun single yarn, 40 threads per 10mm.
2)   4 × 2mm, very crumpled. The weave is unidentifiable.

3)   5 × 1mm. The weave is tabby (plain). System 1, slight Z-spun single yarn, 50 threads per 10mm.
4)   3 × 2mm, very crumpled. The weave is unidentifiable.
5)   5 × 2mm, adhering to a small cinder. The weave is tabby (plain). System 1, slight Z-spun single yarn, about 30 threads per 10mm. system 2, ?-spun single yarn, about 50 threads per 10mm.

Yarn	Fibre	Spin	L	Diam
1	wool	S-plied	3mm	0.5mm
2	wool	S-spun	5mm	1.0mm

ENVIRONMENTAL STUDIES

5.1 INTRODUCTION TO THE RESEARCH PROGRAMME

Coralie M Mills

To the credit of the excavators, environmental archaeologists were consulted and involved from a very early stage of the fieldwork onwards. This allowed for the formulation of a sampling strategy, appropriate to the types of deposits present and to the range of questions being asked of the site, which could be applied throughout the excavations. The environmental work was co-ordinated by the author through the Archaeological Operations and Conservation branch of Historic Scotland.

5.1.1 SAMPLING

Two main types of sample were employed; bulk samples and structured samples. In addition, larger ecofactual material, principally bone, was recovered by hand during excavation.

BULK SAMPLES

Where possible, three large bags (holding about 5 litres) of soil were taken from each context. These were forwarded to AOC for sub-sampling and analysis. The bulk samples were sub-sampled for analyses of soils, pollen, phytoliths and of uncarbonised organic remains such as insects. These sub-samples were placed in cool storage prior to analysis. After sub-sampling, the remainder of each bulk sample, generally two large bags, was sieved using a water separation machine (see Table 21, 5.2mf, 2:B1–2). This allowed for the retrieval of small ecofacts and artefacts which would generally not be retrieved by hand. In this process carbonised material (the 'flot'; charcoal, seeds etc), is recovered separately from the non-floating material (the 'retent'). No chemicals are used in the process so that retrieved materials may be safely used for radiocarbon dating. Flots and retents were sorted in advance of analyses of plant remains, bone and shell. Artefactual and industrial materials were also retrieved and forwarded for analysis. Amongst these were tiny fragments of charred textile (see 4.4.6).

STRUCTURED SAMPLES

These were taken with Kubiena cans or as larger monoliths of sediment by using 'peat' tins. These samples were used for investigations of the structure, content and mode of formation of the major deposits through the methods of soil micromorphology (see Soils Report 5.5 below).

5.1.2 ASSESSMENTS AND ANALYSES

During excavation it was not certain whether the preservation conditions at the site would allow for the survival of the less robust classes of remains. For this reason, assessments were undertaken for pollen (see Akhtar & Tipping, 5.5.3mf, 2:F3–5) and for insect remains. The insect assessment, on a small selection of the more promising samples, was undertaken by Dr H Kenward of the Environmental Archaeology Unit at York. The samples proved to be barren of both pollen and insects; this probably largely reflects the well-drained, and hence well-aerated, nature of the deposits.

A small quantity of land snail fragments was recovered from the flots and retents; this assemblage was assessed by Steven Carter and was found to be too small to be worthy of further analysis. Marine shells were a common find, and were catalogued (see Russell, 5.4.3mf, 2:D8–12).

Analyses proceeded on a range of materials relevant to the investigation of the origin, composition and formation processes of the deposits and of the economy and environment of the site through time. The soil micromorphology work has proved particularly useful in unravelling site formation processes. The work on carbonised plant remains and on animal bone has provided insights into economy, diet and the exploitation of the Castle's hinterland through time. In the general absence of the survival of pollen and uncarbonised plant macro-remains, the phytolith work (see Powers, 5.5.4mf, 2:F6–14) has allowed investigation of the now invisible plant component which originally would have been a major constituent of most of the deposits.

5.2 THE CHARRED PLANT REMAINS FROM MILLS MOUNT

Sheila Boardman with Susan Ramsay

Only Mills Mount produced soil deposits which contained organic materials in contexts which could confidently be related to the history of the use of the Castle.

81 soil samples were processed following the methods used by Historic Scotland's Archaeological Operations and Conservation facility for the recovery of environmental remains, dating material and artefacts. 74 samples produced charred plant remains. The richest came from Phases 2, 3 and 5. Only six samples contained more than 100 components. Four of these were from hearths. A further ten samples had 50–100 components. These are concentrated across Phases 1–5. Aspects of Medieval and post-Medieval plant economy (Phases 6–9) are therefore not illuminated by this evidence.

Table 22 summarises the overall composition of the samples and Table 23, the cereal species present in each phase. Nomenclature follows Clapham *et al* (1982) and for the sedges (*Carex* sp.), Berggren (1969). The plant remains are presented sample by sample in Tables 24–29mf (2:B3–12). A complete list of taxa represented at Edinburgh Castle can be found in Table 30.

5.2.1 CULTIVATED SPECIES (Tables 22 and 23)

Barley, the principal cereal species, was represented almost entirely by grains. The latter were identified as hulled six row barley (*Hordeum vulgare* L.), naked six row barley (*H. vulgare* var. nudum), or simply barley (hulled, naked and indeterminate grains). Rachis internodes from a single Phase 4 sample (S124) were identified as *H. vulgare* L. On the basis of grain morphology, this appears to be the main species, but with so few chaff fragments, the presence of other species (eg *H. distichon* L) cannot be excluded. Indeterminate chaff fragments and culm nodes were also recovered.

The wheats included emmer (*Triticum dicoccum* Schubl), bread/club wheat (*T. aestivum* s.l.) and possibly spelt (*T.* cf *spelta* L). Grain was again the principal component. Many grains could not be assigned to a single species. Glume bases and rachis internodes, identified as emmer (*T. dicoccum*) and wheat (*T. sp*) respectively, were recovered from a single Phase 2 sample (S077), together with unidentifiable rachis internodes and awns.

Floret bases indicate the possible presence of bristle oat (*Avena strigosa* Schreb) by Phase 3, and by Phase 5, of three oat species: bristle oat, cultivated oat (*A. sativa* L), and wild oat (*A. fatua/sterilis*). Oat grains were present throughout the deposits but the paucity of chaff fragments prevented identification of most beyond *Avena* sp.

Cultivated flax (*Linum usitatissimum* L) was present in samples from Phases 1, 2, 3 and 5, usually with a range of other cultivated species. Flax may have been utilised for oil, fibre and food (human and animal).

Many small-seeded legumes could not be identified beyond vetch/pea (*Vicia/Lathyrus*) so their status at the site remains uncertain. Common vetch (*Vicia sativa* L) and meadow vetchling (*Lathyrus pratensis* L) are frequent in managed grasslands (Greig 1984, 1988), and in hedgerows and grassy places generally. Larger-seeded pulses, such as the horse bean (*Vicia faba* var. minor) and cultivated pea (*Pisum sativum* L), were confined to the later phases (5 and beyond). Legumes may have had importance as animal fodder or human food. They also restore soil nitrogen which is vital for sustained agriculture on poor soils.

Table 22 Mills Mount: Major components of the macroplant samples

Phase	CEREAL GRAINS	CHAFF + GW	CHAFF + FT	CULM NODES	OTHER SEEDS	TOTAL COMPS	Hordeum	CEREAL GROUPS:		
								Triticum	Avena	Indet
1	224	–	–	1	28	252	76.5%	15%	5%	3.5%
2	362	4	–	1	107	469	92%	3%	1.5%	3.5%
3	686	–	–	–	549	1235	94.5%	1.5%	2.5%	1.5%
4	1312	–	1	–	359	1671	82%	0.5%	11.5%	6%
5	365	–	–	1	53	418	62%	10%	22%	6%
6	108	–	–	–	32	140	48.5%	28.5%	19.5%	3.5%
7	88	–	–	–	21	109	26%	41%	15%	18%
8	14	–	–	–	3	37	–	7%	64.5%	28.5%
9	34	–	–	–	3	37	79.5%	–	3%	17.5%

KEY: +GW = glume wheats (*Triticum dicoccum* & *T spelta*): chaff includes glume bases only.
+FT = free theshing cereals (*T aestivum* & *Hordeum vulgare*): chaff includes rachis internodes only.
Cereal percentages are calculated from total cereal components and are approximated to the nearest 0.5%

Table 23 Detail of cereal species represented at Mills Mount

Phase	Hordeum vulgare	H. sp.	Triticum dicoccum	T. aestivum	T. dicoccum /aestivum	T.dicoccum /spelta	T. cf spelta	T. sp.	Avena sp.
1	43%	36%	5%	10%	0.5%	–	–	0.5%	5%
2	47%	48%	2%	0.5%	–	–	–	1%	1.5%
3	36.5%	60%	+	1%	–	+	–	0.5%	2%
4	54%	33.5%	+	+	–	–	–	+	12.5%
5	29.5%	33%	0.5%	8.5%	–	–	1%	2%	25.5%
6	14.5%	35.5%	–	27%	–	–	–	3%	20%
7	14%	18%	–	40.5%	–	–	–	9.5%	18%
8	–	–	–	8%	–	–	–	–	92%
9	14.5%	82%	–	–	–	–	–	–	3.5%

KEY: ★ Samples include *T* cf *dicoccum* or *T* cf *aestivum* grains. Percentages exclude indeterminate grains and fragments

5.2.2 WILD SPECIES (Table 30)

These are discussed more fully in the next sections. There were many common weeds of cultivation, and species associated with disturbed ground generally. Some species are suited to growth in dry, basic conditions whilst others prefer damper ground. Many would have flourished on the nitrogen rich soils provided by the site itself. As well as weedy vegetation, the charred remains indicate grassland, heath, woodland and some wetland habitats. There were few remains of wild edible plants, and few species which could be considered 'exotic' in this context.

Table 30 The taxa represented in the Mills Mount charred plant remains

Ranunculus acris L (meadow buttercup)
R. sardous Crantz (hairy buttercup)
R. sp. (buttercup)

Fumaria officinalis L (common fumitory)

Brassica nigra (L) Koch (black mustard)
Sinapis cf *alba* L (possible white mustard)
Brassica/Sinapis (cabbage/mustard)
Raphanus raphanistrum L (wild radish/charlock, runch)
Thlaspi arvense L (field penny cress)

Stellaria media (L) Vill (chickweed)
S. sp. (chickweed/stitchwort)

Chenopodium polyspermum (all-seed)
C. album type (fat hen)
C. cf *glaucum* L (glaucous goosefoot)
Atriplex sp (orache)
Chenopodium/Atriplex (goosefoot/orache)
Sherardia arvensis L (field madder)
Linum usitatissimum L (cultivated flax)

Trifolium repens L (white/dutch clover)
Vicia hirsuta (L) SF Gray (hairy tare)
V. tetrasperma (L) Schreb (smooth tare)

V. sativa L (common vetch)
Vicia faba var minor (horse bean)
Vicia sp. (vetch)
Lathyrus pratensis L (meadow vetchling)
L sp. (pea/vetchling)
Vicia/Lathyrus (vetch/pea)
Pisum sativum L (garden/field pea)

Rubus idaeus/fruticosus (raspberry/bramble)
Potentilla cf *palustris* (L) Scop (march cinquefoil)
P reptans (L) (creeping cinquefoil)
P sp (cinquefoil)
Fragaria vesca L (wild strawberry)
Aphanes arvensis (parsley piert)
Aphanes sp.
Prunus domestica s.l. (bullace/plum)

Epilobium sp. (willow-herb)
Umbelliferae undiff

Polygonum aviculare agg (knotgrass)
P. persicaria L/*lapathifolium* L (persicaria)
P. hydropiper L (water-pepper)
P. (Bilderdykia) *convolvulus* L (black bindweed)
P. sp. (knotgrass/bindweed)

Rumex acetosella agg (sheep's sorrel)
R. crispus L (curled dock)
R. obtusifolius L (broad leaved dock)
R. crispus/obtusifolius
R. sp. (dock)
Polygonaceae/Cyperaceae (knotgrasses/sedges)

Corylus avellana L (hazel)

Calluna vulgaris (L) Hull (ling)

Anagallis arvensis L (scarlet pimpernel)

Hyoscyamus niger L (henbane)
Rhinanthus minor agg (yellow-rattle)
Mentha sp. (mint)
Stachys/Galeopsis (woundwort/hemp-nettle)
Galeopsis tetrahit agg (common hemp-nettle)
Plantago lanceolata L (ribwort plantain)

Galium aparine L (goosegrass/cleavers)
Galium sp. (bedstraw)

Centaurea cf *cyanus* (cornflower/bluebottle)
Lapsana communis L (nipplewort)

Eleocharis palustris (L) Roem */uniglumis* (Link) Schult (spike-rush)

Scirpus sp. (club-rush)
Carex Sect Paludosae Fr (after Berggren 1969)
C sp. (biconvex)
C sp. (trigonous)
Cyperaceae undiff

Poa sp.
Bromus mollis agg.*/secalinus* L. (lop-grass/rye-brome)
B. (*Anisantha*) *sterilis* L (barren brome)
Triticum dicoccum Schubl (emmer wheat)
T. spelta L (spelt wheat)
T. dicoccum/spelta (emmer/spelt)
T. aestivum L (bread wheat)
T. dicoccum/aestivum (emmer/bread wheat)
T. sp. (indet wheat)
Triticum/Hordeum (wheat/barley)
Hordeum vulgare L (hulled six row barley)
H. vulgare var. nudum (naked six row barley)
H. sp. (indet. barley)
Avena fatua L*/sterilis* L (wild oat)
A. strigosa Schreb (bristle/black oat)
A. sativa L (cultivated oat)
A. sp. (indet oat)
Cerealia indet
Gramineae undiff

Seaweed *Fucus* sp. (wrack)

5.2.3 ANALYSIS BY PHASE

PHASE 1

Late Bronze Age – Early Iron Age Occupation (Table 24mf, 2:B3–4)

Samples came from the putative natural soil, occupation debris, and the scant remains of features cut into the natural soil. The latter included a drain, postholes, pits and a pit/ditch.

I) THE NATURAL SOIL

Sample 76 produced single grains of barley and oats, and a limited range of wild species including possible hairy tare (*Vicia* cf *hirsuta* L), fat hen (*Chenopodium album* type), goosefoot/orache (*Chenopodium/Atriplex*) and mint (*Mentha* sp.). These are all frequent arable weeds. The remains indicate that the natural soil had become contaminated by human-related material, probably through invertebrate mixing (also see Powers 5.5.4mf, 2:F6–14).

II) OCCUPATION DEBRIS: SAMPLES 105 AND 138

Both samples contained a few barley grains and hazel (*Corylus avellana* L) nutshell fragments. S105 produced predominantly naked barley, the only such sample from the site, plus single grains of indeterminate wheat and oats. As in S076, there were too few remains to indicate specific crop-related activities.

III) THE PITS: SAMPLES 133, 135, 136 AND 137

Samples from the pits were similarly poor. Wheat grains in S135 and S136 included emmer (*Triticum dicoccum* Schubl) and bread wheat (*T. aestivum* s.l.). The latter is unusual for this period. Cleavers (*Galium aparine* L), often a noxious weed of autumn sown crops (Hillman 1981, 146), was also present. This species is known from a variety of disturbed habitats, also woodland and hedgerows.

IV) OTHER DEPOSITS: SAMPLES 140, 142, 144, 145 AND 146

Two samples produced more than 50 plant remains. S140, from the stone built drain, contained hulled barley, wheat and an oat grain. S144, from a pit or posthole, produced mostly hulled barley. Bread wheat was present in both samples. The wild species included cabbage/mustard (*Brassica/Sinapis*), fat hen (*Chenopodium album* type) and woundwort/hemp-nettle (*Stachys/Galeopsis*), again representing common cultivation weeds. Pale persicaria (*Polygonum lapthifolium* L) and most of the sedges (*Carex* spp.) have a preference for moist, even wet conditions. Meadow buttercup (*Ranunculus acris* L) is often abundant in damp meadows and calcareous grassland.

S145 and S146 from the other postholes, produced sparser but apparently similar remains. The concentrations of hazelnut shell fragments in S142 and S145 suggest that these contexts were latterly used for refuse. Charred nutshells are typical of floor or hearth sweepings. The associated cereals may similarly represent food processing waste, swept up and discarded onto fires. S145 produced the largest concentration of bread wheat for this phase, plus a single grain of flax (*Linum usitatissimum* L).

PHASE 1 SUMMARY

The mixed nature and paucity of the Phase 1 samples suggests considerable post-depositional disturbance. The plant material probably bears little relation to the original functions of the various contexts. Barley was generally dominated by hulled grains. Naked barley, bread wheat, emmer and oats were also present.

PHASE 2

Iron Age Settlement (Table 25mf, 2:B5–6)

I) HEARTHS: SAMPLES 125, 132 AND 148

Phase 2 produced some of the richest samples from the site. Three samples contained more than 50 plant components and two had more than a 100. The richest sample came from a hearth. There were fewer oat and bread wheat grains than in the Phase 1 samples.

The association of hulled barley grains and hearths is of some interest. This crop is unlikely to have been deliberately burnt. The quantity of grains in some samples also suggests more than mere cooking accidents. Whole cereal ears may have been parched to ease threshing and winnowing, or 'graddened' to avoid threshing and winnowing altogether (Fenton 1977, 94). Grain dehusking is another possible activity, although this is normally carried out with the grains slightly moist (Fenton 1977, 99; Hillman 1981, 134–7). Barley used in malting also would have required heating to halt the germination, and in the moist climate of Scotland, grain is often dried before it is ground (Fenton 1977, 94).

The absence of chaff and straw remains from the hearth samples suggests that grains had been threshed and winnowed prior to charring. The presence of weed seeds hints at only partial crop cleaning, or that sieving and hand-picking by-products were added to the hearths.

The range of wild plants was wider than before. Parsley piert (*Aphanes arvensis* L) is found in arable fields and on bare ground. Ribwort plantain (*Plantago lanceolata* L), another shade intolerant species, is common in prehistoric crop assemblages but it is better known today as a plant of grassland, over neutral to basic soils. Seeds of cabbage/mustard (*Brassica/Sinapis*) represent other common cultivation weeds, plus culinary herbs and an oil plant (*Brassica nigra* (L) Koch). Cabbage/mustard seeds were very abundant in S132.

II) 'OCCUPATION DEBRIS'/MIDDEN: SAMPLES 77 AND 141

S077 from beneath the lowest cobbling layer produced one of the few glimpses of cereal chaff from the site but the overall quantity was low. Some of the barley grains were also very small and there were a number of detached, sprouted cereal embryos. Spoiled grain seems to have been mixed and burnt with crop processing debris and other refuse, eg the leaves and stems of ling (*Calluna vulgaris* (L) Hull) and seaweed. The seaweed was too fragmentary to identify so its purpose at the site remains unclear.

Ling was present in charcoal samples from the same context. This is found today on acid soils, on heaths, moors and in bogs and open woodland (Clapham *et al* 1962). It may have been brought to the site for a variety of purposes, including thatching, bedding, broom making and for dye production (Edlin 1974; see below Charcoal Report 5.3).

The sample from the deep accumulation overlying the final paved surface (S141) produced remains of hulled barley, isolated grains of emmer wheat and oats as well as many weedy species seen previously.

PHASE 2 SUMMARY

The denser barley deposits, particularly those from hearths, may represent grain accidentally burnt during parching. One sample was relatively free of wild species (S141) so may constitute final crop products. Another sample contained more mixed cereals and proportionally more 'weeds' (S132). This suggests less thorough crop cleaning, or in the case of the *Brassica/Sinapis* seeds, that the weeds were desirable. One sample may represent spoiled grain destroyed with other refuse (S077).

The absence of charred plant remains from some layers and quite high concentrations in others suggests limited soil homogenisation. Wheat was more poorly represented than in Phase 1. Samples from Phase 2 also contained much other material: stone, bone, pottery, coprolite, coal and slate. These suggest a wider range of activities than before.

PHASE 3

Roman Period Midden (Table 26mf, 2:B7–9)

This phase is characterised by hearth deposits, burnt soil and an extensive, fibrous layer, an apparent rapid accumulating midden. Two bulk samples were analysed from this fibrous layer. The soil micromorphology description suggests that F497 was a dump of almost pure plant material, principally decayed grass culms or leaves; carbonised plant tissues were only rarely present (see Soils Report 5.2). The phytolith analysis links S061 with other Phase 3 samples (S068, S069, S131) and a Phase 2 midden sample (S077), important components of which appear to be cereal culm, leaf, and root (Powers 5.5.4mf, 2:F6–14).

The fibrous deposit was checked for the presence of identifiable uncharred plant fragments. A sub-sample was gently washed through a 0.5mm sieve and the retent observed under a low power light microscope. No identifiable fragments were retrieved and the plant material appears to have been broken down, probably though the processes of decay.

I) FIBROUS LAYER: SAMPLES 61 & 71

S061 produced a few hulled barley grains and fragments, and some 400 seeds of wild plants. These represent a variety of habitats and soil types which are discussed below. In contrast, S071 produced only a handful of barley grains and few other seeds. Both samples contained non plant domestic refuse (animal bone, marine shell). S071 also contained slag and coal/shale. Some small-scale activity involving these may account for the lack of plant remains.

Arable fields, disturbed ground

Chickweed (*Stellaria media* (L) Vill), field penny-cress (*Thlaspi arvense* L), the knotgrasses (*Polygonum* spp.) and the Chenopodiaceae (*Chenopodium/Atriplex*), were among the most frequent weeds in S061. Together with parsley piert (*Aphanes*), bedstraw (*Galium* spp.) and the vetches (*Vicia* spp.), these form a small, fairly unspecialised weed flora, seen in association with cereals in many samples elsewhere at Edinburgh Castle. As well as cultivated fields, these plants are found today in disturbed and waste places, grassland, woodland, hedgerow and scrub. They are all common components of ancient crop assemblages (Greig 1991).

Pale persicaria (*Polygonum lapathifolium* L) and hairy buttercup (*Ranunculus sardous* Crantz) may represent damper cultivation conditions, and water-pepper (*P. hydropiper* L), the sedges (*Carex* ssp) and club-rush (*Scirpus* sp.) are possible components of marshy field margins, ditches, and/or moist grassland. This is in contrast to the lighter soils indicated by parsley piert. The latter is now mainly a weed of autumn sown crops, while field penny-cress and many of the goosefoots are common today as weeds of summer crops.

Grassland, heath

Species typical of grassland include meadow buttercup (*Ranunculus acris* L), white clover (*Trifolium repens* L) and yellow-rattle (*Rhinanthus minor* agg). The latter is typical of tall growth in hay meadows rather than closely cropped pastures. Meadow buttercup and yellow rattle are frequently found on damp basic soils, whilst white clover is common on heavier soils and clays.

Other possible components of grassland include many of the weedy taxa above, plus the Gramineae, many cinquefoils (*Potentilla* spp), docks (*Rumex* spp.) and vetches/peas (*Vicia/Lathyrus*). Marsh cinquefoil (*Potentilla palustris* (L) Scop) is more typical of fens and marshes. It is also common in heathland, as are raspberry and bramble (*Rubus* spp.).

Other habitats/uses

Plants common in woodland, hedgerows and scrub include raspberry and bramble, creeping cinquefoil (*Potentilla reptans* L) and bedstraw (*Galium* sp.). None of these are confined to woodland. A few common weed species will also grow wild close to the sea, eg knotgrass (*Polygonum aviculare* agg), curled dock (*Rumex crispus* L) and some oraches (*Atriplex* spp.). Other than the berries, there were few obvious edible plants. Also, the seeds of these would normally be eaten with the fruit so another mode of arrival is likely.

II) HEARTHS: SAMPLES 62A, 62B, 66, 67 AND 129

The hearth samples were particularly rich in grains of hulled barley, as were the hearth samples discussed under Phase 2. Rare grains of wheat and oats were also present. Henbane (*Hyoscyamus niger* L) dominated one hearth sample, S062A. This species grows on sandy soils, especially close to the sea, and in farmyards and other disturbed places (Clapham *et al* 1962). Henbane is unusual in Britain today and it has been cited as evidence of thermophilous weed communities (Greig 1991, 304, 307). The deposit may have resulted from a tidying exercise, or from careful crop cleaning to remove the poisonous seeds. Alternatively, henbane may have been used for its medicinal properties. This sample also preserved a single fragmentary stone of plum/bullace (*Prunus domestica* L).

The associated sample, S062B, was dominated by hulled barley grains and well preserved seeds of cultivated flax. S062A and S062B seem to represent distinct activities, possibly related to two features, or distinct episodes in the use of one feature.

III) BURNT SOIL LAYERS: SAMPLES 65, 68, 69, 72

Two samples (S065, S068) from these putative 'occupation debris' layers produced few plant remains. S072, from just above the lowest cobbling layer, S069 and S131 were relatively rich in material. The three samples were dominated by hulled barley with small amounts of oats. S072 and S131 also contained grains of wheat. There were also possible weeds: goosefoot/orache (*Chenopodium/Atriplex*), bedstraw (*Galium* sp.) and dock (*Rumex* sp) along with Poa grass (*Poa* sp.) which may have originated from damp grassland. A single seed of field madder (*Sheradia arvensis* L) (S131) may indicate basic soil conditions.

PHASE 3 SUMMARY

Two samples were relatively free of wild species (S066, S131) so may constitute final crop products. Sample S072 contained more mixed cereals and proportionally more 'weeds'. This suggests less thorough crop cleaning. The other concentrations, of henbane (S062A) and flax (S062B), are less easy to tie to specific activities. S061 is one of the few 'weed rich' samples from the site. The phytolith study (5.5.4m, 2:F6–14) indicates that cereal chaff was not present. However, charred cereal grains and the many cultivation weeds in this sample suggests a strong link with arable fields. The remains in S061 may represent the straw fraction of the harvest, the straw component of which had decomposed or burned away. Straw and/or grass stems are indicated by the phytolith and soil micromorphology studies. However, each study was focused on very small parts of the total layer. This is likely to have varied horizontally so that the material observed in each case was slightly different.

The charred remains include some classic indicators of grassland including meadows. Evidence for hay is rare in archaeological assemblages of charred plants. In general, context 497 seems to have contained much material which is typical of byres, ie straw and grassy material. However, similar remains might be expected from human habitations, after use in bedding, furnishings, thatch, etc. The widespread layer may represent wholesale clearance from a variety of buildings and deposits. Only a small fraction of this seems to have become charred.

PHASE 4

Early Medieval Midden
(Table 26mf, 2:B7–9)

SUMMARY OF THE REMAINS: SAMPLES 124, 130

Midden accumulation continued after the Phase 3 horizon and the overlying layer was rich in animal bones. This was also sampled twice but only one sample (S130) produced plant remains. These included hulled six row barley, two wheat grains (including possible emmer) and a few poorly preserved weed seeds (including *Vicia/Lathyrus*). Little can be said about the midden layer on the basis of these few remains. S124, the richest sample from the site, produced wild, cultivated and bristle oats. The latter was widely cultivated in Scotland's past. Other possible crops plants include the cultivated pea and common vetch. Cultivated flax was also present in at least two samples (S050, S119). In S124, approximately one sixth of the hulled barley grains, the dominant cereal, showed signs of germination. There were also many detached sprouted embryos. This crop may have been deliberately destroyed, although whether this was fully cleaned prior to charring is uncertain. The other cultivated plants and wild species may have been contaminants of the barley crop, or the result of separate crop cleaning exercises. None of the other remains showed signs of germination and there were conflicting habitat preferences among the wild species.

Arable fields, disturbed ground

Typical cornfield weeds include the possible cornflower (*Centaurea* cf *cyanus* L) and common fumitory (*Fumaria officinalis* L)

Wild radish (*Raphanus raphanistrum* L) indicates more acid conditions. The other weedy species tend to be tolerant of a range of habitats and soils. Damper cultivation conditions, ditch or streamside vegetation, may again be indicated by pale persicaria (*Polygonum lapathifolium*) and the sedges (*Carex* spp.). Barren brome (*Bromus sterilis* L) is common in gardens today and many knotgrasses and goosefoots also could have grown on rich soils provided by the site itself.

Grassland, heath

Species associated with grassland were common in S124. Meadow vetchling (*Lathyrus pratensis* L) is characteristic of flood meadows (Greig 1984, 1988). Common vetch (*Vicia sativa* L) and creeping cinquefoil (*Potentilla reptans* (L) are also found in managed grasslands (Greig 1984, 1988), but all three are common in grassy places generally, and in hedgerows. Ribwort plantain (*Plantago lanceolata* L) is more typical of shorter, grazed turf. Meadow vetchling, ribwort plantain and creeping cinquefoil (*Potentilla reptans* L) are found predominantly on neutral to basic soils. Sheep's sorrel may have come from acid grassland or heath.

Other habitats/uses

Black mustard (*Brassica nigra* (L) Koch), an important oil and flavouring plant, was well represented in S124.

PHASE 4 SUMMARY

Agriculturally significant in Phase 4 is the appearance of a range of new cultigens, including the cultivated pea, cultivated oat and possibly black mustard. The processing sequence for the pulses provides few opportunities for accidental charring so these may be under-represented elsewhere at Edinburgh Castle. Despite the greater range of plants, the status and importance of many species from Phase 4 remains unclear.

The charred remains contain much material seen previously, also new cultigens and a seed of possible cornflower (*Centaurea* cf *cyanus*) which is unusual prior to AD1100 (Greig 1991, 326).

PHASE 5

Medieval Industrial
(Table 26mf, 2:B7–9)

Samples came from the levelling deposits and from features located within the levelling. These included hearths, a ditch and a drain.

SUMMARY OF THE REMAINS

Samples 40, 50, 57, 59, 64A, 64B, 115, 116, 119, 122, 123

Again, there is no clear patterning in the remains from different deposit types. One sample produced more than 100 remains but eight had less than 50. Hulled barley was the main cereal overall. One hearth sample (S115) was dominated by oats (*Avena* sp), then bread wheat (*Triticum aestivum* s.l.). Another poorer sample (S116) had near equal proportions of the three cereals.

Other possible crop plants include the cultivated pea (S116, S119, S122), horse bean (S116), common vetch (S115, S119) and a variety of other legumes. Cultivated flax was also present in at least two samples (S050, S119).

Crop processing by-products and a succession of parching/cooking accidents may be represented elsewhere in Phase 5. There was a wider range of wild species than in previous samples and as in Phase 3, these represent a variety of different habitats.

Typical cornfield weeds include scarlet pimpernel (*Anagallis arvensis* L, field madder (*Sheradia arvensis* L) and smooth tare (*Vicia tetrasperma* (L) Schreb). Generally, these have a preference for light, neutral to basic soils. Scarlet pimpernel grows today mainly as a weed of autumn sown crops, while many goosefoots and cabbage/mustard species are common as weeds of spring sown crops (Greig 1991).

PHASE 5 DISCUSSION AND SUMMARY

The soil deposits here were more homogenised than in previous phases, a fact observed in the pottery assemblage. The phytoliths suggest that some Phase 5 deposits contain reworked Phase 3 & 4 midden material. It is not possible to separate material from different ages and activities which makes generalisations about the phase as a whole difficult. However, Phase 5 seems to be the final phase in which quantities of different crops were present, even as rubbish, on Mills Mount.

PHASE 6

14th-Century smithy
(Table 27mf, 2:B10)

Samples came from a floor, a posthole, the fill of an iron box, midden layers and hearths.

SUMMARY OF THE REMAINS

Samples 30, 39, 43, 51, 114, 127, 139, 147 and 149

There was a marked decrease in the quantity of remains, reflecting departure from previous use of the area. Proportionally wheat, all probably bread wheat, and oats were better represented. There were few wild species, except in S139 from a hearth. These are all very general weeds (see above). S139 may be the only *in situ* deposit for this phase, with other material coming from domestic contexts located some distance away, and from reworked deposits.

PHASES 7, 8 & 9

Late Medieval Redeposited Midden & Post-Medieval Levelling Deposits
(Tables 28mf & 29mf, 2:B11–12)

The Phase 7 samples came from floor layers of the reused Smithy, redeposited midden layers and discrete deposits associated with these. The Phase 8 samples came from redeposited midden layers, also pit-fills and postholes of a later structure. There was only one productive sample from Phase 9, again from redeposited midden infill.

PHASES 7–9 SUMMARY

The results indicate an even sparser spread of plant remains across the excavated area. Some material may have come from domestic refuse used as tinder or fuel. S014, from the Phase 7 midden overlying the Smithy floor, produced a small deposit of charred seaweed, mostly flattened thallus fragments with few diagnostic elements, although this seems to have included a wrack (*Fucus* sp). This may have been used as a flux material prior to being dumped in the old Smithy area.

The economic species from these phases are unlikely to be fully representative of plants being utilised by this time. Whilst they hint at some continuity from previous phases, this may be largely due to landfill operations and continual reworking of the area.

5.2.4 GENERAL DISCUSSION

CROP PROCESSING

For free threshing cereals such as barley and bread wheat, a single threshing and winnowing will normally separate the grain from the rachises and straw (Hillman 1981, 1984; Jones 1984). Weed seeds and minor contaminants of rachises and straw are generally removed from the grain by sieving and hand-picking.

For the glume wheats, emmer and spelt, the processing sequence is slightly different. Threshing of whole crops will normally separate only the straw from the cereal ear, and break the latter into individual spikelets (grains still surrounded by their protective glumes, each attached to a single rachis internode). Spikelets require a separate threshing or pounding to release the grain, a practice that in cool, damp climates normally takes place on a day-to-day basis, as grain is required (Hillman 1981).

Cereal grains were the main component of the Edinburgh Castle samples. The grains are more likely to survive charring than are cereal chaff (glume bases, rachis internodes) and straw (culms). However, even where chaff and straw have completely burned away, they may leave behind other traces, in the form of silica phytoliths (Boardman & Jones 1990). The phytolith study conducted on this material is based on recent experimental work. This has demonstrated the possibility of identifying chaff and straw components in archaeological contexts, and some of the likely species involved (Harvey & Powers, forthcoming).

All of the samples analysed for phytoliths proved to be very productive, indicating that deposits contained large quantities of decayed plant material. Much of this appears to be of cereal origin, although currently there are limited modern comparatives for the wide range of wild grass species. Fewer samples were studied for phytoliths than macrofossils, and only one context which produced charred chaff remains (F535) was also analysed for phytoliths. The combined results of the two studies are nevertheless significant.

In S077, where charred *Triticum* glumes and rachises were present, the phytoliths do not indicate that these were more widespread prior to charring. The inflorescence (ear) of cereals is the most silicified part of the plant so this is unlikely to be a taphonomic effect. None of the phytolith samples contained a significant chaff component. All of the material seems to fall into the categories of cereal leaf, culm and root, and within this group, leaf and culm are most likely (Powers, 5.5.4mf, 2:F-6-14).

The absence of rachises from the straw fractions at the Castle, and awns which are also very distinctive when silicified, suggests that straw and ears were processed, and probably harvested separately. The evidence from both phytoliths and charred plant remains also suggests that dehusking of glume wheat spikelets did not occur at Mills Mount. This probably took place soon after threshing and winnowing, closer to cultivated fields.

It is significant that the same cereal species are indicated by both phytoliths and charred plant remains, ie *Hordeum vulgare* L and *Triticum*, including *T. dicoccum* Schubl. We may be looking at different products from the same crops, ie the straw and the grain. Although impossible to prove, it is likely that these were grown locally. Straw is bulky and difficult to transport great distances. The longevity of settlement also argues for a strong, local agricultural base.

THE REGIONAL LANDSCAPE

Pollen analyses from sites located on and around the Antonine Wall have indicated clearance of the native oak and birch woodland, possibly up to 300 years before the Roman military occupation (Boyd 1984). A secondary light woodland of predominantly alder and hazel developed. There are also indications of substantial open grassland, including pasture and heath. The latter aspect of the vegetation seems to have been kept under control by intensive grazing throughout the Iron Age and Romano–British periods. Evidence for local cereal cultivation is scant (Boyd 1984; Clapham, unpub; Dickson & Dickson 1988; Dickson 1989).

At Blackpool Moss, Whitlaw, in south eastern Scotland, major woodland clearance seems to have taken place at a much earlier date, possibly the Neolithic (Butler 1992). This is accompanied by cereal-type pollen at low frequencies. By the Iron Age, much of the area around the hillforts at Dunion and Eildon, in the southern uplands, appears to be open grassland, meadow and pasture. Cereal and poppy (*Papaver*) type pollen from Blackpool Moss hints at some local cereal agriculture. Land pressure in the hillfort area apparently continued until around the 3rd century AD, when some hazel regeneration occurred (Butler 1992).

There are no pollen diagrams for the Edinburgh area covering the later prehistoric and early historic periods. Substantial reductions in tree cover indicated for other parts of southern Scotland, with a dearth of cereals from archaeological sites, supports a hypothesis of an economy focused on animal husbandry. However, this picture also reflects the choice of pollen sites, often in agriculturally marginal areas, and of archaeological sites, which have frequently been on hilltops. The plant macrofossil evidence from Edinburgh Castle suggests a stronger commitment to crop agriculture and some stability in the conditions of cultivation through time.

The published crop record suggests that hulled six row barley as the principal crop on Scottish Iron Age sites. Emmer wheat has been recorded as a secondary cereal on sites from the Forth Valley to the Northern Isles (Boyd 1988). Oats first occur widely on Iron Age sites and by the Roman period this seems to include the cultivated oat and the bristle oat, also widely cultivated in Scotland's past (Boyd 1988; Greig 1991). At Fairy Knowe in the Forth valley, bread/club wheat was also recorded (Boyd 1982–3).

Spelt is very rare on Scottish prehistoric sites, although grains and chaff have been recovered from the late Bronze Age site of Oakbank crannog on Loch Tay (Clapham & Scaife 1988). Emmer and spelt seem to be important components of the Roman military diet, both in Scotland (eg Dickson 1989) and elsewhere. Bread/club wheat is recorded at York (Buckland 1976), South Shields (van der Veen 1988), and at Castlecary and Rough Castle on the Antonine Wall (Dickson 1989). This is often regarded as a contaminant, or a longer distance import (eg van der Veen 1988). Some emmer and spelt grains may also fall into this category as they are frequently found with more exotic items, eg horse bean, lentil and fig (Dickson 1989; Clapham, unpublished). At most military sites barley is a minor element and there has been a tendency to regard this crop merely in terms of beer making, animal fodder or punishment food (eg Davis 1971).

Samples from the Roman fort at Elginhaugh, near Dalkeith were dominated by hulled barley but this may be related to their origins near stable blocks. Wheat grains, with roughly equal proportions of emmer and spelt, dominated the annexe samples and the majority of bran fragments from the site were identified as wheat/rye (*Triticum/Secale*). However, barley bran fragments were present, suggesting that this crop was also consumed by humans (Clapham in Hanson, in prep).

Six-row barley dominates the Phase 1 samples from Edinburgh Castle, a pattern which continues through to Phase 5. Wheat comprises 15% of the Phase 1 cereals and over half are probable bread/club wheat. The latter is unusual away from the Roman military sites, although not unique (cf Boyd 1982–82 and above). Other possible crops from phase 1 were emmer, oats and flax. By Phase 2 at Edinburgh Castle, wheat has decreased in relation to barley, and emmer is more frequent than bread wheat. There was a single occurrence of possible spelt. Barley is the major crop from Phase 3, which also produced wheat and oats. In Phase 4 barley is accompanied by fairly high amounts of oats.

There are then few detailed plant records predating the high medieval period, where the bulk of the evidence comes from large urban excavations. At the two rural medieval sites of Nethermills and Castlehill of Strachan, both in Grampian Region (Boyd 1986), small deposits of mostly hulled barley were accompanied by indeterminate wheat, bristle oats and a range of weedy plants. At the rural medieval site of Castle of Wardhouse, Aberdeenshire, the assemblage was almost entirely cultivated oats, although hulled six row barley, and traces of wheat and rye were also present (Boardman in prep).

The main crops at medieval urban sites (eg Perth, Glasgow, St Andrews, Elgin and Aberdeen) are hulled barley, bristle oat, cultivated oat and bread/club wheat (Boyd 1988; Greig 1991). At St Andrews, rye and emmer were also present, reflecting optimal cultivation conditions along this narrow coastal strip (Boyd unpublished, in Boyd 1988, 105). Despite a patchwork of regional differences, barley and oats seem to remain the staple crops in Scotland until the recent past. By Phase 5 at Edinburgh Castle, wheat and oats have obtained greater prominence. Wheat is dominated, from this phase, by bread/club wheat. Both cultivated oat and bristle oat seem to be present. With the cultivated pea and the horse bean, more diversified crop agriculture is suggested. Oats are suited to poor, acidic and infertile soils and the leguminous species may have helped sustain agriculture in such areas (Jones 1981). Hulled barley remained dominant overall.

The wider range of cultivated plants in Phase 5 may equally reflect material coming from further afield. This phase extends over some 500 years (c AD 600–1100) so observed changes may be very gradual. Also, as mentioned before, samples may include reworked Iron Age material, plus contamination from above.

After the Wars of Independence in the late 13th century, Edinburgh Castle was rebuilt and established as a royal palace. By this time, however, crop related activity and domestic rubbish disposal seem to have moved well away from Mills Mount. The sparse cereal remains from Phase 6 onwards suggest only ephemeral dumping, or earlier material which was redeposited via landscaping operations. The supply of agricultural goods to the royal household and the types of foodstuffs are likely to have been very much more complex than before. The only clues to these come from sparse and somewhat later documentary records.

The Castle gardens were apparently on the sites of the current Grassmarket, King's Stables Road and Castle Terrace. Orchards extended from the Grassmarket and King's Stables to Liberton in the S, and from the

Burgh Muir to the King's Farm at Dalry. In 1335, the King's Farm was recorded as some 260 acres in extent (Malcolm 1925, 101–102).

While it cannot be argued that charred cereals from the later midden deposits came from this area, such a pattern of land use may have been established much earlier. Hay was sent to the Castle stables from the King's Meadows at Dalry and Liberton. The kitchen gardens in the Grassmarket produced onions, leeks, cabbages, peas, beans and garlic. Fruits included apple, pear, cherry, strawberry and plum. Many flowers were also grown. The Grassmarket gardens were covered by housing in the 14th century and, by the 15th century, the other gardens of the Castle were derelict (Malcolm 1925, 102–113).

THE WEED FLORA

There was a fairly wide range of weeds from Phases 2, 3, 4 and 5, and from isolated samples elsewhere. This would seem to reflect the myriad different soils and conditions available within the immediate Edinburgh Castle area. For the later phases, charred plants could equally reflect material brought in from further afield, although none of the plant species need necessarily have come from more than a few miles away.

The prominence of knotgrasses (*Polygonum* spp.) and the Chenopodiaceae in the grain samples, and of chickweed (*Stellaria media*) in S061 (Phase 3), is suggestive of good, nitrogen rich soils. There were many species suited to light, neutral to basic soils, possibly reflecting cultivation over base rich drift and basaltic parent materials. Cultivated fields also do not seem to have been without their damper elements and the presence of many small seeded legumes suggests some nitrogen depletion.

In Phase 5, species associated with light, neutral to basic soils and nitrogen rich conditions are found alongside plants indicative of more acidic soils (eg *Raphanus raphanistrum* L and *Rumex acetosella* agg). There were also many more legumes, suggesting greater nitrogen depletion or cultivation of more impoverished soils.

Some weed species are likely to have grown on the site, or arrived via animal fodder, building materials, fuel and other collected plants. Species typical of grassland were fairly common. Charred remains are normally poor indicators of types of grassland exploited, although these may have included damp ground, even flood meadows, and drier pastures. Ling (*Calluna vulgaris* L), from heath or acid grassland, represents areas which may have been exploited for animal grazing, as today.

As regards other habitats, marine shells (Russell 5.4.3mf, 2:D8–12) and seaweed indicate seashore resources, but no other plant species are confined to this habitat. The charcoal evidence (Crone 5.3 below) also suggests the presence throughout, of nearby mixed deciduous woodland. There were few typical woodland plants. Hazel nutshells, common on archaeological sites of all ages, were represented only in the early phases. If widely utilised in later periods, the nutshells do not seem to have reached domestic fires.

CONCLUSIONS

Striking throughout is the important role played by hulled six-row barley. This remained the Scots staple for bread until this century. The grain and straw of this crop, together with other cereal species, seem to have arrived separately at the site. Local cultivation is likely during the early phases but this could not be demonstrated.

Throughout the phases, a variety of cultivated species were added or lost to the record reflecting changes in local tastes and possibly, cultivation practices. For the Romano–British period, the absence of 'exotic' imports may reflect the site's native status. For the later phases, after Edinburgh Castle had been established as a royal palace, this absence is likely to be taphonomic.

The deposits at Edinburgh Castle have offered a rare opportunity to investigate charred plant remains from the Iron Age through to the medieval period. The plant assemblage is not rich by conventional archaeobotanical standards and the picture so far revealed is partial. Further work at this important site, particularly for the later phases of settlement, may prove to be interesting and very much more revealing.

5.3 THE CHARCOAL FROM MILLS MOUNT
Anne Crone

In all, charcoal from 19 samples representing 16 contexts, all from Mills Mount, was analysed (see Tables 31 and 32mf, 2:B13–14).

The material analysed here comes from contexts ranging in date from the late Bronze Age to the medieval period. Many of the samples produced insufficient charcoal to enable any comment to be made. For this reason Phases 7 and 8 are excluded from this discussion. There are a number of features worthy of comment.

The range of species within each sample varies little from phase to phase. Oak and hazel are the predominant species in every phase, accompanied, in varying quantities, by willow, alder, birch, elm, ash and wild cherry. This range of species would be at home in a mixed oak woodland with the possible exception of willow which may have been found on the riverine margins of such a woodland. This lack of variation over time suggests that the same type of woodland was being exploited and, also, that continual exploitation had not had a great impact on the composition of the woodland.

There are two species present which are 'exotic' in this context. The sample of heather in Phase 2 could have been brought into the settlement for any number of purposes including thatching, bedding, broom-making, as packing material or even for the production of dyes (Edlin 1973, 117 & 169). The Scots pine in Phase 6 includes a few twigs and could represent the trimmings of pine logs brought into the town for building purposes. By the 14th century there was some trade in timber within Scotland so the pine could have been carried some distance (Anderson 1967, 146). It is unlikely to have been found locally. There are now no truly native pinewoods S of Perthshire and it probable that this was always the case (Stevens & Carlisle 1959, 5).

The other feature of the assemblage is the variation within the samples. Even in those samples where it has been only possible to identify a few fragments, as many as five species have been identified. This has various implications as to the type of wood and woodland being exploited. It seems unlikely that the wood was coming from coppiced woodland. Although there is no documentary references to coppicing in Scotland until the 13th century (Lindsay 1974), it has been argued that, prior to the advent of a formal coppicing system, the exploitation of adventitious coppice would have taken place (Crone 1988). However, within coppiced woodland the different species tend to grow in patches and thus cropping of stools within coppiced woodland usually results in one, possibly two, species being utilized. The mixture of species within the samples would, therefore, indicate a different origin. Unfortunately, the sample size is so small that other interpretations are as likely. The wood may have been brought in from a wide range of sources or, alternatively, the deposits have been mixed and represent the debris from several fires.

Table 31 Analysis of charcoal from Mills Mount

Phase	S No	weight	species	quantity	C14	Comments
1	592	18.96	*Corylus av.*	5	GU-2579	
			Quercus sp.	3		
			Fraxinus ex.	1		
			Alnus glut	1		
1	592		*Quercus* sp.	5		Small twigs av diam = 5mm
			Prunus avium	4		twig 14mm diam
			Corylus av.	3		7mm diam
			Betula sp.	1		
2	534	7.64	*Quercus* sp.	5	GU-2661	Some small twigs
			Alnus glut	2		
			Corylus av.	2		
			Betula sp.	1		
2	535	24.47	*Calluna vul*	100%	GU-2580	Same context as 104
2	1225	29.83	*Alnus glut*	8	GU-2663	Some small twigs and cereal
			Pomoideae	6		
			Fraxinus ex.	3		Salix sp
			Corylus av.	1		
			Betula sp.	2		
2	535	3.32				Fragments too small to ID

Phase	S No	weight	species	quantity	C14	Comments
3	520	3.13				Fragments too small to ID
3	521		*Quercus* sp.	100%		All oak wide-ringed, avg 4-6 rings per cm
3	519	29.56	*Corylus av.*	100%		Complete, stems av. diam = 1.5cm
3	519c	5.46	*Quercus* sp.	7		Coal found in sample
			Salix sp.	2		rejected for C14
			Corylus av.	1		
3	522	17.4	*Alnus glut*	6	GU-2581	
			Salix sp.	2		
			Corylus av.	1		
			Quercus sp.	1		
3	522	9.5	*Quercus* sp.	4	GU-2664	Much was twigs with some cereal
			Betula sp.	6		
3	1417		*Quercus* sp.	5		rest of sample too small to ID
			Corylus av.	4		
			Salix sp.	2		
4	461	8.78	*Salix* sp.	5	GU-2662	Some small twigs
			Quercus sp.	3		
			Prunus sp.	2		
4	1385		*Quercus* sp.	10+		Sample is entirely oak
			Alnus glut	4		except for fragments
			Corylus av.	4		identified here
			Salix sp.	2		
5	1361		*Salix* sp.	6		Bulk of sample is coal
			Corylus av.	4		twig diam. 15mm
			Betula sp.	2		
			Alnus glut	1		
5	1362		*Quercus* sp.	4		Bulk of sample is coal
			Ulmus sp.	2		
			Fraxinus ex.	1		
			Salix sp.	1		
			cf *Pomoideae*	1		
5	1443		*Quercus* sp.	6		very small fragments
			Salix sp.	4		
			Prunus avium	3		
			Corylus av.	3		
			Betula sp.	2		
6	1444		*Ulmus* sp.	2		Only small fragments of charcoal
			Betula sp.	2		bulk of sample is coal
			Fraxinius ex.	1		
			Quercus sp.	1		
6	1440		*Corylus av.*	1		Fragments too small to ID
			Quercus sp.	1		coal in sample
6	406/420		*Quercus* sp.	99%		Bulk of sample is oak wide-ringed.
						3–7 rings per cm.
			Pinus syl	9		twig 16mm, 28mm and 30mm diam.
			Corylus av.	4		twig 5mm diam
			Salix sp.	1		twig 7mm diam.
7	440		*Quercus* sp.	100%		Branches and larger twigs 30mm diam. Many narrow-ringed 8–12 rings per cm. Others show pattern of compression and fast growth
8	301		*Quercus* sp.	4		Sample all coal/slag.

5.4 THE FAUNAL REMAINS FROM MILLS MOUNT
Finbar McCormick

The excavations in Mills Mount produced medium-sized bone assemblages but as the material came from over 100 separate contexts the individual samples were small. This greatly reduces the potential information that can be acquired from the study of the material. Only nine samples produced more than 200 identifiable fragments and only for these samples are the bones listed and the minimum individuals (MNI) estimated (Tables 44–52mf, 2:C3–D3). In the remainder of the contexts only the frequency of specimens from each species is listed (Table 43mf, 2:C1–2). The pre-Roman Iron Age (Phase 1) and late Medieval/post-Medieval layers (Phase 9) produced only insignificant samples and will not be discussed further. Phase 5 contexts produced reasonable quantities of bone but unfortunately contained a mixture of Dark Age and medieval material thus making them unsuitable for zooarchaeological study.

In the present study the minimum number of individuals was based exclusively on the frequency of the most commonly occurring skeletal element in each bone sample. No attempt was made to modify the calculation on the basis of bone size or on the state of bone fusion in the samples. The fragments total for each species is the sum of all identifiable fragments, less vertebrae and ribs. The single exception is sample F350/363/383 where eight horse vertebrae are noted as no other identifiable horse remains were present in the sample. The measurement abbreviations used are those of von den Driesch (1976).

5.4.1 GENERAL RESULTS

DISTRIBUTION AND CONDITION

Comparison of the distribution of fragments and minimum numbers of individuals (MNI) were undertaken for those samples containing more than 200 identifiable fragments (Tables 33 and 34) and as these samples are still relatively small the results should be treated with extreme caution. For the purpose of this discussion the site is divided into three broad phases. Phase 2 dates to the pre-Roman Iron Age, Phases 3 and 4 date to the Roman period/Dark Age while Phases 6–8 are of Medieval date.

Table 33 Distribution of fragments from samples containing in excess of 200 fragments (based in Tables 44–52, 5.4.1mf).

(One of the fox fragments (F431) is probable rather than certain.)

	Cattle	Horse	Sheep/Goat	Pig	Dog	Cat	Red Deer	Others
Phase 2								
510+	302	9	106	117	4	31	-	1 (Wild pig)
1387	401	10	102	64	2	-	14	2 (Badger)
								2 (Human)
Total	703	19	207	181	6	-	45	5
Total %	60.3	1.6	17.8	15.5	0.5	-	3.0	0.4
Phase 3–4								
431	291	6	78	110	2	1	29	1 (Beaver)
418	297	6	66	158	3	-	18	2 (Roe Deer)
1382	199	3	33	94	3	-	7	2 (Fox)
493	129	3	24	71	-	-	27	
1360	133	7	38	38	-	-	6	
Total	1049	25	239	471	8	1	87	5
Total %	55.8	1.3	12.7	25.0	0.4	-	4.6	-
Phase 6–8								
330	685	6	658	94	6	4	10	3 (Roe deer)
381	131	1	61	33	2	1	5	3 (Hare)
								3 (Rabbit)
								3 (Rat)
								1 (Human)
Total	816	7	719	127	8	5	15	13
Total%	47.7	0.4	42.0	7.4	0.5	0.3	0.9	0.8

Table 34 Distribution of minimum numbers of individuals (MNI) from samples containing in excess of 200 fragments (based on Tables 44–52, 5.4.1mf).

One of the fox bones (F431) probable rather than certain.)

	Cattle	Horse	Sheep/Goat	Pig	Dog	Cat	Red Deer	Others
Phase 2								
510+	8	1	6	9	1	-	2	1 (Wild Pig)
1387	12	1	6	5	1	-	1	1 (Badger)
								1 (Human)
Total	20	2	12	14	2	-	3	3
Total %	35.7	3.6	21.4	25.0	3.6		5.3	5.3
Phase 3–4								
431	7	1	5	5	1	1	2	2 (Fox)
418	9	1	9	8	1	-	1	2 (Roe Deer)
1382	5	1	5	4	1	-	1	1 (Beaver)
493	4	1	3	6	-	-	3	
1360	4	1	3	3	-	-	2	
Total	29	5	25	26	3	1	9	5
Total %	28.2	4.9	24.3	25.2	2.9	1.0	8.7	4.9

	Cattle	Horse	Sheep/Goat	Pig	Dog	Cat	Red Deer	Others
Phases 6–8								
330	15	1	25	7	1	1	1	2 (Roe deer)
381	6	1	3	3	1	1	1	2 (Hare)
								1 (Rabbit)
								1 (Human)
								1 (Rat)
Total	21	2	28	10	2	2	2	7
Total %	28.4	2.7	37.8	13.5	2.7	2.7	2.7	9.4

The MNI distributions indicated in Tables 33 and 34 show a general similarity between the Roman Iron Age and Dark Age assemblages, although this masks some intra-phase variation. During the Roman Iron Age cattle are dominant with sheep/goat and pig present in roughly equal proportions. During the Dark Ages the three principal domesticates are present in roughly equal numbers. Red deer hunting seems to have increased slightly between the Roman Iron Age and the Dark Ages. The medieval period differs greatly from the previous phases in that sheep/goats become the dominant animals present mostly at the expense of pig. There is also a decline in red deer during this period. Few goat remains were noted in the assemblage so it is assumed that the great majority of caprovine (sheep/goat) remains are those of sheep.

Nearly all of the bones displayed evidence of butchery or breakage clearly indicating that it represented discarded food. Very occasionally, sawn bone or antler indicated that the material represented industrial waste while the presence of a single human bone in two Roman Iron Age samples (F592;1387) and one medieval sample (F330) can best be interpreted as intrusions from nearby burial areas.

PERIOD DISCUSSION

The condition of the bone varied considerably. The bones from Roman Iron Age (F510+), for instance, survive as much bigger fragments than those of medieval date (F330). Detailed examination of the bones from these two contexts indicated that the intense fragmentation in the medieval context was not due to post-depositional taphonomic factors but instead reflected more acute butchery. The bones in F330 had been chopped into smaller pieces with articular areas being split vertically, so that all the marrow present could be extracted. This degree of exploitation of the bone can be interpreted as a sign of impoverishment, or at least a situation where the meat was in limited supply. It implies that meat was more readily available to the Iron Age inhabitants of the area than it was to those of the medieval period.

Roman Iron Age

Comparative material from Iron Age sites in the south of Scotland is extremely rare. The large assemblage from Broxmouth hillfort has yet to be published in any detail although it has been stated that cattle fragments were more numerous than sheep which in turn were more numerous than pig (Barnetson 1982, 102). This is the general trend as noted at Edinburgh Castle but without MNI details more useful comparison is not possible. At the Roman fort at Mumrills, near Falkirk, cattle remains greatly outnumbered sheep/goat and pig but again direct comparison is impossible. Even this level of comparison cannot be undertaken with earlier samples excavated from Bar Hill, Dunbartonshire (MacDonald & Park 1906) and Newstead (Ewart 1911) where quantitative analyses did not occur. The best comparative material comes from a civilian settlement beside the Roman fort at Inveresk (Barnetson 1988) which lies 9km SE of Edinburgh Castle. Direct comparison is possible when the MNI values from different Roman period contexts at both sites are amalgamated (Table 35).

Table 35 Comparison between the MNI distribution of the main domesticates from Inveresk and the Roman levels at Edinburgh Castle (after Barnetson 1988, Table 5).

	No.	Cattle %	Sheep/Goat %	Pig %
Inveresk	73	58.9	16.4	24.7
Edinburgh Cas	46	43.5	26.1	30.4

The results show that cattle were slightly more numerous and sheep slightly less so at Inveresk but there is no significant difference in the livestock farming practices represented by the two assemblages.

The distribution of the main domesticates from the Iron Age levels at Inveresk and Edinburgh Castle differs greatly from that of Iron Age sites in southern England. In the latter sheep were generally the dominant animal present (Grant 1984, 117). Grant (ibid, 116) suggests that the production of wool was the principal reason for the dominance of sheep in England. Perhaps the dominance of sheep is best viewed as an attribute of the development of a cash-crop economy, as occurred later, in the medieval period in Scotland (below). Grain was probably the most important cash-crop but its continued production requires a constant supply of dung. Sheep dung is the richest dung of the domesticates containing greater quantities of nitrogen, phosphorus and potassium than that of cattle (White 1970, 127–128). A predominance of sheep may be expected in truly marginal areas where they fare better than cattle or pigs for purely environmental deterministic reasons, but in the south of England it must be regarded as a necessary consequence of the development of a cash economy in a location that had large areas of cultivable land. The limited evidence from Edinburgh Castle, Inveresk and presumably Broxmouth suggests that this was not the case in Iron Age or Roman southern Scotland and the evidence from Iron Age Thorpe Thewles in Cleveland, where cattle were also dominant, also suggests that such an economy had yet to develop in north-east England (Rackham 1987).

Dark Age

The data from this period differs from the preceding period, in terms of MNI, in that cattle are now only marginally more important than the other two principal domesticates and the three species are essentially present in equal numbers. Comparative material from southern Scotland is rare. The very small sample from Clatchard Craig again suggests the dominance of cattle but the samples are too small to be trustworthy (Barnetson 1986). It is perhaps interesting that at Dunadd the 'greater numbers of remains belong to the pig, followed by the ox, and that by the sheep' (Ritchie 1930, 126). A predominance of pig may be due to the high status of this Dal Riada site as Lucas (1989, 4), on the basis of the literary evidence, concluded that the 'doughtiest Irish warriors relied on pig-meat for their intake of protein'. Heavy oak woodland in the area could also account for the high incidence of pig.

There is evidence for the increased hunting of red deer during the Dark Age period. These represent nearly 9% of the MNI totals. Most of the bones were not antler, which could have been brought to the site independently of the carcass, so the assemblage represents an unusually high level of hunting. Again, direct comparisons are unavailable from southern Scotland and comparisons with the 'highland' areas of the north and west are invalid because of the area's different topography. In contemporary Ireland, despite the high profile of hunting in the heroic literature, the incidence of red deer is never as high as at Edinburgh and in any case the majority of red deer bones almost invariably consist of antler fragments. At Moynagh crannog, a high status site in County Meath which has produced a large sample, red deer comprise only 0.6% of the MNI (McCormick 1987). Similarly at Knowth, Co Meath, red deer accounted for 1.1–1.5% of the MNI totals from the 'Dark Age' levels. It is difficult to explain these differences between Irish and Scottish Dark Age assemblages. At Edinburgh it is clear that the interest in deer hunting was already well established by the Iron Age as red deer constituted 5.3% of the MNI total. Hunting, while dominated by, was not confined to red deer as roe deer, beaver and fox are also present in the Dark Age levels while badger and wild pig were present during the Roman Iron Age phases.

Medieval period

The medieval samples, in terms of MNI, attest to the importance of sheep in Scotland's medieval economy. The passing of the old order and its replacement by feudalism meant that food rent was replaced by cash rent. This had occurred in Scotland by the late 11th or early 12th century and for the reasons mentioned in the context of the Iron Age, above, this led to a great expansion in sheep flocks. Wool, as a cash crop, became the most important item of English foreign trade (Lloyd 1977) and was probably as important in Scotland. The contemporary documentation shows that the monasteries of southern Scotland took to sheep rearing and wool production with determined enthusiasm. This brought them into conflict with the remainder of the population whose interests often lay in other forms of agriculture. The monks of Melrose can be seen during the late 12th and early 13th century to be involved in the 'ruthless pursuit of grazing rights' in order to reap the profits of the wool trade (Duncan 1975, 420). Mutton, although essentially a secondary product, found a ready market in urban areas. The meat diet of the towns was, in consequence, dictated to a certain degree by the agricultural practices and not vice versa. The importance of sheep in Scotland is reflected in the bone assemblages of the period. Sheep are not only dominant at Edinburgh Castle but also in a series of samples of 13th-/15th-century date from the site of the Scandic Hotel in the High Street (Chaplin & Barnetson 1976, 234). Sheep were also dominant in a sample from medieval deposits at St Ann's Lane, Perth (Hodgson & Jones 1982, 451) and also generally outnumber the other domesticates at 45 Canal St, Perth (*ibid*, 1983, 515). Cattle, however, outnumber sheep at another Perth site, High St, and also in medieval levels in Elgin and Aberdeen (*ibid* 515; *ibid* 1984, fiche 4:B3). Cattle also dominate in a small 14th-/15th-century sample from Inverkeithing (Smith & Hodgson 1982, 543). This suggests that intensive wool production was limited to the southern part Scotland which is consistent with the theory that sheep manure for cereal crops was an important factor in determining regional animal husbandry practices. All of these assemblages are small, and larger samples are necessary to test the hypothesis.

One observation that can, however, be made with reasonable confidence is that pig played a minor role in the diet. The remains are less numerous than either cattle or sheep/goat in Edinburgh, Perth, Elgin and Aberdeen.

SPECIES DISCUSSION

Cattle

Cattle provided the bulk of the meat consumed at the site during all periods. The small size of the individual samples precludes detailed study of butchering techniques but the high incidence of head and foot fragments indicates that the animals were generally brought to the site either on the hoof or as complete carcasses. This is supported by the documentary evidence, as the food stores for Edinburgh Castle on October 17, 1298 included 'of the carcasses of oxen – 20' as well as '100 live oxen' (Dickinson *et al* 1952, 200). It should be remembered that Area H lay outside the castle until approximately AD 1560–1575 and it is probable that animals were slaughtered outside the Castle walls. There was, however, no evidence in the faunal assemblage to suggest that any of the samples represented specialised butchering waste. In the Roman Iron Age sample, F510, the angle of the chop-marks on the lumbar vertebrae indicated that the carcass was lying on the ground during butchery and not hanging by its hind legs as is the modern practice. The cattle of this period were also butchered by chopping through the transverse processes of the vertebrae thus sectioning the carcass into two sides and a joint consisting of the vertebral column which was consequently chopped laterally into smaller portions. There was also evidence for this in the medieval samples but the medial splitting of the vertebrae of a hung carcass, as is practised today, was also noted. Examples of this type of butchery were also occasionally noted in medieval deposits from Leith (Barnetson 1985, fiche 3). The continual occurrence of both prime parts, eg scapula and pelvis, and waste parts, eg skull and feet, of the skeleton, together, was a feature of this site and, indeed, is generally the pattern noted on medieval sites. This seems to reflect a lack of specialisation on the part of the consumer as far as specific joints of meat are concerned. The presence of retail butchers in Medieval Scottish towns is well attested in the Burgh Laws which legislate for the sale of meat on market stalls or from their house windows (Innes 1868). The regularisation of the meat market and the stipulation that the butcher must sell meat openly '. . in thair bothys and thair wyndowis beande opyn . . .', at a fixed price '. . . the price salbe set and the assis . . .' and to allcomers '. . . al men als well gangand as cummand what somevir . . .' (*ibid*, 32–33, 140) suggests that meat was generally in short supply and demand outstripped supply. In such circumstances the consumer could not consistently exercise selectivity in their choice of meat joints but simply bought what was available. This could explain the complete range of bones found in Edinburgh and other sites and the evolution of such unappetising recipes as sheep's head pie : '2 sheep's heads and trotters, singed and well cleaned, then soaked overnight etc.' (Hope 1987, 156).

As already stated, the data for the ageing of the cattle was very limited. Both mature and sub-adult animals tended to dominate with calves being occasionally present. The age distribution of animals from the Roman Iron Age and Dark Age are shown in Table 36. The acute fragmentation of the medieval bones meant that no ageing data could be calculated for the period.

Table 36 Cattle age distribution based on Higham (1967) and Grant (1982).

Phase No	Higham stage of eruption	Grant M3 wear stage	Approx Age (in months)
Iron Age			
1	8	-	15–16
1	13	-	24–30
1	15	B	30
3	20+	GKJ	40+
Dark Age			
3	3–4	-	1–6
1	6	-	7–9
2	10	-	17–18
2	15	B	30–31
1	16	C	31–32
5	20+	G	40+
1	20+	H	
1	20+	M	

The sex of cattle is best determined by the metrical analysis of complete metacarpals. Only a few of these were found during excavation so the, less satisfactory, distal width (Bd) of the metacarpal was used (after McCormick 1992). The probable distribution of the sex of cattle is shown in Table 37.

Table 37 Probable sex distribution of cattle on the basis of the distal width of the metacarpal. Those less than 55mm are regarded as female while those greater than 57mm are male

Period	Female	Male
Iron Age	6	4
Roman/Dark Age	5	2
Medieval	6	2
17th century	3	1

The sample provides little information other than to indicate that the higher incidence of cows during the post-Iron Age period may be a product of the development of dairying (McCormick 1992).

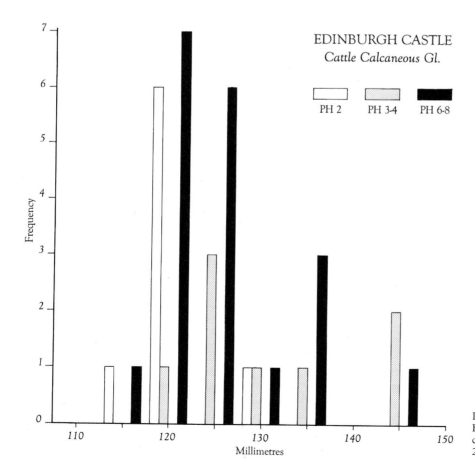

Illus 145
Bar chart comparing the Gl of cattle calcaneous from Mills Mount Phases 2, 3 & 4 and 6 & 8.

The bovine metrical data are listed in Table 53mf (2:C11–12). Analysis of the calcaneus (illus 145) indicates that there was a general increase in cattle size after the Roman Iron Age. The Romans were agricultural improvers, as evidenced by the extensive treatise on agriculture written by Columella which remained in vogue until the Agricultural Revolution. In some areas in Europe an increase in cattle size was noted during the Roman period with a decline in the post-Roman period (Bokonyi 1974, 115). In Britain the evidence is less convincing, while the Edinburgh Castle data suggest that cattle underwent no improvement at this time.

Table 38 Estimated withers heights of cattle based on metacarpal and metatarsal lengths (GL).

The metacarpals are all female and use a multiplication factor of 6. The factor used for all the metatarsals (5.45) is that used when the sex is undeterminable (after von den Driesch & Boessneck 1974).

Bone	Phase	GL (in mm)	Multiplication Factor	EWH (in cm)
Metacarpal				
	Iron Age	182.3	6	109.4
		167.3	6	100.4
		185.3	6	111.2
		177.9	6	106.7
	Dark Age			
		191.4	6	114.8
		181.1	6	108.7
		184.6	6	110.2
	Medieval			
		180.0	6	108.0
		181.7	6	109.0
Metatarsal				
	Iron Age			
		211.6	5.45	115.3
		202.3	5.45	110.3
	Dark Age			
		236.9	5.45	129.1
		228.6	5.45	124.5
		217.1	5.45	118.3
		211.9	5.45	115.4
		240.1	5.45	108.6
	Medieval			
		236.6	5.45	128.9

It should be noted that due to the acute fragmentation of the animal bone few complete cattle longbones survived. The complete metapodials along with the estimated withers heights (EWH) are given in Table 38. The EWH based on metatarsals are higher for metatarsals than metacarpals but this is simply due to the fact that multiplication factor used for female is less than that used for male or when the male or indeterminate sex is used. No complete metapodia were present the medieval excavations at Bernard St, Leith (Barnetson 1985) or from S of High St, Edinburgh (Chaplin & Barnetson 1975–6) but the other metapodia measurements indicate that the cattle fall within the same size range. Occasional large instances were noted and a radius with a Bp of 94.9mm in the 13th-century context F389 etc. is almost certainly a post-Medieval if not a modern intrusion. Several complete sheep metapodia were found on the site and these are listed below.

Only a few instances of palaeopathology were noted on the cattle bones and these were generally limited to the hind limb. Osteo-arthritis, with pitting and exostosis, was noted on one proximal metatarsal surface (Phase 7) while the fusion of the centroquartal to the second/third tarsal (Phase 7), again with pitting and exostoses of the centroquartal, is also probably due to the same cause. Two distal ends displayed slight eburnation and exostosis while pitting and exostosis was noted on two phalanges (Phase 6). These arthritic conditions were probably caused by the use of the animals for traction. One metacarpal displays swelling at the point of distal epiphyseal fusion. Again the bone is incomplete so it is not known if the articular surface is effected. The latter is from a 17th-century context (F237).

There was only one instance of the use of cattle bone as a raw material. This consists of a sawn horn core from F330 (Phase 8), indicative of the careful removal of the horn sheath for horn-working.

Sheep/Goat

The problem of differentiating between sheep and goat is well attested but generally, in the present instance, few identifiable goat bones were present. In the largest sample, F330 etc, no goat bones were noted while many could be definitely attributed to sheep. The only definite goat bones were a radius from F530, a female goat horn from F418, and a male horn and humerus from F431, all of Dark Age date. Polled sheep were noted only in F330 which dates to about the 15th century. The late appearance of polled sheep was also noted off the High Street in Edinburgh (Armitage 1975–6, 239) where they were present in the 15th-century levels but were absent in the earlier medieval contexts.

It is extremely difficult to differentiate between the mandibulae of sheep and goat so the attempted reconstruction of age-slaughter patterns for caprovines can be highly dubious. The low incidence of goat in the sample, however, suggests that sheep age/slaughter patterns can be attempted with reasonable confidence (Table 39).

Table 39 Ageing data for caprovine mandibulae based on Higham (1967) and Grant (1982).

Date No	Higham stage of eruption	Approx Age (in months)
Iron Age		
1	10	10–11
1	12	12–21
1	13	21–24
1	14 (C)	25–26
2	15+ (GG)	26+
Roman/Dark Age		
1	6	5
1	12	12–21
2	13	21–24
2	14 (DD)	24–26
3	15+ (GHJ)	26+
Medieval		
2	4	3
2	11	11–12
1	12	12–21
1	13	21–24
5	14 (BCCCD)	24–26
1	15 (E)	26+

The small sample from the Roman Iron Age levels shows a general similarity to Inveresk where most of the sheep were semi-mature or adult at time of death (Barnetson 1988) although no very young animals were present. The samples from both sites are, however, small.

The samples from the Dark Age and medieval Edinburgh are slightly larger and also differ from each other. In the Dark Age sample the sheep were predominantly fully grown or old animals with few young individuals being present. In the medieval layers there is a peak in the slaughter of animals of about one year and two years with few older animals being killed. This may represent the selection of sheep for the meat market at ages which are most cost effective for the producer. The age/slaughter pattern is essentially the same as that noted at Kirk Close, Perth (Smith & Hodgson 1987, 197–8) although there is a higher proportion of young animals at Edinburgh. The peak represents the slaughter of prime meat animals for consumption.

A neonatal caprovine bone was present in the Dark Age sample F1360 while some extremely young caprovines were present in F1382, which dates to the same period. There was no evidence for goat in either sample so it is likely that this is evidence of the breeding of sheep in the vicinity of the site during this period.

The metrical data for sheep are shown in Table 55mf (2:D1–2). The data did not show any significant change in the size of sheep during the period under study.

Table 40 Sheep metapodial dimensions (in mm) and estimated withers heights (in cm).

(Data from F330 etc is omitted. Only a small sample of material produced metrical data and the more important of these are shown in Table 39.) The multiplication factor for metacarpels is 4.89 and for metatarsals is 4.54.

Bone	Phase	Gl	Bp	Bd	SD	EWH
Metacarpal						
	Iron Age	128.2	22.2	25.5	16.1	62.7
	Roman/Dark Age	120.1	22.1	25.0	13.5	58.7
		120.9	22.1	25.8	15.9	59.1
	Medieval					
		117.4	–	21.5	11.4	57.4
		117.3	23.2	24.9	13.5	57.3
		104.1	20.5	23.3	17.3	50.9
Metatarsal						
	Roman/Dark Age	122.9	20.8	25.1	13.9	55.8
		139.5	19.9	24.0	13.1	68.2

Chop or knife marks were rare on the sheep bones. There were occasional instances, however, of caprovine bones being chopped cleanly through (Phase 8) while in one Iron Age context (F520) a sheep skull has been bisected medially for the removal of the brain.

Pig

Pigs were never dominant during any of the phases represented in the present samples. Pig, unlike cattle or sheep, could be reared within the medieval town and therefore reduced dependence on outside producers. Pigs, however, were a troublesome animal to keep, and the Burgh Laws of Scotland state that a burgher could only keep pigs if they were confined to a sty or allowed to roam only in the presence of a keeper (Innes 1868, 41). The Records of the Burgh of Edinburgh record that in 1450 and 1490 edicts were issued to try to curtail the menace of pigs roving the streets of the city (Edinburgh Burgh Recs, I, 12, 58–59). The faunal remains also provide evidence for the breeding of pigs within the town. In the Phase 8 sample F330 four neonatal pig bones were present indicating that pigs were being bred in the immediate vicinity. Neonatal bones were also present in some Dark Age contexts.

A small sample of mandibulae were recovered and the ageing data based on these are shown in Table 41.

Table 41 Ageing data for pig mandibulae based on Higham (1967) and Grant (1982).

Date No	Higham stage of eruption	Approx Age (in months)
Iron Age		
1	13	11–12
1	14–17	12–17
3	18	17–19
5	20 (B)	21–23
2	22 (C)	25–27
2	23 (D)	27–29
2	24+ (F/GH)	30+
Roman/Dark age		
1	8	6–7
3	11	9–10
3	14–17	12–17
2	18	17–19
3	19	19–21
2	20	21–23
3	22	25–27
1	24+ (J/K)	30+
Medieval		
1	9–10	7–9
1	11	9–10
1	14–17	12–17
1	18	17–19
1	20	21–23
1	22	25–27
1	24+ (J+)	29+

The data indicate that the great majority of pigs were killed between the ages of six months and two years with few, presumably breeding stock, surviving into old age. Three instances of palaeopathology were noted.

One metacarpal (F297, 7) displays exostoses on the shaft probably due to inflammation caused by penetrating trauma. In the second instance, a calcaneus displays almost complete inflammation with only the proximal fusion area unaffected (F433, and finally, a mandible (F389, Phase 5) displayed fracture and successful mending immediately behind the canine; the animal was male. The last two instances came from a phase that contained both Dark Age and medieval material. The metrical data (Table 54mf, 2:C13) indicated no significant change in size during the periods studied.

Table 42 Pig measurements (in mm).

Bone	Phase/date	GL/GL1	Bp	Bd	Bt
Humerus					
	2/Iron Age			41.4	32.3
	4/Dark Age			39.9	33.1
	5/11–13th cent			39.0	33.1
				34.4	27.4
				43.5	32.1
				37.6	30.4
				36.2	27.8
	7/14th cent			37.8	28.4
	9/17th cent			37.5	27.3
Tibia					
	2/Roman IA			27.1	
	4/Dark Age			32.0	
	5/11–13th cent			30.9	
				29.7	
				20.1	
	6/14th cent			27.6	
	8/16–17th cent			33.0	
Calcaneus					
	4/Dark Age	76.4			
	7/16th century	80.9			
Astragalus					
	2/Iron Age	39.9		25.6	
	5/13th cent	42.6		26.0	
		41.2		–	
		41.2		25.8	
Radius					
	2/Iron Age		28.1		
			31.5		
			29.0		
	4/Dark Ages		31.8		
	6/14th cent		29.5		

Pelvis		LAR			
	2/Iron Age	34.9			
	4/Dark Age	33.1			
		34.5			
		34.7			
	6/14th cent	33.9			

Teeth		L. 3rd lower molar			
	4//Dark Age	32.1			
	5/11–13th cent	33.3			
		34.0			

Other domesticates

Horse, dog and cat bones were present in only small numbers. Horse and dog were present from the earliest Roman Iron Age levels but the cat does not appear until the Dark Ages. A femur from F431 has a Bp of 16.4 mm which falls well within the range of early domesticated cats. The cat was a Roman introduction into Britain and its absence from Edinburgh, the civilian settlement at Inveresk, as well as at the Roman Forts at Newstead, Bar Hill and Mumrills suggests that it is possible that it had not reached Scotland until a later period. Cat's paw marks are present on a brick at Mumrills Fort near Falkirk (Macdonald & Curle 1925, 571). They were made by a leaping animal on the soft clay prior to firing. The large size of the prints, however, indicate that they were of the wild cat rather than the domesticated variety. Wild cat are notoriously shy and the presence of the claw marks suggests that the bricks were made in a very isolated area.

Dog bones were occasionally found on the excavation but bones with gnawing marks, presumably caused by dogs, were present in most contexts. Ageing data was rare but both young and mature individuals were present in the Roman Iron Age levels. The remains provided no metrical data so it is not possible to estimate the size of the dogs present.

The presence of butchered horse bone suggests that horse were at least occasionally consumed. A metacarpal from a Roman Iron Age context (F1387) displays a chop mark while medieval context (F383) produced a horse metatarsal that had been split medially for the extraction of marrow. Butchered horse bones have also been noted on medieval sites in Perth, Inverness and Inverkeithing (Smith 1989). In most instances the horses were several years of age at time of death but an individual of approximately a year and a half was present in context F433 (Phase 5). The eating of horse had been regarded as taboo since the Early Christian period. When St Boniface informed Pope Gregory III in about AD 732 that the English ate horse the latter replied, telling him to use all powers within his means to suppress this 'filthy and abominable practice' (Emerton 1940, 58). Horse eating, however, continued into the Medieval period but probably only in times of extreme food shortage. It is quite possible that the medieval horse bones at Edinburgh Castle represent periods of siege. There is certainly documentary evidence for this at Berwick on Tweed. On the 18th of February, 1315, Maurice de Berkley wrote to Sir William Ingge to inform him that:

'No town was ever in such distress as Berwick, short of being taken or surrendered. The garrison are deserting daily, and there are none left in the town, save only such of the garrison of the castle that are slain or dead of hunger. Whenever a horse dies in the town the men-at-arms carry off the flesh, and boil and eat it not letting the foot(men) touch it until they have had what they will. Pity to see Christians leading such a life' (Cal Docs Scot III, 90).

Horse bones tend to be found in small quantities in Leith (Barnetson 1985, 425).

Wild animals

A wide range of wild animals were present. These included red deer, roe deer, wild pig, hare, beaver, badger, rabbit, rat and possibly fox. The wild pig is from the Roman Iron Age levels and consists of a third metacarpal (GL 94.9mm). A further wild pig bone was found in the Phase 5 mixed Dark Age and early medieval deposits (F493) and consisted of a scapula fragment (GLP 48.4 SLC 38.5mm). Wild pig was also found at Roman forts at Newstead (Ewart 1917, 376) and Bar Hill (Macdonald & Park 1906, 530) but was absent from Inveresk, Mumrills and the Iron Age fort at Broxmouth (P Hill pers comm). The presence of wild pig at the site is indicative of a forested environment in the vicinity. Boar survived into the medieval period in Scotland and is listed as among the preserved beasts in the royal forest at Falkland but the paucity of documentary references to them in the context of hunting indicates that they had become very scarce by the 15th century (Gilbert 1979, 98).

Red deer are present in all phases of the site. Usually red deer remains on urban sites consist of antler fragments, reflecting its use as an industrial raw material. This is clearly not the case in the present instance as post-cranial bones are well represented at all levels indicating the exploitation of the animal primarily for food. During the Iron Age and Dark Ages the site was essentially rural so the presence of a wide range of wild animals is not unexpected. Deer, both red and roe, continue to be present during the medieval period but in smaller quantities than the earlier phases. Although the site was essentially at the edge of an urban centre their presence still indicates continued access to rural areas. Small quantities of deer bone were also present in the medieval levels on High Street (Chaplin & Barnetson 1976, 234). While the latter may represent trade in venison it is possible that some of the game found at the Castle represents deer taken in Royal game reserves. The nearest Royal parks were at Seton and Dalkeith (Gilbert 1979, 365) although the origin legend of Holyrood Abbey suggests that hunting was practised in the immediate vicinity of Salisbury Crags (Cummins 1988, 52). Rather surprisingly, the presence of English venison at Edinburgh cannot be discounted. King Edward I brought casked venison from England during his Scottish campaign in 1299–1300. The game was caught in Sherwood Forest, shipped from there to London for salting and hence to Scotland (Topham 1787, xvii).

A beaver incisor was found in the Dark Age level F1382. Beaver remains are extremely rare on Scottish archaeological sites. It is not certain when the beaver became extinct in Scotland. Geraldus Cambrensis in *The history and topography of Ireland*, written in about 1188, states that the beaver was still present in Scotland

(O'Meara 1982, 49), a claim which is supported by the inclusion of Beveris amongst skins being taxed for export in the Assis de tolloneis of King David I who reigned from 1124 to 1153 (Innes 1868, 101). The latest reference to the beaver is by Hector Boece (d. 1536) who states that beavers were present and hunted in Loch Ness. His descriptions of Loch Ness are, however, unreliable and Samuel Johnson (1777, 53) doubted that he ever visited the area.

Both the rat (presumably *rattus rattus*) and the rabbit were Norman introductions to Scotland and none were found in pre-Medieval levels in the excavation.

5.5 MILLS MOUNT SOIL MICROMORPHOLOGY
Discussion and interpretation of the thin section descriptions
Stephen P Carter

SUMMARY

Three groups of soil thin sections have been prepared from Areas H and X covering selected contexts from Phases 1 to 8 (see illus 24 for sample locations). It was originally intended that these would be discussed by phase, addressing specific questions relevant to each phase. However, the interpretation of the section descriptions questions both the site interpretation of individual contexts and the overall phasing. This makes a phase by phase analysis of the thin sections impossible. An interpretation of events in Mills Mount up to the start of medieval deposits, based on the thin sections and information provided by the excavators is summarised below. Detailed descriptions of the thin sections are to be found in fiche (5.5.1mf, 2:E1–14).

Area H (Shallower deposits, upslope at S end of trench).

1 Formation of soil in mixed glacial drift over basalt.
   (Sections 99/4, 99/5, 99/6; Contexts 535, 536)
2 Iron Age occupation and limited disturbance of original soil. Equivalent to Phases 1 and 2
   (Sections 99/4, 99/5; Context 535)
3 Period of restricted or no activity with development of soil over Iron Age structures. Equivalent to late Phase 2.
   (Section 99/1; Context 522)
4 Rapid accumulation of midden containing ashes and plant waste with bone, shell and coprolites. Equivalent to late Phase 2 and Phases 3, 4 and 5.
   (Sections 1593, 1594; Contexts 516, 497, 493)
5 Period of unknown activity and duration, due to subsequent truncation of deposits.
6 Levelling of area and start of medieval industrial activity. Phase 6.
   (Sections 1595/1, 1595/2; Contexts 389, 344)

Area X (Deeper deposits, downslope at N end of trench).

1 Formation of soil in mixed glacial drift over basalt.
   (From results in area H)
2 Iron Age occupation and limited disturbance of original soil. Equivalent to Phases 1 and 2.
   (From results in Area H)
3 Apparently uninterrupted slow accumulation of sediment incorporating midden material with no evidence for significant change up to and including Phase 7 deposits.
   (Sections 143/A–F; Contexts 1352, 1353, 1356, 1360, 1382, 1387)

The most important difference between this sequence of events and the on-site interpretation of the stratigraphy is that the group of contexts identified as parts of a turf line (Phase 3) is now interpreted as a layer of organic refuse within a midden. This midden accumulated after the abandonment of the Iron Age structures and its top was lost through later (Phase 6) activity. Therefore some of the contexts at present assigned to Phases 2, 3, 4 and 5 are part of the same rapidly accumulating midden.

The stratigraphy and phasing of the deposits in Area X could not be confirmed by soil micromorphology and it seems that their nature and depositional environment did not change significantly from late Phase 2 to Phase 7. They are interpreted as slowly accumulating midden derived sediments totally mixed by invertebrate and plant root action.

DETAILED DESCRIPTION

PHASE 1

The natural soil

The natural soil survived under the Iron Age deposits except at the upper S end of Area H. It consisted at most of two layers, 535 and 536 forming a profile up to *c* 0.4m thick over the irregular surface of the solid basalt of the Castle Rock. These layers were sampled at the N end of Area H, 535 in sample 99/4 and 99/5, and 536 in sample 99/6.

In thin section, the mineral fraction of this soil is a mixture of basalt rock fragments and minerals derived from the basalt with common silt and fine sand-sized quartz grains and rare sedimentary and metamorphic rock fragments. This mixture indicates that the soil parent material was glacial drift consisting of local basalt, nearby Carboniferous sedimentary rocks and more distant types. The differences between 535 and 536 were in the organic fraction and the organisation of the groundmass. 535 had frequent fragments of amorphous polymorphic organic matter and a high concentration of organic pigment but 536 contained little of either. The groundmass in 535 was porphyric and in 536 it was chitonic.

It is concluded that 535 is the A horizon and 536 the B horizon of a freely draining brown soil. The degree of disturbance noted in these thin sections was low. It was limited to ash and charcoal-rich soil fragments introduced as excrement filling vertical earthworm burrows which penetrated to the base of the profile. Elsewhere in Area X, layer 535 was absent indicating that the soil was either truncated or severely disturbed here. The degree of disturbance is clearly variable, ranging from minor contamination to total destruction at the S end of Area H.

PHASES 2, 3, 4 & 5

Deposits Accumulated over the Iron Age Structures

As indicated in the summary, the site phasing at this point becomes difficult to follow. The key thin sections for the interpretation of these phases are samples 1593 and 1594 so these will be discussed first.

Sections 1593 and 1594 sampled the stratigraphic sequence of contexts 493 over 497 over 516. This sequence is very clear in thin section and in addition, 516 may be divided into two layers.

CONTEXT 493

This layer is dominantly mineral in composition. The coarse mineral fraction is dominated by very fine to medium sand-sized quartz grains with few basalt rock fragments, olivine derived from the basalt and rare sedimentary rock fragments. The fine mineral fraction is dominated by phytoliths with a few quartz grains and diatoms.

The coarse organic fraction consists of common fragments of wood charcoal and phlobophane-filled plant tissue with a few fragments of lignified plant tissue. The fine organic fraction is dominated by carbonised cells and cell fragments with common non-carbonised cell fragments.

Included in this groundmass are small fragments of bone, marine shell and coprolite which judging by its nature is carnivore coprolite (Courty *et al* 1989, 114).

The fine groundmass, dominated by phytoliths and very fine charcoal fragments indicates that the bulk of 493 is ash (in the general sense) from fires. Actual plant ash (Calcium Carbonate) is absent, presumably because of subsequent solution, but the surviving residues show that the fuel included broadleaved wood (charcoal) and grasses (phytoliths). The other components of 493 confirm that it consists of domestic refuse with bone, shell and plant waste.

The presence of abundant quartz in the coarse mineral fraction is not so simple to interpret. Although single mineral grains of quartz are present in the drift on the Castle Rock (see thin sections 99/4–6, 5.5.1mf), in 493 they are larger and much more abundant relative to the basalt derived minerals. Individual grains reach medium sand size in 493 but only very fine and fine sand is present in the drift derived soil. These features would seem to rule out a drift source for the quartz so an anthropic source is most likely. It is important to note that the quartz is present as single grains only. Possible sources include:

1   Sandstone quernstones.
2   Sandstone hearth slabs.
3   Turves from quartz-rich soils used to bank up fires.
4   Sandstone buildings.

Option 3 is the least likely as it would have also resulted in the formation of abundant burnt soil fragments which are absent from 493. Option 2 would account for the association of the quartz with ashes scraped from hearths. Only one sandstone quernstone was found in Areas H and X in the Phase 2 context 529 (Find No 204) and it has not been examined to determine the texture of the quartz grains. Grinding could generate the single mineral grains with no larger rock fragments. A source in the sweepings from sandstone floors and house walls is attractive but cannot be tested.

Although the various midden components are easily identified in 493, the deposit has been affected by post-burial processes. The complex crumb/spongy microstructure and heterogeneity of the groundmass indicate invertebrate mixing, probably by earthworms. This is also suggested by the fine fragmentation of the coprolites (none larger than 2mm) and the absence of groups of phytoliths preserving their original plant tissue structure. The invertebrate mixing predates the creation of abundant thick typic coatings of clay and fine silt sized phytolith and charcoal fragments. These coatings are a common feature of layers containing abundant ash (Courty *et al* 1989, 113) and their formation may have followed the decalcification of the ashes. The deposit has subsequently been partially recalcified by the precipitation of microsparitic calcite in hypocoatings, impregnating the typic coatings described above. It has also become waterlogged presumably as a result of deep burial and this has led to the formation of iron/organic matter mottles and iron/phosphate mottles. The phosphatic mottles have generally developed around a nucleus of plant tissue, bone or coprolite.

CONTEXT 497

This layer is dominantly organic in composition. Areas of dominantly mineral groundmass are mamillated excrement mixed into the layer by earthworms. Excluding these areas, 497 is a layer of non-carbonised elongate plant fragments forming a horizontal mat. The larger fragments (up to 10mm long) contain well preserved vascular tissue connected to poorly preserved parenchymatous tissue. The tissue types and elongate shape of the fragments suggest that these are plant stems. Smaller tissue fragments are comminuted pieces of similar organs and are generally less well preserved. Carbonised plant tissue is rare in both the coarse and fine fraction and the fine groundmass is made up of dark brown cell residues and amorphous organic matter. The only common mineral components are the plant derived phytoliths which are concentrated in bands with amorphous organic matter up to 1mm thick. These are the residues of decayed grass culms or leaves. Other midden components present include rare carnivore coprolite fragments and bone fragments. 497 has been affected by post-burial processes although these differ from those in 493. Invertebrate mixing has introduced mineral matter as excrement but has only partially disrupted the plant stems which are still in horizontal layers. The plant tissues have been affected by microbial decay, particularly the parenchymatous tissues. Phosphatic pedofeatures are common and include crystalline vivianite (Iron phosphate) infillings and amorphous phosphate mottles like those in 493. 497 is discontinuous as a layer in thin section with a sharp vertical break. This indicates a large scale disturbance that must also have affected 493 and it was probably created by mammals (man, dog or small mammals).

CONTEXT 516

Thin section 1594 includes the top 60mm of this layer and two distinct bands are present. The upper band, immediately below the organic layer 497, is only 20mm thick and consists almost entirely of mineral components. The coarse fraction is dominated by quartz grains up to medium sand-size and the fine fraction by phytoliths. As in context 493 this suggests that ash is the main component of the band but in this case there is relatively little charcoal. Other midden components such as bone and plant fragments are very rare and there are no coprolite fragments. This is therefore more or less pure hearth waste and the presence of abundant quartz re-enforces its link with hearths.

Post-burial physical alteration of this band by invertebrates has been limited as it retains sharp upper and lower boundaries, there is internal banding of the coarse components and some phytoliths are organised into small fragments of plant tissue pseudomorphs. Typic coatings are present but very rare and thin.

The lower band of 516 which occupies the remainder of section 1594 is very similar to 493. It is therefore a groundmass of ash with other domestic refuse. There is more charcoal (both large fragments and fine material) than in 493 indicating variation in the proportions of different fuels contributing to the ash. 516 also contains very rare small fragments (less than 1mm) of what appears to be pottery. The same processes of decalcification of ash and typic coating formation have occurred but in 516 these have been accompanied by the general slaking and collapse of the soil structure. This has created a dense groundmass with embedded layered coatings broken by partially infilled rounded vughs and this has removed most of the evidence for invertebrate mixing.

DISCUSSION OF CONTEXTS 493, 497, 516

From the analysis of the thin sections it is clear that these contexts are a series of well-stratified primary midden deposits. The sharp boundaries between all the layers show that the impact of invertebrate mixing is limited and the original nature of the layers is clear. The combined processes of invertebrate consumption and microbial attack have reduced the proportion of organic components in these layers but it is concluded that 493 and 516 are multiple dumps of ash mixed with organic domestic refuse and 497 is a single dump of pure plant debris. The midden that they form part of must have accumulated sufficiently fast to preserve these thin dumps which would have otherwise been destroyed by invertebrates and plant roots. The sequence of pedofeatures identified in 493 and 516 shows that the mixing that

did occur ended before the decalcification and slaking of the ashy groundmass and no further mixing took place. This is consistent with a temporary phase of disturbance as the midden accumulated and these layers were still close to the surface.

The excellent preservation of 493 indicates that the overlying context 433 must be part of the same midden accumulation. The top of 433 was cut away at the start of phase 6 leaving a minimum thickness of 0.8m of midden. The size of this primary midden is best shown by the extent of the organic layer 497 and the equivalent contexts 373, 382, 384, 400, 511, 518, 532 and 1386. Except for the isolated patch (1386) in Area X this layer extends S for 9m from a point c 7m S of the Cartshed S wall before it is destroyed by later cuts.

According to the drawn W section of Area H, the base of 497 and equivalent contexts is only 0.1–0.2m above Iron Age layers (Phase 2), represented here by 529 and 531 with lower midden layer 516 directly overlying 531. Therefore there is apparently little or no accumulation of sediment between the Iron Age structures and the base of the midden in this area. A few metres downslope of the limit of the organic layer 497, the midden, represented by contexts 418 and 520 (an ash layer according to the field description by Ian Mate), overlies 522. This is a 0.25m deep layer that in turn overlies the Iron Age cobbling 529 and it was described in thin section 99/1.

CONTEXT 522

In thin section, two different areas could be identified. Area 1 occupies the top 60mm of the section and is dominantly mineral in composition. The coarse mineral fraction is dominated by quartz with frequent basalt rock fragments and basalt derived mineral grains. The fine mineral fraction is a mixture of common phytoliths with basalt derived olivine and plagioclase and frequent quartz. Organic components are dominated by charcoal in the coarse and fine fractions. In addition there are very few small fragments of bone and pottery and possibly coprolite.

The fabric of the groundmass is heterogeneous, and this combined with a crumb/granular microstructure is evidence for considerable earthworm activity. Although this deposit contains fragments of refuse (charcoal, pottery, bone, coprolite) they are small and not abundant. The fine groundmass resembles that of the A horizon of the natural soil (535, sections 99/4 and 99/5) but with a higher concentration of phytoliths and fine charcoal. It is concluded that this deposit is the top of the natural soil heavily disturbed and contaminated by the addition of midden material which has then been well mixed by earthworms and probably roots also.

Area 2 which occupies the bottom 20mm of section 99/1 is similar in its basic components to context 535, the A horizon of the natural soil. It differs primarily in microstructure being apedal rather than having a crumb structure. Area 2 of 522 is therefore probably part of the trampled top to 535 and represents the Phase 2 Iron Age surface at this point.

If contexts 418 and 520 have been correctly interpreted as part of the rapidly accumulating midden (it should be noted that there are no micromorphological data to confirm this) then 522 represents a phase of soil development with minor refuse accumulation between the occupation of the Roman Iron Age structures and the start of rapid midden accumulation. This need not imply a period with no activity in the area as it may have taken time for the main midden to spread downslope to this area and 522 could have formed at the periphery of a growing midden.

SAMPLE 143

The micromorphology of deposits contemporary but downslope of the Area H midden was examined in Area X. A vertical series of six thin sections (sample 143) was prepared from c 1m thick of sediments dated from the junction of Phases 7 and 8 down to Phase 2.

The most striking feature of these six thin sections is their similarity. They all have essentially the same basic mineral and organic components arranged into the same microstructure and these are like those described for the upper area of context 522. The phytolith and fine charcoal content indicate an ash component and fragments of plant tissue, bone, shell and coprolite demonstrate the presence of other domestic refuse. However, as in context 522 they do not have a pure ash groundmass like that of contexts 497 and 493. There is no evidence for discrete bands or lenses of contrasting material in the sediment and this suggests total mixing of the soil components. The presence of invertebrates is confirmed by abundant mamillated excrement from earthworms and re-working of this into smaller excrement by other invertebrates. Mixing by plant roots certainly occurred in the Phase 7 context 1353 as ancient roots have been preserved in vertical channels and it probably affected the other contexts in this sequence as well.

It is concluded from these various lines of evidence that the source of most of the basic components in these deposits is a midden but the rate of accumulation has been slow allowing the total mixing of components. This suggests either infrequent dumping of refuse in Area X or the slow movement of material downslope off the Area H midden into Area X.

The similarity of the deposits from context 1387 (Phase 2) up to 1352 (Phase 9) indicates that either conditions did not change during this period or that episodes of slow sediment accumulation were frequent enough to destroy any discrete strata that formed. The failure to identify any context boundaries in thin section is puzzling, particularly the compacted surface 1360 (Phase 5) which should have had a distinctive microstructure at least.

It is concluded that following the abandonment of the Phase 2 structures, Area X was peripheral to any activity right through to Phase 8. Sediments accumulated through infrequent dumping of refuse or redeposition from middens upslope. No activity in the area created features substantial enough to survive the intense mixing processes in these enriched soils.

GENERAL CONCLUSIONS
(illus 41)

Iron Age occupation (Phases 1 and 2) in Areas H and X has left features dug into or on a soil developed in glacial drift. Little or no sediment accumulated during these phases. These features are buried under up to 1m of sediment which consists predominantly of mineral and organic domestic refuse. This is present as either primary midden or sediments derived from middens. The source of the midden material is, not surprisingly, upslope of the excavated area. Little or no sediment separates the Phase 2 features from the primary midden and this could result from either soil stability during a period of abandonment or continuity of activity. The fact that all the accumulated sediments that were examined are anthropogenic suggests that natural sediment accumulation did not occur on this slope. The top of the midden deposits in Area H was removed at the start of Phase 6 when it was prepared for industrial activity so the nature and duration of activity prior to this is not known. In Area X, soil thin section data suggest continuity of activity, or rather lack of activity from Phase 2 through to Phase 8 and this appears to contradict the on-site interpretation of the stratigraphy.

6

THE HUMAN REMAINS · THE COAL YARD CEMETERY
Dick Grove

Excavation of the area which was formerly the Coal Yard for Edinburgh Castle was precipitated by construction work at the immediate entrance of the new tunnel. One major discovery was a cemetery of 14 skeletons. It is clear that this cemetery extended to the E and N over the backfilled medieval defensive ditches of which only the E portion was located. The S margin may have been disturbed by the later construction of casemates. To the W, there is the wall which formerly contained the presumed entrance to the Castle, the blocking of which had rendered the area redundant and thus made it available for use as a cemetery. This latter limit forms the only definite boundary.

There are a number of features which suggest that this cemetery belongs to a single phase and the individuals could, therefore, represent the victims of a particular event such as a siege or the ravages of an infectious disease. All graves are positioned along the same alignment (E–W) so as not to overlap with each other and indeed, given the small number of individuals present, are placed in neat rows, thus indicating that the location of the preceding burials was known and, therefore, probably recent. Other common features are wooden coffins joined by iron nails, the position of the arms by the side or hands placed over the pelvis and the common use of shroud pins. As will be discussed below, the suggestion that this is a single-phase cemetery is lent further support by the number of common features to be found among the skeletal remains themselves.

The majority of burials have survived intact, but a number of loose, disarticulated bones, in levels disturbed by the building operations, suggest that there were more burials in the area. However, the disturbance of several graves (1106, 1168 and 1173 in particular) provides the possibility that these loose bones may well come from the identified burials. There were also a small number of disarticulated human bones found in the grave fills themselves. This need not detract from the conclusion that the excavated graves are from a single phase of burials. It is possible that these bones come from burials of a different date in the area. There were, for example, two skeletons discovered outwith the Castle walls, in Princes St Gardens North. They are recorded in photographs housed in the National Monuments Record of Scotland (illus 108). Judging from their proximity they may well be part of the cemetery. From the photographs they appear to be adult but unfortunately no further details are available.

DETAILS OF THE SKELETONS

CONDITION

In the majority of cases all areas of the skeleton were recovered; three in particular (1114 (illus 109, 1129 and 1146) were in excellent condition. Often, however, the smaller bones of the hands and feet were poorly represented. The bone itself is well preserved although some thinner areas, in particular the articular surfaces, are pitted with decay. The disturbance and breakage of bones seems to have been largely due to the movement of heavy vehicles over the cemetery, as the skeletons themselves lay only just below the surface of the coal yard. As a consequence, the more fragile bones, the skulls (with the exception of the more robust mandibles), ribs, vertebrae, scapulae and innominate, had usually been broken. This certainly contributed to the loss of fragments during excavation. In addition, a number of skeletons were discovered by the building contractors. (The condition and further details of individual skeletons can be found in the archive report.)

One skeleton (1106) had been severely damaged as a result of the construction of a manhole some 25 years ago. Here the majority of bones which have survived come from the right side, including the humerus (the only large complete bone), fragments of the ulna, a number of handbones, femur, tibia and fibula and a fragment of the right innominate. The skull, cervical vertebrae and most of the thoracic vertebrae, clavicles and scapulae of 1168 are missing. In the case of 1173 only the upper region of the skeleton has survived and the only longbones are fragments of the left humerus and ulna.

ESTIMATED AGE AT DEATH AND SEX

With some reservations, detailed below, a general picture of the age at death and sex of the individuals has emerged. All appear to be male and the majority died when young adults. In both aspects the degree of preservation, in particular of the skull and pelvis, has a direct relation to the reliability in the diagnosis of both age and sex. In only one case was the skull complete (1146) but, at the other extreme, one skull was in a total of 73 fragments rendering reconstruction impractical and often in some cases impossible due to the warping of the bone as the (presumed) result of the pressure of heavy machinery. The pelvis was also a major victim of these disturbances. Nevertheless all those with appropriate surviving bones seemed to be male using the criteria discussed by Genoves (1963) and Krogman (1962). One exception to this is 1143 which possessed ambivalent characteristics in the morphology of both the skull and pelvis which may, however, be related to the developmental defects of the skeleton (cf below); the individual does, nevertheless, appear to be male on the criteria identified by Phenice (1967). The sex of Skeleton 1106 could not be identified; the robust appearance of the surviving bones suggest it is possibly male.

All individuals are adults although a number have not reached full skeletal maturity. In particular, Skeletons 1122 and 1158 have a number of unfused epiphyses. In the case of the latter, the epiphyses of the proximal humerus, distal radius and ulna and distal femur as well as those which tend to fuse later – the annular rings of the vertebrae, the clavicles and the secondary centres of the innominate and scapulae – are unfused. The majority of the main epiphyses which have thus fused indicate that the age of this individual would be approximately 18–20 years. In the example of 1122 both the distal ends of the radii and ulnae are unfused; the annular rings of the vertebrae are partially fused as are a number of secondary centres. In both the wear of the teeth suggest an age of 17–25 (Brothwell 1981). In the case of Skeleton 1158, where the pubic symphysis, has survived the estimated age at death can be refined to 17–20 years.

In a number of individuals (1129, 1143, 1159 and 1173) the secondary epiphysis on the clavicle has remained unfused; this usually occurs by the 25th year (Todd & D'Errico 1928) and more rarely will remain completely or partially unfused usually until approximately the 30th year (McKern & Stewart 1957; both quoted in Krogman 1962). Some corroborative evidence to support the estimated age at death comes from the degree of tooth attrition which in all these individuals falls within the range of 17–25 (Brothwell 1981). In the case of three individuals (1129, 1143 and 1159) the pubic symphyses have survived to give further information (18–23, 17–20 and 20–24 respectively) (Mckern & Stewart 1957).

Full skeletal maturity in the remaining eight individuals has been reached (this probably includes both 1106 and 1168 whose skeletons are poorly preserved). In the case of two (1114 and 1146) both teeth and pelves were recovered. In Skeleton 1168 only the pubic symphysis was available. The remainder (except 1106 which can only be given the approximate estimated age at death as adult and 1100 whose extent of dental disease obscures the degree of wear (but which nevertheless has an unworn appearance)), have their ages assessed from the degree of toothwear only. This is between 17 and 25 years. The one exception to this is Skeleton 1117 who appears to be older. The wide range of the estimated age at death for this individual is due to the unusual pattern of tooth wear and the extent of dental disease.

The above discussion of the estimated age at death of these individuals is given at some length because it has recently been argued that toothwear, which in this sample has provided the greatest available criterion, can only give an approximate and possibly misleading estimate of the age at death. In the cases where, however, other evidence has been available, either from the stage of skeletal maturity or the morphology of the pubic symphysis, the degree of tooth attrition has tended to be in agreement. In addition the inferred age of the majority of individuals is supported by the frequency of epiphyseal lines still visible and the paucity (with the fortuitous exception of 1117) of degenerative change and periodontal disease (see below). All these secondary criteria are not conclusive evidence but they do, however, lend support to the argument that the majority of these individuals are young adults.

STATURE

The following estimates of stature are based upon the calculations of Trotter & Gleser (1958). The imperial measurements are to the nearest inch.

Table 77 Estimate of stature

1100	1.686m	–	5ft 6ins
1103	1.829m	–	6ft–
1106	1.763m	–	5ft 7ins
1114	1.677m	–	5ft 6ins
1117	1.778m	–	5ft 10ins
1122	1.702m	–	5ft 7ins
1129	1.708m	–	5ft 7ins
1143	1.68m	–	5ft 6ins
1146	1.716m	–	5ft 8ins
1158	immature		–
1159	1.750m	–	5ft 9ins
1168	1.723m	–	5ft 7ins
1173	?		–
1175	1.682m	–	5ft 6ins

The lower limb bones of Skeleton 1158 have not completely fused; those of 1122 have fused and are therefore included despite the immature stage of the upper limbs. It is probable that Skeleton 1143 and to a lesser extent 1175 were, in fact, shorter because of the unusual curve of their spines (cf below).

PATHOLOGY

DENTAL PATHOLOGY

Of the 14 individuals, 12 have complete or partial surviving dentitions; the exceptions are 1106 and 1168. As mentioned above, only one skull was recovered intact (1146). Of the remainder, the mandible was often in good condition while the maxillary area was usually fragmentary. In many cases the post-burial damage removed areas of the tooth sockets and sometimes the teeth themselves had been lost.

Of the 12 individuals, 11 have suffered from a total of 26 carious lesions (the exception is 1122). Eight of these are occlusal, seven buccal and eight are interproximal. A further three have eroded the enamel to such an extent that the initial site of the lesion is unknown and a total of 12 teeth are missing *ante-mortem* some of this loss is doubtless due to caries destroying enamel and loosening teeth. This pattern of caries is worthy of remark. The presumed age at death of these individuals, in part, explains the frequency of occlusal caries. As young adults little wear has occurred on the occlusal surface of the molars; areas of stagnation which would form ready sites for caries are therefore still present amongst almost all skeletons. Such a pattern would not be found amongst a group of older individuals. Of greater interest is the incidence of caries occurring between teeth (interproximal) and in addition the number of carious lesions on the sides of teeth, both

Table 76 Summary of age at death

Skeleton	Teeth	Pelvis	Epiphyses
1100	17–25?	–	adult
1103	17–25	–	adult
1106	–	–	adult
1114	17–25	22–28	adult
1117	25–35	33–45	adult
1122	17–25	18–20	
1129	17–25	18–23	under 30
1143	17–25	17–20	under 30
1146	17–25	20–24	adult
1158	17–25	17–20	18–20
1159	17–25	20–24	under30
1168	22–28	–	adult
1173	17–25	–	under 30
1175	17–25	–	adult

lingual and buccal. These latter are not sited on the dentino-enamel border which is usually associated with gingival disease but positioned on the mid surface of the enamel. This incidence of caries forms a pattern reminiscent of that found among populations with diets high in refined carbohydrates such as is common in the Western world today. The 17th century saw the initial beginnings of the sugar trade (the first English sugar plantation was founded on Barbados in 1640) but it is unlikely that carbohydrates formed a substantial part of the diet during the remainder of the century. It would not be acceptable, however, to make use of this feature to establish the date of burial.

One probable consequence of untreated caries is the death of the pulp and the spread of the infection to the root of the tooth thus forming a local periodontitis; the pus formed by this pattern of infection usually escapes through the thinnest area of bone which is the buccal side of the maxilla or mandible forming a sinus in the process. These sinuses are visible on 1100 (1), 1117 (3) and 1159 (2). In the case of the latter the upper right 1st molar has lost approximately three quarters of its enamel and a sinus, opening bucally, has formed with great loss of bone. One sinus has formed in association with the lower left 1st incisor of 1117. The source of this infection is through the pulp which has been exposed through excessive wear. In only one instance is there a caries at the dentino-enamel border on the lower left second molar which is characteristically wide and shallow. This individual, 1103, displays moderate alveolar resorption subsequent to periodontal disease; the condition probably following the irritation and infection caused by the formation of calculus which may have been much more extensive than is now visible. The resorption of bone has doubtless contributed to the loss of the lower right 1st and 2nd molars.

The age of the individuals does have a bearing on the pattern of dental disease. Tooth loss is largely due to caries rather than periodontal disease. With the exception of Skeleton 1103, calculus is slight although some has evidently chipped off *post-mortem*. Resorption of bone tends to increase with age if there is a propensity for gum disease. Evidence for this can be found in only six individuals and in these cases it is only slight (Brothwell, 1981, 155).

PATHOLOGY OF THE SKELETON

The estimation that the majority of individuals in this group died when young adults has, as with the incidence of dental disease, a direct influence on the pattern of disease visible on the skeletons. There is, for example, very little degenerative change. In the case of three skeletons very few vertebrae were recovered but in all the remaining individuals a common pattern was evident. Typically degenerative change, in the form of the development of osteophytes and the discolouration and indentations on the body surfaces known as Schmorl's nodes, was evident from the 5th or 6th thoracic vertebrae and often continued down to the first few lumbar vertebrae. It is worthy of note that even in the two youngest individuals slight degeneration in this area is evident – even before the annular rings of the vertebral bodies have fused. In all but one case it is confined to the lower thoracic vertebrae. The exception is Skeleton 1117, which, significantly, was probably the oldest at death; degenerative change is also visible on the lower cervical vertebrae. In addition he is the only individual with evidence of degeneration – possibly the early stages of osteoarthritis – on other parts of the skeleton; in this case lipping on the inner edge of the condyles of the femora.

The vertebrae are also the site of a number of developmental anomalies, some of which may have contributed to the appearance of degenerative change. Skeleton 1146 has an extra (6th) lumbar vertebra which itself has an overdeveloped left transverse process. This has formed a false joint with the left ala of the sacrum. Another common variation, visible on 1129, is the 5th lumbar fused to the sacrum. In addition the 4th lumbar exhibits spondylolysis - a failure of the posterior arch and inferior articular surfaces to be joined with the remaining part of the vertebra. This is less common on the 4th than the 5th. 'The defect has hitherto

been regarded as congenital [but] it is now widely believed that it may be caused by injury; or it may be the result of a stress fracture in childhood or adolescence' (Adams 1981, 211).

The abnormalities affecting Skeleton 1143 are more complex. The sacrum, although damaged, is clearly bifid. The 5th lumbar is similarly affected but both sides of the spinous process meet without fusing. this condition need not, however, have produced any symptoms. The spine is also distinguished by a lateral curvature (scoliosis) towards the right in the area of the mid thoracic; the 4th thoracic and the 9th thoracic are shaped so as to compensate for the curve. (1175 has a slight curvature in the region of the upper thoracic.) There are a number of possible causes for this condition: one is that this is a case of idiopathic scoliosis which progresses during skeletal growth but which ceases at skeletal maturity. Another is that the deformity is caused by the paralysis of muscles following the infection of poliomyelitis. Unfortunately a correct diagnosis is not possible.

Skeleton 1143 is also blessed with a further anomaly – the retention of the deciduous second molar on the right mandible – and because there is still a gap in the teeth on the left side, it would appear that the opposite tooth has only just been shed a short time before death. In the case of 1114, the deciduous 2nd incisors of the maxilla have been retained and the permanent teeth have failed to erupt.

A significant finding amongst this group of individuals is the number of injuries they appear to have suffered during their lifetime. Probable injuries to bone cover most areas of the skeleton, although evidence from the skull is somewhat limited owing to their fragmentary condition. These are described below.

Skeleton 1129 appears to have sustained a blow to the teeth. The maxillary left 1st incisor has a slightly rounded indentation while its neighbour, the right 1st incisor, has a smaller notch with a small 'hook' of enamel. It is this latter feature, in particular, which suggests injury due to a blow or a fall as opposed to abnormal wear caused by a regular habit of holding objects by the teeth such as a pipe.

In Skeleton 1146 there has been a well healed fracture of the upper mid shaft of both left radius and ulna. The fracture is commonly called a parry fracture. Both bones are shorter than their opposites (the radius by 9mm). and there is also slight mal-alignment of the shafts. In addition there is a small raised nodule of bone on the left side of the ulna. The X-ray hints at the location of the line of the original break in the radius.

A clearer case of injury is evident on the left tibia and fibula of Skeleton 1114 (illus 150). Both have been broken in the upper mid shaft; the fibula has a slight area of raised bone and an alteration in the alignment of the shaft at this point. In the same position, at the point of the nutrient foramen, the tibia has an area of raised bone some 56mm long around the posterior and medial sides. The fact that both are at the same position on the leg would suggest a transverse rather than a rotational injury (Adams 1987, 254). The appearance of the raised area of bone is not smooth but pitted with pinprick holes in an uneven 'striated' surface. This would suggest that the wound had become infected, although there are no sinuses for the drainage of pus to suggest that it was very serious. The infection of the tibia is not unusual following a fracture because the bone lies so close to the skin. The most likely cause of this infection is the bacteria reaching the surface of the bone via an open wound caused at the same time as the breakage. There is a similar appearance on the bone surface – pitting and 'striations' running along the length of the bone shaft which is sometimes slightly raised – this so-called periostitis (Manchester 1983, 37) most typically affects the shafts of the tibiae (1100, 1106, 1146 and 1168). The proximal fibulae of Skeleton 1103 and the shafts of the femora of 1143 and 1175 also have a similar appearance. It is considered that this is a low grade infection often caused by persistent trauma or irritation.

Skeleton 1114 had also suffered an injury to the left foot. The

Illus 150
Skeleton 1114 under excavation
showing healed fracture to left tibia.

shafts of the 2nd to 5th metatarsals are thickened and uneven when compared to those of the right. A similar condition is evident on possibly all metatarsals of the right foot and also on the 2nd left metatarsal of 1103. In addition one proximal phalanx has fused at right angles with its mid phalanx although its position on the foot is unclear. Fractures of the metatarsal shafts can be caused by a heavy object falling upon the foot or by repeated stress from prolonged walking or running, thus the popular term to describe this condition as a 'march fracture'. 1103 also has an abnormal development of bone on the right innominate. Its opposite side, for comparison, is unfortunately missing. It may represent a fracture of the wing of the ilium. There is also slight lipping at the sacroiliac junction presumably acting to compensate for the stress of the injury.

It is not known at what age these injuries took place except to state that all, with one possible exception, have completely healed (which renders diagnosis more difficult); the younger the individual, the quicker and more effective the mend is likely to be. What can be stated is that none, with the exception of the infection of the tibia, has been life threatening or apparently beset by complications (eg compound or multiple fractures) and indeed those injuries to the hip and feet could be treated in modern medical practice by rest alone.

SUMMARY

On the grounds of the positioning of graves, style of burial and similarities in age, sex and pathology it has been suggested that the burials from this cemetery represent the victims of a single event. The majority of individuals would appear to have been young male adults, many with a history of injuries, some of which have popular terms such as 'parry fracture' and 'marching fracture'. Obviously it is probable that they are soldiers and tempting to conclude that they are victims of a siege although there is no reason to discount other events such as the presence of diseases.

The most significant dating evidence was the discovery of a coin which dated to 1682/86, in a context through which the graves had been cut. The most obvious siege would therefore be that of 1689. In such circumstances there would be no great necessity to exclude females from the group: in the 1689 siege '. . . a gunner's wife falling in labour, the Governour caused beat a parley to send in a midwyfe, which was refused . . .' (Bannatyne Club 1928, 195). It is unlikely that women were absent from the Castle in any siege in its history. Nor, if it was a siege, need the absence of evidence of cause of death cause surprise particularly in a type of warfare where injuries are not primarily caused by edged weapons. One is equally likely, if not more so, to die of some other cause as did the first casualty (except the 'governours cow') of the 1689: siege '[Colin Sutherland] a private centinell in the garrison, after a tedious sickness, dyed, and 8th day was buryed, with thrie volleys of small shott.' (In the siege of 1640 a substantial number of the garrison died as a consequence of eating contaminated salt pork.) There is, unfortunately, little other evidence of the types of injuries and numbers of casualties at this particular siege.

7

DISCUSSION
A RETURN TO THE OPENING THEMES

The discussion of the results of the excavations returns to the themes introduced in the prologue to the report. The themes are arranged chronologically, but we have resisted the temptation to try and produce a new narrative account of the history of the Castle, because the excavations themselves do not provide the basis for a complete re-evaluation. A full account of the Castle's history can be read elsewhere (MacIvor 1993).

THEME 1 · THE PREHISTORIC SETTING AND SIGNIFICANCE

The discovery of prehistoric deposits on Castle Rock, dating back to the late Bronze Age or early Iron Age, naturally excited much interest and was widely reported in the national press. The reasons for this have little to do with the intrinsic quality of the materials discovered and everything to do with their location. As a source for Iron Age evidence, Edinburgh Castle is surpassed by a number of sites in the east of Scotland which had better preserved and more extensive remains, the most noteworthy perhaps being Broxmouth (Hill 1982a). Indeed, it is these neighbouring sites which provide the key to interpreting the deposits and structures attributed to Mills Mount Phases 1 and 2. What makes the site unique, and is the source of the great interest, is, of course, the later history of this location. To begin with, we will consider the setting of the site, how it may have related to its surrounding landscape in later prehistoric times, and what the earliest settlement may have looked like.

The density of enclosed settlements in the Lothians is represented in the two location maps (illus 3 and 4) which illustrate the preponderance of fortified or enclosed settlements known to survive in the Lothians either as upstanding monuments or as cropmarks. Many of these sites have been discussed on an individual basis (Harding 1982; Rideout et al 1992), and have also formed part of recent synthetic discussions (Macinnes 1982, 1984a, 1984b; Hill 1982c). The map of the later prehistoric environs (illus 4) makes it clear that the Castle is but one of many settlements existing at that time in the region. The question that immediately arises is: can any reason for its later eminence be adduced from its geographical setting? There can, of course, be no certain answers to such questions, but two aspects of the site are made plain by the map. Firstly, the Castle Rock occupies a position where the coastal strip of Midlothian is pinched to its narrowest – only about 10km – between the Pentland Hills and the Forth. This places the Castle in the midst of a naturally-created boundary zone through which land traffic moving between East Lothian and central Scotland would pass. The specific route which this traffic followed was probably determined by local topographic features, some of which can be reconstructed.

Pollen analysis indicates that, by the early first millennium, large-scale forest clearance had already taken place, leading to the development of grassland, heath and bog during the Iron Age (Boyd 1984). The boggy areas which separated the stretches of potentially arable land are significant and have been represented with the running and standing water in the map of prehistoric Edinburgh (illus 3). It seems likely the main E–W route would have taken the traveller N of the Castle across fords between Arthur's Seat and the Castle Rock. The occupants of the Iron Age settlement on Castle Rock were apparently well placed to observe traffic in order to protect themselves and to develop both local and seaborne trading networks. It must be recognised that, with respect to E–W traffic, the Castle Rock is in no better position than the more prominent Arthur's Seat, which was sufficiently advantageous to have attracted four prehistoric enclosed settlements.

Ancient remains on Arthur's Seat (illus 151), including fortified sites and cultivation terraces, have long been known (Stevenson 1947, 158–70), but the full extent of the fortified settlements is only now being explored

Illus 151
Aerial view of Arthur's Seat showing the cultivation terraces in the foreground. (Copyright: Royal Commission of the Ancient and Historical Monuments of Scotland; NMRS neg ED/14798.)

(Ian Morrison pers comm; Wickham-Jones 1996). Nether Hill and Arthur's Seat are enclosed on the E side by a pair of substantial ramparts, with a well-defined entrance on that side. The circuit may have continued around the other three sides to enclose a very rocky 20 acres, relatively little of which could have been built upon. The slopes below the ramparts are covered in cultivation terraces, which are undated. Arthur's Seat overlooks Dunsapie Hill, immediately to the NE, which is surmounted by a smaller fort with a large annex to the E. The promontory of Salisbury Crags, to the N of the Seat, is enclosed by widely-spaced ramparts, the inner of which is the more visible, being comprised chiefly of large stones. Finally, the discovery of a Roman intaglio ring, of the 1st century BC, led to the identification of the fourth fort on a ledge at Samson's Ribs, to the S of Arthur's Seat (Stevenson 1970, 294).

This series of seemingly unrelated, or at least non-contiguous, enclosed settlements scattered about the hill argues for a long history of settlement. Judging from the reduced and denuded condition of the earthworks, all are arguably prehistoric. Moreover, one is forced to conclude that these were not especially successful settlements, since they do not show any evidence of having been modified and rebuilt. While the sheer mass and altitude of Arthur's Seat makes it a far more prominent topographic feature than the Castle Rock, the sites found there give the impression of instability and insignificance. The fact that, rather than one prominent, successful establishment, there are several rather ephemeral ones may be an index of the lesser importance of these various fortified settlements. The evidence from Arthur's Seat is in marked contrast to Traprain Law and apparently to the Castle itself. The Castle Rock's appeal, when compared with that of Arthur's Seat, is that, although craggy and impressive from most perspectives, it is over 100m lower and is thus more comfortable and convenient. It also provides a more compact and defensible site by virtue of the crags to the N and S.

During the later prehistoric period, the settlement on Castle Rock was presumably an enclosed village (ie hillfort), but only one of a number in the immediate Edinburgh region. In addition to the sites on Arthur's Seat, contemporary hilltop settlements may have existed on Corstorphine Hill and on Calton Hill (where, in the 19th century, Samian and 'Roman urns' were discovered), although there is no visible evidence of fortifications at either site now. Slightly further afield there certainly were hillforts on Blackford Hill, Wester Craiglockhart Hill, Castle Law at Hillfoot, Kaimes Hill and Dalmahoy (illus 3). Therefore it would seem that in the later prehistoric era the settlement on the Castle Rock was just one of a number of enclosed sites in this pivotal region, which formed a link between the East Lothian Plain and the Central Belt. Arguably, the Castle settlement occupied the most attractive site when the various considerations of natural security, visual prominence, proximity to the traffic and convenience to farm lands are weighed up. Unfortunately, available evidence does not provide enough information to determine why it became the most successful.

Besides the fortified sites, the Castle environs included open settlements consisting of isolated round houses or small clusters of two or three buildings. Apart from aerial photography, these sites on the lower ground have not received much attention. Examining the later prehistoric environs of Edinburgh (illus 3), it can be seen that they have been commonly recorded only in the Esk Valley, where they are observed as cropmarks. The overwhelming prominence of fortified sites in the Lothians has tended to overshadow these sites and it seems likely that, as in Fife and Angus, they made up a significant proportion of the settlements (however see Macinnes 1982 and 1984 for a divergent view). It is reasonable to expect that the area now occupied by the City of Edinburgh was well-settled by the Iron Age and that the settlement took the form of small farms set in a landscape of cultivated fields, broken up by woodlands, scattered small lochs and patches of boggy ground. Exactly how these open settlements articulated with the hillforts remains to be explored and to do so will require the excavation and publication of some of these open settlements.

The evidence relating to the early Castle settlement is indeed slight. No traces of early ramparts survive, as a consequence of the frequent and often extensive rebuilding programmes over the past 500 years. However it would be unusual, to say the least, for a hilltop settlement in this region to be unenclosed. We should probably imagine that it was fully enclosed despite the natural protection provided by the crags. Traprain Law, for example, is not unusual amongst hillforts in having ramparts which run along even its most precipitous slopes. Not only should we imagine ramparts but we should imagine them in a practically constant state of being repaired. At Broxmouth the defences were almost continuously remodelled from its inception in the late Bronze Age until a century or so before the arrival of the Romans, so the precise form of the supposed Castle Rock defences at any given time is beyond speculation (we have provided no reconstruction for this reason).

As the description of the early phases of the Mills Mount trench make clear, only fragments of buildings were revealed. For the best impression of what the interior settlement of the Castle was like we must turn to the more extensive excavations of forts in the Lothians. Principal amongst these are of course Traprain Law and Broxmouth, although the excavations at Wester Craiglockhart Hill, Kaimes Hill and the Dunion all have points of interest.

We will return to consider the relationship of Traprain Law to the Castle below, because the more recent and more comprehensive excavations at Broxmouth provide the best guide to how the Castle interior may have developed. We have speculated that the medieval ditches cutting off the E approach to the Castle may have had Iron Age predecessors. If so, they may have resembled the final defended phase at Broxmouth (in the pre-Roman Iron Age) when the defences were remodelled to create ditch terminals which were revetted with

Illus 152
View of the interior of Broxmouth under excavation, with the partially excavated triple ramparts to the top.

drystone walling and a dual portal timber gateway, with earthworks forming an extended inward passage (Hill 1982b, 168). In the subsequent and final phase, sub-circular, stone-walled, sunken-floored houses were built on what may have been the stances of earlier ring-groove houses (illus 152). One house had a paved porch, and paving was also used extensively for floor and yard surfaces. These features together with the nature of their construction, the polygonal stone hearths, and the raised threshold or door-check are strongly reminiscent of the houses on Mills Mount. Similar houses have been reported at the Iron Age coastal fort above the harbour at Dunbar including stone-built round houses grouped around a paved yard (Holdsworth 1991, 315). In the final occupation of Broxmouth, houses overlay the rampart. The excavations of the small dun-like structure at Wester Craiglockhart Hill revealed structural elements of houses, built over the collapsed ramparts, which included stone-flagging around a hearth of orthostats set on edge (G Maxwell pers comm), again corresponding to the hearths from Mills Mount.

These house fragments from Mills Mount appear to belong to a type identified by Jobey (1966) as typifying Votadinian settlement in Northumbria. In his study Jobey recorded many examples with similar features and common traits, notably stone-lined basins, the basal stones of rotary querns (reused as door pivots?), raised stone benches (possibly represented at Mills Mount), internal wooden partitions and double doors. These houses, like the Broxmouth examples, measured on average 8–10m in diameter. The evidence from the Castle is too meagre to allow for absolute confidence in applying Jobey's model (with or without Hill's further modifications (1982c)); nevertheless it remains our best indication of what was probably there.

THEME 2 • THE POLITICAL GEOGRAPHY OF THE EDINBURGH REGION IN ROMAN TIMES

The discovery that the Castle Rock supported a settlement which prospered during the first few centuries AD calls for a reconsideration of both the significance of Roman artefacts and the ways in which the Castle related to the other known settlements and military establishments.

Within the limitations of the evidence, we have argued for the presence of a hillfort, which was a typical Iron

Age creation. However the structures of that settlement, the houses of Mills Mount Phase 2, are stratigraphically earlier and cannot be directly linked with the use of the Roman goods. All of the Roman artefacts which were recovered from a primary context came from the midden which engulfed the abandoned and demolished houses. The evidence for the Roman period settlement consists of the midden itself. The contents of the midden demonstrate that settlement on the Rock continued from the Iron Age (or resumed). However it also suggests that the settlement in Roman times was smaller, perhaps confined to the summit now occupied by the Palace block, the Scottish National War Memorial and St Margaret's Chapel.

The imported artefactual assemblage from the Roman period settlement includes sherds representing over fifty vessels (about 37 coarse ware and 14 fine ware), two sherds of glass and ten objects of cast bronze. The bulk of the coarse and fine wares dates to the period from about AD 80 to 160; however a significant number of fine wares date to the 3rd–4th century. This pattern is mirrored in the other categories of artefacts: there are examples of later Roman glass and metalwork. This seems to point to a continued access to imported goods after the military withdrawal. It should also be noted that amongst the few iron objects from the Roman period are a fragment of a spearhead and a probable spear butt, which might be taken to indicate the presence of a warrior or militarised element in the settlement.

To make sense of the evidence for this settlement we must look further afield and enter into the debate about the nature of Roman impact on the Lothians. Put baldly, the traditional position argues that, having been subdued by the Romans, the native Votadini abandoned the practice of fortifying their settlements, although some continued to be occupied but unenclosed (Hanson & Maxwell 1983, 35–6). At a couple of sites there was an episode of refortification in the late 4th century (traditionally interpreted as the consequence of the Votadini having *foederatus* status). Feachem, for instance, proposed such an explanation for the late defences at Traprain Law (1956, 289). Since these positions were advanced, more dating evidence has become available and a new picture is emerging. Most Roman specialists would now agree that many hillforts were in disrepair by the late 1st century AD (Breeze 1982). However, the body of evidence relating to the late occupation of hillforts is rarely deployed in the context of identifying high status sites of the Roman period. Apart from the unique case of Traprain Law, attention has focused upon the more compact fortified sites, the so-called lowland brochs (see Macinnes 1984a, 1989).

Traprain Law is without question the most impressive hillfort in the Lothians (illus 153). Its sheer bulk dominates the immediate landscape and, with respect to the finds which have been made there, it has no close rivals. Traprain at 40 acres is ten times as large as Edinburgh Castle Rock and the main area excavated by Curle and Cree was over 0.6ha, which is about twenty times the size of the Mills Mount trench. Despite differences of scale and the obvious difficulties of working with old excavations, it nevertheless invites comparison, if for no other reason than because its principal occupation extends from later prehistory into the late Roman period and thus is contemporary with the settlement on the Castle Rock. Traprain's spectacular treasure of late Roman silver plate has ensured that it commands a large place in the discussion of the history of the Roman occupation of Scotland. The interpretation of the site has been much considered in recent years starting with George Jobey's comprehensive review (1976), followed by Dr. Close-Brook's analysis of the late rampart sequence revealed by Bersu (1983b) and most importantly by the debate initiated reluctantly by Sekulla (1982) and continued by Peter Hill (1987).

In his analysis of the coin assemblage from Traprain, Sekulla recognised that the characteristics of the coins did not resemble those of a hoard, but were more characteristic of votive offerings made over an extended period although he could not bring himself to accept the conclusion that there was a temple at Traprain (1982, 288). Hill, however, has strengthened the case for a religious focus to the Law by drawing into the discussion the remarkable assemblage of Roman period artefacts and manufacturing debris material from Traprain. Hill suggests that these do not derive from settlement debris, but are evidence of religious practices. He offers the hypothesis '. . . that Traprain Law was primarily a ceremonial centre in the Roman period . . .' (1987, 90), a suggestion warmly supported with comparative evidence from Ireland by Aitchison, but disputed by Close-Brooks (1987, 92–4). Aitchison makes the additional observation, that if Traprain is regarded as a ceremonial site as opposed to a settlement site, then '. . . the brochs of central and southern Scotland emerge as by far the richest domestic settlements, in terms of quantities of Roman material, on the northern frontier . . .' (1987, 96). Increasingly these lowland brochs have come to be seen as expressions of social distinction emerging from the Iron Age architectural tradition which owe little or nothing to the Roman world (for both sides of the debate see Mackie 1971, Barrett 1982, Macinnes 1984a).

Illus 153
Traprain Law from the air.
(Copyright: Royal Commission of
the Ancient and Historical
Monuments of Scotland; NMRS neg
EL/5080/CN.)

On topographic grounds Edinburgh Castle Rock could fall into the hilltop ritual site category as easily as it could be the setting for a 'lowland' broch. Much rests on the objects themselves and what we make of them. The datable artefacts are mostly from the 2nd century AD and, with the possible exception of the dragonesque brooch, they are not individually uncommon or remarkable. However as a group they assume some importance. They indicate that the residents of the Castle Rock had access to the earliest Roman pottery to be available in north Britain and that they continued to maintain that access despite the fluctuations of Roman military arrangements. Although the absolute numbers of fine wares is not high, the density is impressive. Nevertheless the complete Roman period finds assemblage from the Castle does not look like one twentieth of the Traprain assemblage. Rather the Castle finds look like a particularly large set of domestic objects, comparable to those which have been recovered from the other lowland brochs as well as from less distinguished settlements. Traprain's collection on the other hand can be regarded as having a strongly non-domestic quality. Significantly, in view of Hill's suggestion that the manufacture of jewellery may be an indication of the ceremonial function of Traprain, there was no convincing evidence for metalworking at Mills Mount and the styles of the identifiable bronzework are not local. The dragonesque brooch is not paralleled in the large collection from Traprain and arguably was made in southern Britain.

Goods similar to those from Mills Mount have been recovered from relatively humble rural establishments, some of which are well beyond the Antonine Wall (for example, the Ardestie settlement in Angus (Wainwright 1963)). Interestingly, they occur alongside pottery and other objects of local manufacture. As far as can be seen, these Roman objects are being used in a domestic context and, although they represent an exotic element introduced into the traditional material cultural assemblage, it is by no means clear that they were used in order to emulate or participate in Mediterranean dietary practices.

As with many of the Roman finds discovered on native settlement sites (Robertson 1970), much of the Castle material may be the result of trade, which was an inevitable consequence of the presence of large numbers of

Illus 154
Edin's Hall Broch from the air. (Copyright: Royal Commission of the Ancient and Historical Monuments of Scotland; NMRS neg BW/2969.)

soldiers. This is particularly true for the coarse wares which dry up around AD160 with the withdrawal from the Antonine Wall. The high proportion of fine wares and non-local metalwork may indicate a more significant commerce or even diplomatic gifts to the local chief; however, the collection seems to reflects the Castle Rock's ability to attract merchants independent of the military.

Although the arguments on this point are inconclusive, we would suggest that the Roman period settlement at Edinburgh Castle Rock took the form of a lowland broch, perhaps on the model of Edin's Hall or Turin Hill where the broch was located within earlier ramparts (illus 154). If the appropriate comparison of the Roman material from Edinburgh is with the excavated lowland brochs such as Hurly Hawkins (Taylor 1982) or Leckie (MacKie 1987) rather than Traprain Law, then how does it rate? Edinburgh Castle emerges as the richest of these Iron Age sites in terms of quantities of finds. Even when proximity to the sources of Roman material is taken into account, the Castle Rock looks to be one of the pinnacles of native political authority – if material wealth can be equated with political power at this time.

THEME 3 • THE DARK AGES AND THE CONTINUITY QUESTION

These excavations allow us to reconsider how Scotland passed from prehistory into the Middle Ages. The evidence at Mills Mount provides the Castle with the longest continuous settlement of any comparable site in the country. Of course continuity must be qualified; we know, for instance, that Robert the Bruce slighted the defences after he recaptured the Castle in 1314 and that for a period of 22 years the Castle was apparently a ruin. At earlier times it is possible that breaks of a century could go undetected, particularly given the restricted area of the excavations and the problems of dating in the Iron Age or early medieval periods. Indeed the early history of Edinburgh almost requires that we postulate periods of abandonment as the Castle changed hands; these were perhaps similar to the early 14th-century hiatus. Until these excavations, the continuity question took as its starting point the *Gododdin* elegies and informed discussion was the preserve of scholars of the ancient Celtic language. Discussions about the origins of the Castle have now shifted somewhat into the domain of prehistorians, but questions still remain about the post-Roman era. What happened to the Votadini? What role did the Angles play? Can a case be made for the Castle Rock having been an uninterrupted seat of authority prior to the 12th century?

Unfortunately, our most attractive early documentation, the *Gododdin* elegies (Williams 1938, Jackson 1969) cannot be regarded as a sound basis for constructing an historical narrative, and they must be used with caution as a source of circumstantial detail. Not only must we allow for poetic language, but we must remain aware of the great distance between the 6th-century society which the *Gododdin* describes and its transmission. Jackson attempted to minimise these concerns to provide a window on the north British Dark Ages, but such optimistic readings have come to be questioned because of the problems raised by detailed linguistic studies. Dumville thinks that later linguistic details undermine any confidence in the historicity of the poetic material (1988), while Alcock has drawn attention to how the poets' hyperbole can obscure the true nature of the material culture: for example, the description of some of the heroes' gold jewellery is clearly anachronistic (1981; 1987, 234–54). Nevertheless, it is widely accepted that the poems provide the most immediate representation that is ever likely to be available to us of the aristocratic values of north British society during the transition from the Iron Age to the medieval world (Charles-Edwards 1978).

In addition, detailed linguistic analysis now allows us to be more positive about the historical value of the *Gododdin* than Dumville has argued, because it is possible to extract the earlier material from the later. John Koch has identified three main strands of composition within the surviving manuscript (1994, 293–7), the earliest of which he believes was composed before AD 638 (the traditional date for the fall of Din Eidyn, see below). In addition, he argues that the material has a sufficiently western perspective to suggest that it was composed in Strathclyde, when the power of the Gododdin polity was in terminal decline (Koch 1993, 82–6). He also notes that the earliest recension (the Ur-text) does not indicate that the focal battle at Catraeth was against the Anglo-Saxons and nor is it described as a defeat. The catastrophic destruction of the warband and the identification of the enemy as English, which are amongst the most familiar of the themes of the *Gododdin* elegies, belong to later strands composed in North Wales. Apart from recasting these general points, there are a number of points specific to the Castle. Firstly, the long-standing identification of Mynyddawg Mwynfawr as the lord of Din Eidyn must now be abandoned. Independently Koch (1993, 86–7) and Graham Issac (1990) have recognised that *mynyddawg mwynfawr* are adjectives meaning 'pertaining to a mountain' and 'of great wealth' or 'luxurious', which are used repeatedly in the collection of verse to qualify Eidyn and its retinue, but should not be taken as a personal name. If we still require a named ruler of Eidyn, Koch offers us a certain Yrfai son of Wolstan, who is described as 'lord of Eidyn' in one of the Ur-text elegies (1994, 299). Apart from changing the name of the ruler of Eidyn, and implying an early Anglian presence in the Lothian aristocracy, this name change is perhaps not so significant. Potentially more important are the political inferences about the scale and position of the kingdom which emerge from Koch's work. The earliest elements of the collection of poems indicates that the Gododdin warband came from the Rock of Lleu's tribe, which is described as being on the frontier of the Gododdin, near to the Forth. This seems to suggest that Eidyn was the principal stronghold of a kingdom within the greater territory of the Gododdin (Koch 1994, 297). We might speculate that the tribe of Lleu's occupied what is now the Lothians, or approximately the area represented in illustration 4, but it would appear that in the 7th century the lords of Eidyn did not hold sway over all of the Gododdin.

The archaeological evidence for the Dark Age or early medieval period at the Castle includes no significant structural remains. It consists entirely of the midden deposits, which in themselves present only oblique evidence that an aristocratic household flourished there. The artefacts from the midden were scarce and their dating equivocal. For instance, the dating of the combs is not beyond question (L Alcock (pers comm) prefers a date later than the one we suggest). However, and this is the key piece of evidence, these objects come from a midden which shows no clear sign of a break from Roman times.

The contents of the later levels (Mills Mount Phase 4) of the primary midden do seem noticeably different from the Iron Age with respect to the faunal remains. During the Roman or Early Historic period (it would

Illus 155
The hunting scene from the Aberlemno
roadside cross-slab. (Copyright: Royal
Commission of the Ancient and Historical
Monuments of Scotland; NMRS neg
A/35024.)

be impossible to define this more closely on the basis of the excavated evidence) there was an increase in the consumption of wild fauna, principally deer. This provides circumstantial evidence that the inhabitants were of noble status. In the Middle Ages hunting was an aristocratic pastime. This linking of the hunt to the nobility appears to happen quite early in northern Britain: certainly the hunting motif is one of the most widespread and consistently rendered themes on Pictish sculpture (illus 155; Allen & Anderson 1903). The location of the midden on the main route to the summit may even have served to display conspicuous feasting habits.

Given the lack of a break in the midden deposition and the previous argument for a Roman period aristocratic residence on the summit, it seems probable that the hall of the Gododdin evolved from the late Roman establishment. What form this took, like the putative broch discussed above, is a matter for speculation. Before the excavation took place, Alcock and MacIvor created a conjectural nuclear fort for the Castle (Alcock 1987, 243). The point of their exercise was merely to demonstrate that the Castle Rock provided a suitable setting for the construction of a '. . . lofty enclosed nucleus surrounded by subordinate enclosures'. Its craggy eminence included several natural terraces; it was of a moderate size and was prominent without being windswept: in short, it represents the setting for a typical nuclear fort, entirely consistent with the excavated evidence and comparable with the prototype nuclear fort at Dalmahoy (Stevenson 1949). The discussion of nuclear forts has recently moved forward with further examples being dated. The implications of this are discussed in some detail in the Dundurn excavation report (Alcock *et al* 1989); here, we need only repeat that there is good evidence that such places were occupied during the 6th century, as for instance at Dumbarton (Alcock & Alcock 1990) and Dundurn. More pertinent to this case are the sitings of some of the lowland brochs, such as Edin's Hall, Turin Hill, and Hurley Hawkin, in former Iron Age forts and the suggestion that other Iron Age hillforts, such as Clatchard Craig, Fife (Close-Brooks 1986), Dundonald, Ayrshire (Ewart 1988) and Moncrieff Hill, Perthshire (Feacham 1955, 80) were also transformed into early medieval aristocratic residences.

The exact form of the early medieval settlement will remain a mystery; certainly, structures such as those found at Dunadd or Dundurn would not survive building works like those which have taken place over the last five centuries at Edinburgh. The characteristic drystone masonry is simply too fragile. On balance it seems likely that, at least while it was a British stronghold, the structure was predominantly stone-built. However the buildings in the interior may well have been timber. Substantial timber structures on aristocratic sites are known from the relative proximity of Doon Hill (Hope-Taylor 1980) and Dunbar (Holdsworth 1991) and from further afield at Dundurn and Yeavering (Hope-Taylor 1977). The period of Anglian occupation may have led to the introduction of buildings similar to the halls which were being erected in Northumbria.

More significant than the archaeological argument for continuity is the question of the relationship between the royal residence and the administrative centre established by the later 11th century. The early attribution of political significance to Edinburgh Castle rests entirely on the identification with the Din Eidyn of the *Gododdin* (Alcock 1981, 165–6). If this is accepted it makes the Castle a place of some importance by the late 6th century. Almost nothing can be said of the fate of the Castle during the Anglian conquest of the Lothians. The Iona Annal for AD 638, noting the siege of Etin, may indicate when it fell to the Anglians (Anderson 1922, 163–4). The Chronicles of Clonmacnoise for 934 AD say that Aethelstan 'spoiled the kingdom to Edinburgh' (Anderson 1922, 426) implying the existence of a fortified establishment then. The Old Scottish Chronicle notes that the fortress of Eden was evacuated and abandoned to the Scots during the reign of Indulf (AD 954–62) (Anderson 1922, 468). The material from these excavations sheds no new light on this extremely dark period of Northumbrian ascendancy. By the 10th century it would seem that some form of noble household is in residence on the Rock, but what form it took and whether it was fortified is unknown.

The fort became a Scottish royal castle in the 11th century. On Mills Mount the earlier midden was sealed by the construction of the kerbed path which ran from the W towards the summit. The topography suggests (and the scant dating evidence does not contradict it) that this was the route by which the body of the saintly Queen Margaret was secreted out of the Castle to be buried in her church in Dunfermline.

THEME 4 • THE ECONOMIC SETTING OF THE CASTLE

Nothing makes the changing significance of the Castle over time more apparent than a consideration of the changing scales of the economic relationships in which it participated. A sober consideration of the evidence that has been recovered from these excavations does not encourage sweeping generalisations. Preservation conditions were variable, some of the contexts were unusual and the assemblages were generally small, but they are all we have. These limited data become all the more important when we recall that there is no other site in Scotland approaching the Castle in longevity that provides a comparable set of economic and environmental evidence.

Although in some instances we have been able to refine our chronological control of the archaeological deposits to a few calendar years, by and large we are working at a much broader scale. For the purposes of this discussion we will organise our comments into five broad time spans: the Iron Age, the Roman period, the early medieval, the High Middle Ages and the Modern age. In the circumstances, these broad categorisations are all that the data can justify and in any case will be helpful for visualising the major changes over time.

IRON AGE

The economy of the Iron Age (800 BC–100 AD) was apparently a locally based agrarian regime with very little evidence of long-distance commerce. For the prehistoric period, since there were few artefacts, the nature of the economy is revealed almost entirely by the plant and animal remains, none of which could be described as exotic. Clearly subsistence depended upon the cultivation of barley with wheat and oats, with barley probably being the most important to judge by the predominance of naked barley in the sample from the occupation level. This type of barley and wheat prosper in the better drained lands of the Lothian plain, while the presence of oats points to contact with areas with less favourable ground, perhaps towards the Pentlands. The arable weeds in these samples are entirely to be expected even had they been processed off-site, so they provide no indication of how closely involved in the arable process the inhabitants were. In the absence of any indications to the contrary, we must assume that the inhabitants were the farmers and that they worked the lands immediately around the Castle.

We may also presume that their agriculture extended to silviculture. The hazelnut shells in any case are likely to have come from managed coppices. Although there is little other evidence of wild plant exploitation, the earlier levels are less conducive to the survival of macro-plant remains than some of the later midden deposits; so, despite their absence, we may presuppose the consumption of berries.

Little can be said about animal husbandry because of the small size of the samples, but the major domesticates are all present and wild fauna account for only a small proportion of the bones.

The economic evidence provided by the agricultural residues indicates that the Castle's occupants in the Iron Age participated in a system of production which may not have extended more than a few miles from the Rock. This impression of a localised small-scale economy is reinforced by the other finds. Pottery, iron, flint, quernstones and whetstones may have been acquired from some distance away, but none need have travelled more than a dozen miles. There is thus nothing to distinguish the village on Castle Rock from any of the myriad enclosed hilltop settlements which were typical of the later prehistoric period in the Lothians.

THE ROMAN PERIOD

The later Iron Age merges with the Roman period in so far as we can distinguish between their stratigraphic deposits. The most important are those which accumulated on the ruins of the earlier settlement remains and contain objects from southern Britain which can be dated to the 2nd or 3rd century AD. These midden deposits proved particularly good for the preservation of both plant and animal remains.

The evidence for agriculture in this period shows an expansion of the types of cultigens and the sorts of weeds characteristic of a wider range of habitats. This may simply reflect the better preservation conditions, but equally may represent some real development in farming practices. Although barley still dominates the assemblage, it may be that the food consumed on site was being drawn from a wider hinterland.

The animal remains occur in much larger quantities and provide some index to the pattern of consumption, even if they are inadequate to inform us of the herd structure. Cattle provided the major proportion of the meat, but pigs were almost as numerous as the sheep or goats. Pigs were perhaps the second most important source of meat. Deer and other wild fauna were relatively scarce. The full skeletons were represented, butchery seems to have taken place on site. Every part of the beast was fully utilised – the larger bones were all smashed to extract the marrow and there is evidence for the crude working of bone on site.

Although the agriculture shows little sign of change between the earlier and later Iron Ages, the economic horizons had certainly expanded by the end of the 2nd century AD. The presence of such a range of pottery fabrics may not be entirely explained by contact with the military, but argues for prolonged commercial contacts. Moreover, it seems likely that some of the later objects were acquired outwith the military context, either down the line via a series of overland exchanges or as a result of specific trading expeditions with the south. Nevertheless we should probably not regard this as a profound change: local networks were not abandoned, they were merely augmented by bringing the communities attached to Roman forts into the system. It is not even clear that the local patterns of production and exchange were significantly altered to service the new trade networks.

THE EARLY MEDIEVAL

In agricultural terms there is nothing particularly new to distinguish the coming of the Middle Ages, but there is the hint of a significant change in the consumption and procurement of meat in the early medieval contexts. Bearing in mind that the absolute number of animal bones is small and the minimum numbers of individuals is tiny, there seems to be a perceptible rise in the representation of wild fauna. Hunting is of course a pastime which is firmly associated with medieval nobility, and is indeed a striking feature of Pictish sculpture. The presence of more wild beasts in the Castle rubbish may indicate that it had become the seat of the local aristocracy, but it was certainly not a hunting lodge. The overwhelming proportion of the meat consumed was still provided by domestic fauna.

Turning to the artefacts, there is no indication of a radical social change; methods of livelihood and production were still essentially those of the Iron Age. As if to emphasise this, we have identified the possibility that locally produced hand-made pottery was still in use. The decoration on the combs indicates that the inhabitants were familiar with fashions elsewhere, but certainly does not suggest that they were dependent on far-flung commercial transactions or even had regular access to long distance trade. Indeed in some ways they show less evidence of access to material imported from outwith Scotland than in the Roman period.

THE HIGH MIDDLE AGES

It is clear that there is a desperate lack of evidence for the key economic and social transitions to the medieval economy. This transformation occurred between the 11th and 13th centuries when little or nothing was happening on Mills Mount. By the time there is good medieval evidence, the Castle had assumed its position as the centre of the most important burgh in the country and a key possession of the king. Moreover, a great deal of the evidence for the medieval activity comes from deposits which may have originated outwith the Castle walls.

The archaeological evidence hardly reflects the Castle's importance, but it does show its urban character and provides evidence that the Castle was part of increasingly specialised and interdependent manufacturing networks. The pottery, for instance, is still probably made locally, possibly in the same places where it had always been made, but is the refined product of specialist craftsmen. Not only is the pottery quite serviceable – if not exactly beautiful – it is also plentiful. Although the craftsmen resident in a royal castle would have been a skilled and varied bunch, the wide variety of specially made objects from knives to locks are likely to have been made elsewhere and purchased in the market place. Indeed, even the iron used in the smithy was smelted elsewhere and procured for the Castle as pig iron. Most small objects of bone and bronze were probably brought in ready-made, as was the food.

The medieval plant remains contain a much higher proportion of oats. Not only is this suggestive of a different pattern of acquiring foodstuffs, it also carries implications about the class of people consuming the food. Oats were cultivated in less fertile ground and imply that more marginal land had been brought under plough. Oats were not a particularly high-status food and would be more appropriate in the diet of a servant than a lord. The other significant change which typifies this assemblage is the relative increase in the importance of sheep. Sheep take over from cattle as the best represented animal, although beef may have remained the most common meat. The popularity of sheep was achieved at the expense of pigs and must reflect the availability of mutton which coincided with the growth of the wool industry, and may perhaps indicate a decline in the extent of woodland.

What is most striking about the medieval assemblage is that, despite its relative poverty of items which may have played a visible role in the royal household, it still shows that the Castle was part of an extensive economic system, one which was more long-lasting and more pervasive than the Roman system. Between the royal household, the needs of the royal armoury and the requirements of the court, the Castle must have been a major magnet for trade. This helped to stimulate and maintain the economic system which became associated with town life in the 15th and 16th centuries.

THE MODERN AGE

No analysis of modern plant or faunal remains was conducted, partially because the latest contexts tended to be disturbed, but also because the available documentation about the supply of the Castle diminishes the value of such studies. From the 17th century onwards, the Castle housed a garrison which augmented and then replaced its administrative and ceremonial importance. MacIvor notes that the last mention of royal accommodation was in a plan drawn in 1719 (1993, 92). However, for all the military presence, there is less uniformity than might be expected. Certainly there are the buttons and cartridges issued by the army and there were also goods manufactured specifically for the garrison. The clay pipes with themes designed to appeal to the Castle soldiery are the most clear-cut example of such targeted objects. However, beyond the military hardware (some of which was still made in the Castle), the personal items are less uniform. For example the mass-produced crockery was not standardised. Most personal items reflected individual choice, choice which increased as the industrial revolution went on and Britain became wealthier. These goods are most informative about the domestic lives of the soldiers and their families and are indicative of the financial condition of much of the army. These goods, although varied, were few, because the soldiers were by and large poor. This is, of course, well known from textual sources. What is most striking is that although the soldiers participated in the most developed economic system to have occupied the Castle, with the most far-flung networks of commerce, most of the Castle's residents did not enjoy the benefits of the system. Prosperity as measured in goods was not that different from that experienced by most of the medieval residents of the Castle.

THEME 5 • THE EVOLUTION OF THE MEDIEVAL DEFENCES FROM ROYAL CASTLE TO GARRISON FORTRESS

The defences are the most conspicuous thing about the Castle and yet they are amongst the most difficult features to interpret. During the Middle Ages the Castle experienced more than its fair share of sieges, which caused repeated and serious damage to the fabric. These are charted below. Building and repair campaigns followed the sieges, which helps us understand why so little survives from before the 17th century. Both the extensive rebuilding programmes of the past and the more recent restoration works contribute to making interpretation difficult. There are no drawings or plans which pre-date the 16th century and, before the 18th century, few which are completely accurate or reliable, so archaeology does play a significant role in contributing to the understanding of even the later defences.

In these investigations the major discoveries relate to the entrance and NE defences, but some surprising evidence for defensive works was also found at Mills Mount. Most of these discoveries relate to the post-medieval period when the Castle underwent a transformation from a royal residence and administrative centre into a specialised garrison. The defences were never purely functional and the ideological values probably always guided the works. The context in which the various modifications took place was thus changing (see MacIvor 1993 for an overview), so it is instructive to look at our new evidence in light of the existing scheme and the uses to which the defences were being put.

As was discussed above, the earliest historically attested presence on the rock has left little physical evidence and no trace of the early medieval defences survive either. All that we can be sure of is that the ramparts would have been dry-stone structures which are unlikely to survive anywhere in the vicinity of the existing ramparts. Where the foundations of either medieval or post-medieval defences were investigated, they have been either built directly on the rock or deeply bedded in the subsoil. Substantial mortared buildings were probably first constructed during the reign of Malcolm III Canmore (1057–93), when we have the first evidence that the Castle had become the principal royal centre where the king and court spent significant periods each year. A defensive circuit is suggested by the presence of a western postern through which the corpse of the saintly Margaret was said to have been smuggled by Prince Edgar.

The first meeting of the embryonic Scottish Parliament took place in the Castle during David I's reign (1124–53). A hall suitable for this clearly existed, possibly standing close to a Norman-style keep. It has been argued that St Margaret's Chapel is all that remains of the southern part of a square stone keep built by David (Fernie 1986, 401). It is likely that activity focused here, since much of the southern citadel, now occupied by the Great Hall and parts of the Palace, was unsuitable for building on until the vaults created a level platform here in the later 15th century. The northern part was better suited, and the site of the postulated keep is a logical one, in a prominent position yet sheltered from attack from the east. It should be recognised that this postulated tower of David I would have been one of the most substantial and impressive non-ecclesiastical buildings in Scotland. Its Norman form would have been quite novel and expressive of the European setting in which the king had spent much of his youth.

During the wars with England in the early 14th century, both Edward I and Robert the Bruce (1306–29) besieged the Castle. In 1296 Edward's giant siege engines caused considerable damage to structures which may have been rebuilt and possibly enlarged on during the 17 years the English held the Castle. In 1300 the garrison of knights, soldiers, priests and servants totalled 347 in number. It was recaptured in 1314, and then, like so many other castles, Bruce ordered the defences to be slighted. By this time it is likely that these defences included the massive double ditches cutting off the approach from the east side. During the next 22

Illus 156
Main entrance to David's tower now encased in the Half Moon Battery. The vault seen here is that of a 19th-century water tank.

years, the site lay derelict with repairs being recorded only on St Margaret's Chapel. Indeed, during this period the site was let for grazing!

In 1335 the castle was recaptured twice by Edward III and held by the English with a garrison of around 115 men until 1341. Repairs were recorded on St Margaret's Chapel, the Great Chamber, the defences and the stables. At this time John de Kilbourn, the noted English architect, was engaged on building works in the Castle.

Upon his release by the English in 1356, David II (1329–71) began the major campaign of building and repair which changed the face of the Castle. He repaired St Mary's Church (on the site now occupied by the National War Memorial); had the Well House Tower built in 1362 to safeguard one element of the always problematic water supply. Some of the works exposed to the NW of Mills Mount (Area T) may have served to link the Castle to the well.

In 1368, David II began the construction of the tower. It was not completed until after his death, and, although now buried beneath the Half Moon Battery, it still bears his name (illus 156). This tower aggressively fronted the defences and, besides providing comfortable new royal lodgings, also dominated the burgh visually as is plain in the earliest representations (illus 72). Like the work of the earlier David, this tower had a dramatic symbolic impact and may be thought of as the original inspiration for many of the typical Scottish towerhouses to be built during succeeding centuries.

It seems likely that the original gatehouse, which was contained within the entrance Flanker with the flattened relieving arch, was constructed during this period of refurbishment. This would have provided the grand approach required by a major royal establishment. It was of course built to reflect contemporary military concerns. Such a well-defended entrance was essential if the Castle was to serve as a secure royal residence able to withstand sieges. Indeed, all David II's work – the towerhouse, the defended well and the possible gateway – seems geared to ensuring that no future siege could succeed. And none did until 1573 when the medieval ramparts were demolished by a sustained artillery assault.

The armaments industry, based in the Castle, comes into focus under Robert II's reign (1371–90). Bows, crossbows, and throwing engines were being produced in workshops, and it is entirely possible that one of these was the smithy excavated on Mills Mount. Robert II is probably also responsible for introducing the first guns into the Castle. The most significant structural development in this period was the building of the new inner gate tower. The Constable's Tower was at the opposite end of the curtain wall, running S from David II's tower, which provided a visual balance as well as enhancing the strength of the Castle. An integral part of the tower appears to have been the Lang Stair which provided the most direct access to the summit.

The 15th century saw the construction of more elaborate royal apartments, not the least to accommodate James I (1406–37) who spent much time in the Castle. As well as repairing the curtain walls, James I built a new Great Chamber which later evolved into the Palace block on the E side of Crown Square. Later in the century, James III (1460–88) is credited with initiating an ambitious building programme the aim of which was to aggrandize the Castle as 'royal residence and centre for great affairs of state'. Edinburgh's status as chief burgh was confirmed under his reign, as every Parliament except one met here, either in the town's Tolbooth or in the Hall at the Castle. The site of the old hall on the citadel is unknown although it was clearly large and grand enough to accommodate the Parliament.

At the end of the century James IV (1488–1513) completed the replanning of Crown Square as the grand royal courtyard. The vaults were constructed S of St Mary's to form a level building platform with ample space for storage, workshops and prisons below. The new Great Hall was built here between 1503 and 1513, with the old hall being transformed into a workshop and foundry. A house of artillery is recorded located to the W of the vaults (Caldwell 1983).

By the end of the 15th century the Castle was a fully developed royal medieval castle which performed a number of roles: fortress, palace, arsenal, treasury, national archive, state prison and residence of state officials. It was also on the verge of obsolescence in terms of a royal residence, with the lodgings at Holyrood Abbey being increasingly favoured.

The half-hearted siege of 1544 during Henry VIII's 'Rough Wooing' of Mary Queen of Scots (1542–67) heralded a significant change in the visual appearance of the Castle. After this the Scots were quick to realise that modern artillery defences were needed to improve on the last phases of old work executed in the 1380s. The angle-pointed artillery fortification, the Spur, was constructed in front of the entrance on what is now the Esplanade. This along with other outworks may have been built under the direction of the Italian engineer Ubaldini. In addition, the medieval curtain wall (now the Forewall Battery) was looped for heavy guns from David's Tower to the Constable's Tower. Above and behind this was another looped rampart which ran between the Munitions House and St Margaret's Chapel. These works, completed in the 1550s, transformed the Castle into 'one of the strongest artillery defences in Britain'. By 1566 the ramparts bristled with at least 25 cast bronze guns. Although it maintained contemporary standards of defence, this was at the cost of architectural grandeur and comfort. In 1561, when Mary began her rule, she took up residence in Holyrood. Although Holyrood and Linlithgow now outstripped the Castle in comfort, they did not carry the same symbolic weight or prestige, because Mary was careful to return to the Castle for the birth of the future James VI.

It is probably during the course of the 'Rough Wooing' that Mills Mount was substantially remodelled. The old smithy shed was swept away and Mills Mount transformed into a makeshift battery. The rude rubble defences, consisting of quantities of shattered whinstone, perhaps quarried from the Rock itself, seem to mark the first attempt to defend this key vantage point facing towards St Cuthbert's to the NW of the Castle. Even this area saw some remodelling during the 17th century. The scale and orientation of the large ditch suggests that the reworking was substantial, although its overall form remains a mystery.

After the Wars of Independence the most disastrous events for the Castle were those associated with the Lang Siege which was only concluded in 1573 following the arrival of English artillery. These guns caused terrible

Illus 157
Aerial view of the Castle in 1994. (Copyright: Royal Commission of the Ancient and Historical Monuments of Scotland; NMRS neg C/40325/CN.)

damage to the Forewall Battery, David's Tower and the Spur. All were shot to pieces. Repairs and rebuilding were carried out for most of the rest of the century, the main works being: the rebuilding of the Spur; the construction of the Half Moon Battery built around and atop David's Tower; and the replacement of Constable's Tower by the Portcullis Gate, complete with a fine Renaissance facade. These transformations were visible at all levels within the Castle. The entrance Flanker was very badly damaged, probably in 1573, and was substantially rebuilt. This Flanker was redesigned to serve as both entrance and an artillery bastion. Thus the skyline of the late medieval Castle was transformed essentially into what is seen today (illus 157).

In the 17th century, the chief function of the Castle as a military fortress garrisoned by a standing army was confirmed. Nowhere is this clearer than in the arrangements made at the entrance. In the early 17th century, the medieval Flanker was completely rebuilt into a purely artillery battery. This 'slimline' Flanker was more compact and built of massive walls over 5m thick and with foundations dug over 2m through the boulder clay to the bedrock and it was filled with masses of soil. Traffic no longer passed through it, as this Flanker was dedicated to housing guns and to withstanding their fire. This remains substantially intact and despite the 19th-century Guardhouse modifications it still dominates the approach from the NE.

The fabric suffered further during the sieges of 1639 and 1640 by the Covenanters. The Castle was left in a state of disrepair following Cromwell's siege in 1650. By now the Spur was demolished, and access followed a road line further up the Rock which approached the Castle Rock more centrally. This is the route which is followed today. The new approach was designed to get men and guns in and out fast, therefore the measures for controlling access became increasingly mechanised. A complex lifting bridge was introduced at the Inner Barrier which was controlled by sentries housed in the Port Guard.

This tendency towards the tighter regulation of movement within the Castle and the formalisation of the defences perhaps reached its peak with the works constructed by John Slezer. The Inner Traverse which zigzagged across Mills Mount was the most substantial part of his elaborate scheme that was realised. It effectively defined a great military area between the Constable's Tower/Portcullis Gate and Hospital Brae, which was maintained to the present. This area was probably left open as a parade ground and important buildings like the Storekeeper's House were set behind the Traverse, where they were protected by being located more deeply within the Castle's defences.

Even in the modern era the Castle remained an object of desire to those wishing to assert political authority. The last serious siege was mounted in 1689 and is grimly commemorated in the cemetery found in the Coal yard. Prior to the excavations these burials, no doubt made under the most extreme conditions, had been forgotten.

The remainder of the modifications can be understood firstly in the context of the formalisation of the military installations and, from the middle of the 19th century, with the increasing symbolic role of the Castle, most splendidly as the home of the rediscovered regalia (MacIvor 1993, 104–7). The introduction of large numbers of soldiers (who required to be controlled and disciplined) and the housing of prisoners were probably contributory factors in the construction of new guardhouses, first opposite the Argyll Battery in 1801 and then at the Inner Barrier in 1853, in what had been the slimline Entrance Flanker. Both contained accommodation for a 24-hour watch and cells for locking up unruly soldiers for short periods.

The growth of the army presence was in part to bring the Highlands tightly under the rule of law and state control. At Edinburgh Castle this was represented by the construction of the Cartshed on Mills Mount which was used to house the fleet of carts employed to supply the Highland garrisons.

The final Gatehouse which stretches across the whole eastern approach (1888) is primarily a ceremonial entrance. It should probably be seen as an expression of the same romantic motives which were articulated in the refurbished Argyll Tower. This building with its drawbridge over the dry-ditch and its elaborate Scottish Baronial style with the sculptures of Wallace and Bruce (added later in 1929) could be said to be the first piece of the Castle consciously intended to appeal to tourists eager to encounter Scotland's heroic heritage.

Overall these excavations have added considerable detail to the already rich body of historical knowledge about the Castle. The unexpectedly extensive surviving deposits have provided answers to questions previously thought unanswerable, such as: when was the Castle first occupied? The excavations have also clarified some of the most opaque architectural features, particularly those around the entrance. All of these new discoveries are significant, but most of all we hope that the material presented here will encourage new lines of historical enquiry, which will extend outwith the Castle into the region and the country beyond.

REFERENCES

Adams, J 1981 *Outline of orthopaedics*. 9 edn. London: Churchill Livingstone.

Adams, J 1987 *Outline of fractures*. 9 edn. London: Churchill Livingstone.

Aitken, WG 1970 'Excavations of bloomeries in Rannoch, Perthshire and elsewhere', *Proc Soc Antiq Scot*, 107 (1970), 188–204.

Alcock, L 1981 'Early Historic Fortifications in Scotland', *in* Guilbert, G (ed) *Hill-fort Studies*, Leicester Univ Press, 150–80.

Alcock, L 1987 *Economy, society and warfare*. Cardiff: Univ of Wales Press.

Alcock, L, Alcock, E, & Driscoll, ST 1989 'Excavations at Dundurn, St Fillan's, Perthshire, 1976–77', *Proc Soc Antiq Scot*, 119 (1989), 189–226.

Alcock, L & Alcock, EA 1990 'Reconnaissance excavations on Early Historic fortifications and other royal sites in Scotland, 1974–84; 4, Excavations at Alt Clut, Clyde Rock, Strathclyde, 1974–75', *Proc Soc Antiq Scot*, 120 (1990), 95–150.

Alcock, L & Alcock, EA 1992 'Reconnaissance excavations on Early Historic fortifications and other royal sites in Scotland, 1974–84; 5:C, Excavations at Dunnottar, Kincardineshire, 1984', *Proc Soc Antiq Scot*, 122 (1992), 267–82.

Allen, JR & Anderson, J 1903 *The Early Christian Monuments of Scotland*. Edinburgh: Soc Antiq Scot.

Anderson, AO 1922 *Early Sources of Scottish History. AD 500–1288*. Edinburgh (1990 Reprint Stamford: Paul Watkins).

Anderson, H, Crabb, PJ & Madsen, HJ 1971 *Århus Søndervold. En byarkeologisk undersøkelse*. Copenhagen.

Anderson, ML 1967 *A history of Scottish forestry*. Edinburgh: Nelson.

Anderson, RR 1913 'Notice of Plans and a Bird's-Eye Perspective, believed to be the Oldest Authentic View of Edinburgh Castle, now in the King's Library, British Museum', *Proc Soc Antiq Scot*, 47 (1912–13), 17–29.

Arbman, H 1943 *Birka I: die Gräber*. Stockholm.

Ardwidsson, G 1984 *Birka II: 1 systematische analysen der gräberfunde*. Stockholm.

Armitage, PL 1976 'Seven sheep skulls and inferences from them', *in* Schofield, J 'Excavations south of Edinburgh High Street, 1973–4', *Proc Soc Antiq Scot*, 107 (1975–6), 239.

Armstrong, P, Tomlinson, D & Evans, DH 1991 *Excavations at Lurk Lane, Beverley, 1979–82*. Sheffield: Collis. (= *Sheffield Excav Rep*, 1.)

Atkin, M, Carter, A & Evans, DH 1985 *Excavations in Norwich 1971–78*, Part II. (= *East Anglian Archaeol*, 26.)

Atkinson, D & Oswald, A 1969 'London clay tobacco pipes', *J Brit Archaeol Assoc*, 13s, 32 (1969), 171–227.

Atkinson, DR & Oswald, A 1980 'The dating and typology of pipes bearing the royal arms', *in* P Davey, *The archaeology of the clay tobacco pipe*, 3, 363–91.

Aitchison, NB 1987 'Roman wealth, native ritual', *Scott Archaeol Rev*, 4 (1987), 95–8.

Ayers, B 1988 *Excavations at St Martin-at-Palace Plain, Norwich, 1981*. (= *East Anglian Archaeol*, 37.)

Baart, J *et al* 1977 *Opgravingen in Amsterdam, twintig jaar stadskernonderzoek*. Amsterdam.

Bain, J (ed) 1887 *Calendar of Documents Relating to Scotland*. Vol III (1307–1375). Edinburgh: HMSO.

Bain, J (ed) 1898 *Calendar of the State Papers Relating to Mary Queen of Scots 1547–1603, presented in the Public Records office, the British Museum and elsewhere in England*. Vol I (AD 1547–1563). Edinburgh: HMSO.

Ballin Smith, B 1994 *Howe. Four millennia of Orkney prehistory*. Edinburgh: Soc Antiq Scot. (= *Soc Antiq Scot Monogr Ser*, 9.)

Barker, PA & Higham, RA 1982 *Hen Domen Montgomery: a timber castle on the English–Welsh border*. London: Roy Archaeol Inst Monogr.

Bannatyne Club (ed) 1928 'The Portrait of a True Loyalty Exposed in the Family of Gordon with a Copious Relation of the Siege of the Castle of Edinburgh, 1689. By WR 1691', *Extracts from Bannatyne Club Publications. Book of the Old Edinburgh Club*, 16 (1928), 171–213.

Barnetson, LPD 1982 'Animal husbandry – clues from Broxmouth', *in* D Harding (ed), *Later prehistoric settlement in south-east Scotland*, 101–5. Edinburgh: Univ: Univ Edinburgh (= *Edinburgh Occas Pap*, 8.)

Barnetson, LPD 1985 'Faunal remains', *in* Holmes, NMcQ 'Excavations south of Bernard St, Leith 1980', *Proc Soc Antiq Scot*, 115 (1985), 401–28, fiche 1: E1–F11; 424–5 & fiche 1: F1–11.

Barnetson, LPD 1986 'The animal bones from Clatchard Craig', *in* J Close-Brooks 'Excavations at Clatchard Craig', *Proc Soc Antiq Scot*, 116 (1986), 178, fiche 1, C6–C14.

Barnetson, LPD 1988 'Animal bones', *in* GD Thomas 'Excavations at the Roman civil settlement at Inveresk, 1976–77', *Proc Soc Antiq Scot*, 118 (1988) 171–2, Fiche 2, C3–D4.

Barrett, JC 1981 'Aspects of the Iron Age of Atlantic Scotland: a case study in archaeological interpretation', *Proc Soc Antiq Scot*, 111 (1981), 204–19.

Barrett, J, Fitzpatrick, A & Macinnes, L (eds) 1989 *Barbarians and Romans in North-West Europe.* Oxford: BAR (= *BAR Int Ser*, 471.)

Barton, KJ & Holden, EW 1977 'Excavations at Bramber Castle, 1966–67', *in* Saunders, AD (ed), 'Some castle excavations: reports on the Institute's research projects into the origins of the castle in England', *Archaeol J*, 134 (1977), 11–79.

Beresford, G 1987 *Goltho: the development of an Early Medieval Manor c 850–1150.* London: English Heritage. (= English Heritage *Archaeol Rep*, 4.)

Bergrren, G 1969 *Atlas of seeds and small fruits of Northwest-European plant species.* Pt 2. *Cyperaceae.* Stockholm: Swedish Natur Sci Res Counc.

Biddle, M 1990 *Object and economy in Medieval Winchester: artefacts from Medieval Winchester.* Oxford: Univ Press. (= *Winchester Stud*, 7ii.)

Biddle, M & Barclay, K 1990 'Sewing pins and wires', *in* Biddle, 1990, 560–71.

Biddle, M & Hinton, DA 1990 'Points', *in* Biddle, 1990, 581–9.

Biddle, M & Hinton, DA 1990 'Copper-alloy bells', *in* Biddle, 1990, 725–8.

Bidwell, PT 1985 *The Roman Fort of Vindolanda.* London: HBMCE. (= *Historic Buildings Monuments Commission England Rep*, 1.)

Blockley, K 1989 *Prestatyn 1984–5, an Iron Age farmstead and Romano–British industrial settlement in North Wales.* Oxford: BAR (= *Brit Ser*, 210).

Board of Artillery Officers 1864 *Instruction for Field Artillery.* Philadephia.

Boardman, SJ & Jones, GEM 1990 'Experiments on the effects of charring on cereal plant components', *J Archaeol Sci*, 17 (1990), 1–11.

Boardman, S (in prep) 'The charred plant remains from Castle of Wardhouse, Aberdeenshire', *in* Yeoman, P (forthcoming) *Excavations at Castle of Wardhouse, Aberdeenshire 1988.*

Bokonyi, S 1974 *History of domestic mammals in Central and Eastern Europe.* 1988 edn. Budapest.

Boyd, WE 1983 'Botanical remains of edible plants from the Iron Age broch at Fairy Knowe, Buchlyvie, near Stirling', *Forth Naturalist Historian*, 7 (1982–3), 77–83.

Boyd, WE 1984 'Environmental change and Iron Age land management in the area of the Antonine Wall, Central Scotland: a summary', *Glasgow Archaeol J*, 11 (1984), 75–81.

Boyd, WE 1986 'Minor cereal finds at two rural Medieval archaeological sites in north-east Scotland', *Circaea*, 4 (1986), 39–42.

Boyd, WE 1988 'Cereals in Scottish antiquity,' *Circaea*, 5 (1988), 101–110.

Boyd, WK (ed) 1905 *Calendar of the State Papers relating to Scotland and Mary Queen of Scots 1547–1605 preserved in the Public Record Office, the British Museum and elsewhere in England.* Vol IV (1571–1574). Edinburgh: HMSO.

Brailsford, JW 1962 *Hod Hill I. Antiquities from Hod Hill in the Durden Collection.* London: Brit Mus.

Breeze, DJ 1982 *The Northern Frontiers of Roman Britain.* London: Batsford.

Breeze, DJ 1990 'The impact of the Roman Army on the native peoples of North Britain', *in* Vetters & Kandler (eds), 85–97.

Britnell, WJ 1990 'Capel Maelog, Powys: Excavations 1984–87', *Medieval Archaeol*, 34 (1990), 27–96.

Brooks, C 1980 'Medieval pottery from the kiln site at Coulston, E Lothian', *Proc Soc Antiq Scot*, 110 (1978–80), 364–403.

Brothwell, DR 1981 *Digging up bones.* 3 edn. Oxford: Brit Mus, Oxford Univ Press.

Buckland, PC 1976 'The environmental evidence from the Church Street Roman sewer system', *in* PV Addyman (ed) *The past environment of York. The archaeology of York*, 14, 1–44.

Bulleid, A & Gray H St G 1917 *The Glastonbury Lake Village.* II. Glastonbury Antiq Soc.

Bullock, P, Federoff, N, Jongerius, A, Stoops, G & Tursina, T 1985 *Handbook for soil thin section description.* Wolverhampton: Waine Research Publications.

Bushe-Fox, JP 1915 *Excavations at Hengistbury Head, Hampshire, in 1911–12.* London: Soc Antiq London (= Soc Antiq London Res Rep, 3).

Bushe-Fox, JP 1916 *Third report on the excavations on the site of the Roman town at Wroxeter, Shropshire, 1914.* Oxford: Soc Antiq London (= Soc Antiq London Res Rep, 4).

Butler, S 1992 'Vegetational history and land use', *in* Rideout, JS, *et al* (eds), 1992, 7–14.

Cal Docs Scot *see* Bain, J (ed) 1887.

Cal State Papers Scot *see* Bain, J (ed) 1898 for Vol I AD 1547–1563; *see* Boyd, WK (ed) 1905 for Vol V AD 1571–1574.

Carter, A 1984 *World bayonets 1800 to the present.*

Caldwell, DH 1981 'Metalwork', *in* Good & Tabraham 1981, 106–16.

Caldwell, DH 1983 'The Royal Scottish Gun Foundry in the Sixteenth Century', *in* O'Connor, A & Clarke, DV (eds), *From the Stone Age to the 'Forty-Five*: studies presented to RBK Stevenson, 427–39. Edinburgh: John Donald.

Caldwell, DH & Dean, V 1981 'Post-Medieval pottery industry at Throsk, Stirlingshire', *Scot Pot Hist Rev*, 6 (1981), 21–7.

Caple, C 1983 'Pins and wires', in Mayes & Butler 1983, 269–78.

Care-Evans, A (ed) 1983 *The Sutton Hoo ship-burial.* III. London: Brit Mus.

Cat Nat Mus Antiq Scot 1982 *Catalogue of the National Museum of Antiquities of Scotland 1892.* Edinburgh.

Chaplin, RE & Barnetson, L 1976 'The animal bones' in Schofield, J 'Excavations south of Edinburgh High Street, 1973–4', *Proc Soc Antiq Scot*, 107 (1975–6), 229–39.

Charles-Edwards, TM 1978 'The Authenticity of the Gododdin: an historian's view', *in* R Bromwich & R Brinley Jones (eds) *Astudiathau ar yr Hengerrod. Studies in Old Welsh Poetry*, 44–71. Cardiff: Univ Wales Press.

Charlesworth, D 1966 'Roman square bottles', *J Glass Stud*, 7 (1966), 26–40.

Cheeney, RF 1977 *Report on aspects of the geology of Edinburgh Castle Rock.* Unpub rep, Univ Edinburgh.

Christison, D 1905 'Report on the Society's excavations of forts on the Poltalloch Estate, Argyll, in 1904–15', *Proc Soc Antiq Scot*, 39 (1904–5), 282–9.

Christy, M 1926 *The Bryant and May museum of fire-making appliances. Catalogue of exhibits.* London.

Clapham, AR, Tutin, TG, & Moore, PD 1982 *Flora of the British Isles.* 3 edn. Cambridge: Univ Press.

Clapham, AJ & Scaife, RG 1988 'A pollen and macrofossil investigation of Oakbank crannog, Loch Tay, Scotland', in Murphy, P & French, C (eds) *The exploitation of wetlands*, 293–325. Oxford: Brit Archaeol Rep. (= Brit Archaeol Rep Brit Ser, 186.)

Clapham, A forthcoming 'The environmental evidence; the macroplant remains', in Hanson, WS (forthcoming).

Clarke, G 1979 *The Roman cemetery at Lankhills.* Oxford: Univ Press. (= *Winchester Stud*, 3:ii.)

Clarke, H & Carter, A 1977 *Excavations in King's Lynn, 1963–70.* London: Soc Medieval Archaeol. (= *Soc Medieval Archaeol Monogr Ser*, 7.)

Clay, P 1981 'The small finds – non structural', in Mellor & Pearce 1981, 130–45.

Close-Brooks, J 1983a 'Some early querns', *Proc Soc Antiq Scot*, 113 (1983), 215–53.

Close-Brooks, J 1983b 'Dr Bersu's excavations at Traprain Law 1947', *in* O'Connor, A & Clarke, DV (eds) *From the Stone Age to the 'Forty-Five*, 206–24. Edinburgh: John Donald.

Close-Brooks, J 1986 'Excavations at Clatchard Craig, Fife', *Proc Soc Antiq Scot*, 116 (1986), 117–84.

Close-Brooks, J 1987 'Comment on Traprain Law', *Scott Archaeol Rev*, 4 (1987). 92–4.

Coad, JG & Streeten, ADF 1982 'Excavations at Castle Acre Castle, Norfolk, 1972–77', *Archaeol J*, 139 (1982), 138–301.

Collingwood, RG 1930 'Romano-Celtic Art in Northumbria', *Archaeologia*, 80 (1930), 37–58.

Cool, HEM 1982 'Later prehistoric farming in south-east Scotland', *in* Harding 1982, 92–100.

Cool, HEM 1990 'Roman metal hair pins from southern Britain', *Archaeol J*, 147 (1990), 148–82.

Cotton, MA 1947 'Excavations at Silchester 1938–9', *Archaeologia*, 92 (1947), 121–67.

Courty, MA, Goldberg, P & Macphail, R 1989 *Soils and micromorphology in archaeology.* Cambridge: Univ Press.

Cowgill, J 1987 'Manufacturing techniques', *in* Cowgill *et al*, 1987, 8–39.

Cowgill, J, de Neergaard, M & Griffiths, N 1987 *Knives and scabbards. Medieval finds from excavations in London 1.* London: Mus London Publications.

Cox, E, Haggarty, G & Hurst, JG 1984 'Ceramic material', *in* Tabraham, 1984, 381–98.

Cramp, F & Simmons, KEL 1980 *Handbook of the birds of Europe, the Middle East and North Africa 2.* Oxford: Univ Press.

Crone, BA 1988 *Tree-ring analysis and the study of crannogs.* PhD thesis, Univ Sheffield.

Cronyn, JM 1990 *The elements of archaeological conservation.* London: Routledge.

Crossley, DW (ed) 1981 *Medieval industry.* London: Counc Brit Archaeol. (= *CBA Res Rep*, 40).

Crowdy, A 1986 'The pottery', *in* Dixon 1986, 10.

Cruden, S 1940 'The ramparts of Traprain Law: excavations in 1939', *Proc Soc Antiq Scot*, 74 (1939-40), 48–59.

Cruden, S 1952 'Scottish Medieval pottery: the Bothwell Castle collection', *Proc Soc Antiq Scot*, 86 (1951–52), 140–70.

Cruden, S 1953 'Scottish Medieval pottery: the Melrose Abbey collection', *Proc Soc Antiq Scot*, 87 (1952–53), 161–74.

Cruden, S 1956 'Scottish Medieval pottery', *Proc Soc Antiq Scot*, 89 (1955–6), 67–82.

Crummy, N 1983 *The Roman small finds from excavations in Colchester, 1971–9*. Colchester: Colchester Archaeol Trust. (= *Colchester Archaeol Rep*, 2.)

Cummins, J 1988 *The Hound and the Hawk*. London.

Curle, CL 1982 *Pictish and Norse finds from the Brough of Birsay*. Edinburgh: Soc Antiq Scot. (= *Soc Antiq Scot Monogr Ser*, 1.)

Curle, J 1911 *A Roman frontier post and its people: the fort of Newstead in the parish of Melrose*. Glasgow.

Daniels, C (ed) 1978 *Handbook to the Roman Wall with the Cumbrian Coast and Outpost Forts*. Newcastle: J Collingwood Bruce.

Dannell, GB & Wild, GB 1987 *Longthorpe II, The military works-depot: an episode in landscape history*. London: Soc Roman Stud. (= *Britannia Monogr Ser*, 8.)

Davey, PJ 1981 'Guidelines for the processing and publication of clay pipes from excavations', *Medieval and Later Pottery in Wales*, 4 (1981), 65–88.

Davey, PJ (ed) 1981a *The archaeology of the clay tobacco pipe. 5. Europe 2*. Oxford: BAR. (= *BAR Int Ser*, 106(i).)

Davey, PJ (ed) 1981b *The archaeology of the clay tobacco pipe 6*. Oxford: BAR (= *BAR* Brit Ser, 97.)

Davey, PJ (ed) 1987 *The archaeology of the clay tobacco pipe. 10*. Oxford: BAR (= *BAR* Brit Ser, 178.)

Davis, RW 1971 'The Roman military diet', *Britannia*, 11 (1971), 122–42.

Déchelette, J 1904 *Les Vases céramiques ornés de la Gaule romaine*. Paris.

Dickinson, WC, Donaldson, G & Millne, I 1954 *A source book of Scottish history*. London: Nelson.

Dickson, CA & Dickson, JH 1988 'The diet of the Roman army in deforested central Scotland', *Plants Today*, Jul–Aug 1988, 121–6.

Dickson, CA 1989 'The Roman army diet in Britain and Germany', *in* Korber-Grohne, U & Kuster, H (hrsg), *Archäobotanik Dissertationes Botanicae*, 133 (1989), 135–154.

Dixon, P 1986 *Excavations in the fishing town of Eyemouth 1982–1984*. Kelso: Borders Burghs Archaeol Survey.

Dodwell, GR (ed) 1961 *Rogerus Theophilus' De Diversis Artibus*. London: Nelson.

Dolley, M 1975 'The coin-weight', *in* Platt & Coleman-Smith, 1975, 250–2.

Dool, J, Wheeler, H & Mackreth, D 1985 'Roman Derby: excavations 1968–1983', *Derbyshire Archaeol J*, 105 (1985), 155–314.

Douglas, WS 1898 *Cromwell's Scotch Campaigns 1650-51*. London: Elliot Stock.

Driesch, A von den 1976 *Guide to the measurement of animal bones from archaeological sites*. Cambridge Mass: Peabody Mus.

Driscoll, ST 1987 *The Early Historic landscape of Strathearn: the archaeology of a Pictish kingdom*. Unpub PhD thesis: Univ Glasgow.

Driscoll, ST 1996 'Excavations at Dundee Law 1992', *Proc Soc Antiq Scot*, 125, 1091–1108.

Düco, DH 1981 'De Kleipijp in de Zeventiende Eeuwse Nederlanden', *in* Davey, PJ (ed) 1981, 111–468.

Düco, DH 1987 *De Nederlandse Kleipipp. Handbook voor dateren endeterineren*. Leiden: Pijpenkaninet.

Dumville, D 1988 'Early Welsh poetry: problems of historicity', *in* Brinley, F Roberts (ed) *Early Welsh poetry studies in the Book of Aneirin*, 1–16, Aberystwyth: Univ Wales Press.

Dunbar, JG 1969 'Three little known early drawings of Edinburgh Castle', *Book of Old Edinburgh Club*, 33 (1969), 10–12.

Duncan, AMM 1975 *Scotland: the making of a Kingdom*. Edinburgh: Oliver & Boyd.

Duncan, HB 1982 *Aspects of the Early Historic Period in south-west Scotland: a comparison of the material cultures of Scottish Dal Riada and the British kingdoms of Strathclyde and Rheged*. Unpub MLitt thesis: Glasgow Univ.

Duncan, HB & Spearman, RM 1984 'Small finds', *in* Yeoman 1984, 354–60.

Dunlevy, M 1988 'A classification of early Irish combs', *Proc Roy Ir Acad*, 88C, 11 (1988), 341–422.

Edinburgh Burgh Recs Edinburgh City Corporation 1927–67 *Extracts from the records of the Burgh of Edinburgh published for the Corporation of the City of Edinburgh*. Vol IV (1642–1655). Edinburgh: Oliver & Boyd.

Edlin, HL 1974 *Woodland crafts in Britain*. Newton Abbot: Country Book Club.

Edwards, L 1988 'Seventeenth and eighteenth century Tyneside tobacco pipe makers and tobacconists', *in* Davey, PJ (ed) *The archaeology of the clay tobacco pipe*, 11. Oxford: BAR. (= *BAR Brit Ser*, 192.)

Emerton, E 1940 *The Letters of St Boniface*. New York: Columbia Univ Press.

Ewart, G 1980 'Excavations at Stirling Castle 1977–78', *Post-Medieval Archaeol*, 14 (1980), 23–51.

Ewart, G 1988 'Dundonald Castle', *Discovery Excav Scot*, 1988, 52. Edinburgh: Counc Scott Archaeol.

Ewart, JC 1911 'Appendix: animal remains, equidae and bovidae', *in* Curle, 1911, 362–77.

Exch Rolls *see* Stuart, J *et al* (eds), 1878–1908.

Farmer, P 1979 *An introduction to Scarborough Ware and a reassessment of Knight jugs*. London: P Farmer.

Fawcett, R 1994 *Scottish architecture from the accession of the Stewarts to the Reformation 1371–1560*. Edinburgh: Univ Press.

Feachem, RW 1955 'Fortifications', *in* Wainwright, FT (ed) *The Problem of the Picts*, 66–86. Edinburgh: Nelson.

Feachem, RW 1956 'The fortifications on Traprain Law', *Proc Soc Antiq Scot*, 89 (1955–56), 284–9.

Feachem, RW 1963 *A guide to prehistoric Scotland*. London: Batsford.

Fenton, A 1977 *Scottish country life*. Edinburgh: John Donald Ltd.

Fernie, E 1986 'Early Church architecture in Scotland', *Proc Soc Antiq Scot*, 116 (1986), 393–411.

Ford, B 1987 'Iron objects', *in* Holdsworth 1987, 130–41.

Ford, B & Walsh, A 1987 'Iron nails', *in* Holdsworth 1987, 138–9.

Foster, SM 1990 'Pins, combs and the chronology of later Atlantic Iron Age settlement', *in* I Armit (ed) *Beyond the brochs*, 143–74. Edinburgh: Univ Press.

Fox, Sir C 1958 *Pattern and purpose*. Cardiff: Univ Wales Press.

Fox, R & Barton, KJ 1986 'Excavations at Oyster Street, Portsmouth, Hampshire, 1968–70', *Post-Medieval Archaeol*, 20 (1986), 31–255.

Fremersdorf, F 1959 *Römisches Gläser mit Fadenauflage in Köln. Die Denkmaler des römanischen Köln*. 5. Cologne.

Gallagher, DB 1987a 'Edinburgh pipemakers in the seventeenth century: the documentary evidence', *in* Davey, P (ed) 1987, 3–13.

Gallagher, DB 1987b 'Tobacco pipemaking in Glasgow, 1667–1967', *in* Davey, P (ed) 1987, 35–109.

Gallagher, DB 1987c 'The 1900 List of the Pipe Maker's Society', *in* Davey, P (ed) 1987, 142–63.

Gallagher, DB 1987d 'Edinburgh, Tron Kirk', *in* Davey, P (ed) 1987, 269–71.

Gallagher, DB 1987e 'Kelso', *in* Davey, P (ed) 1987, 279–91.

Gallagher, D & Price, R 1987 'Thomas Davidson & Co, Glasgow', *in* Davey, P (ed) 1987, 110–38.

Gallagher, DB & Sharp, A 1986 *Pypes of Tabaca: Edinburgh tobacco pipemakers and their pipes*. Edinburgh.

Gallagher, DB 1989 'TW pipes, their origins and development', *Soc Clay Pipe Res Newsletter*, 22 (April 1989), 1–5.

Geddes, J 1980 'The well cover', *in* Saunders, 1980, 165–7.

Genoves, S 1963 'Sex determination in earlier man', *in* Brothwell, DR & Higgs, E (eds) *Science in archaeology*, 429–39. London: Thames & Hudson.

Gifford, J, McWilliam, C, Walker, D & Wilson, C 1984 *Edinburgh*. London: Penguin.

Gilbert, JM 1979 *Hunting and hunting reserves in Medieval Scotland*. Edinburgh: John Donald.

Good, G & Tabraham, C 1981 'Excavations at Threave Castle, Galloway 1974–78', *Medieval Archaeol*, 25 (1981), 90–140.

Goodall, AR 1980 'Copper alloy objects', *in* Palmer 1980, fiche 2 B13–C05, figs 23–8.

Goodall, AR 1983 'Non-ferrous metal objects', *in* Mayes & Butler 1983, 231–9.

Goodall, AR 1984 'Non-ferrous metal objects', *in* Rogerson & Dallas 1984, 68–75.

Goodall, AR 1991 'The copper alloy and gold', *in* Armstrong, Tomlinson & Evans 1991, 148–54.

Goodall, IH 1980 'Objects of copper alloy', *in* Wade-Martins 1980, 499–505.

Goodall, IH 1981 'The Medieval blacksmith and his products', *in* Crossley (ed), 1981, 51–62.

Goodall, IH 1982 'Iron objects', *in* Coad & Streeten 1982, 227–36.

Goodall, IH 1983 'Iron objects', *in* Mayes & Butler 1983, 240–52.

Goodall, IH 1984 'Iron objects', *in* Rogerson & Dallas 1984, 76–106.

Goodall, IH 1987 'Objects of iron', *in* Beresford 1987, 177–87.

Goodall, IH 1990 'The medieval iron objects from Winchester', *in* Biddle 1990, 36–41.

Goodall, IH 1991 'The iron', *in* Armstrong, Tomlinson & Evans 1991, 131–46.

Goodall, IH & Carter, A 1977 'Iron objects', *in* Clarke & Carter 1977, 291–8.

Gooder, E 1984 'Finds from the cellar of the Old Hall, Temple Balsall, Warwickshire', *Post-Medieval Archaeol*, 18 (1984), 149–249.

Grant, A 1982 'The use of tooth wear as a guide to the age of domestic ungulates', *in* Wilson, B *et al* (eds) *Aging and sexing animal bones from archaeological sites*, 91–108. Oxford: BAR. (= *BAR Brit Ser*, 109.)

Grant, A 1984 'Animal husbandry in Wessex and the Thames Valley', *in* Cunliffe, B & Miles, D 1984, *Aspects of the Iron Age in Central Southern Britain*, 102–19. Oxford: Univ Comm Archaeol.

Greenacre, MJ 1984 *Theory and application of correspondence analysis*. London: Academic Press.

Greenock, Lord 1833 'A General View of the Phenomena displayed in the neighbourhood of Edinburgh by the Igneous Rocks . . . . the south side of the Castle Hill', *Trans Roy Soc Edinburgh*, 13 (1833), 39–45.

Greig, JRA 1984 'The Palaeoecology of some British hay meadow types', *in* van Zeist, W & Casparie, WA (eds) *Plants and ancient man: studies in palaeoethnobotany*, 213–26. Rotterdam: AA Balkema.

Greig, JRA 1988 'Some evidence of the development of grassland plant communities', *in* Jones, M (ed) *Archaeology and the flora of the British Isles: human influence on the evolution of plant communities*. Oxford: Univ Comm Archaeol. (= *Oxford Univ Comm Archaeol Monogr*, 4).

Greig, JRA 1991 'The British Isles', *in* van Zeist, W & Casparie, WA (eds) *Plants and ancient man: studies in palaeoethnobotany*, 213–66. Rotterdam: Balkema.

Grieg, S 1933 *Middelalderske byfund fra Bergen og Oslo*. Oslo.

Griffith, FM 1986 'Salvage observations at the Dark Age site at Bantham Ham, Thurlestone, in 1982', *Proc Devon Archaeol Soc*, 44 (1986), 39–57.

Griffiths, N 1986 *Horse harness pendants*. London: Medieval Finds Res Gr 700–1700. (= *Medieval Finds Res Gr Datasheet*, 5.)

Groves, M 1990 'Silver and copper-alloy tacks', *in* Biddle 1990, 1102–1114.

Haggarty, G 1980a 'The pottery', *in* Ewart 1980.

Haggarty, G 1980b 'Post-Medieval pottery in Scotland', *Scot Pot Hist Rev*, 5, 45–61.

Haggarty, G 1984 'Observations on the ceramic material from Phase I Pits BY and AQ', *in* Tabraham, 1984, 10.

Haggarty, G & McIntyre, A forthcoming 'Excavation and watching brief at Newbigging Pottery, Musselburgh, East Lothian', *Proc Soc Antiq Scot*, forthcoming.

Hall, RA (ed) 1978 *Viking Age York and the North*. London: Counc Brit Archaeol. (= *Counc Brit Archaeol Res Rep*, 27).

Hann, R de & Krook, W 1988 'Amsterdam', *in* Tymastra, F & Meulen, J van der 1988, 16–38.

Hanson, WS (forthcoming) *Elginhaugh. A Roman fort and its annexe*.

Hanson, W & Maxwell, G 1983 *Rome's North West Frontier*. Edinburgh: Univ Press.

Hamilton, JRC 1956 *Excavations at Jarlshof*, Shetland. Edinburgh: HMSO. (= *Ministry of Works Archaeol Rep*, 1.)

Harden, DB 1987 *Glass of the Caesars*. Milan: Olivetti.

Harding, D (ed) 1976 *Hillforts: later prehistoric earthworks in Britain and Ireland*. London: Academic Press.

Harding, D (ed) 1982 *Later prehistoric settlement in south-east Scotland*. Edinburgh: Univ Dept Archaeol. (= *Edinburgh Dept Archaeol Occas Pap*, 8.)

Harvey, K & Powers AH (forthcoming) *Phytolith suite analysis of Triticum, Hordeum and Panicum: an archaeological application*.

Hartley, BR 1972 'The Roman occupations of Scotland: the evidence of Samian Ware', *Britannia*, 3 (1972), 1–55.

Hartley, BR 1989 'Samian potters' stamps and decorated ware', *in* Frere, SS & Wilkes, JJ *Strageath*, 212–18. London: Soc Roman Stud. (= *Britannia Monogr Ser*, 9.)

Harvey, Y 1975 'The small finds: catalogue', *in* Platt & Coleman-Smith 1975, 254–93.

Haynes, EB 1959 *Glass through the ages*. Harmondsworth: Penguin.

Hencken, H 1950 'Lagore Crannog: an Irish Royal Residence of the 7th to 10th Centuries AD', *Proc Roy Irish Acad*, 53C, 1–247

Henshall, A 1982 'The finds', *in* Taylor, DB 'Excavations at Hurly Hawkin, Angus', *Proc Soc Antiq Scot*, 112 (1982), 215–53.

Higham, CFW 1967 'Flock rearing as a cultural factor in prehistoric Europe', *Proc Prehist Soc*, 33 (1967), 84–106.

Hill, P 1982b 'Broxmouth hillfort excavations 1977-78: an interim report', *in* Harding 1982, 141–88.

Hill, P 1982a 'Settlement and chronology', *in* Harding 1982, 4–43.

Hill, P 1982c 'Towards a new classification of early houses', *Scott Archaeol Rev*, 1 (1982), 24–31.

Hill, P 1987 'Traprain Law: the Votadini and the Romans', *Scott Archael Rev*, 4 (1987), 85–91.

Hillman, GC 1981 'Reconstructing crop husbandry practices from the remains of crops', *in* Mercer, RJ (ed) *Farming practices in British prehistory*, 123–62. Edinburgh: Univ Press.

Hillman, GC 1984 'Interpretation of archaeological plant remains: the application of ethnographical models from Turkey', *in* Zeist, W van & Casparie, WA (eds) *Plants and ancient man: studies in palaeoethnobotany*, 1–41. Rotterdam: Balkema.

Hinton, DA 1990a 'Buckles and buckle-plates', *in* Biddle 1990, 506–26.

Hinton, DA 1990b 'Harness pendants and swivels', *in* Biddle 1990, 1047–53.

Hinton, DA 1990c 'Copper-alloy and tin chains', *in* Biddle 1990, 1089–91.

Hobley, B 1969 'A Neronian-Vespasianic military site at "The Lunt", Baginton, Warwickshire', *Trans Proc Birmingham Archaeol Soc*, 83 (1969), 65–129.

Hobley, B 1973 'Excavations at "The Lunt" Roman Military Site, Baginton, Warwickshire, 1968–71, Second Interim Report', *Trans Proc Birmingham Archaeol Soc*, 85 (1971–1973), 7–92.

Hodgson, GWI & Jones, A 1982 'Report on the animal bones', *in* Thoms, LM 'Trial excavations at St Ann's Lane, Perth', *Proc Soc Antiq Scot*, 112 (1982), 449–53.

Hodgson, GWI & Jones, A 1983 'Report on the animal remains from the Medieval levels', *in* Blanchard, L 'An excavation at 45 Canal Street, Perth, 1978–9', *Proc Soc Antiq Scot*, 113 (1983), 514–17.

Hodgson, GWI & Jones, A 1984 'The animal bone', in Murray, H 'Excavations at 45-47 Gallowgate, Aberdeen', *Proc Soc Antiq Scot*, 114 (1984), Fiche 4: A11–B10.

Holdsworth, P 1987 *Excavations in the Medieval Burgh of Perth, 1979–81*. Edinburgh: Soc Antiq Scot. (= *Soc Antiq Scot Monogr Ser*, 5.)

Holdsworth, P 1991 'Dunbar', *Current Archaeol*, 127 (1991), 315–17.

Holmes, N (forthcoming) *Report on excavations at Cramond 1975–78*.

Hope, A 1987 *A Caledonian Feast: Scottish cuisine through the ages*. Edinburgh: Mainstream.

Hope-Taylor, B 1977 *Yeavering*. London: HMSO.

Hope-Taylor, B 1980 'Balbridie . . . . . and Doon Hill', *Current Archaeol*, 71 (1981), 18–19.

Horton, MC, Higgins, DA & Oswald, A 1987 'Clay Tobacco Pipes from the Scottish Darien Colony (1698–1700)', *in* Davey, P 1987, 239–51.

Hughes, BP 1969 *British Smooth-bore Artillery*.

Hull, MR & Hawkes, CFC 1987 *Pre-Roman bow brooches. Corpus of ancient brooches in Britain*. Oxford: Brit Archaeol Rep. (= *BAR Brit Ser*, 168.)

Hume, IN 1970 *A Guide to artifacts of Colonial America*. New York: Alfred A Knopf.

Hume, JR 1991 'Firing quill from the Duke of Cumberland's Bastion, Fort George', *Proc Soc Antiq Scot*, 121 (1991), 423–5.

Hurst, JG 1977 'Spanish pottery imported into Medieval Britain', *Medieval Archaeol*, 21 (1977), 68–105.

Hurst, JG 1979 *Wharram: a study of settlement of the Yorkshire Wolds*. London: Soc Medieval Archaeol. (= *Soc Medieval Archaeol Monogr Ser*, 8.)

Innes, C (ed) 1868 *Ancient Laws and Customs of the Burghs of Scotland. 1 (1124–1424)*. Edinburgh: Scott Burgh Records Soc.

Isaac, G 1990 'Mynyddawg Mwynfawr', *Bull Board Celtic Stud*, 37 (1990), 111–13.

Jackson, K 1969 *The Gododdin, the oldest Scottish poem*. Edinburgh: Univ Press.

Jelks, EB 1973 *Archaeological explorations at Signal Hill, Newfoundland 1965–66*. Ottawa: Canadian Historic Sites. (= *Occas Pap Archaeol Hist*, 7.)

Jennings, S (ed) 1982 *Eighteen centuries of pottery from Norwich*. (= *East Anglian Archaeol*, 13.)

Jobey, G 1966 'Homesteads and settlements of the frontier area', *in* Thomas, C (ed), 1–14.

Jobey, G 1976 'Traprain Law: a summary', *in* Harding (ed), 191–204.

Johnson, S 1777 *A Journey to the Western Islands of Scotland*. 1984 edn. Harmondsworth: Penguin.

Jones, GEM 1984 'Interpretation of archaeological plant remains: ethnographic models from Greece', *in* Zeist, W van & Casparie, WA (eds), *Plants and ancient man. Studies in palaeoethnobotany*, 43–61. Rotterdam: Balkema.

Jones, M 1981 'The development of crop husbandry', *in* Jones, M & Dimbleby, G (eds), *The environment of man: the Iron Age to the Anglo-Saxon Period*, 95–127. Oxford: Brit Archaeol Rep. (= *BAR Brit Ser*, 87.)

Jones, NW & Courtney, P 1990 'Medieval ironwork', *in* Britnell 1990, 27–96.

Kenward, HK, Hall, AR, & Jones, AKG 1980 'A tested set of techniques for the extraction of animal and plant macrofossils from waterlogged archaeological deposits', *Sci Archaeol*, 22 (1980), 3–15.

Koch, J 1993 'Thoughts on the Ur-Gododdin: rethinking Aneirin and Mynyddawc Mwynvawr', *Language Sciences*, 15 (1993), 81–9.

Koch, J 1994 *The Celtic Heroic Age literary sources for ancient Celtic Europe and Early Ireland and Wales*. Malden Mass: Celtic Studies Publications.

Krogman, WM 1962 'The human skeleton', *in* Thomas, CL (ed) *Forensic medicine*. Chigaco, Illinois.

Laing, L 1975 *The archaeology of late Celtic Britain and Ireland c 400–1200 AD*. London.

Laws, A & Oswald, A 1981 'The kiln of William Heath, eighteenth century Brentford pipemaker', *in* Davey, P (ed), 1981-, 25–66.

Lawson, G 1978 'Medieval tuning pegs from Whitby, N Yorkshire', *Medieval Archaeol*, 22 (1978), 139–41.

Lawson, G 1990 'Pieces from stringed instruments', *in* Biddle, 1990, 711–8.

Lawson, G 1991 'The tuning peg', *in* Armstrong *et al*, 1991, 188–9.

Lawson, RG 1975 'Clay pipes', *in* Holmes, NMMcQ 'Excavations within the Tron Kirk, Edinburgh, 1974', *Post-Medieval Archaeol*, 9 (1975), 149–52.

Lawson, RG 1980 'The clay tobacco-pipes', *in* Holmes, NMMcQ 'Excavations at St Mary's Street, Edinburgh', *Post-Medieval Archaeol*, 14 (1980), 171–4.

Le Cheminant, R 1981 'Armorials from Paul's Wharf', *in* Davey, P (ed) 1982, 102–26.

Le Cheminant, R 1982 'The development of the pipeclay hair curler: a preliminary study', *in* Davey, P (ed) 1982, 102–26.

Leach, P 1982 *Ilchester Vol 1. Excavations 1974–1975: the Roman and Medieval Town*. Bristol: West Archaeol Trust. (= *Excav Monogr*, 3.)

Lewis, J 1984 'The charcoal-fired blast furnaces of Scotland: a review', *Proc Soc Antiq Scot*, 114 (1984), 433–81.

Lewis, J & Ewart, G 1995 *Jedburgh Abbey: the archaeology and architecture of a Border Abbey*. Edinburgh: Soc Antiq Scot. (= *Soc Antiq Scot Monogr Ser*, 10).

Lindsay, JM 1974 *The use of woodland in Argyllshire and Perthshire between 1650–1850*. Unpub PhD thesis: Univ Edinburgh.

Lloyd, TH 1977 *The English wool trade in the Middle Ages*. Cambridge: Univ Press.

LMMC 1967 *London Museum Medieval catalogue*. London: Mus London.

Lotbiniere, De S 1984 'Gunflint recognition', *Int J Nautical Archaeol Underwater Exploration*, 13.3 (1984), 206–9.

Long, A & Long, E 1983 'Nails', *in* Mayes, P & Butler, L 1983, 279–80.

Lucas, AT 1989 *Cattle in ancient Ireland*. Kilkenny: Borthius Press.

Lynch, M, Spearman, RM & Stell, G (eds) 1988 *The Scottish Medieval town*. Edinburgh: John Donald.

McCormick, F 1992 'Early faunal evidence for dairying', *Oxford J Archaeol*, 11 (1992), 201–209.

Macdonald, ADS & Laing, LR 1975 'Excavations at Lochmaben Castle, Dumfriesshire', *Proc Soc Antiq Scot*, 106 (1974–75) 124–57.

Macdonald, G & Curle, A 1929 'The Roman fort at Murmills near Falkirk', *Proc Soc Antiq Scot*, 63 (1928–29), 396–575.

Macdonald, G & Park, A 1906 'The Roman forts at Bar Hill, Dunbartonshire excavated by Mr Alexander Whitelaw of Gartshore', *Proc Soc Antiq Scot*, 40 (1906–6), 403–546.

MacGregor, A 1974 'The Broch of Burrian, North Ronaldsay, Orkney', *Proc Soc Antiq Scot*, 105 (1973–74), 63–118.

MacGregor, A 1985 *Bone, antler, ivory & horn. The technology of skeletal materials since the Roman world*. London: Croom Helm.

MacGregor, A 1978 'Industry and commerce', *in* Hall, RA, 1978, 37–57.

Macinnes, L 1982 'Pattern and purpose: the settlement evidence', *in* Harding (ed), 57–74.

Macinnes, L 1984a 'Brochs and the Roman occupation of lowland Scotland', *Proc Soc Antiq Scot*, 114 (1984), 235–49.

Macinnes, L 1984b 'Settlement and economy: East Lothian and the Tyne-Forth province', *in* Miket, R & Burgess, C (eds) 1984, 176–98.

Macinnes, L 1989 'Baubles, bangles and beads: trade and exchange in Roman Scotland', *in* Barrett, JC *et al* (eds) 1989, 108–16.

MacIvor, I 1981 'Artillery and major places of strength in the Lothians and the East Border', *in* Caldwell, D (ed) *Scottish weapons and fortifications 1100–1800*, 94–152. Edinburgh: John Donald.

MacIvor, I 1983 *Edinburgh Castle*. London: Batsford.

Mackie, E 1971 'English migrants and Scottish Brochs', *Glasgow Archaeol J*, 2 (1971), 39–71.

Mackie, E 1987 'Leckie Broch – the impact on the Scottish Iron Age', *Glasgow Archaeol J*, 14 (1987), 1–18.

Mackreth, D 1985 'Brooches from Roman Derby', *in* Dool, J *et al*, 1985, 281–99.

Mackreth, D 1989 'Brooches', *in* Blockley, K 1989, 87–99.

Mackreth, D forthcoming 'Brooches', *in* Garrod & Atkin, forthcoming *Kingsholm, Coppice Corner, Gloucester Excation Report*.

Malcolm, CA 1925 'The Gardens of the Castle', *Book Old Edinburgh Club*, 14 (1925), 101–20.

Manchester, K 1983 *The archaeology of disease*. Bradford: Univ Bradford.

Martens, I 1981 'Some reflections on the production and distribution of iron in Norway in the Viking Age', *in* Wilson, DM & Caygill, ML (eds), *Economic aspects of the Viking Age*, 39–43. London: Brit Mus. (= *Brit Mus Occas Pap*, 33.)

Martin, CJM 1987a 'A group of pipes from the Dutch East Indiaman Kennemerland, 1664', *in* Davey, P (ed), 1987, 211–24.

Martin, CJM 1987b 'Pipes from the wreck of HMS Dartmouth, 1690, a re-assessment', *in* Davey, P (ed), 1987, 225–32.

Marwick, JD (ed) 1869 *Extracts from the Record of the Burgh of Edinburgh, 1403–1528*. Edinburgh.

Maltby, JM 1981 'Iron Age, Romano British and Anglo-Saxon Animal Husbandry – a review of the faunal evidence', *in* Jones, M & Dimbleby, G (eds), *Environment of man: the Iron Age to the Anglo-Saxon period*, 155–203. Oxford: Brit Archaeol Rep. (= *Brit Archaeol Rep Brit Ser*, 87.)

Manning, WH 1985 *Catalogue of the Romano-British Iron Tools, Fittings and Weapons in the British Museum*. London: Brit Mus.

Margeson, S 1985 'The small finds', *in* Atkin, M *et al*, 1985, 52–66 & 201–213.

Mayes, P & Butler, L 1983 *Sandal Castle excavations, 1964–1973*. Wakefield: Historical Publications.

McCormick, F 1986 'Interim report on the animal bones from Maynagh Lough', *in* Bradley, J 'Excavations at Maynagh Lough 1984', *Riocht na Midhe*, 74 (1986), 86–90.

McMillan, AA (ed) 1987 *Building stones of Edinburgh*. Edinburgh: Geol Soc.

Mellor, JE & Pearce, T 1981 *The Austin Friars, Leicester*. London: Counc Brit Archaeol. (= *Counc Brit Archaeol Res Rep*, 35).

Metcalf, DM (ed) 1977 *Coinage in Medieval Scotland (1100–1600)*. Oxford: Brit Archaeol Rep. (= *Brit Archaeol Rep Brit Ser*, 45.)

Meulen, J van der 1988 'Leiden', *in* Tymstra, F & Meulen, J van der, 1988, 113–22.

Miket, R & Burgess, C (eds) 1984 *Between and beyond the Walls*. Edinburgh: John Donald.

Millett, M & Russell, D 1982 'An Iron Age burial from Viables Farm, Basingstoke', *Archaeol J*, 139 (1982), 69–90.

Moorhouse, S 1970 'Finds from Basing House, Hampshire (c 1540–1645): Part One', *Post-Medieval Archaeol*, 4 (1970), 31–91.

Morales, A & Rosenlund, K 1979 *Fish bone measurements*. Copenhagen: Streenfturtia.

Munro, R 1882 *Ancient Scottish lake-dwellings or crannogs*. Edinburgh: David Douglas.

Munro, R 1901 'Notice of an Ancient Kitchen-Midden near Largo Bay, Fife, excavated by W Baird Esq of Elie', *Proc Soc Antiq Scot*, 35 (1900–1901), 281–99.

Murray, JEL 1977 'The Black Money of James III', *in* DM Metcalf (ed), 115–30.

Musty, J 1969 'The excavation of two barrows, one of Saxon date, at Ford, Laverstock, near Sailsbury, Wiltshire', *Antiq J*, 49 (1969), 98–117.

Mylne, RS 1893 *The Master Masons to the Crown of Scotland and their works*. Edinburgh.

Neal, DS, Wardle, A & Hunn, J 1990 *Excavation of the Iron Age, Roman and Medieval settlement at Gorhambury, St Albans*. London: Eng Heritage. (= *Eng Heritage Archaeol Rep*, 14.)

Neergaard, M de 1987 'The use of knives, shears, scissors and scabbards', *in* Cowgill *et al*, 1987, 51–61.

Oakley, GE 1979 'The copper alloy objects', *in* Williams, 1979, 248–64.

Oakley, GE & Hunter, J 1979 'The glass', *in* Williams, 1979, 296–302.

Oldrieve, WT 1914 'Account of the recent discovery of the remains of David's Tower at Edinburgh Castle', *Proc Soc Antiq Scot*, 12 (1914), 230–70.

O'Meara, JJ 1982 *Gerald of Wales: the history and topography of Ireland*. Harmondsworth: Penguin.

Oswald, A 1975 *Clay pipes for the archaeologist*. Oxford: Brit Archaeol Rep. (= *Brit Archaeol Rep Brit Ser*, 14.)

Oswald, A 1981 'Part II: the finds', *in* Laws, A & Oswald, A, 1981, 28–55.

Palmer, NB 1980 'A Beaker burial and Medieval tenements in the Hamel, Oxford', *Oxoniensia* 45, 124–225.

Parkyn, HG 1956 *Shoulder-belt plates and buttons*. Aldershot.

Paton, HM, Imrie, J & Dunbar, JG 1957–82 *Accounts of the Masters of Works for Buildings and Repairing Royal Palaces and Castles*. Edinburgh: HMSO.

Petersen, J 1951 *Vikingetidens redskaper*. Oslo.

Phenice, TW 1967 'A newly developed visual method of sexing the os pubis', *Amer Anthropol*, 30 (1967), 297–302.

Piggott, CM 1948 'Excavations at Hownam Rings, Roxburghshire', *Proc Soc Antiq Scot*, 82 (1947–48), 193–225.

Platt, C & Coleman-Smith, R 1975 *Excavations in Medieval Southampton, 1953–1969*. Leicester: Univ Press.

Potter, T 1977 'The Biglands Milefortlet and the Cumberland Coast Defences', *Britannia*, 8 (1977), 149–83.

Potter, T 1979 *Romans in North-West England, Excavations at the Roman forts of Ravenglass, Watercrook and Bowness-on-Solway*. Kendal: Cumberland Westmorland Antiq Archaeol Soc. (= *Cumberland Westmorland Antiq Archaeol Soc Res Ser*, I.)

Powers, AH & Gilbertson, DD 1987 'A simple preparation technique for the study of opal phytoliths from archaeolocal and Quaternary sediments', *J Archaeol Sci*, 14 (1987), 529–35.

Powers, AH, Padmore, J, Gilbertson, DD 1989 'Studies of later prehistoric and modern opal phytoliths from coastal sand dunes and machair in NW Britain', *J Archaeol Sci*, 16 (1989), 27–45.

Price, DG & Knill, JL 1967 'The engineering geology of Edinburgh Castle Rock', *Geotechnique*, 17 (1967), 411–32.

Rackham, DJ 1987 'The animal bone', *in* Heslop, DH (ed) *The excavation of an Iron Age settlement at Thorpe Thewles, Cleveland (1980–82)*, 99–109. London: Counc Brit Archaeol. (= *Counc Brit Archaeol Res Rep*, 65.)

Rae, TI 1966 'Notes on Edinburgh Castle 1751–1753', *Book Old Edinburgh Club*, 32 (1966), 54–107.

Rainbird, C 1935 'The Flint-Knapping Industry at Brandon', *Antiquity* 9 (1935), 38–56.

RCAHMS 1951 *An Inventory of the Ancient and Historical Monuments of the City of Edinburgh*. Edinburgh: HMSO.

RCAHMS 1956 *An Inventory of the Ancient and Historical Monuments of Roxburghshire with the Fourtheenth Report of the Commission*. I & II. Edinburgh: HMSO.

Rees, SE 1979 *Agricultural implements in prehistoric and Roman Britain*. Oxford: Brit Archaeol Rep. (= *Brit Archaeol Rep Brit Ser*, 69.)

Richmond, I 1968 *Hod Hill. 2. Excavations carried out between 1951 and 1958 for the Trustees of the British Museum*. London: Brit Mus.

Rideout, JS, Owen, OA & Halpin, E (eds) 1992 *Hillforts of Southern Scotland*. Edinburgh: Archaeological Operations and Conservation. (= *AOC Monogr*, 1).

Richie, J 1920 *The Influence of Man on Animal Life in Scotland: A Study of Faunal Evolution*. Cambridge: Univ Press.

Richie, J 1930 'Report on the bones from Dunadd', *in* Craw, J 'Excavations at Dunadd and at some other sites on the Poltalloch estates, Argyll', *Proc Soc Antiq Scot*, 64 (1929–30), 126–7.

Ritchie, Anna 1977 'Excavation of Pictish and Viking-age farmsteads at Buckquoy, Orkney', *Proc Soc Antiq Scot*, 108 (1976–77), 174–227.

Ritchie, JNG 1967 'Keil Cave, Southend, Argyll: a late Iron Age cave occupation in Kintyre', *Proc Soc Antiq Scot*, 99 (1966–67), 104–10.

Ritchie, JNG 1971 'Iron Age finds from Dun an Fheurain, Gallanach, Argyll', *Proc Soc Antiq Scot*, 103 (1971), 100–12.

Robertson, A 1970 'Roman finds from non-Roman sites in Scotland', *Britannia*, 1 (1970), 198–226.

Roes, A 1963 *Bone and antler objects from the Frisian terp mounds*. Haarlem: Tjeenk Willink.

Rogers, GA 1983 *An illustrated history of needlework tools*. Reddich: Needle Mus.

Rogers, GB 1974 'Poteries sigillées de la Gaule centrale', *Gallia Suppl*, 28.

Rogers, HCB 1971 *Artillery through the ages*. London.

Rogerson, A 1977 *Excavations at Scole, 1973*. Norfolk: Gressenhall. (= *East Anglian Archaeol Rep*, 5.)

Rogerson, A & Dallas, C 1984 *Excavations in Thetford 1948–59 and 1973–80*. Norfolk: Gressenhall. (= *East Anglian Archaeol Rep*, 22.)

Rodwell, W 1976 'Iron pokers of La Tene II-III', *Archaeol J*, 133 (1976), 43–9.

Ruckley, NA 1990 'Water supply of Medieval castles in the United Kingdom', *Fortress*, 7 (1990), 14–26.

Russell-Smith, F 1956 'The Medieval "Brygyrdyl"', *Antiq J*, 36 (1956), 218–21

Rygh, O 1885 *Norsk oldsager*. Christiania, Norway.

Samson, R 1982 'Finds from Urquhart Castle in the National Museum, Edinburgh', *Proc Soc Antiq Scot*, 112 (1982), 465–76.

Salzman, LF 1952 *Building in England down to 1540*. Oxford.

Saunders, AD 1980 'Lydford Castle, Devon', *Medieval Archaeol*, 24 (1980), 123–86.

Schofield, J 1976 'Excavations south of Edinburgh High Street 1973–74', *Proc Soc Antiq Scot*, 107 (1975–6), 155–241.

Scott, BG 1990 *Early Irish metalworking*. Belfast: Ulster Mus. (= *Ulster Mus Pub*, 266.)

Sekulla, MF 1982 'The Roman coins from Traprain Law', *Proc Soc Antiq Scot*, 112 (1982), 285–94.

Sharp, A 1984 'The clay tobacco pipe collection in the National Museum', *Rev Scott Culture*, 1 (1984), 34–42.

Shell, CA & Robinson, P 1988 'The recent reconstruction of the Bush Barrow lozenge plate', *Antiquity*, 62 (1988), 248–60.

Silvester, RJ 1981 'An excavation on the post-Roman site at Bantham, South Devon', *Proc Devon Archaeol Soc*, 39 (1981), 89–118.

Simpson, DDA 1969 'Excavations at Kaimes Hillfort, Midlothian', *Glasgow Archaeol J*, 1 (1969), 7–28.

Singleton, HR 1973 *A chronology of cutlery*. Sheffield.

Sissons, JB 1967 'The geomorphology of central Edinburgh', *Scott Geograph Mag*, 87 (1967), 185–96.

Skertchly, SBJ 1879 *On the manufacture of gun-flints, the methods of excavating for flint, the age of Palaeolithic man, and the connexion between Neolithic art and the gun-flint trade*. London: HMSO. (= *Sheet Memoirs- Geological Survey of England and Wales*.)

Smith, C 1989 'Perth, the animal remains', *in* Stones, J (ed), 1989, Fiche 13: B2–13.

Smith, C & Hodgson, I 1981 'The animal bones from 1 Bank Street/5–7 Townhall St', *in* Wordsworth, J 'Excavations in Inverkeithing 1981', *Proc Soc Antiq Scot*, 111 (1981), 542–5.

Smith, C & Hodgson, I 1987 'Animal bone', *in* Holdsworth, P (ed) 1987, 196–9.

Southworth, E (ed) 1990 *Anglo-Saxon cemeteries – a reappraisal*. Stroud: Alan Sutton.

Spearman, RM 1982 'The furnace remains', *in* Wordsworth, J 'Excavations at Castle Street, Inverness 1979', *Proc Soc Antiq Scot*, 112 (1982), 346–55.

Spearman, RM 1984 'Ferrous metalworking debris', *in* Yeoman, PA, 'Excavations at Castlehill of Strachan, 1980–81', *Proc Soc Antiq Scot*, 114 (1984), 349–50.

Spearman, RM 1987 'The metalworking debris and moulds and crucibles', *in* Holdsworth, P (ed) 1987, 157–8.

Spearman, RM 1988 'Workshops, materials and debris: evidence of early industries', *in* Lynch *et al*, 1988, 134–47.

Spearman, RM (forthcoming) 'The industrial remains', *in* Lindsay, WJ *Excavations in Elgin*.

Stanfield, JA & Simpson, G 1958 *Central Gaulish potteries*. London.

Stead, IM 1976 *Excavations at Winterton Roman Villa and other Roman sites in north Lincolnshire, 1958–1969*. London: DoE. (= *DoE Archaeol Rep*, 9).

Stead, IM 1980 *Rudston Roman Villa*. Leeds: Yorks Archaeol Soc.

Stevens, HM & Carlisle, A 1959 *The native pinewoods of Scotland*. Edinburgh.

Stevenson, RBK 1947 'Farms and fortifications in King's Park, Edinburgh', *Proc Soc Antiq Scot*, 81 (1947), 158–70.

Stevenson, RBK 1949 'The Nuclear Fort at Dalmahoy and other dark age capitals', *Proc Soc Antiq Scot*, 83 (1949), 186–98.

Stevenson, RBK 1970 'A Roman intaglio ring from a native fort on Arthur's Seat', *Proc Soc Antiq Scot*, 102 (1970), 293–4.

Stones, J 1989 *Three Scottish Carmelite Friaries. Excavations at Aberdeen, Linlithgow and Perth, 1980–86*. Edinburgh: Soc Antiq Scot. (= *Soc Antiq Scot Monogr Ser*, 6).

Stuart, J *et al* (eds) 1878–1908 *Rotuli Scaccarii Regum Scotorum: The Exchequer Rolls of Scotland*. Vol III (1379–1406). Edinburgh: HMSO.

Stuiver, MA & Becker, B 1986 ?? *Radiocarbon*, 28 (1986), 863–910.

Stuiver, MA, Long, A & Kra, RS (eds) 1993 'Calibration issue', *Radiocarbon*, 35 (1) (1993).

Swanton, MJ 1974 *A corpus of pagan Anglo-Saxon spear types*. Oxford: Brit Archaeol Rep. (= *Brit Archaeol Rep Brit Ser*, 7.)

Tabraham, CJ 1984 'Excavations at Kelso Abbey', *Proc Soc Antiq Scot*, 114 (1984), 10.

Tait, D nd *Unpublished notes on wells in Edinburgh, including preparation for a paper on the wells and springs along the line of the Colinton Castle Hill forts*. Edinburgh: Brit Geolog Survey.

Tait, D 1942 'Geological notes on (a) The Nor' loch and (b) The Fore Well in Edinburgh Castle', *Trans Edinburgh Geol Soc*, 14 (1942), 28–33.

Talbot, O 1974 'The evolution of glass bottles for carbonated drinks', *Post-Medieval Archaeol*, 8 (1974), 29–62.

Taylor, DB 1982 'The excavation of a promontory fort, broch and souterrain at Hurley Hawkin, Angus', *Proc Soc Antiq Scot*, 112 (1982), 215–53.

Thomas, C (ed) 1966 *Rural settlement in Roman Britain*. London: Counc Brit Archaeol. (= *Counc Brit Archaeol Res Rep*, 7.)

Thompson, A, Grew, F & Schofield, J 1984 'Excavations at Aldgate, 1974', *Post-Medieval Archaeol*, 18 (1984), 1–148.

Thompson, MW 1967 *Novgorod the Great*. London: Evelyn, Adams & MacKay.

Thorkander, E 1975 'Comment on Medieval Swedish osmund iron', *J Historical Metallurgy Soc*, 9.ii (1975), 68–70.

Topham, J (ed) 1787 *Liber Quotidianus Contrarotaliris garderobae*. London.

Treue, W *et al* (eds) ?? *Das Hausbuch der Mendelschen Zwolfbrudersitiftung zu Nurnberg*. 2 vol. Munchen.

Trotter, M & Gleser, GC 1958 'A re-evaluation of estimation of stature based on measurements of stature taken during life and long-bones after death', *Amer J Phys Anthropol*, 16 (1958), 79–123.

Tymstra, F & Muelen, J van der 1988 *De kleipijp als bodemvondst, pijpelogische Kring Nederland*. Leiden.

Veen, M van der 1988 'Carbonised grain from a Roman granary at South Shields, North East England', *in* Kuster, H (Hrsg), *Der prähistorische Mensch und seine Umwelt (Festschrift U. Körber-Grohne)*, 353–65. (= *Forschungen and Berichete zur Vor- and Frügeschichte in Baden-Wurttemberg*, 31.)

Vetters, H & Kandler, M (eds) 1990 *Der Römische Limes in Österreich*. Heft 36. Vienna: Österreichische Akademie der Wissenschaften. (= *Akten des 14 Internationalen Limeskongresses 1986 in Carnuntum*.)

Wainwright, FT 1963 *Souterrains of Southern Pictland*. London: Routledge, Kegan Paul.

Wardle, A 1990 'Objects of bone' *in* Neal, DS *et al*, 1990, 157–9.

Wade-Martins, P 1980 *Excavations in North Elmham Park 1967–1972*. (= *East Anglian Archaeol*, 9.)

Webster, G 1981 'Final Report on the excavations of the Roman Fort at Waddon Hill, Stoke Abbot, 1963–1969', *Proc Dorset Natural History Archaeol Soc*, 101 (1981), 51–90.

Wheeler, REM 1943 *Maiden Castle, Dorset*. Oxford: Soc Antiq London. (= *Rep Res Comm Soc Antiq London*, 12).

White, KD 1970 *Roman farming*. London: Thames & Hudson.

White, R 1990 'Scrap or substitute: Roman material in Anglo-Saxon graves', *in* Southworth, 1990, 125–52.

Wickham-Jones, C 1996 *Arthur's Seat and Holyrood Park: a visitor's guide*. Edinburgh: HMSO.

Wild, JP 1970 *Textile manufacture in the Northern Roman Provinces*. Cambridge: Univ Press.

Williams, I 1938 *Canu Aneirin*. Cardiff: Univ Wales Press.

Williams, JH 1979 *St Peter's Street, Northampton. Excavations 1973–1976*. Northampton: Development Corporation. (= *Northampton Development Corporation Archaeol Monogr*, 2.)

Williams, V 1988 'Non-ferrous metal objects', *in* Ayers 1988, 63–7.

Wilmott, T 1987 'A note on the heraldic decoration of the scabbards', *in* Cowgill, J *et al*, 1987, 45–50

Woodfield, C 1981 'Finds from the Free Grammar School at Whitefriars, Coventry, *c* 1545–*c* 1557–58', *Post-Medieval Archaeol*, 15 (1981), 81–160.

Works Accounts *see* Paton, HM *et al* (eds) 1957–82.

Yeoman, PA 1984 'Excavation at Castlehill of Strachan, 1980–81', *Proc Soc Antiq Scot*, 114 (1984), 315–64.

Youngs, S (ed) 1989 *The Work of Angels. Masterpieces of Celtic metalwork, 6th–9th centuries AD*. London: Brit Mus Publications.

INDEX

Italicised references at the end of an entry denote illustration numbers

Index prepared by Margot Wright

The S

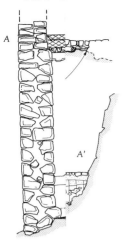

A

A'

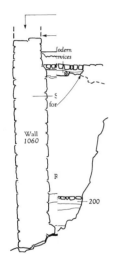

Modern
Services

S
for

Wall
1060

R

—200

EDINBURGH CASTLE

General Key to Illustrations

NOTE: Where necessary, some Illustrations have individual Keys

Limit of Excavations	
Extant Roofed Building	
Top Sloping Masonry	
Flagged Paving	
Top Steps	
Passage or Doorway	

Sand

Silt

Loam

Clay

 Compacted Clay

 Natural Clay

 Metal Filings

 Wood

 Wood Shavings

 Mortar

 Charcoal

Ash

Matted Straw

Stone

 Stone Facing

 Orthostats

 Gravel

 Shattered Bedrock

or Bedrock

 (on all Sections and small scale Plans)

 Brick

Concrete

⊗ Water Pipe

 Bone

 Coal

 Iron object

 Glass

Pottery

 Shell

0

Illus 24
Mills Mount (